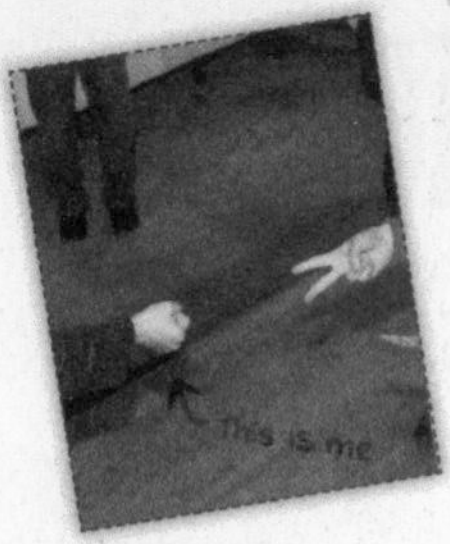
This is me

Even though we mention the reader surveys all the time, I'm too scared to ask for the survey results for *Bakuman。*. People like me are better off trusting their editor to handle that information. In any case, they'll be informed if their manga is performing poorly. Now that's a scary prospect...

—Tsugumi Ohba

Screentones were something I yearned for but couldn't afford as a student. Then I learned that manga artists often used screentone 61. I was so inspired that I rushed out to the store to buy it the very next day.

—Takeshi Obata

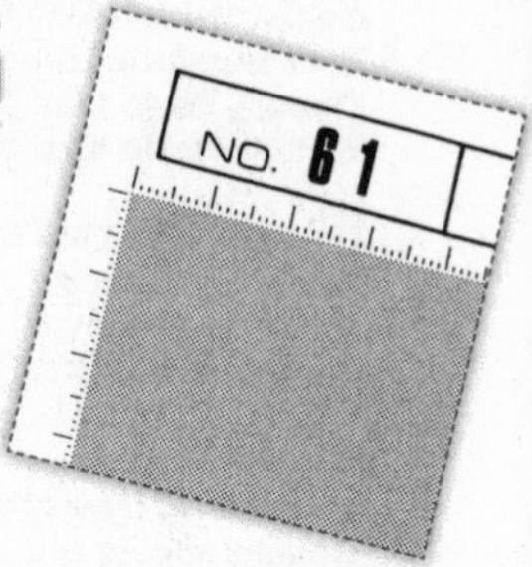
NO. 61

Tsugumi Ohba

Born in Tokyo, Tsugumi Ohba is the author of the hit series *Death Note*. His current series *Bakuman。* is serialized in *Weekly Shonen Jump*.

Takeshi Obata

Takeshi Obata was born in 1969 in Niigata, Japan, and is the artist of the wildly popular SHONEN JUMP title *Hikaru no Go*, which won the 2003 Tezuka Osamu Cultural Prize: Shinsei "New Hope" award and the 2000 Shogakukan Manga award. Obata is also the artist of *Arabian Majin Bokentan Lamp Lamp*, *Ayatsuri Sakon*, *Cyborg Jichan G.*, and the smash hit manga *Death Note*. His current series *Bakuman。* is serialized in *Weekly Shonen Jump*.

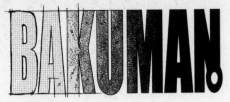

Volume 9

SHONEN JUMP Manga Edition

Story by **TSUGUMI OHBA**
Art by **TAKESHI OBATA**

Translation | **Tetsuichiro Miyaki**
English Adaptation | **Hope Donovan**
Touch-up Art & Lettering | **James Gaubatz**
Design | **Fawn Lau**
Editor | **Alexis Kirsch**

BAKUMAN。© 2008 by Tsugumi Ohba, Takeshi Obata
All rights reserved.
First published in Japan in 2008 by SHUEISHA Inc., Tokyo.
English translation rights arranged by SHUEISHA Inc.

The rights of the author(s) of the work(s) in this publication to be
so identified have been asserted in accordance with the Copyright,
Designs and Patents Act 1988. A CIP catalogue record for this book
is available from the British Library.

Printed in the U.S.A.

Published by VIZ Media, LLC
P.O. Box 77010
San Francisco, CA 94107

10 9 8 7 6 5 4 3 2 1
First printing, February 2012

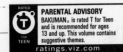

BAKUMAN

9

TALENT and PRIDE

STORY BY

TSUGUMI OHBA

ART BY

TAKESHI OBATA

MAN。 バクマン。 vol. 9

D
C
B
A
LOVE

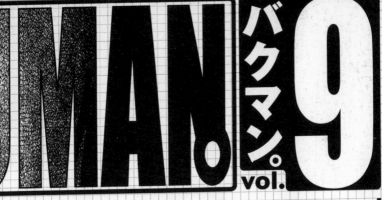

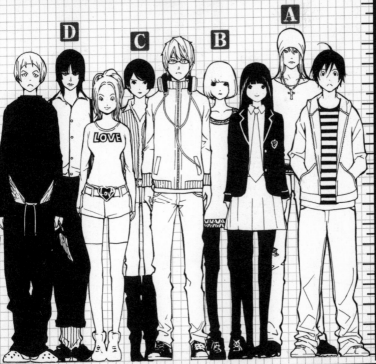

EIJI
Nizuma

A manga prodigy and Tezuka Award winner at the age of 15. One of the most popular creators in *Jump*.

Age: 20

KAYA
Miyoshi

Miho's friend and Akito's girlfriend. A nice girl who actively works as the interceder between Moritaka and Azuki.

Age: 19

AKITO
Takagi

Manga writer. An extremely smart guy who gets the best grades in his class. A cool guy who becomes very passionate when it comes to manga.

Age: 18

MIHO
Azuki

A girl who dreams of becoming a voice actress. She promised to marry Moritaka under the condition that they not see each other until their dreams come true.

Age: 19

MORITAKA
Mashiro

Manga artist. An extreme romantic who believes that he will marry Miho Azuki once their dreams come true.

Age: 18

*These ages are from December 2012.

STORY In order to attain the glory that only a handful of people can, two young men decide to walk the rough "path of manga" and become professional manga creators. This is the story of a great artist, Moritaka Mashiro, a talented writer, Akito Takagi, and their quest to become manga legends!

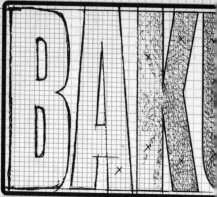

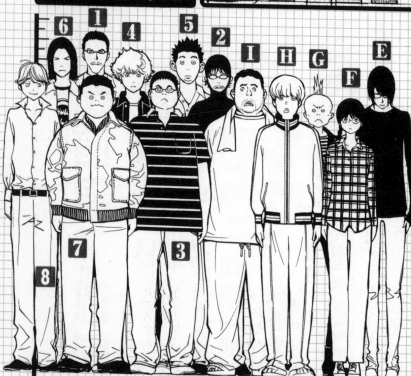

WEEKLY SHONEN JUMP
Editorial Office

1 Editor in Chief Sasaki
2 Deputy Editor in Chief Heishi
3 Soichi Aida
4 Yujiro Hattori
5 Akira Hattori
6 Koji Yoshida
7 Goro Miura
8 Masakazu Yamahisa

The MANGA ARTISTS and ASSISTANTS

A SHINTA FUKUDA
B KO AOKI
C AIKO IWASE
D KAZUYA HIRAMARU
E RYU SHIZUKA
F NATSUMI KATO
G YASUOKA
H SHOYO TAKAHAMA

I TAKURO NAKAI

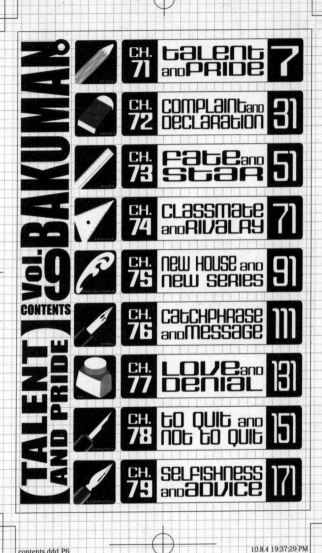

VOL. BAKUMAN。 9 CONTENTS

(TALENT AND PRIDE)

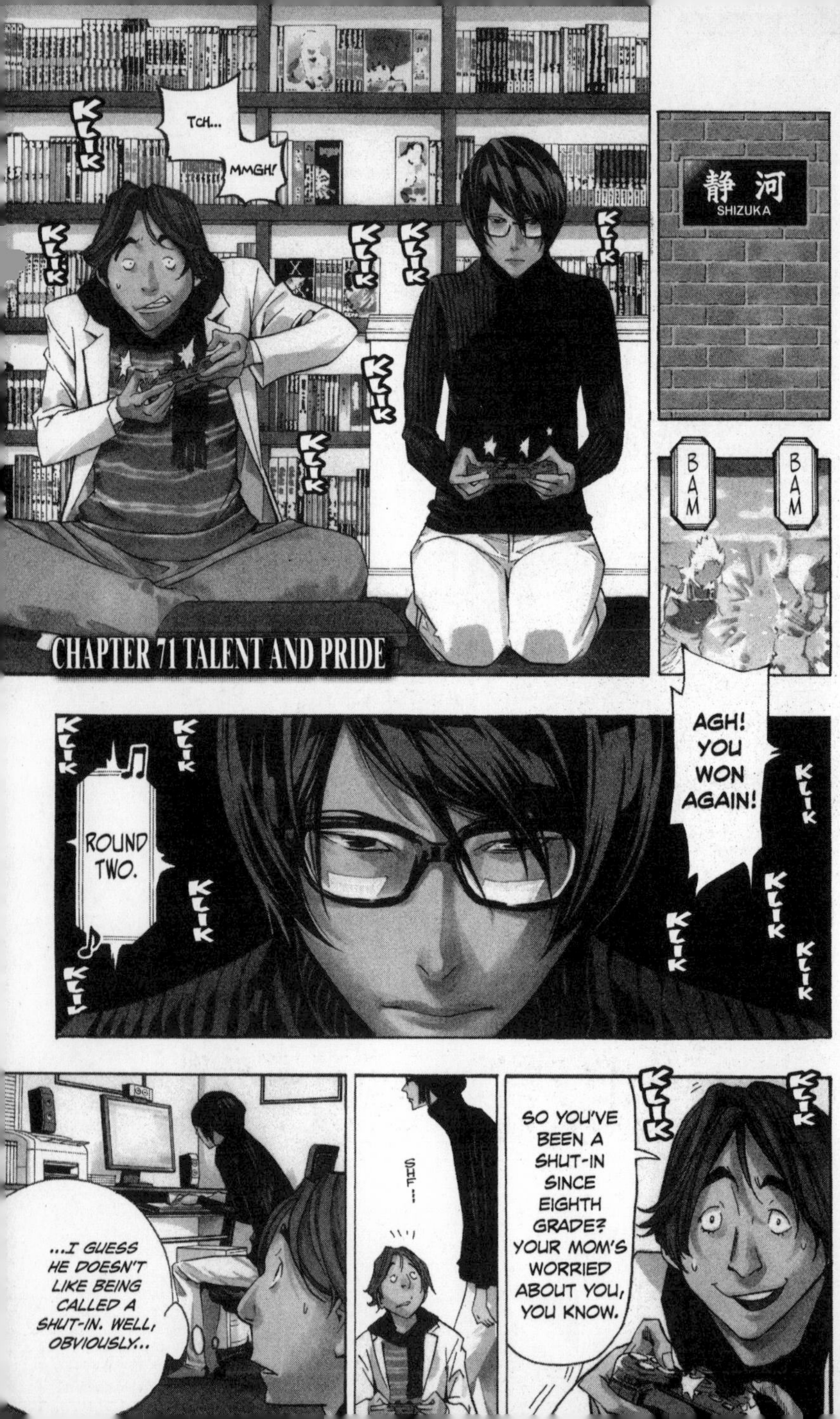
静河
SHIZUKA
BAM
BAM
TCH...
MMGH!
KLIK
KLIK
KLIK
KLIK
KLIK
KLIK
KLIK
CHAPTER 71 TALENT AND PRIDE
AGH! YOU WON AGAIN!
KLIK
KLIK
KLIK
KLIK
ROUND TWO.
KLIK
KLIK
KLIK
KLIK
KLIK
SO YOU'VE BEEN A SHUT-IN SINCE EIGHTH GRADE? YOUR MOM'S WORRIED ABOUT YOU, YOU KNOW.
KLIK
SHF...
...I GUESS HE DOESN'T LIKE BEING CALLED A SHUT-IN. WELL, OBVIOUSLY...

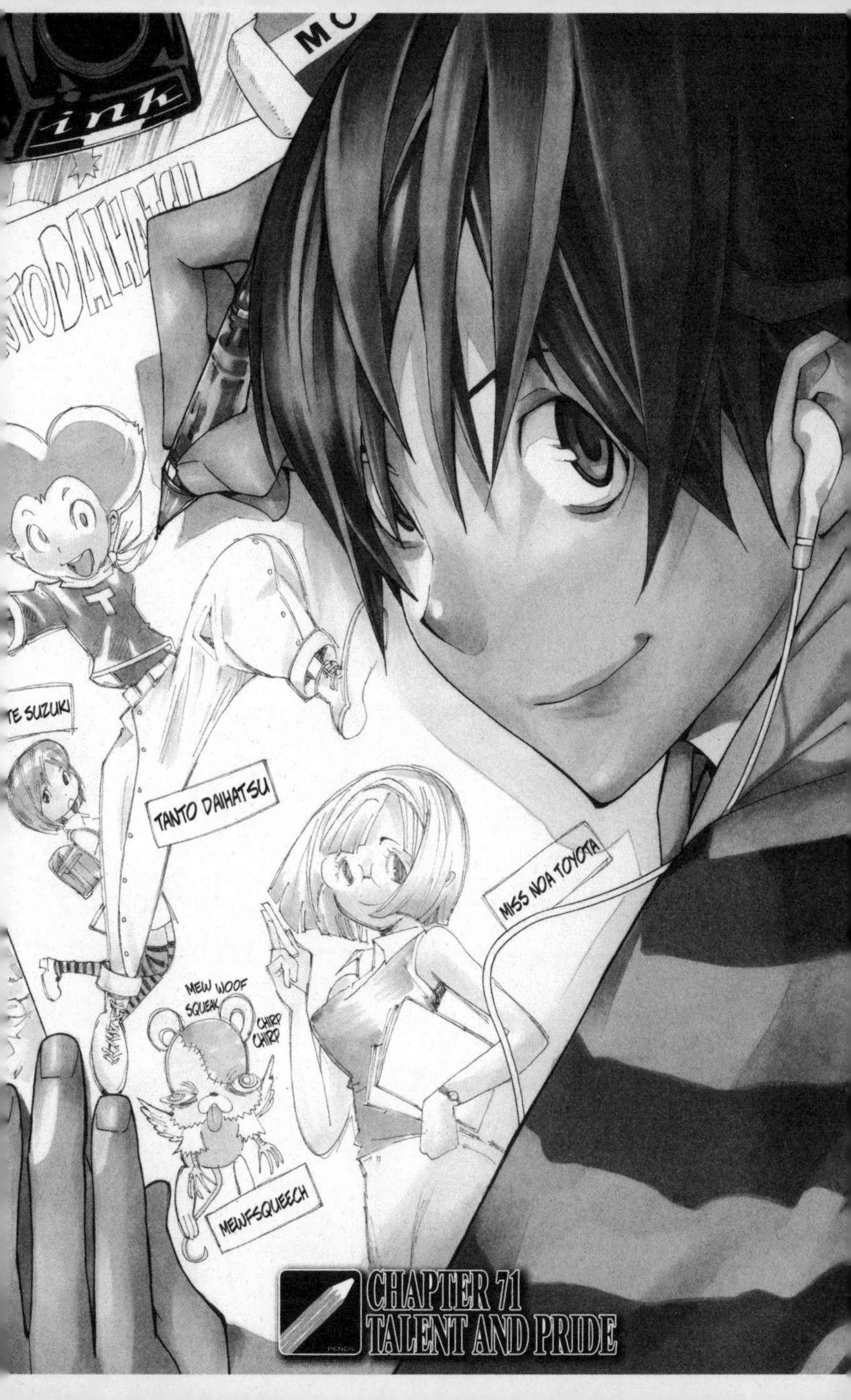
ink
TANTO DAIHATSU
MISS NOA TOYOTA
MEW WOOF
SQUEAK
CHIRP
CHIRP
MEWFSQUEECH
CHAPTER 71
TALENT AND PRIDE

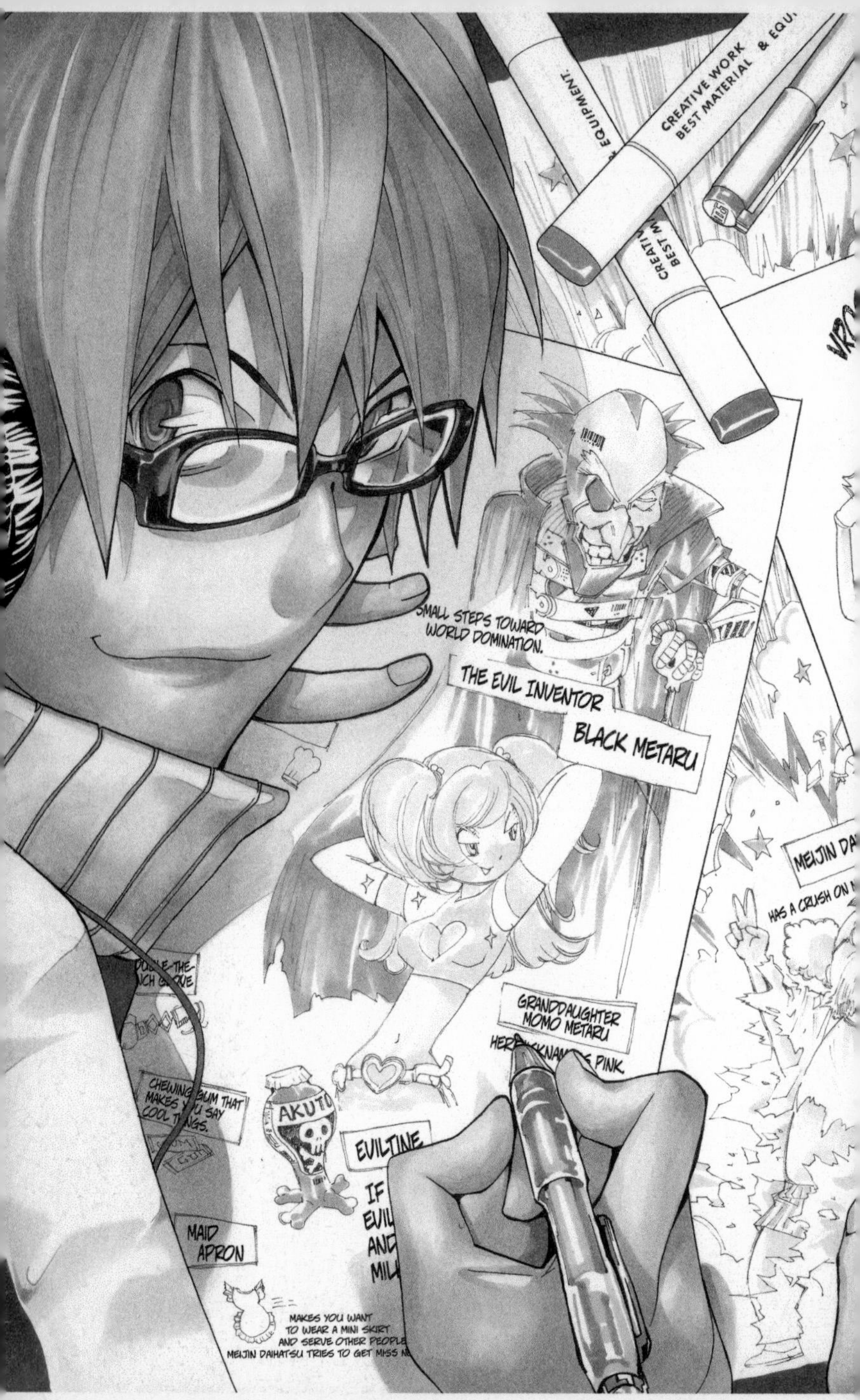
EQUIPMENT.
CREATIVE WORK
BEST MATERIAL
SMALL STEPS TOWARD WORLD DOMINATION.
THE EVIL INVENTOR
BLACK METARU
MEIJIN
HAS A CRUSH ON
GRANDDAUGHTER MOMO METARU
PINK.
CHEWING GUM THAT MAKES YOU SAY COOL THINGS.
AKUTO
EVILTINE
IF
MAID APRON
MAKES YOU WANT TO WEAR A MINI SKIRT AND SERVE OTHER PEOPLE.
MEIJIN DAIHATSU TRIES TO GET MISS

BAKUMAN。

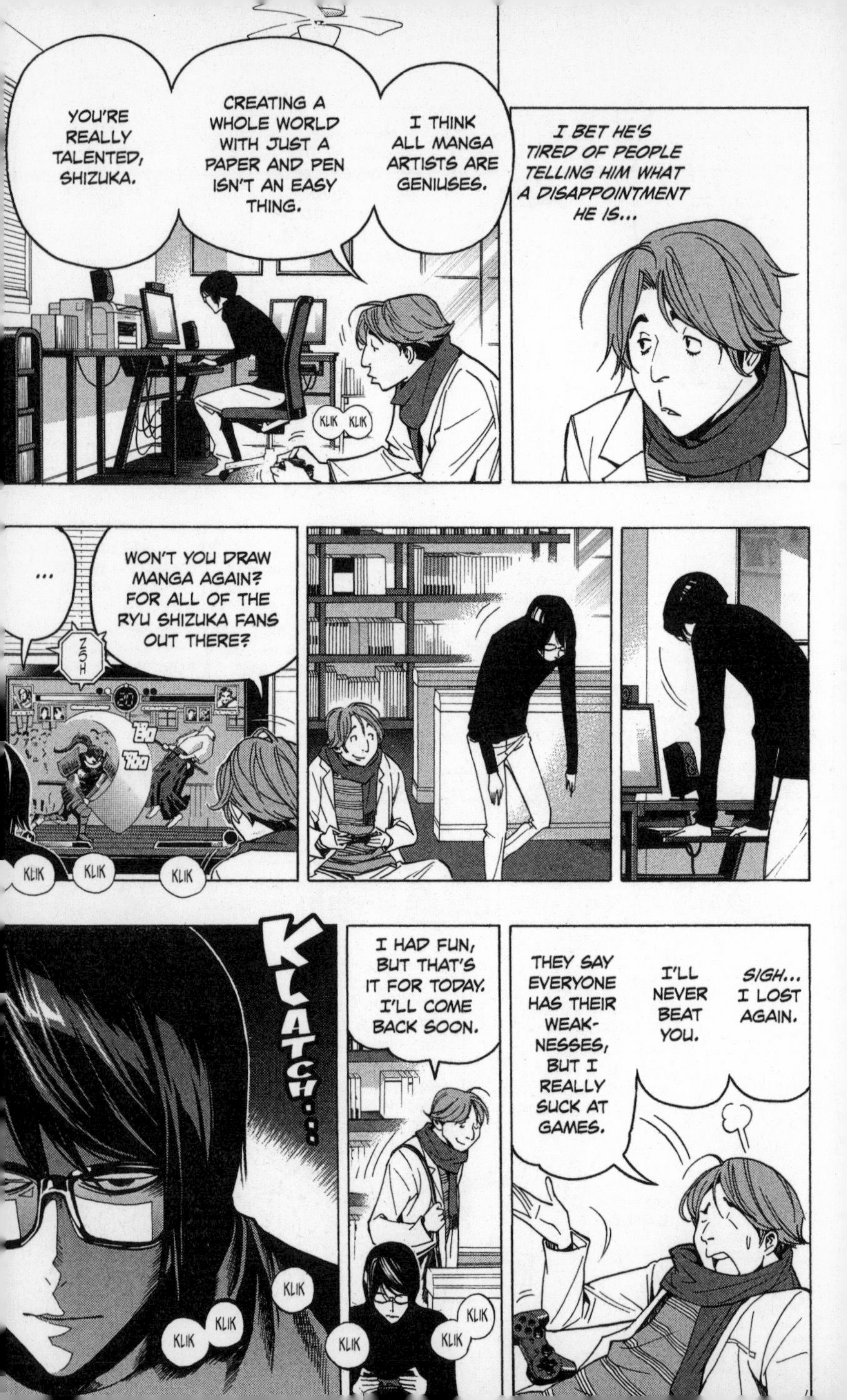

I BET HE'S TIRED OF PEOPLE TELLING HIM WHAT A DISAPPOINTMENT HE IS...
I THINK ALL MANGA ARTISTS ARE GENIUSES.
CREATING A WHOLE WORLD WITH JUST A PAPER AND PEN ISN'T AN EASY THING.
YOU'RE REALLY TALENTED, SHIZUKA.
KLIK
KLIK
WON'T YOU DRAW MANGA AGAIN? FOR ALL OF THE RYU SHIZUKA FANS OUT THERE?
...
ZSH
KLIK
KLIK
KLIK
SIGH... I LOST AGAIN.
I'LL NEVER BEAT YOU.
THEY SAY EVERYONE HAS THEIR WEAK-NESSES, BUT I REALLY SUCK AT GAMES.
I HAD FUN, BUT THAT'S IT FOR TODAY. I'LL COME BACK SOON.
KLIK
KLIK
KLIK
KLATCH...
KLIK
KLIK
KLIK

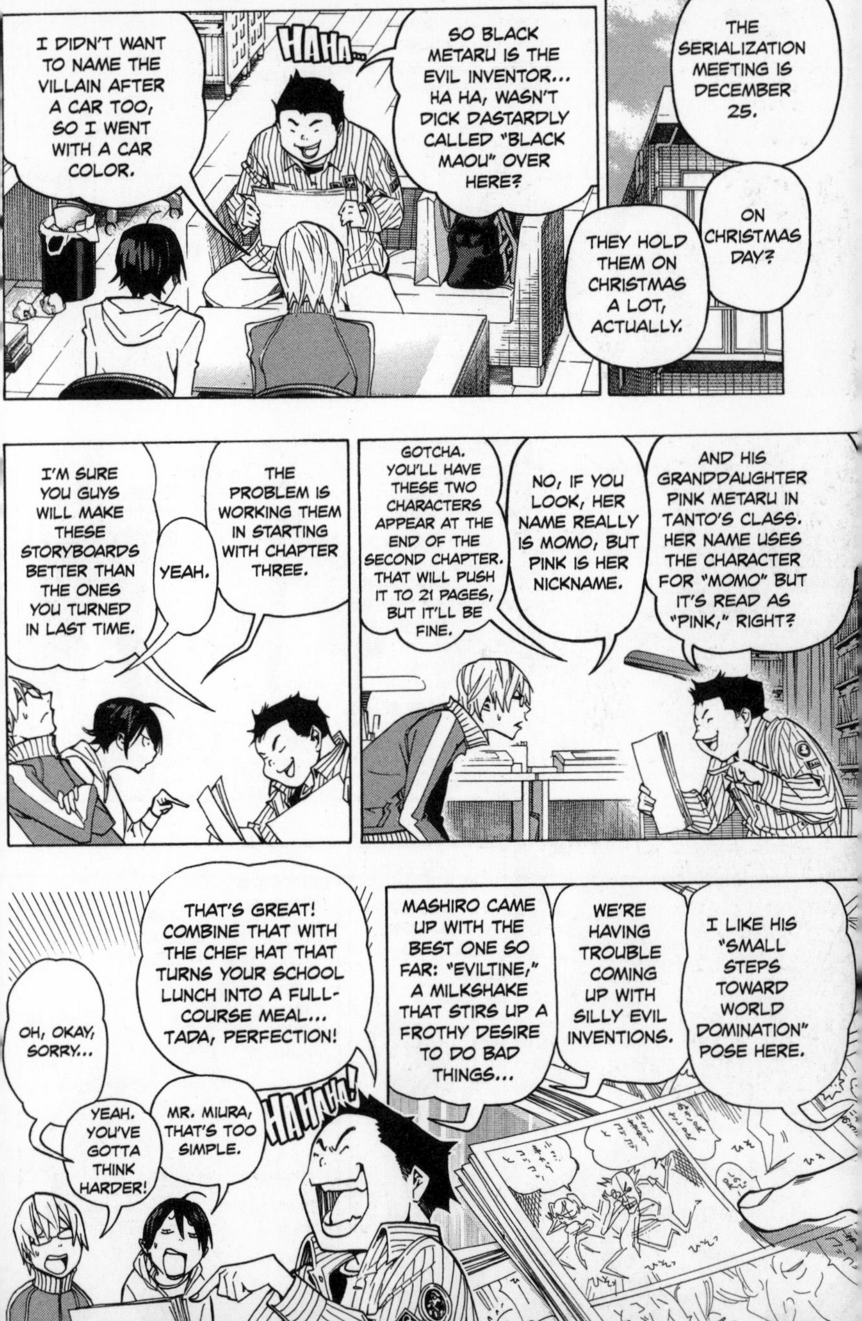
THE SERIALIZATION MEETING IS DECEMBER 25.
ON CHRISTMAS DAY?
THEY HOLD THEM ON CHRISTMAS A LOT, ACTUALLY.
HAHA...
SO BLACK METARU IS THE EVIL INVENTOR... HA HA, WASN'T DICK DASTARDLY CALLED "BLACK MAOU" OVER HERE?
I DIDN'T WANT TO NAME THE VILLAIN AFTER A CAR TOO, SO I WENT WITH A CAR COLOR.
AND HIS GRANDDAUGHTER PINK METARU IN TANTO'S CLASS. HER NAME USES THE CHARACTER FOR "MOMO" BUT IT'S READ AS "PINK," RIGHT?
NO, IF YOU LOOK, HER NAME REALLY IS MOMO, BUT PINK IS HER NICKNAME.
GOTCHA. YOU'LL HAVE THESE TWO CHARACTERS APPEAR AT THE END OF THE SECOND CHAPTER. THAT WILL PUSH IT TO 21 PAGES, BUT IT'LL BE FINE.
THE PROBLEM IS WORKING THEM IN STARTING WITH CHAPTER THREE.
YEAH.
I'M SURE YOU GUYS WILL MAKE THESE STORYBOARDS BETTER THAN THE ONES YOU TURNED IN LAST TIME.
I LIKE HIS "SMALL STEPS TOWARD WORLD DOMINATION" POSE HERE.
WE'RE HAVING TROUBLE COMING UP WITH SILLY EVIL INVENTIONS.
MASHIRO CAME UP WITH THE BEST ONE SO FAR: "EVILTINE," A MILKSHAKE THAT STIRS UP A FROTHY DESIRE TO DO BAD THINGS...
HAHAHA!
THAT'S GREAT! COMBINE THAT WITH THE CHEF HAT THAT TURNS YOUR SCHOOL LUNCH INTO A FULL-COURSE MEAL... TADA, PERFECTION!
OH, OKAY, SORRY...
MR. MIURA, THAT'S TOO SIMPLE.
YEAH. YOU'VE GOTTA THINK HARDER!

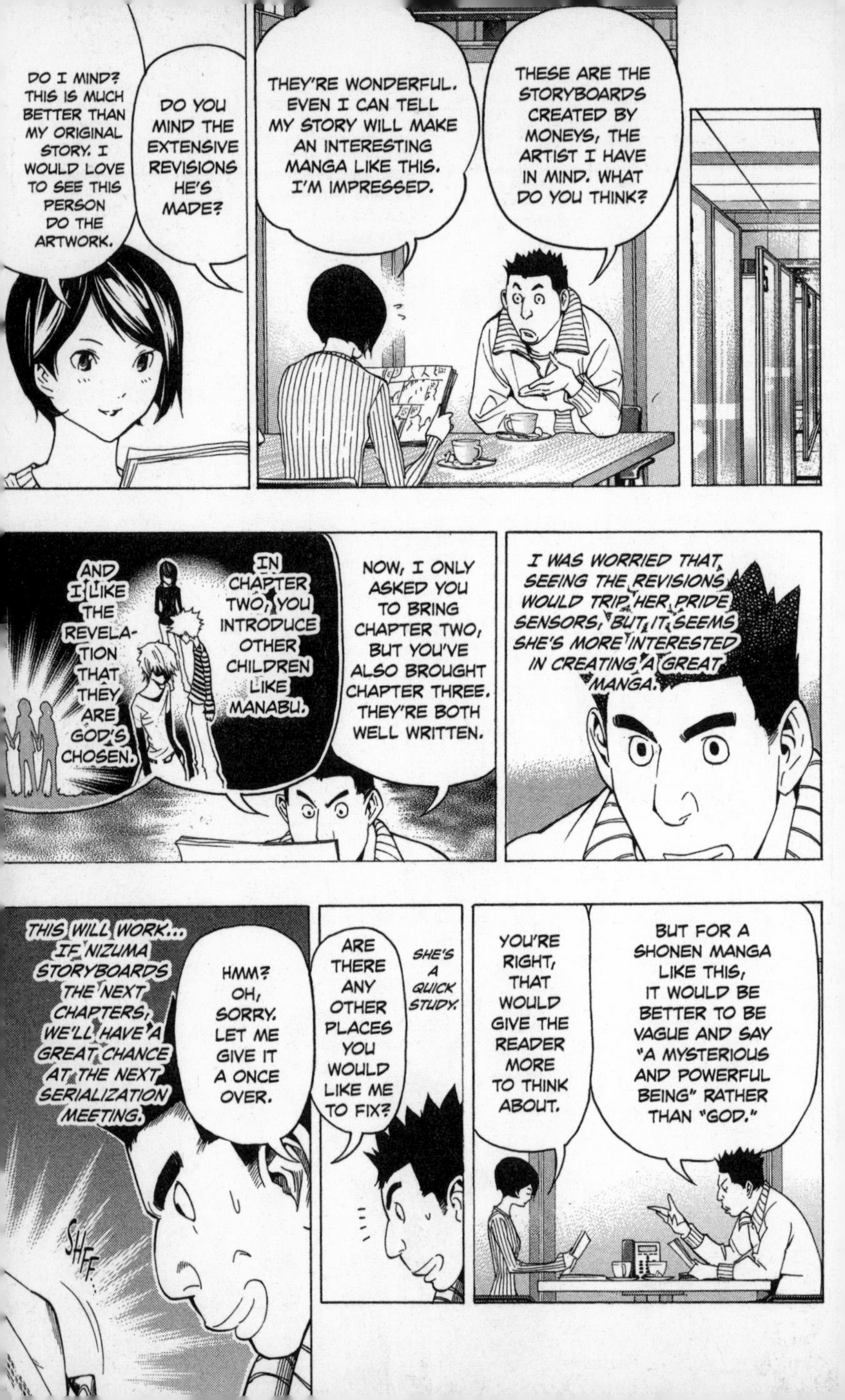
THESE ARE THE STORYBOARDS CREATED BY MONEYS, THE ARTIST I HAVE IN MIND. WHAT DO YOU THINK?
THEY'RE WONDERFUL. EVEN I CAN TELL MY STORY WILL MAKE AN INTERESTING MANGA LIKE THIS. I'M IMPRESSED.
DO YOU MIND THE EXTENSIVE REVISIONS HE'S MADE?
DO I MIND? THIS IS MUCH BETTER THAN MY ORIGINAL STORY. I WOULD LOVE TO SEE THIS PERSON DO THE ARTWORK.
I WAS WORRIED THAT SEEING THE REVISIONS WOULD TRIP HER PRIDE SENSORS, BUT IT SEEMS SHE'S MORE INTERESTED IN CREATING A GREAT MANGA.
NOW, I ONLY ASKED YOU TO BRING CHAPTER TWO, BUT YOU'VE ALSO BROUGHT CHAPTER THREE. THEY'RE BOTH WELL WRITTEN.
IN CHAPTER TWO, YOU INTRODUCE OTHER CHILDREN LIKE MANABU.
AND I LIKE THE REVELATION THAT THEY ARE GOD'S CHOSEN.
BUT FOR A SHONEN MANGA LIKE THIS, IT WOULD BE BETTER TO BE VAGUE AND SAY "A MYSTERIOUS AND POWERFUL BEING" RATHER THAN "GOD."
YOU'RE RIGHT, THAT WOULD GIVE THE READER MORE TO THINK ABOUT.
SHE'S A QUICK STUDY.
ARE THERE ANY OTHER PLACES YOU WOULD LIKE ME TO FIX?
HMM? OH, SORRY. LET ME GIVE IT A ONCE OVER.
THIS WILL WORK... IF NIZUMA STORYBOARDS THE NEXT CHAPTERS, WE'LL HAVE A GREAT CHANCE AT THE NEXT SERIALIZATION MEETING.
SHFF...

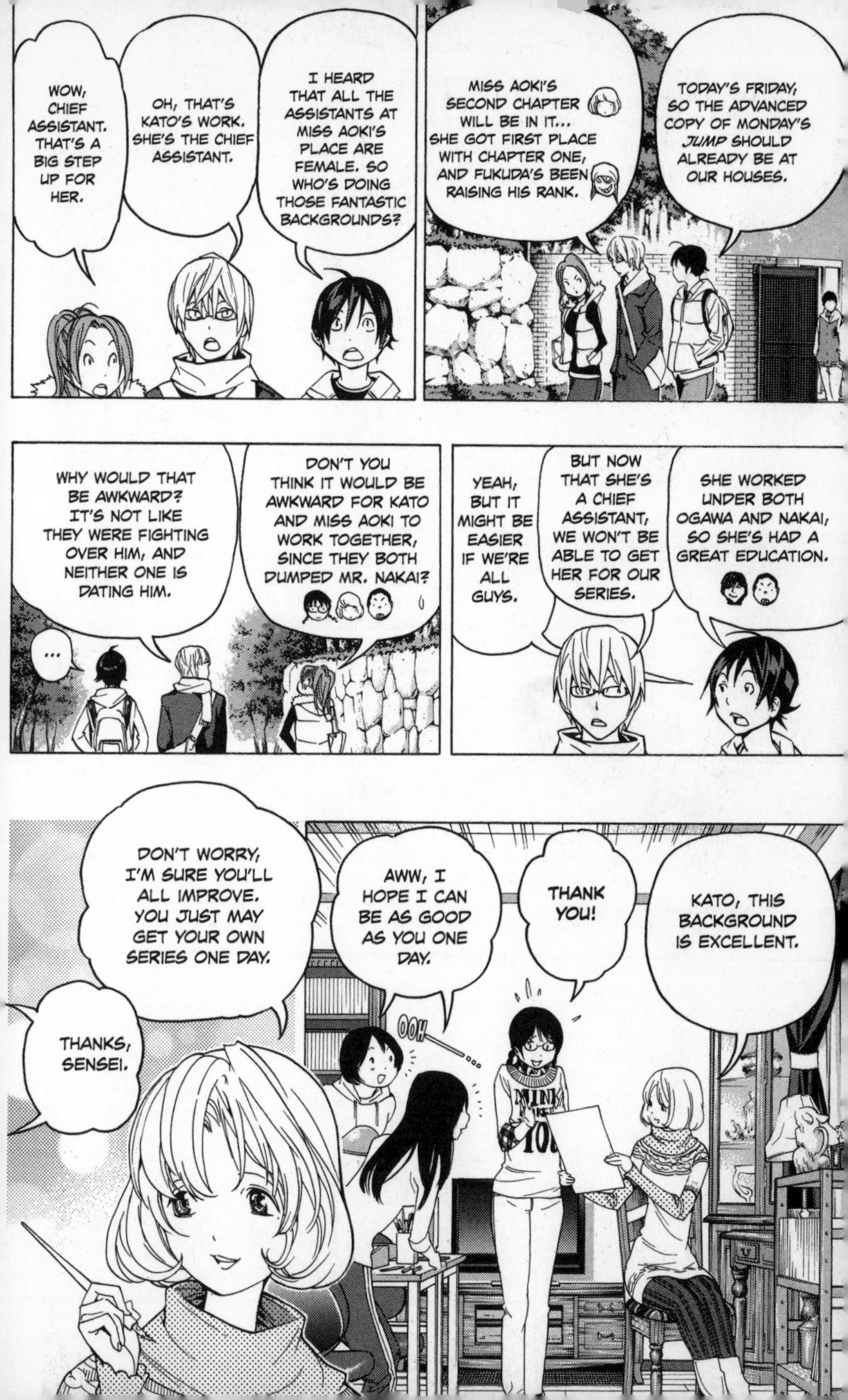
TODAY'S FRIDAY, SO THE ADVANCED COPY OF MONDAY'S *JUMP* SHOULD ALREADY BE AT OUR HOUSES.
MISS AOKI'S SECOND CHAPTER WILL BE IN IT... SHE GOT FIRST PLACE WITH CHAPTER ONE, AND FUKUDA'S BEEN RAISING HIS RANK.
I HEARD THAT ALL THE ASSISTANTS AT MISS AOKI'S PLACE ARE FEMALE. SO WHO'S DOING THOSE FANTASTIC BACKGROUNDS?
OH, THAT'S KATO'S WORK. SHE'S THE CHIEF ASSISTANT.
WOW, CHIEF ASSISTANT. THAT'S A BIG STEP UP FOR HER.
SHE WORKED UNDER BOTH OGAWA AND NAKAI, SO SHE'S HAD A GREAT EDUCATION.
BUT NOW THAT SHE'S A CHIEF ASSISTANT, WE WON'T BE ABLE TO GET HER FOR OUR SERIES.
YEAH, BUT IT MIGHT BE EASIER IF WE'RE ALL GUYS.
DON'T YOU THINK IT WOULD BE AWKWARD FOR KATO AND MISS AOKI TO WORK TOGETHER, SINCE THEY BOTH DUMPED MR. NAKAI?
WHY WOULD THAT BE AWKWARD? IT'S NOT LIKE THEY WERE FIGHTING OVER HIM, AND NEITHER ONE IS DATING HIM.
...
KATO, THIS BACKGROUND IS EXCELLENT.
THANK YOU!
AWW, I HOPE I CAN BE AS GOOD AS YOU ONE DAY.
OOH
DON'T WORRY, I'M SURE YOU'LL ALL IMPROVE. YOU JUST MAY GET YOUR OWN SERIES ONE DAY.
THANKS, SENSEI.

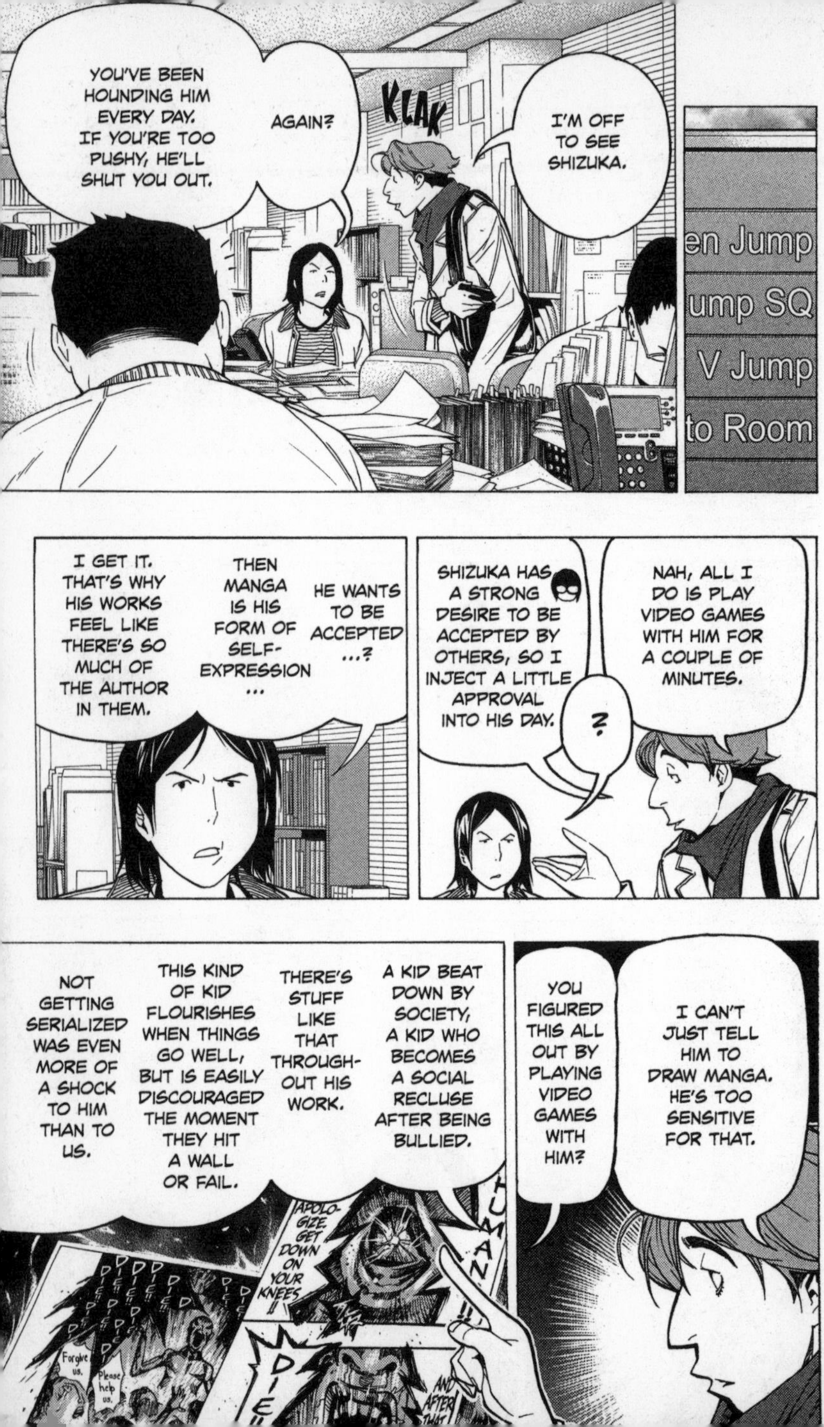
en Jump
ump SQ
V Jump
to Room
I'M OFF TO SEE SHIZUKA.
KLAK
AGAIN?
YOU'VE BEEN HOUNDING HIM EVERY DAY. IF YOU'RE TOO PUSHY, HE'LL SHUT YOU OUT.
NAH, ALL I DO IS PLAY VIDEO GAMES WITH HIM FOR A COUPLE OF MINUTES.
SHIZUKA HAS A STRONG DESIRE TO BE ACCEPTED BY OTHERS, SO I INJECT A LITTLE APPROVAL INTO HIS DAY.
?
HE WANTS TO BE ACCEPTED ...?
THEN MANGA IS HIS FORM OF SELF-EXPRESSION ...
I GET IT. THAT'S WHY HIS WORKS FEEL LIKE THERE'S SO MUCH OF THE AUTHOR IN THEM.
I CAN'T JUST TELL HIM TO DRAW MANGA. HE'S TOO SENSITIVE FOR THAT.
YOU FIGURED THIS ALL OUT BY PLAYING VIDEO GAMES WITH HIM?
A KID BEAT DOWN BY SOCIETY, A KID WHO BECOMES A SOCIAL RECLUSE AFTER BEING BULLIED.
THERE'S STUFF LIKE THAT THROUGH-OUT HIS WORK.
THIS KIND OF KID FLOURISHES WHEN THINGS GO WELL, BUT IS EASILY DISCOURAGED THE MOMENT THEY HIT A WALL OR FAIL.
NOT GETTING SERIALIZED WAS EVEN MORE OF A SHOCK TO HIM THAN TO US.
HUMAN!!
APOLOGIZE. GET DOWN ON YOUR KNEES!!
DIE
Forgive us.
Please help us.

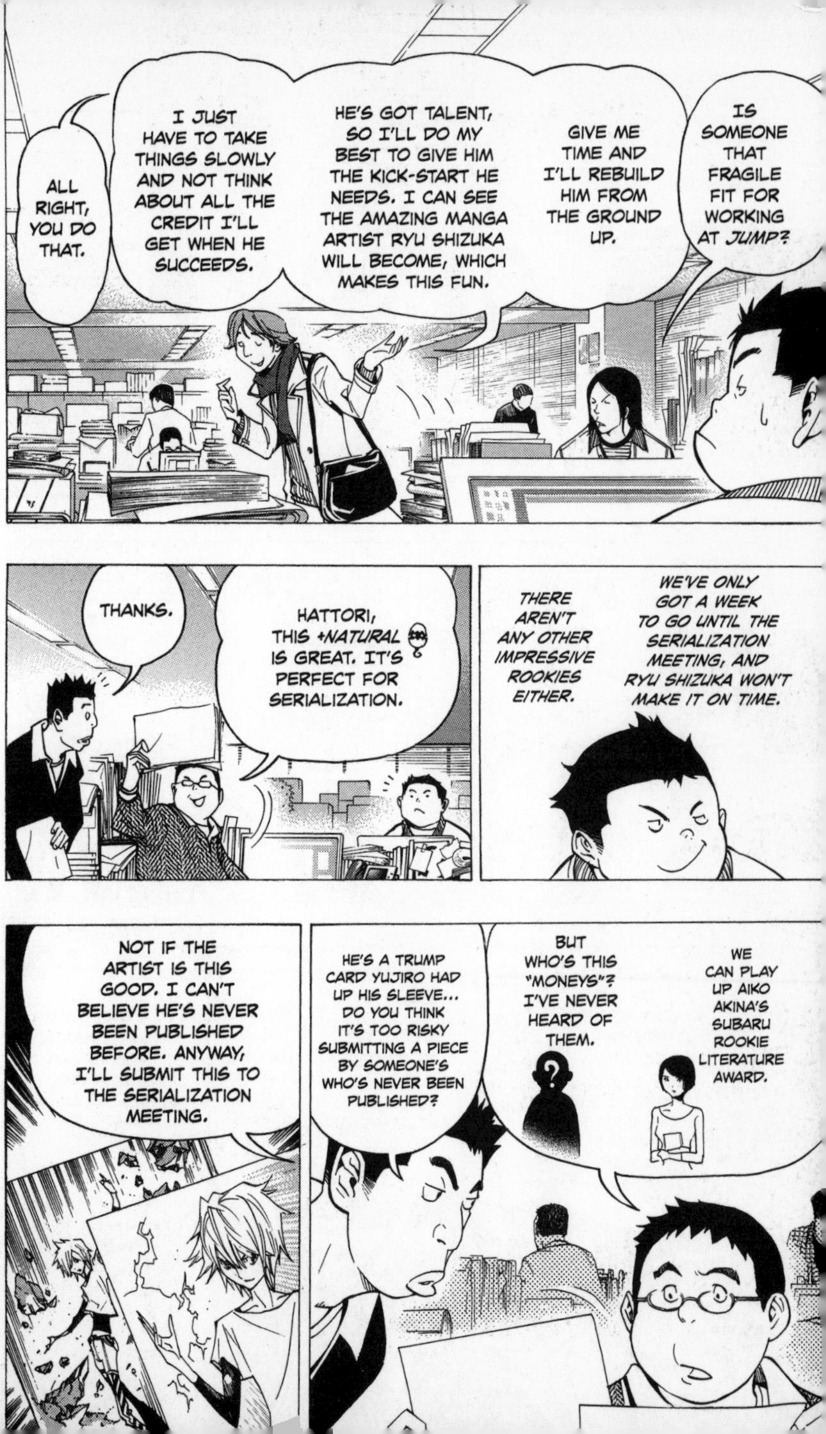
IS SOMEONE THAT FRAGILE FIT FOR WORKING AT *JUMP*?
GIVE ME TIME AND I'LL REBUILD HIM FROM THE GROUND UP.
HE'S GOT TALENT, SO I'LL DO MY BEST TO GIVE HIM THE KICK-START HE NEEDS. I CAN SEE THE AMAZING MANGA ARTIST RYU SHIZUKA WILL BECOME, WHICH MAKES THIS FUN.
I JUST HAVE TO TAKE THINGS SLOWLY AND NOT THINK ABOUT ALL THE CREDIT I'LL GET WHEN HE SUCCEEDS.
ALL RIGHT, YOU DO THAT.
WE'VE ONLY GOT A WEEK TO GO UNTIL THE SERIALIZATION MEETING, AND RYU SHIZUKA WON'T MAKE IT ON TIME.
THERE AREN'T ANY OTHER IMPRESSIVE ROOKIES EITHER.
HATTORI, THIS *+NATURAL* IS GREAT. IT'S PERFECT FOR SERIALIZATION.
THANKS.
WE CAN PLAY UP AIKO AKINA'S SUBARU ROOKIE LITERATURE AWARD.
BUT WHO'S THIS "MONEYS"? I'VE NEVER HEARD OF THEM.
HE'S A TRUMP CARD YUJIRO HAD UP HIS SLEEVE... DO YOU THINK IT'S TOO RISKY SUBMITTING A PIECE BY SOMEONE'S WHO'S NEVER BEEN PUBLISHED?
NOT IF THE ARTIST IS THIS GOOD. I CAN'T BELIEVE HE'S NEVER BEEN PUBLISHED BEFORE. ANYWAY, I'LL SUBMIT THIS TO THE SERIALIZATION MEETING.

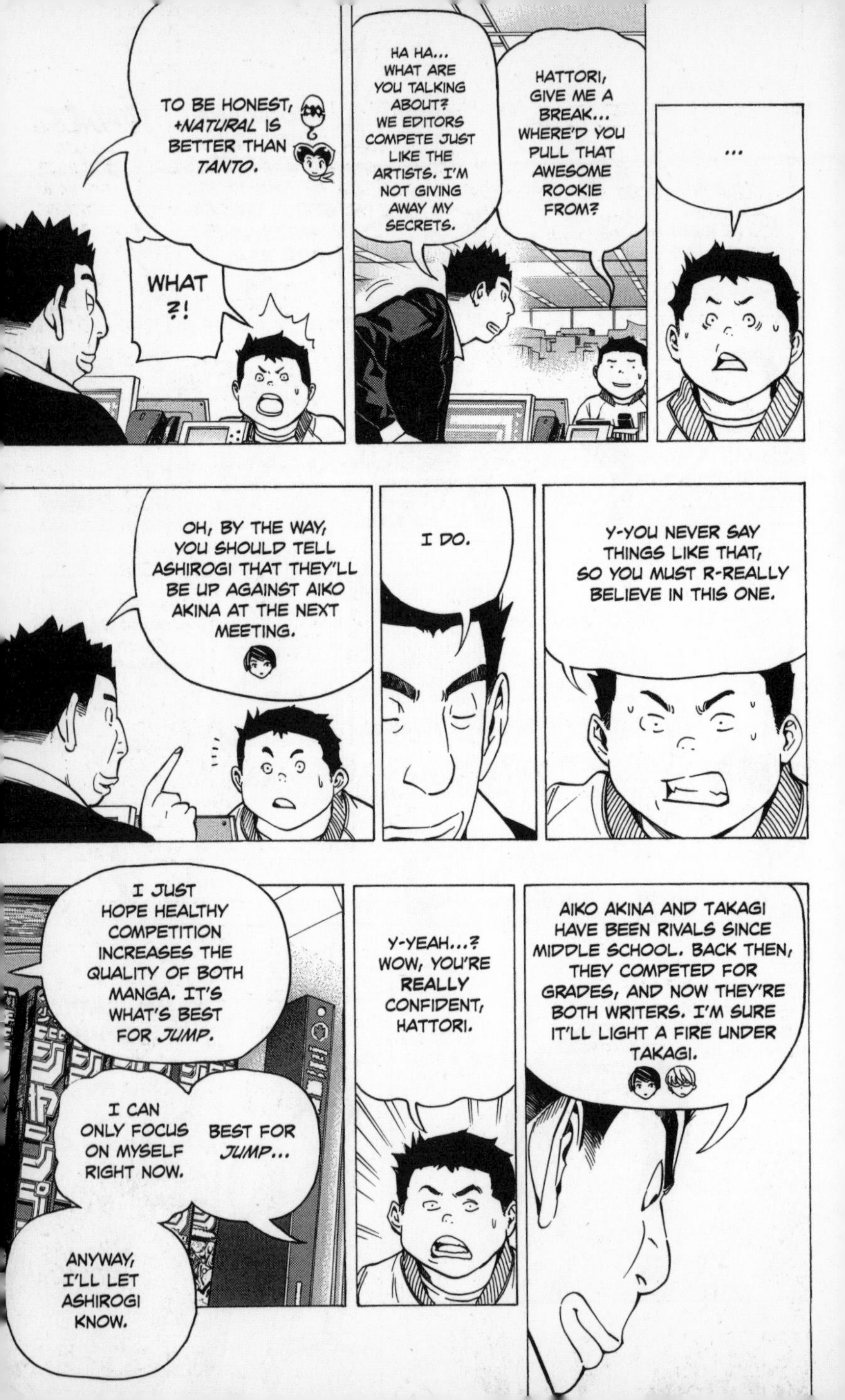
...
HATTORI, GIVE ME A BREAK... WHERE'D YOU PULL THAT AWESOME ROOKIE FROM?
HA HA... WHAT ARE YOU TALKING ABOUT? WE EDITORS COMPETE JUST LIKE THE ARTISTS. I'M NOT GIVING AWAY MY SECRETS.
TO BE HONEST, *+NATURAL* IS BETTER THAN *TANTO*.
WHAT?!
Y-YOU NEVER SAY THINGS LIKE THAT, SO YOU MUST R-REALLY BELIEVE IN THIS ONE.
I DO.
OH, BY THE WAY, YOU SHOULD TELL ASHIROGI THAT THEY'LL BE UP AGAINST AIKO AKINA AT THE NEXT MEETING.
AIKO AKINA AND TAKAGI HAVE BEEN RIVALS SINCE MIDDLE SCHOOL. BACK THEN, THEY COMPETED FOR GRADES, AND NOW THEY'RE BOTH WRITERS. I'M SURE IT'LL LIGHT A FIRE UNDER TAKAGI.
Y-YEAH...? WOW, YOU'RE REALLY CONFIDENT, HATTORI.
I JUST HOPE HEALTHY COMPETITION INCREASES THE QUALITY OF BOTH MANGA. IT'S WHAT'S BEST FOR *JUMP*.
BEST FOR *JUMP*...
I CAN ONLY FOCUS ON MYSELF RIGHT NOW.
ANYWAY, I'LL LET ASHIROGI KNOW.

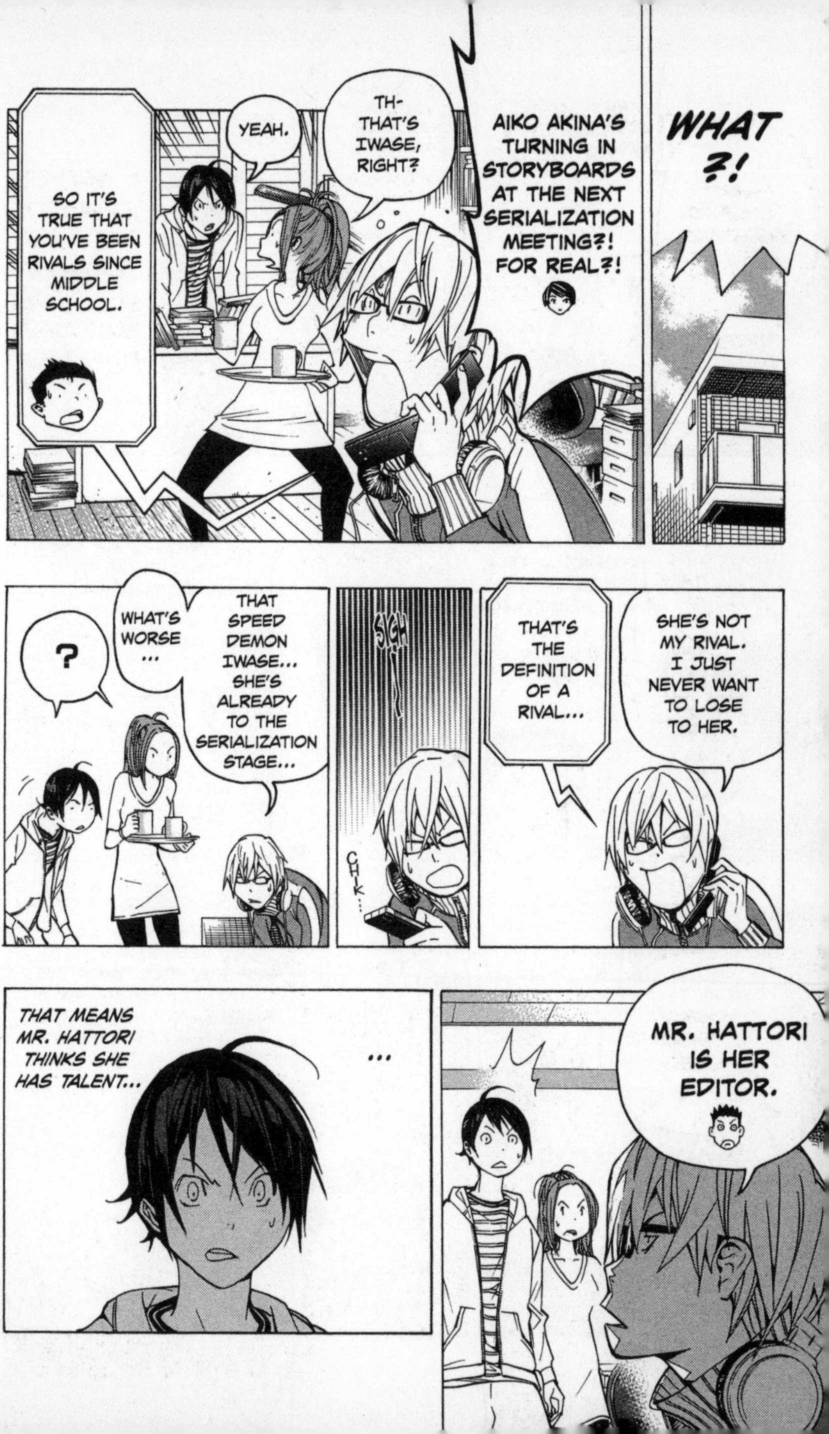
WHAT ?!
AIKO AKINA'S TURNING IN STORYBOARDS AT THE NEXT SERIALIZATION MEETING?! FOR REAL?!
TH- THAT'S IWASE, RIGHT?
YEAH.
SO IT'S TRUE THAT YOU'VE BEEN RIVALS SINCE MIDDLE SCHOOL.
SHE'S NOT MY RIVAL. I JUST NEVER WANT TO LOSE TO HER.
THAT'S THE DEFINITION OF A RIVAL...
SIGH
CHIK...
THAT SPEED DEMON IWASE... SHE'S ALREADY TO THE SERIALIZATION STAGE...
WHAT'S WORSE...
?
MR. HATTORI IS HER EDITOR.
...
THAT MEANS MR. HATTORI THINKS SHE HAS TALENT...

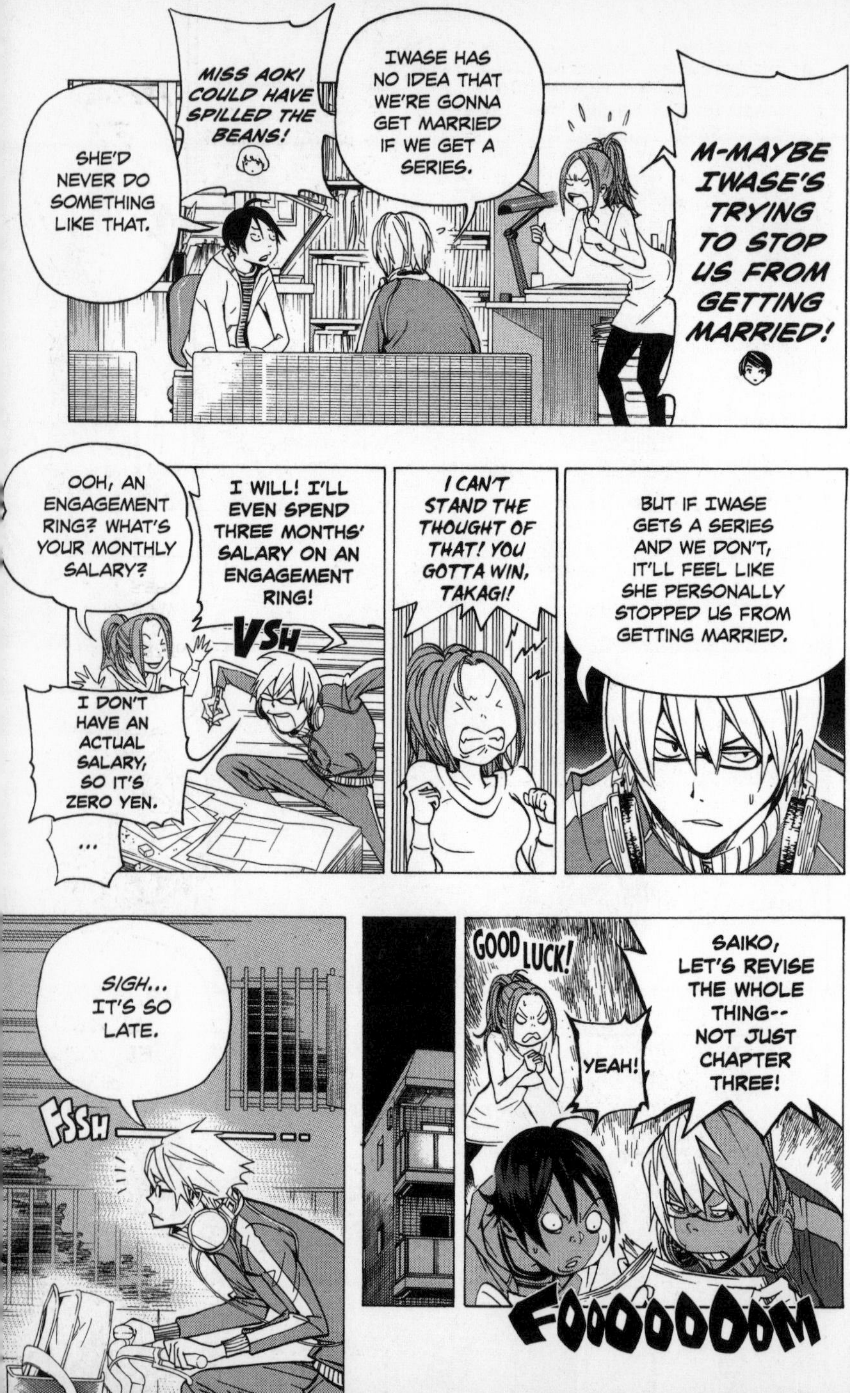
M-MAYBE IWASE'S TRYING TO STOP US FROM GETTING MARRIED!
IWASE HAS NO IDEA THAT WE'RE GONNA GET MARRIED IF WE GET A SERIES.
MISS AOKI COULD HAVE SPILLED THE BEANS!
SHE'D NEVER DO SOMETHING LIKE THAT.
BUT IF IWASE GETS A SERIES AND WE DON'T, IT'LL FEEL LIKE SHE PERSONALLY STOPPED US FROM GETTING MARRIED.
I CAN'T STAND THE THOUGHT OF THAT! YOU GOTTA WIN, TAKAGI!
I WILL! I'LL EVEN SPEND THREE MONTHS' SALARY ON AN ENGAGEMENT RING!
VSH
OOH, AN ENGAGEMENT RING? WHAT'S YOUR MONTHLY SALARY?
I DON'T HAVE AN ACTUAL SALARY, SO IT'S ZERO YEN.
...
SAIKO, LET'S REVISE THE WHOLE THING-- NOT JUST CHAPTER THREE!
GOOD LUCK!
YEAH!
FOOOOOOM
SIGH... IT'S SO LATE.
FSSH

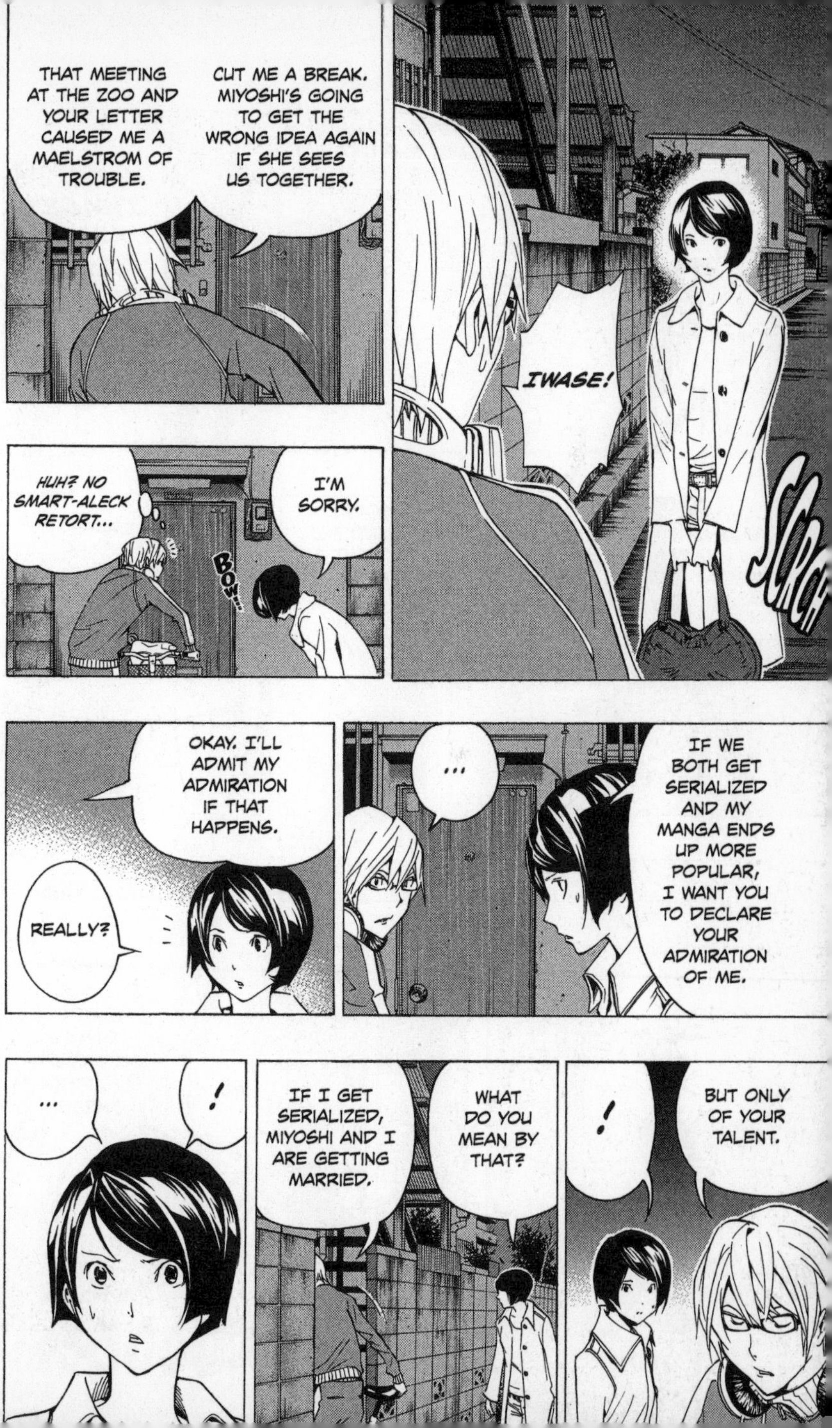
IWASE!
CUT ME A BREAK. MIYOSHI'S GOING TO GET THE WRONG IDEA AGAIN IF SHE SEES US TOGETHER.
THAT MEETING AT THE ZOO AND YOUR LETTER CAUSED ME A MAELSTROM OF TROUBLE.
I'M SORRY.
BOW
HUH? NO SMART-ALECK RETORT...
IF WE BOTH GET SERIALIZED AND MY MANGA ENDS UP MORE POPULAR, I WANT YOU TO DECLARE YOUR ADMIRATION OF ME.
...
OKAY. I'LL ADMIT MY ADMIRATION IF THAT HAPPENS.
REALLY?
BUT ONLY OF YOUR TALENT.
!
WHAT DO YOU MEAN BY THAT?
IF I GET SERIALIZED, MIYOSHI AND I ARE GETTING MARRIED.
!
...

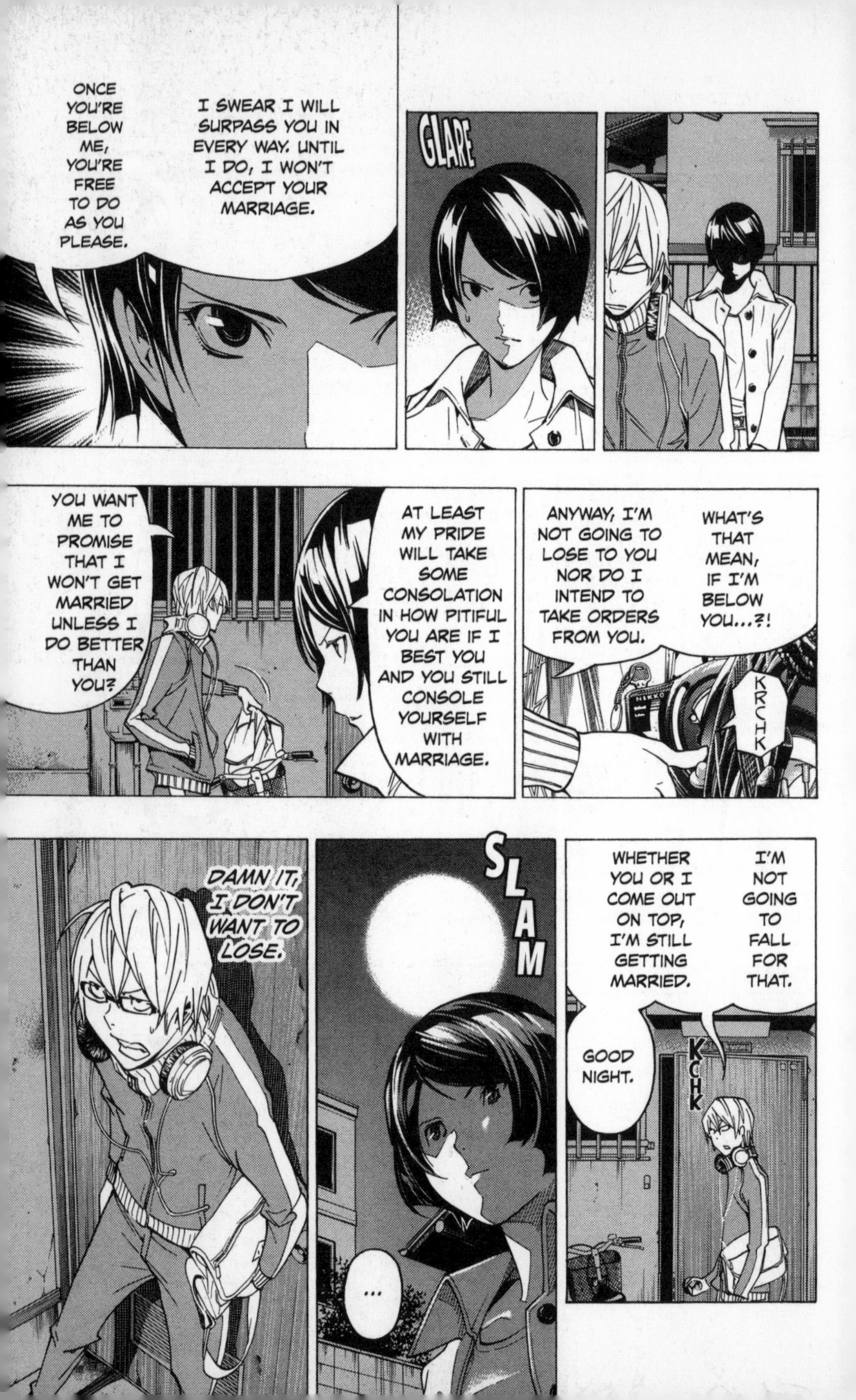
GLARE
I SWEAR I WILL SURPASS YOU IN EVERY WAY. UNTIL I DO, I WON'T ACCEPT YOUR MARRIAGE.
ONCE YOU'RE BELOW ME, YOU'RE FREE TO DO AS YOU PLEASE.
WHAT'S THAT MEAN, IF I'M BELOW YOU...?!
ANYWAY, I'M NOT GOING TO LOSE TO YOU NOR DO I INTEND TO TAKE ORDERS FROM YOU.
KRCHK
AT LEAST MY PRIDE WILL TAKE SOME CONSOLATION IN HOW PITIFUL YOU ARE IF I BEST YOU AND YOU STILL CONSOLE YOURSELF WITH MARRIAGE.
YOU WANT ME TO PROMISE THAT I WON'T GET MARRIED UNLESS I DO BETTER THAN YOU?
I'M NOT GOING TO FALL FOR THAT.
WHETHER YOU OR I COME OUT ON TOP, I'M STILL GETTING MARRIED.
GOOD NIGHT.
KCHK
SLAM
...
DAMN IT, I DON'T WANT TO LOSE.

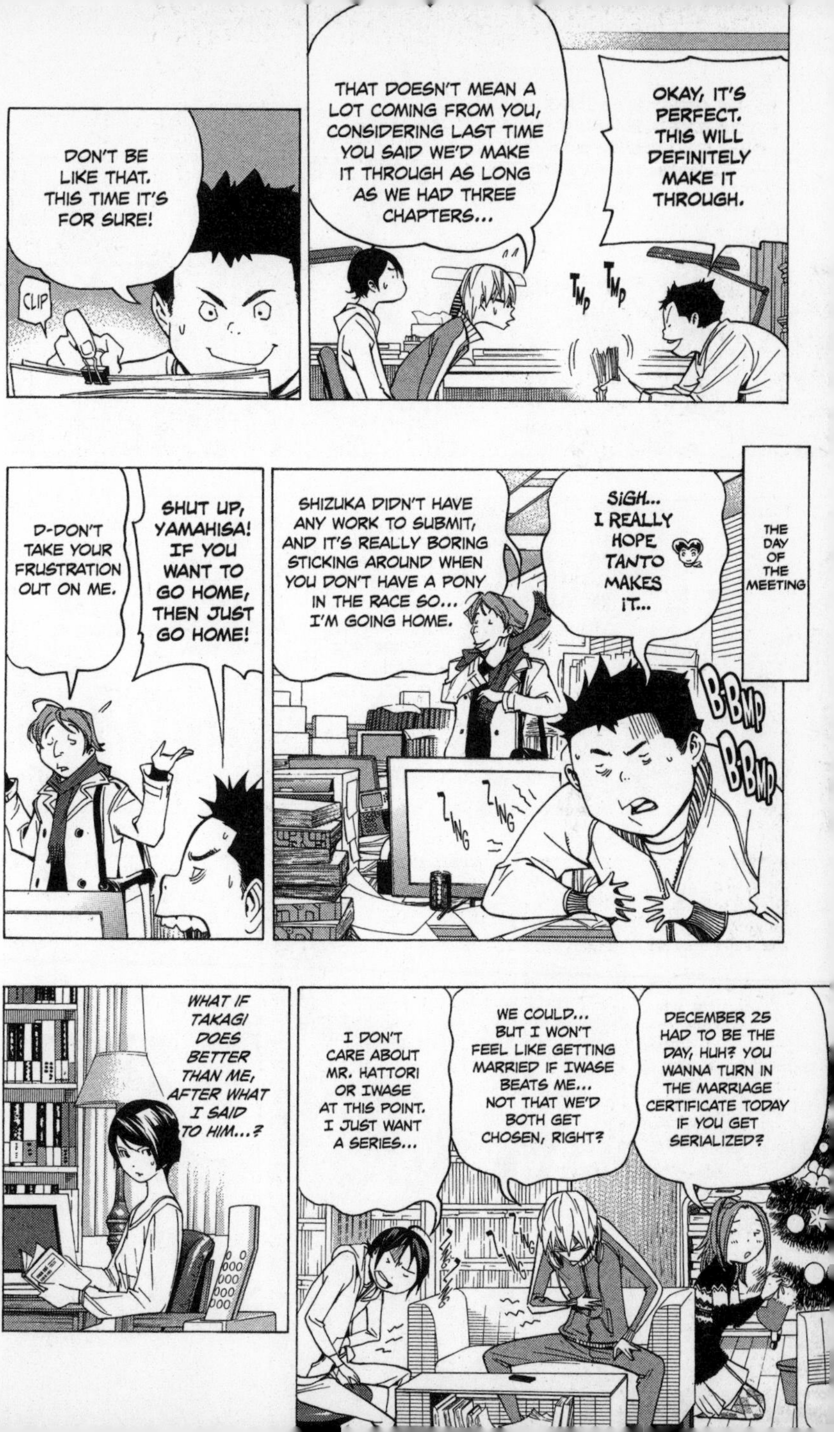

OKAY, IT'S PERFECT. THIS WILL DEFINITELY MAKE IT THROUGH.
TMP
TMP
THAT DOESN'T MEAN A LOT COMING FROM YOU, CONSIDERING LAST TIME YOU SAID WE'D MAKE IT THROUGH AS LONG AS WE HAD THREE CHAPTERS...
DON'T BE LIKE THAT. THIS TIME IT'S FOR SURE!
CLIP
THE DAY OF THE MEETING
SIGH... I REALLY HOPE TANTO MAKES IT...
B-BMP
B-BMP
SHIZUKA DIDN'T HAVE ANY WORK TO SUBMIT, AND IT'S REALLY BORING STICKING AROUND WHEN YOU DON'T HAVE A PONY IN THE RACE SO... I'M GOING HOME.
ZING
ZING
SHUT UP, YAMAHISA! IF YOU WANT TO GO HOME, THEN JUST GO HOME!
D-DON'T TAKE YOUR FRUSTRATION OUT ON ME.
DECEMBER 25 HAD TO BE THE DAY, HUH? YOU WANNA TURN IN THE MARRIAGE CERTIFICATE TODAY IF YOU GET SERIALIZED?
WE COULD... BUT I WON'T FEEL LIKE GETTING MARRIED IF IWASE BEATS ME... NOT THAT WE'D BOTH GET CHOSEN, RIGHT?
I DON'T CARE ABOUT MR. HATTORI OR IWASE AT THIS POINT. I JUST WANT A SERIES...
WHAT IF TAKAGI DOES BETTER THAN ME, AFTER WHAT I SAID TO HIM...?

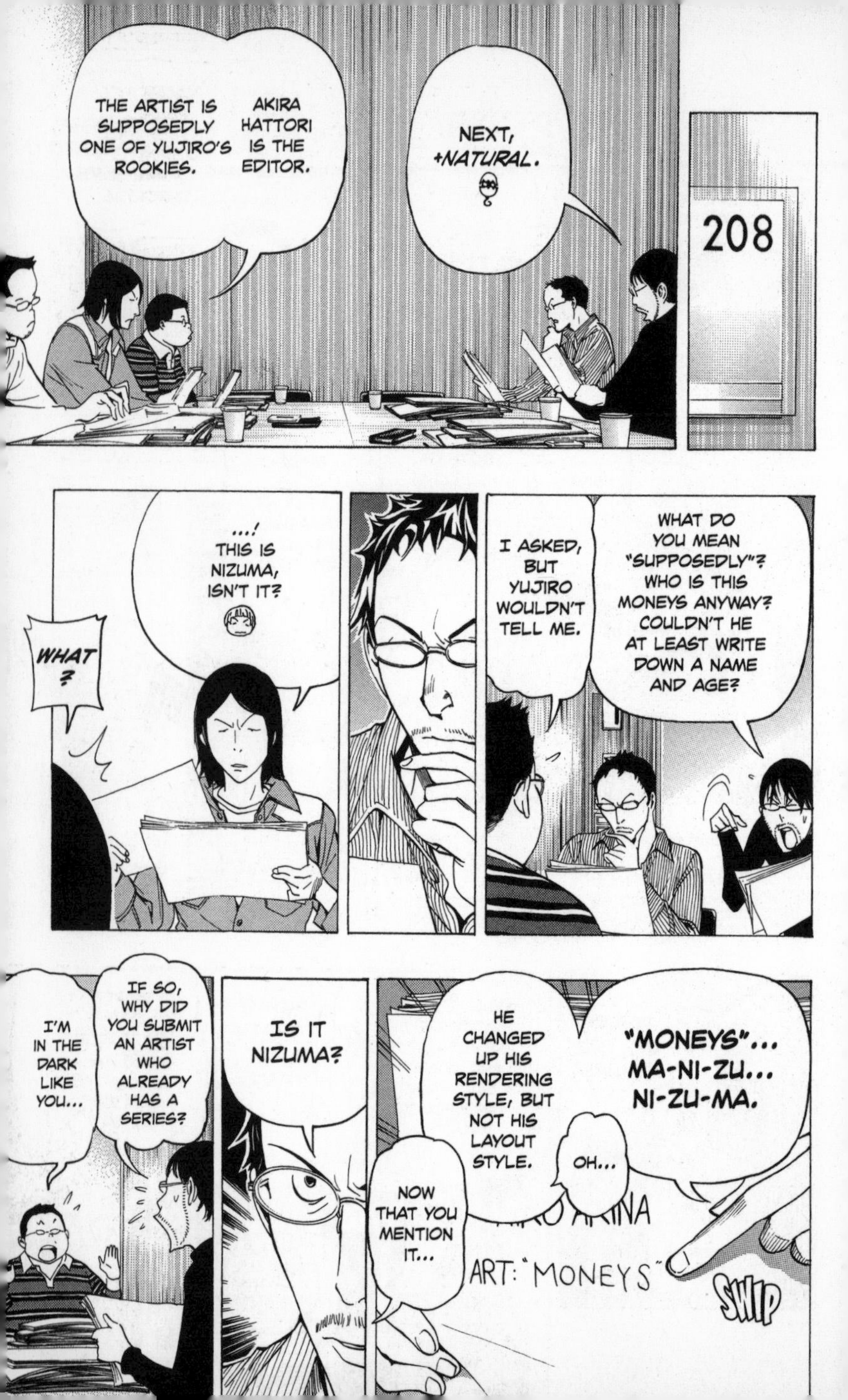
208
NEXT, +NATURAL.
AKIRA HATTORI IS THE EDITOR.
THE ARTIST IS SUPPOSEDLY ONE OF YUJIRO'S ROOKIES.
WHAT DO YOU MEAN "SUPPOSEDLY"? WHO IS THIS MONEYS ANYWAY? COULDN'T HE AT LEAST WRITE DOWN A NAME AND AGE?
I ASKED, BUT YUJIRO WOULDN'T TELL ME.
...! THIS IS NIZUMA, ISN'T IT?
WHAT?
"MONEYS"... MA-NI-ZU... NI-ZU-MA.
HE CHANGED UP HIS RENDERING STYLE, BUT NOT HIS LAYOUT STYLE.
OH...
NOW THAT YOU MENTION IT...
ART: "MONEYS"
SWIP
IS IT NIZUMA?
IF SO, WHY DID YOU SUBMIT AN ARTIST WHO ALREADY HAS A SERIES?
I'M IN THE DARK LIKE YOU...

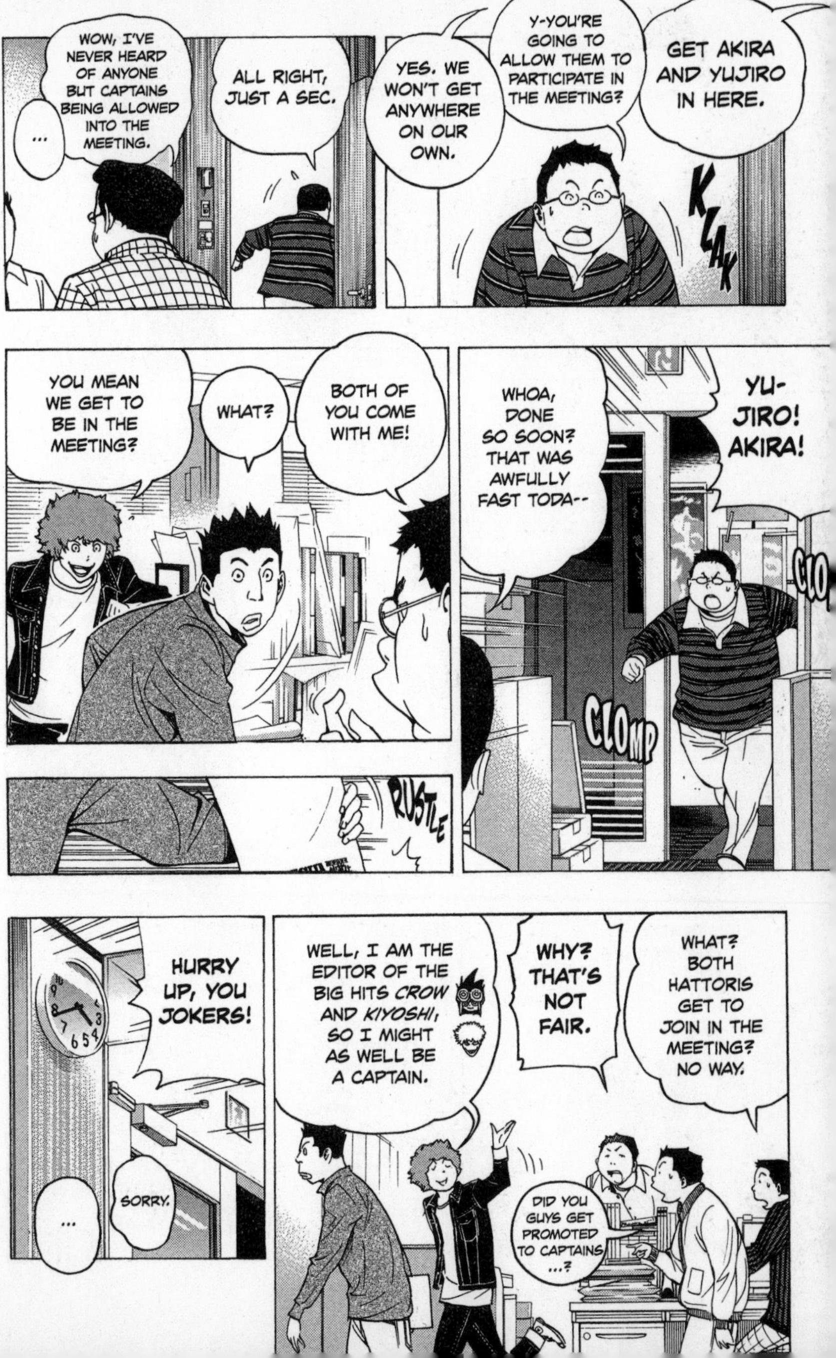
GET AKIRA AND YUJIRO IN HERE.
KLAK
Y-YOU'RE GOING TO ALLOW THEM TO PARTICIPATE IN THE MEETING?
YES. WE WON'T GET ANYWHERE ON OUR OWN.
ALL RIGHT, JUST A SEC.
WOW, I'VE NEVER HEARD OF ANYONE BUT CAPTAINS BEING ALLOWED INTO THE MEETING.
...
YU-JIRO! AKIRA!
WHOA, DONE SO SOON? THAT WAS AWFULLY FAST TODA--
CLOMP
BOTH OF YOU COME WITH ME!
WHAT?
YOU MEAN WE GET TO BE IN THE MEETING?
RUSTLE
WHAT? BOTH HATTORIS GET TO JOIN IN THE MEETING? NO WAY.
WHY? THAT'S NOT FAIR.
WELL, I AM THE EDITOR OF THE BIG HITS *CROW* AND *KIYOSHI*, SO I MIGHT AS WELL BE A CAPTAIN.
DID YOU GUYS GET PROMOTED TO CAPTAINS ...?
HURRY UP, YOU JOKERS!
SORRY.
...

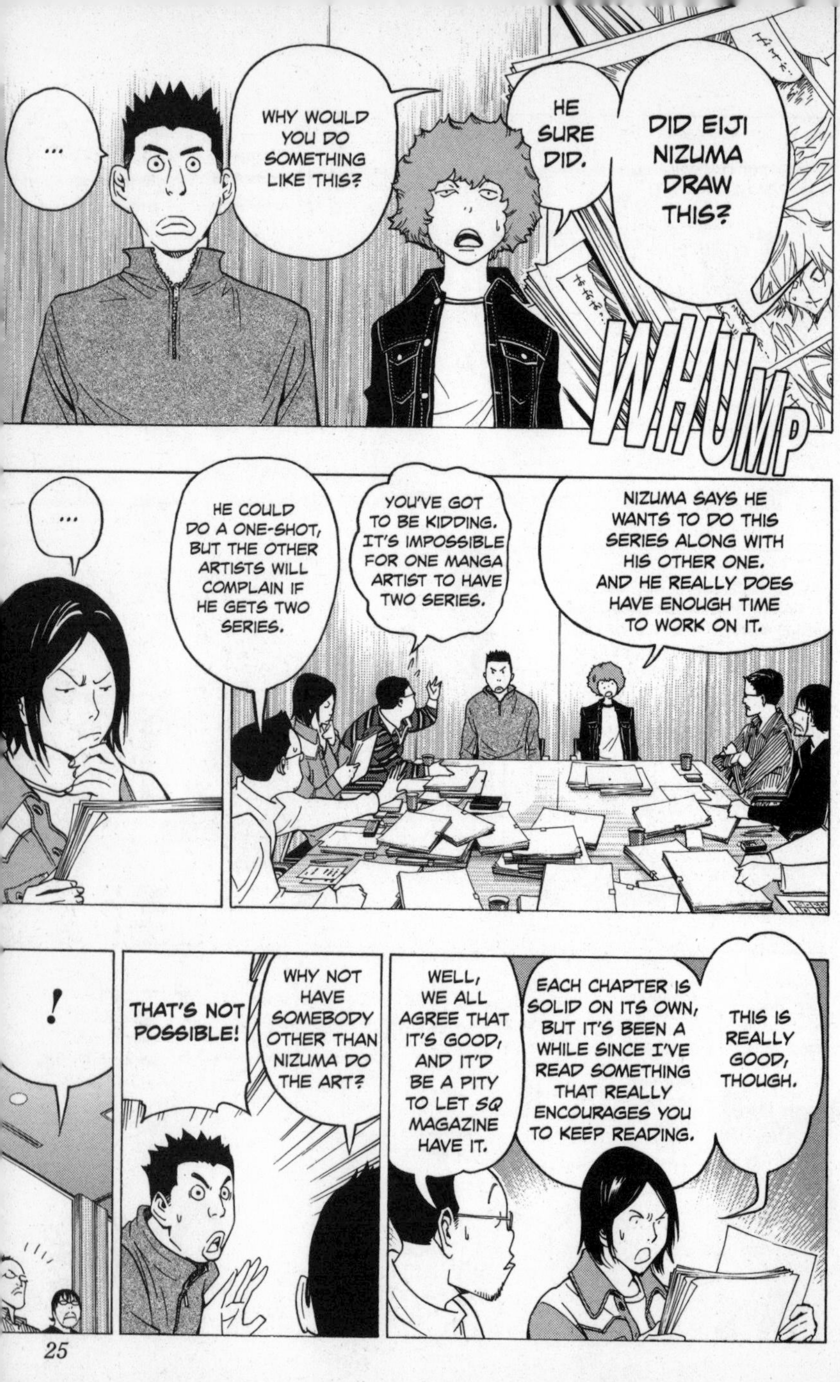
DID EIJI NIZUMA DRAW THIS?
HE SURE DID.
WHY WOULD YOU DO SOMETHING LIKE THIS?
...
WHUMP
NIZUMA SAYS HE WANTS TO DO THIS SERIES ALONG WITH HIS OTHER ONE. AND HE REALLY DOES HAVE ENOUGH TIME TO WORK ON IT.
YOU'VE GOT TO BE KIDDING. IT'S IMPOSSIBLE FOR ONE MANGA ARTIST TO HAVE TWO SERIES.
HE COULD DO A ONE-SHOT, BUT THE OTHER ARTISTS WILL COMPLAIN IF HE GETS TWO SERIES.
...
THIS IS REALLY GOOD, THOUGH.
EACH CHAPTER IS SOLID ON ITS OWN, BUT IT'S BEEN A WHILE SINCE I'VE READ SOMETHING THAT REALLY ENCOURAGES YOU TO KEEP READING.
WELL, WE ALL AGREE THAT IT'S GOOD, AND IT'D BE A PITY TO LET SQ MAGAZINE HAVE IT.
WHY NOT HAVE SOMEBODY OTHER THAN NIZUMA DO THE ART?
THAT'S NOT POSSIBLE!
!

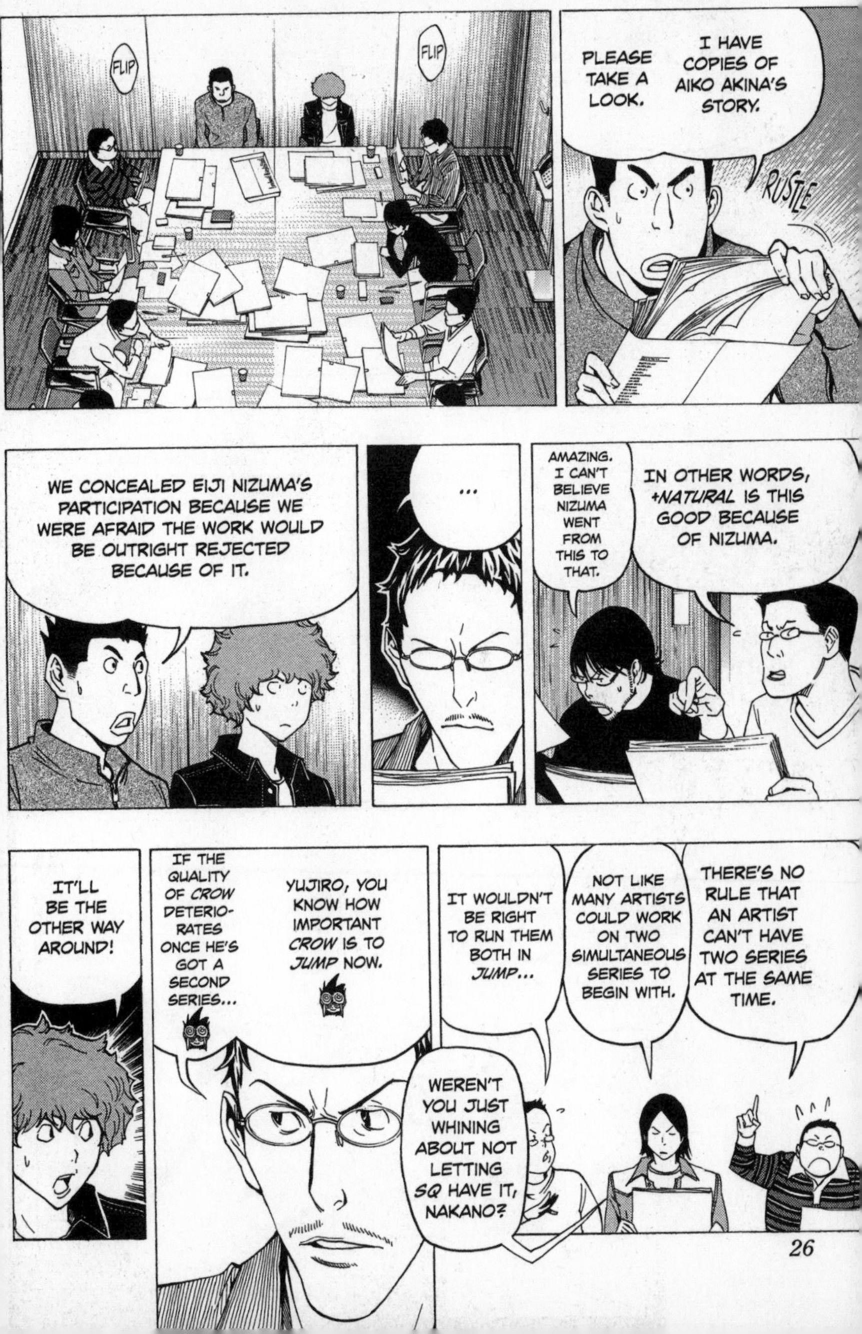
I HAVE COPIES OF AIKO AKINA'S STORY.
PLEASE TAKE A LOOK.
RUSTLE
FLIP
FLIP
IN OTHER WORDS, +NATURAL IS THIS GOOD BECAUSE OF NIZUMA.
AMAZING. I CAN'T BELIEVE NIZUMA WENT FROM THIS TO THAT.
...
WE CONCEALED EIJI NIZUMA'S PARTICIPATION BECAUSE WE WERE AFRAID THE WORK WOULD BE OUTRIGHT REJECTED BECAUSE OF IT.
THERE'S NO RULE THAT AN ARTIST CAN'T HAVE TWO SERIES AT THE SAME TIME.
NOT LIKE MANY ARTISTS COULD WORK ON TWO SIMULTANEOUS SERIES TO BEGIN WITH.
IT WOULDN'T BE RIGHT TO RUN THEM BOTH IN JUMP...
WEREN'T YOU JUST WHINING ABOUT NOT LETTING SQ HAVE IT, NAKANO?
YUJIRO, YOU KNOW HOW IMPORTANT CROW IS TO JUMP NOW.
IF THE QUALITY OF CROW DETERIORATES ONCE HE'S GOT A SECOND SERIES...
IT'LL BE THE OTHER WAY AROUND!

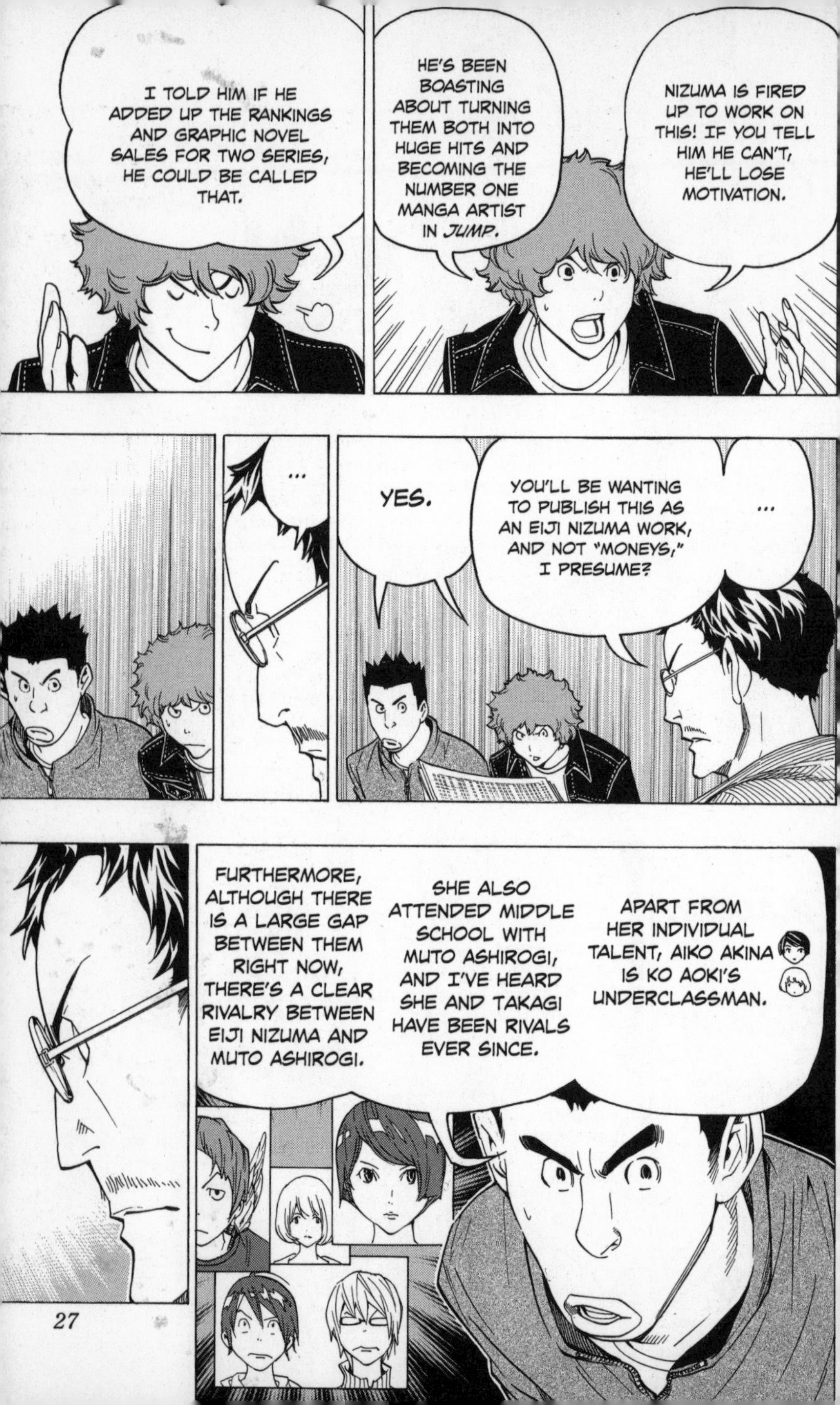
NIZUMA IS FIRED UP TO WORK ON THIS! IF YOU TELL HIM HE CAN'T, HE'LL LOSE MOTIVATION.
HE'S BEEN BOASTING ABOUT TURNING THEM BOTH INTO HUGE HITS AND BECOMING THE NUMBER ONE MANGA ARTIST IN *JUMP*.
I TOLD HIM IF HE ADDED UP THE RANKINGS AND GRAPHIC NOVEL SALES FOR TWO SERIES, HE COULD BE CALLED THAT.
...
YOU'LL BE WANTING TO PUBLISH THIS AS AN EIJI NIZUMA WORK, AND NOT "MONEYS," I PRESUME?
YES.
...
APART FROM HER INDIVIDUAL TALENT, AIKO AKINA IS KO AOKI'S UNDERCLASSMAN.
SHE ALSO ATTENDED MIDDLE SCHOOL WITH MUTO ASHIROGI, AND I'VE HEARD SHE AND TAKAGI HAVE BEEN RIVALS EVER SINCE.
FURTHERMORE, ALTHOUGH THERE IS A LARGE GAP BETWEEN THEM RIGHT NOW, THERE'S A CLEAR RIVALRY BETWEEN EIJI NIZUMA AND MUTO ASHIROGI.

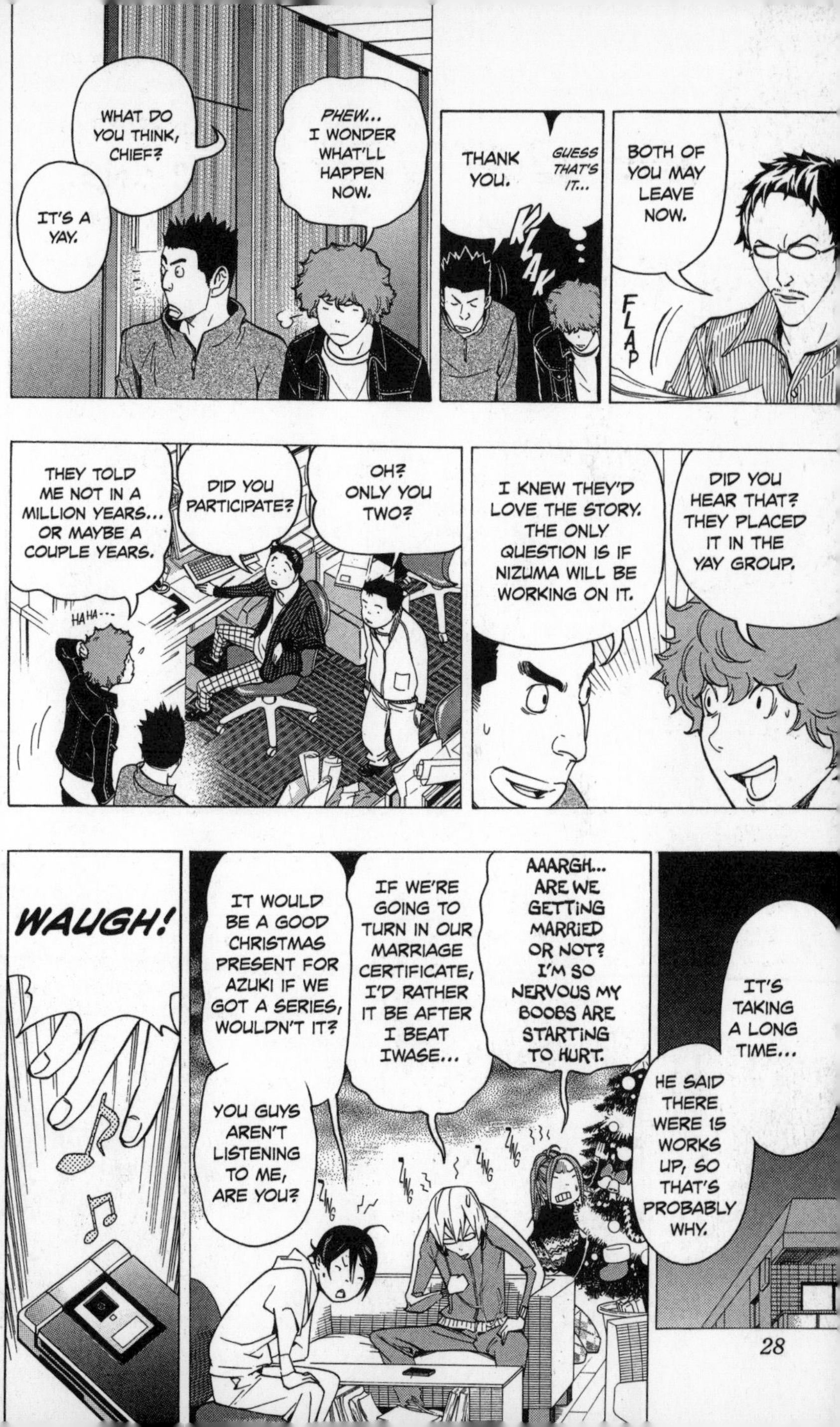
BOTH OF YOU MAY LEAVE NOW.
FLAP
GUESS THAT'S IT...
THANK YOU.
KLAK
PHEW... I WONDER WHAT'LL HAPPEN NOW.
WHAT DO YOU THINK, CHIEF?
IT'S A YAY.
DID YOU HEAR THAT? THEY PLACED IT IN THE YAY GROUP.
I KNEW THEY'D LOVE THE STORY. THE ONLY QUESTION IS IF NIZUMA WILL BE WORKING ON IT.
OH? ONLY YOU TWO?
DID YOU PARTICIPATE?
THEY TOLD ME NOT IN A MILLION YEARS... OR MAYBE A COUPLE YEARS.
HAHA...
IT'S TAKING A LONG TIME...
HE SAID THERE WERE 15 WORKS UP, SO THAT'S PROBABLY WHY.
AAARGH... ARE WE GETTING MARRIED OR NOT? I'M SO NERVOUS MY BOOBS ARE STARTING TO HURT.
IF WE'RE GOING TO TURN IN OUR MARRIAGE CERTIFICATE, I'D RATHER IT BE AFTER I BEAT IWASE...
IT WOULD BE A GOOD CHRISTMAS PRESENT FOR AZUKI IF WE GOT A SERIES, WOULDN'T IT?
YOU GUYS AREN'T LISTENING TO ME, ARE YOU?
ZING
ZING
ZING
ZING
WAUGH!

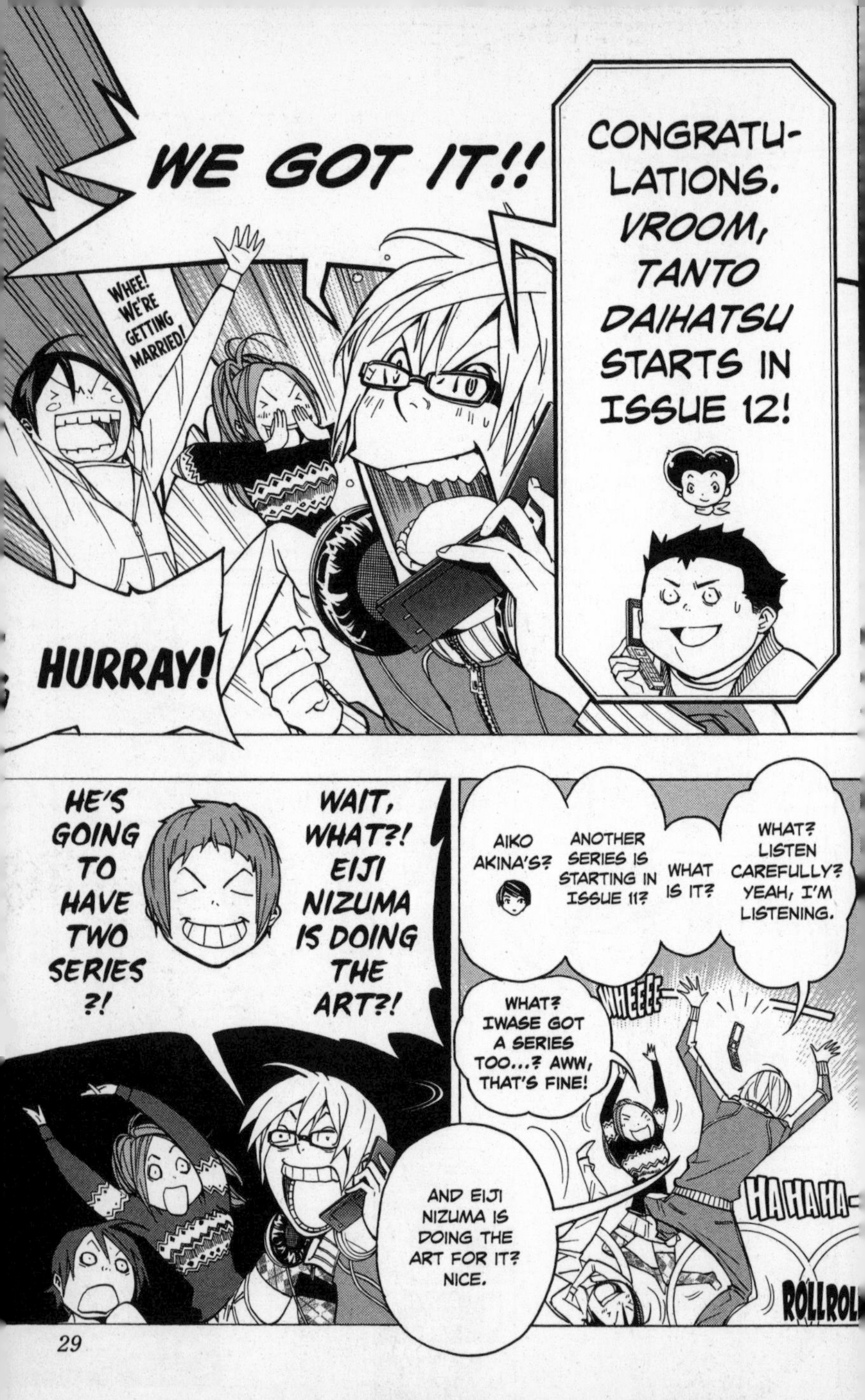
CONGRATU-LATIONS. VROOM, TANTO DAIHATSU STARTS IN ISSUE 12!
WE GOT IT!!
WHEE! WE'RE GETTING MARRIED!
HURRAY!
WHAT? LISTEN CAREFULLY? YEAH, I'M LISTENING.
WHAT IS IT?
ANOTHER SERIES IS STARTING IN ISSUE 11?
AIKO AKINA'S?
WHEEEE
WHAT? IWASE GOT A SERIES TOO...? AWW, THAT'S FINE!
HAHAHA-
ROLLROL
AND EIJI NIZUMA IS DOING THE ART FOR IT? NICE.
WAIT, WHAT?! EIJI NIZUMA IS DOING THE ART?!
HE'S GOING TO HAVE TWO SERIES ?!

OHBA'S STORYBOARD

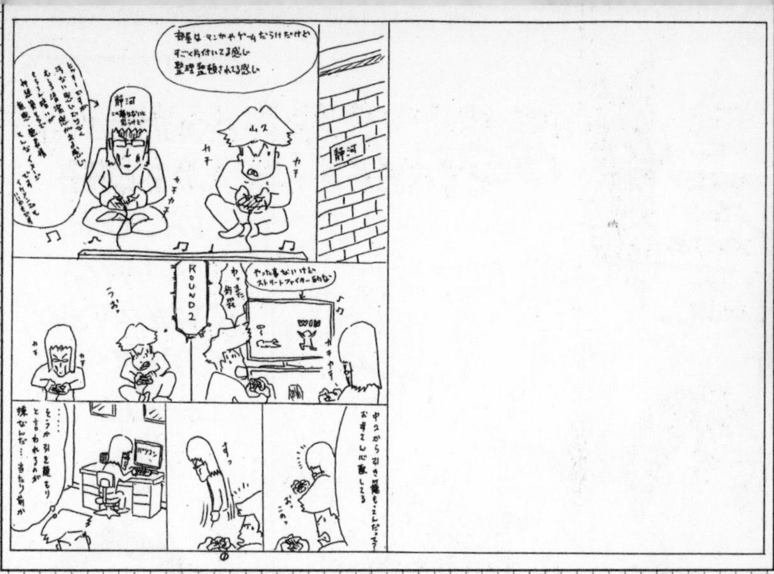

部屋はマンガやゲームだらけだけど
すごく片付いてる感じ
整理整頓されてる感じ
静河
やった事ないけど
ストリートファイター的な
ROUND2

OBATA'S STORYBOARD

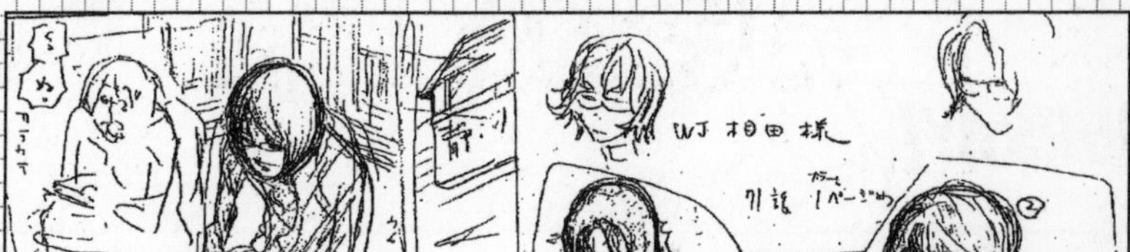

WJ 相田様
ROUND2
静河
マンガ家というより
若手の推理小説家という
なんとなく勝手なイメージです

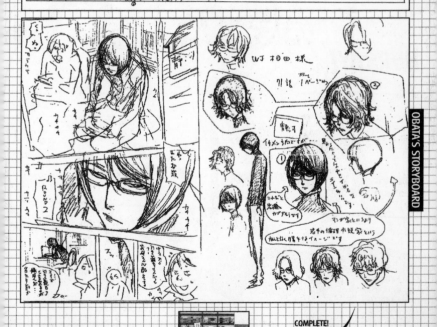

COMPLETE!

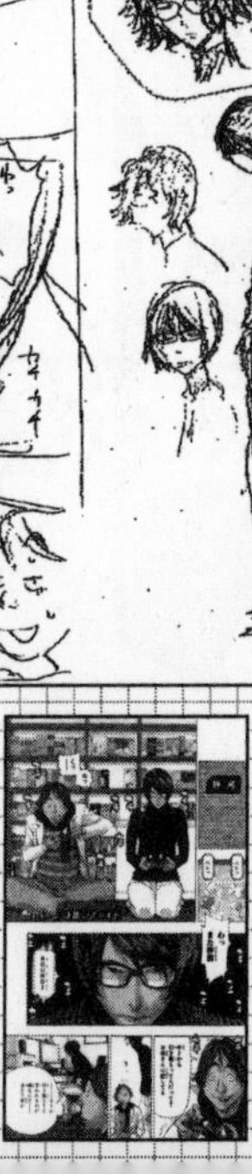

*CREATOR STORYBOARDS AND FINISHED PAGES IN JAPANESE

BAKUMAN。 vol.9

"Until the Final Draft Is Complete"

Chapter 71, pp. 7

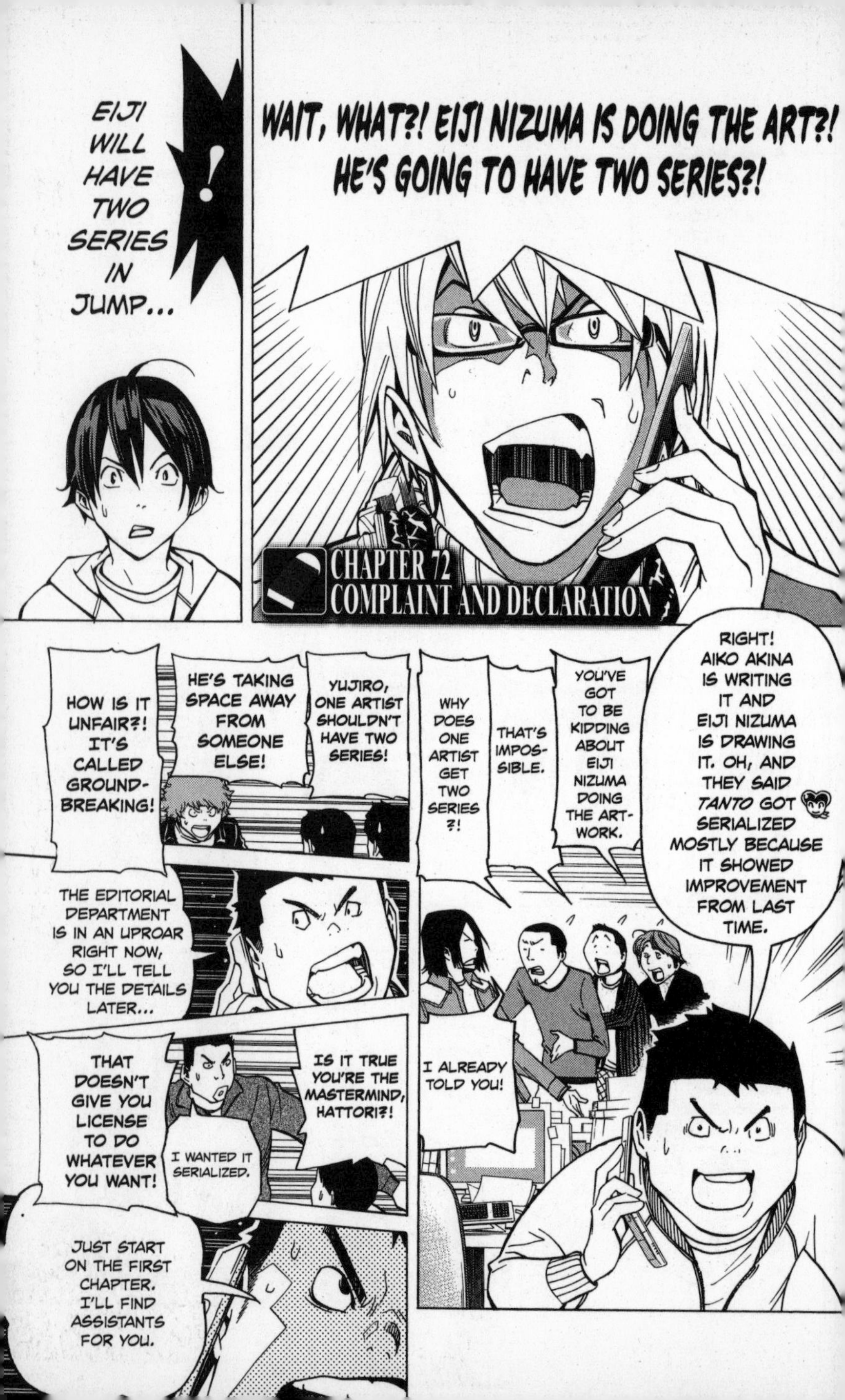
WAIT, WHAT?! EIJI NIZUMA IS DOING THE ART?! HE'S GOING TO HAVE TWO SERIES?!
CHAPTER 72 COMPLAINT AND DECLARATION
EIJI WILL HAVE TWO SERIES IN JUMP...
RIGHT! AIKO AKINA IS WRITING IT AND EIJI NIZUMA IS DRAWING IT. OH, AND THEY SAID TANTO GOT SERIALIZED MOSTLY BECAUSE IT SHOWED IMPROVEMENT FROM LAST TIME.
YOU'VE GOT TO BE KIDDING ABOUT EIJI NIZUMA DOING THE ARTWORK.
THAT'S IMPOSSIBLE.
WHY DOES ONE ARTIST GET TWO SERIES?!
I ALREADY TOLD YOU!
YUJIRO, ONE ARTIST SHOULDN'T HAVE TWO SERIES!
HE'S TAKING SPACE AWAY FROM SOMEONE ELSE!
HOW IS IT UNFAIR?! IT'S CALLED GROUNDBREAKING!
THE EDITORIAL DEPARTMENT IS IN AN UPROAR RIGHT NOW, SO I'LL TELL YOU THE DETAILS LATER...
IS IT TRUE YOU'RE THE MASTERMIND, HATTORI?!
THAT DOESN'T GIVE YOU LICENSE TO DO WHATEVER YOU WANT!
I WANTED IT SERIALIZED.
JUST START ON THE FIRST CHAPTER. I'LL FIND ASSISTANTS FOR YOU.

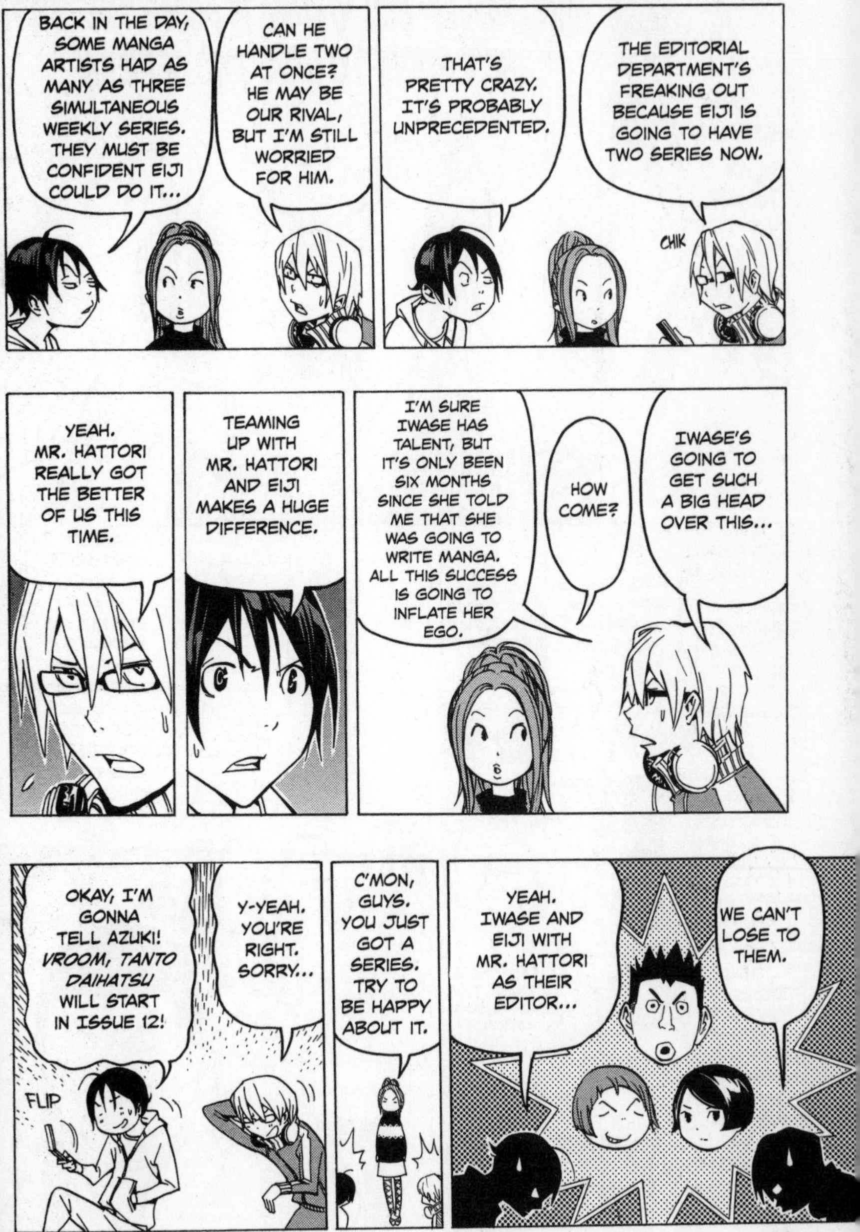
THE EDITORIAL DEPARTMENT'S FREAKING OUT BECAUSE EIJI IS GOING TO HAVE TWO SERIES NOW.
CHIK
THAT'S PRETTY CRAZY. IT'S PROBABLY UNPRECEDENTED.
CAN HE HANDLE TWO AT ONCE? HE MAY BE OUR RIVAL, BUT I'M STILL WORRIED FOR HIM.
BACK IN THE DAY, SOME MANGA ARTISTS HAD AS MANY AS THREE SIMULTANEOUS WEEKLY SERIES. THEY MUST BE CONFIDENT EIJI COULD DO IT...
IWASE'S GOING TO GET SUCH A BIG HEAD OVER THIS...
HOW COME?
I'M SURE IWASE HAS TALENT, BUT IT'S ONLY BEEN SIX MONTHS SINCE SHE TOLD ME THAT SHE WAS GOING TO WRITE MANGA. ALL THIS SUCCESS IS GOING TO INFLATE HER EGO.
TEAMING UP WITH MR. HATTORI AND EIJI MAKES A HUGE DIFFERENCE.
YEAH. MR. HATTORI REALLY GOT THE BETTER OF US THIS TIME.
WE CAN'T LOSE TO THEM.
YEAH. IWASE AND EIJI WITH MR. HATTORI AS THEIR EDITOR...
C'MON, GUYS. YOU JUST GOT A SERIES. TRY TO BE HAPPY ABOUT IT.
Y-YEAH. YOU'RE RIGHT. SORRY...
OKAY, I'M GONNA TELL AZUKI! *VROOM, TANTO DAIHATSU* WILL START IN ISSUE 12!
FLIP

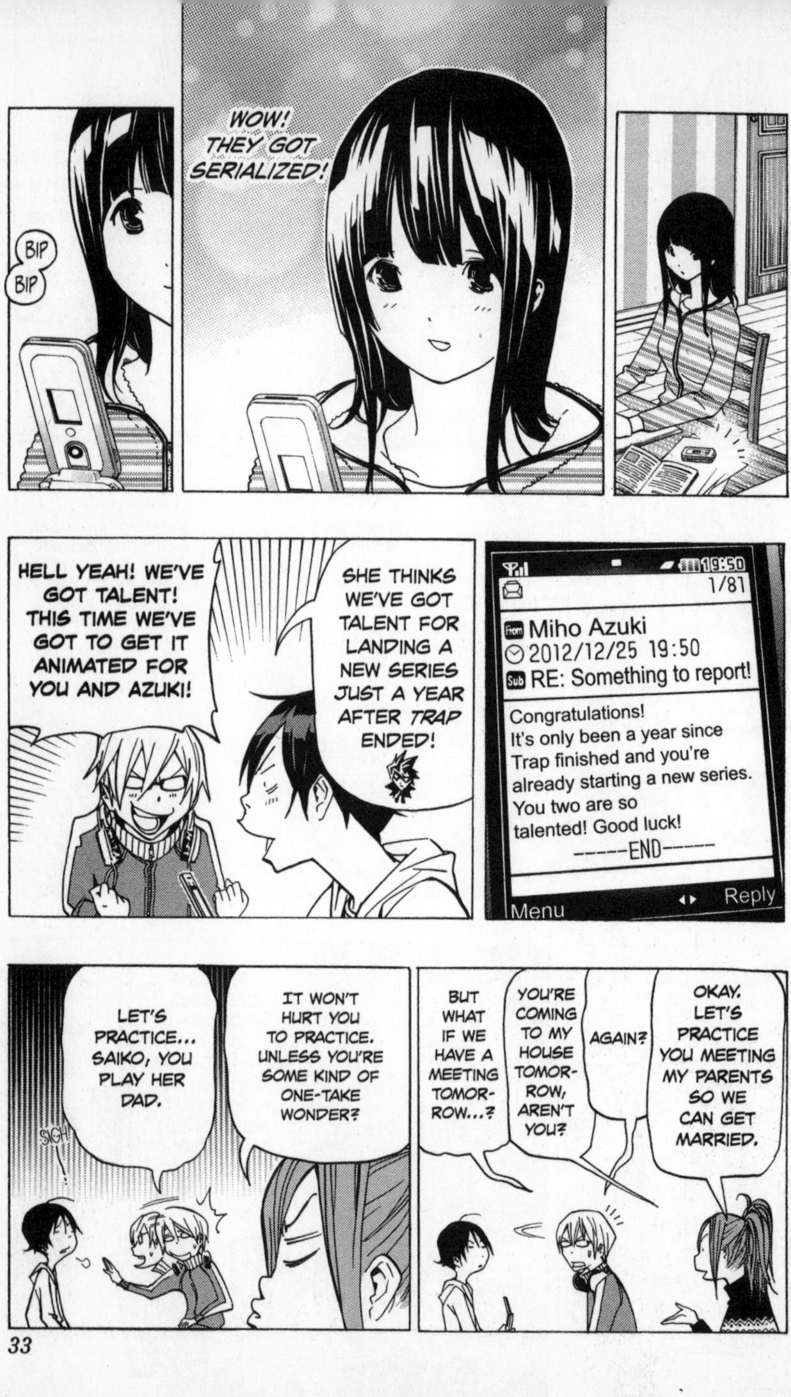
WOW! THEY GOT SERIALIZED!
BIP BIP
19:50
1/81
From Miho Azuki
2012/12/25 19:50
Sub RE: Something to report!
Congratulations!
It's only been a year since Trap finished and you're already starting a new series.
You two are so talented! Good luck!
-----END-----
Menu
Reply
SHE THINKS WE'VE GOT TALENT FOR LANDING A NEW SERIES JUST A YEAR AFTER *TRAP* ENDED!
HELL YEAH! WE'VE GOT TALENT! THIS TIME WE'VE GOT TO GET IT ANIMATED FOR YOU AND AZUKI!
OKAY. LET'S PRACTICE YOU MEETING MY PARENTS SO WE CAN GET MARRIED.
AGAIN?
YOU'RE COMING TO MY HOUSE TOMORROW, AREN'T YOU?
BUT WHAT IF WE HAVE A MEETING TOMORROW...?
IT WON'T HURT YOU TO PRACTICE. UNLESS YOU'RE SOME KIND OF ONE-TAKE WONDER?
LET'S PRACTICE... SAIKO, YOU PLAY HER DAD.
SIGH

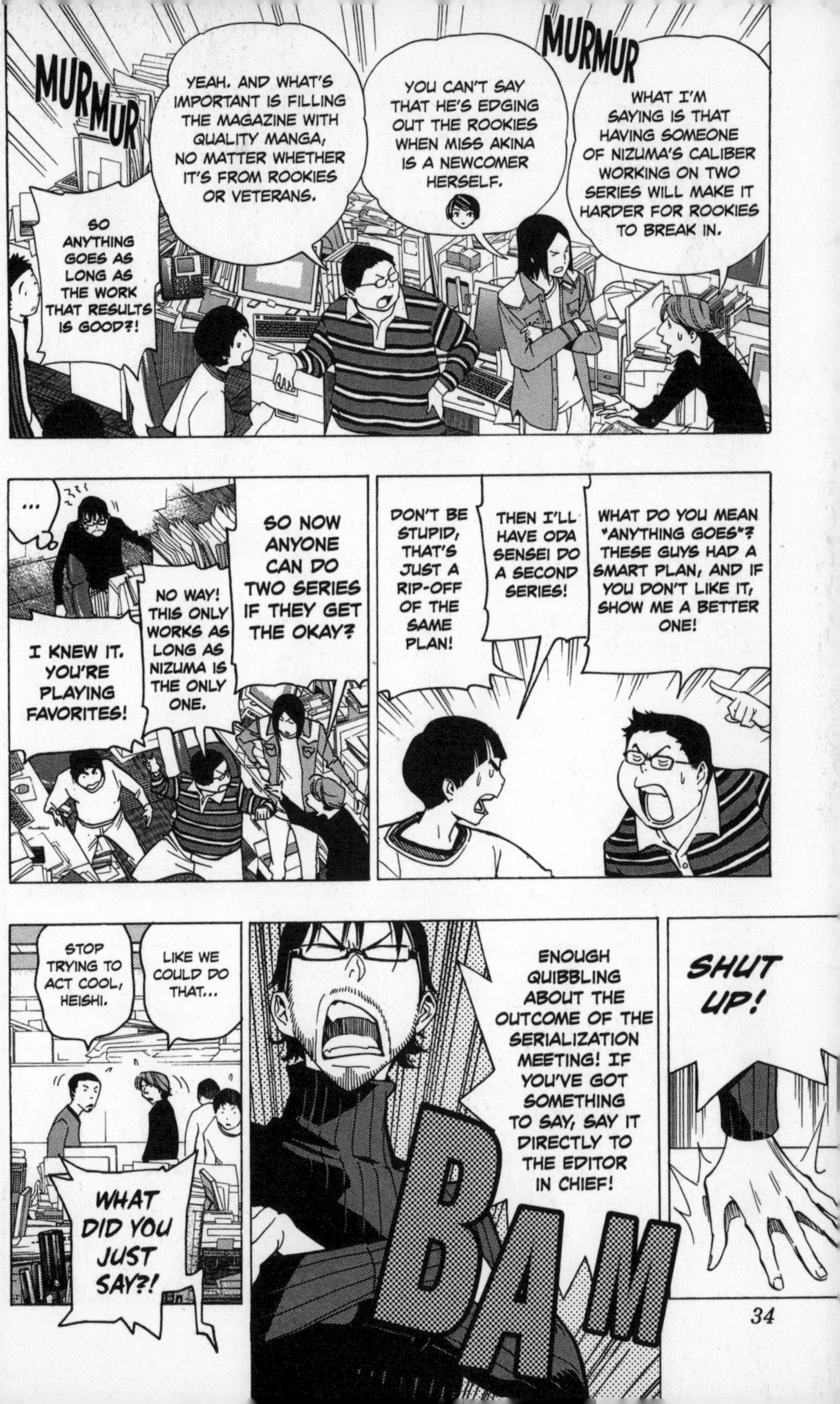
MURMUR
WHAT I'M SAYING IS THAT HAVING SOMEONE OF NIZUMA'S CALIBER WORKING ON TWO SERIES WILL MAKE IT HARDER FOR ROOKIES TO BREAK IN.
YOU CAN'T SAY THAT HE'S EDGING OUT THE ROOKIES WHEN MISS AKINA IS A NEWCOMER HERSELF.
YEAH. AND WHAT'S IMPORTANT IS FILLING THE MAGAZINE WITH QUALITY MANGA, NO MATTER WHETHER IT'S FROM ROOKIES OR VETERANS.
MURMUR
SO ANYTHING GOES AS LONG AS THE WORK THAT RESULTS IS GOOD?!
WHAT DO YOU MEAN "ANYTHING GOES"? THESE GUYS HAD A SMART PLAN, AND IF YOU DON'T LIKE IT, SHOW ME A BETTER ONE!
THEN I'LL HAVE ODA SENSEI DO A SECOND SERIES!
DON'T BE STUPID, THAT'S JUST A RIP-OFF OF THE SAME PLAN!
SO NOW ANYONE CAN DO TWO SERIES IF THEY GET THE OKAY?
NO WAY! THIS ONLY WORKS AS LONG AS NIZUMA IS THE ONLY ONE.
I KNEW IT. YOU'RE PLAYING FAVORITES!
...
SHUT UP!
ENOUGH QUIBBLING ABOUT THE OUTCOME OF THE SERIALIZATION MEETING! IF YOU'VE GOT SOMETHING TO SAY, SAY IT DIRECTLY TO THE EDITOR IN CHIEF!
BAM
LIKE WE COULD DO THAT...
STOP TRYING TO ACT COOL, HEISHI.
WHAT DID YOU JUST SAY?!

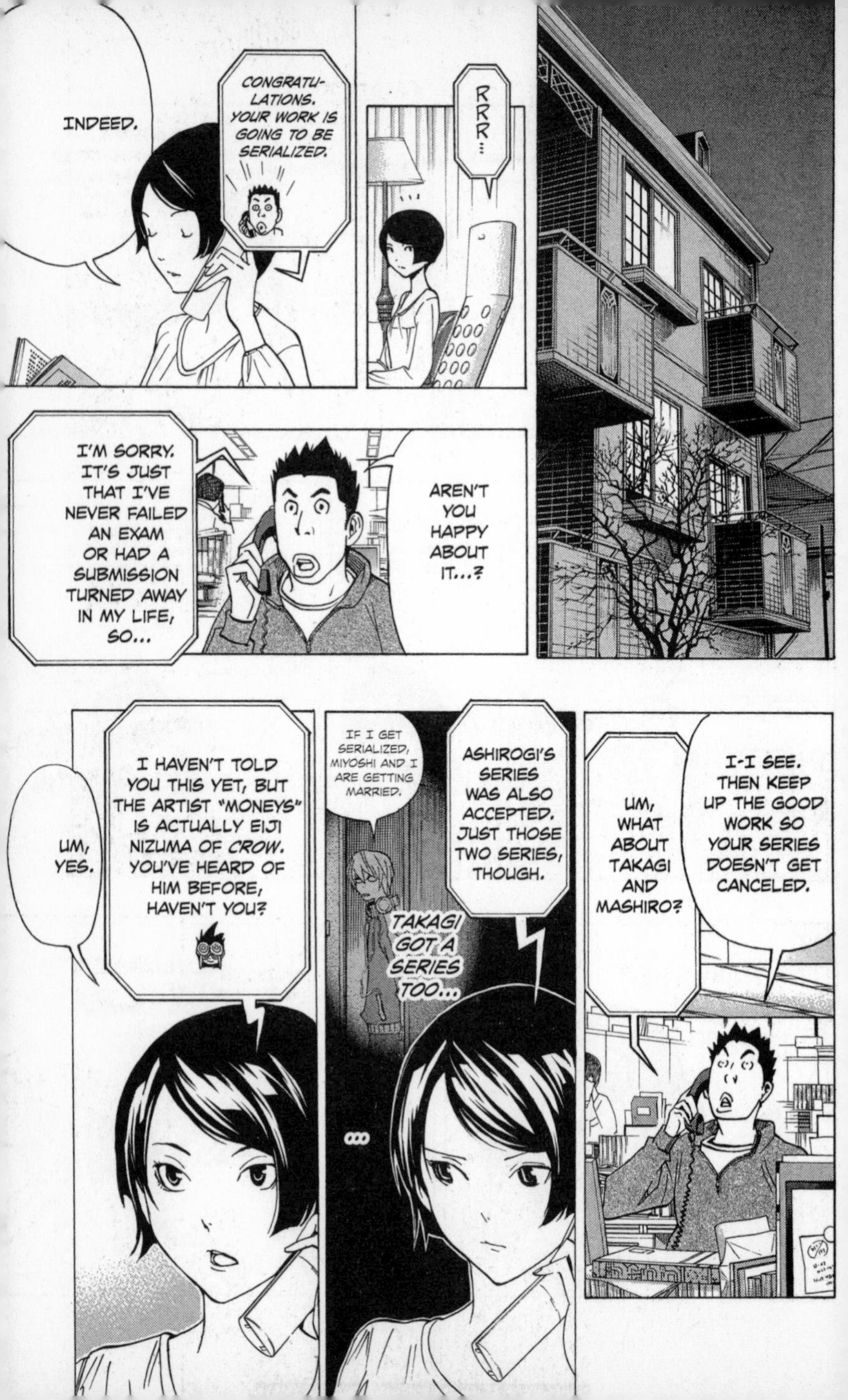
RRR...
CONGRATULATIONS. YOUR WORK IS GOING TO BE SERIALIZED.
INDEED.
AREN'T YOU HAPPY ABOUT IT...?
I'M SORRY. IT'S JUST THAT I'VE NEVER FAILED AN EXAM OR HAD A SUBMISSION TURNED AWAY IN MY LIFE, SO...
I-I SEE. THEN KEEP UP THE GOOD WORK SO YOUR SERIES DOESN'T GET CANCELED.
UM, WHAT ABOUT TAKAGI AND MASHIRO?
ASHIROGI'S SERIES WAS ALSO ACCEPTED. JUST THOSE TWO SERIES, THOUGH.
IF I GET SERIALIZED, MIYOSHI AND I ARE GETTING MARRIED.
TAKAGI GOT A SERIES TOO...
...
I HAVEN'T TOLD YOU THIS YET, BUT THE ARTIST "MONEYS" IS ACTUALLY EIJI NIZUMA OF CROW. YOU'VE HEARD OF HIM BEFORE, HAVEN'T YOU?
UM, YES.

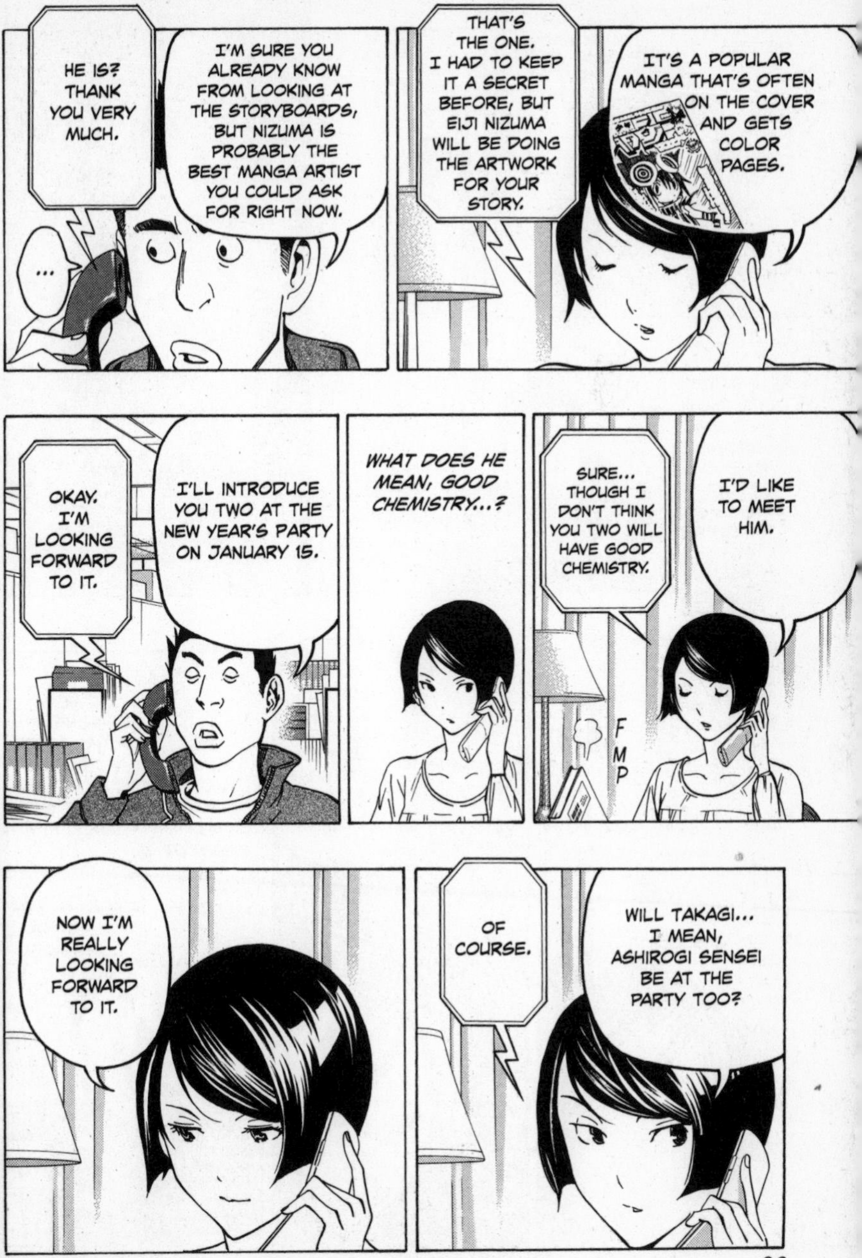
IT'S A POPULAR MANGA THAT'S OFTEN ON THE COVER AND GETS COLOR PAGES.
THAT'S THE ONE. I HAD TO KEEP IT A SECRET BEFORE, BUT EIJI NIZUMA WILL BE DOING THE ARTWORK FOR YOUR STORY.
I'M SURE YOU ALREADY KNOW FROM LOOKING AT THE STORYBOARDS, BUT NIZUMA IS PROBABLY THE BEST MANGA ARTIST YOU COULD ASK FOR RIGHT NOW.
HE IS? THANK YOU VERY MUCH.
...
I'D LIKE TO MEET HIM.
SURE... THOUGH I DON'T THINK YOU TWO WILL HAVE GOOD CHEMISTRY.
FMP
WHAT DOES HE MEAN, GOOD CHEMISTRY...?
I'LL INTRODUCE YOU TWO AT THE NEW YEAR'S PARTY ON JANUARY 15.
OKAY. I'M LOOKING FORWARD TO IT.
WILL TAKAGI... I MEAN, ASHIROGI SENSEI BE AT THE PARTY TOO?
OF COURSE.
NOW I'M REALLY LOOKING FORWARD TO IT.

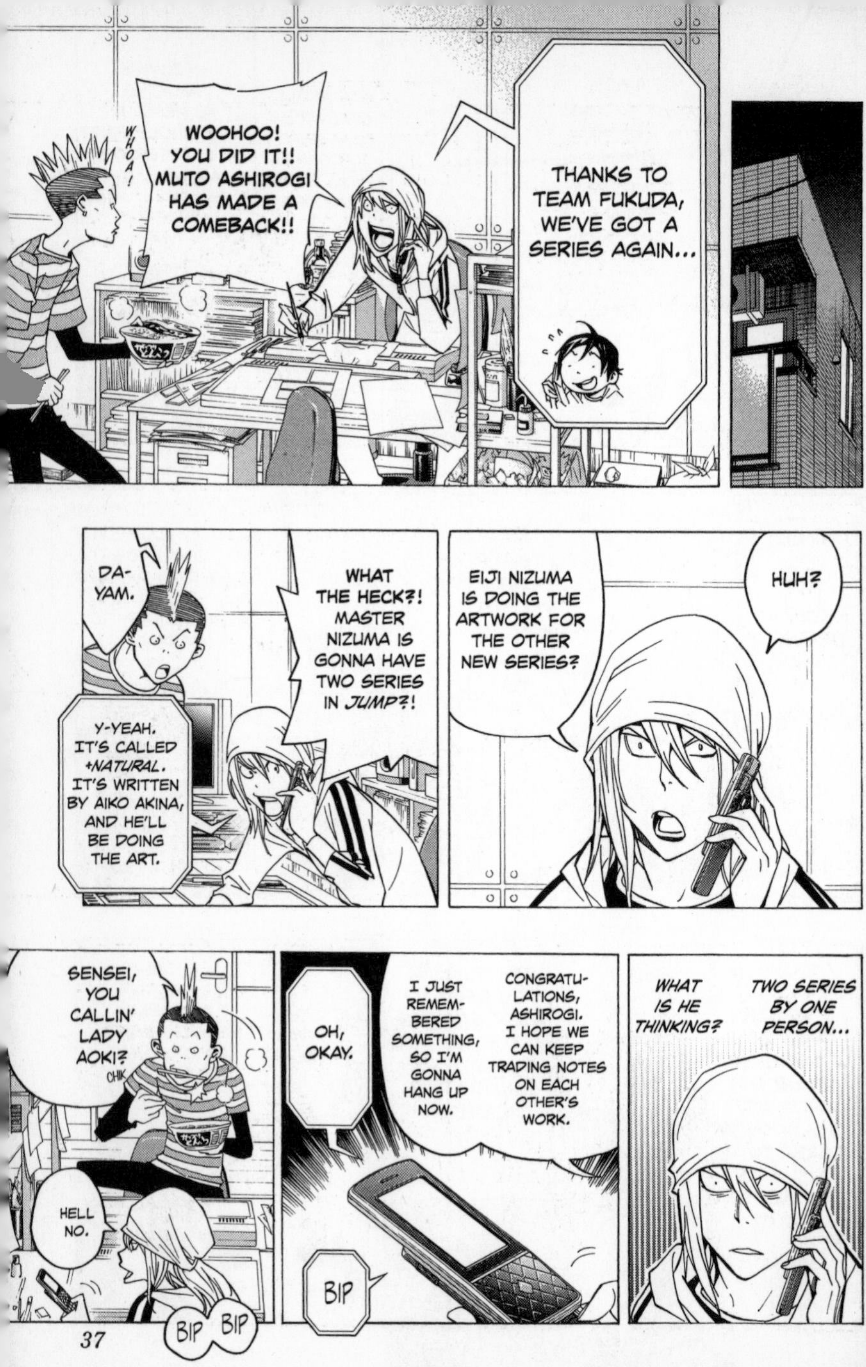
THANKS TO TEAM FUKUDA, WE'VE GOT A SERIES AGAIN...
WOOHOO! YOU DID IT!! MUTO ASHIROGI HAS MADE A COMEBACK!!
WHOA!
HUH?
EIJI NIZUMA IS DOING THE ARTWORK FOR THE OTHER NEW SERIES?
WHAT THE HECK?! MASTER NIZUMA IS GONNA HAVE TWO SERIES IN *JUMP*?!
DA-YAM.
Y-YEAH. IT'S CALLED *+NATURAL*. IT'S WRITTEN BY AIKO AKINA, AND HE'LL BE DOING THE ART.
TWO SERIES BY ONE PERSON...
WHAT IS HE THINKING?
CONGRATULATIONS, ASHIROGI. I HOPE WE CAN KEEP TRADING NOTES ON EACH OTHER'S WORK.
I JUST REMEMBERED SOMETHING, SO I'M GONNA HANG UP NOW.
OH, OKAY.
BIP
SENSEI, YOU CALLIN' LADY AOKI?
CHIK
HELL NO.
BIP BIP

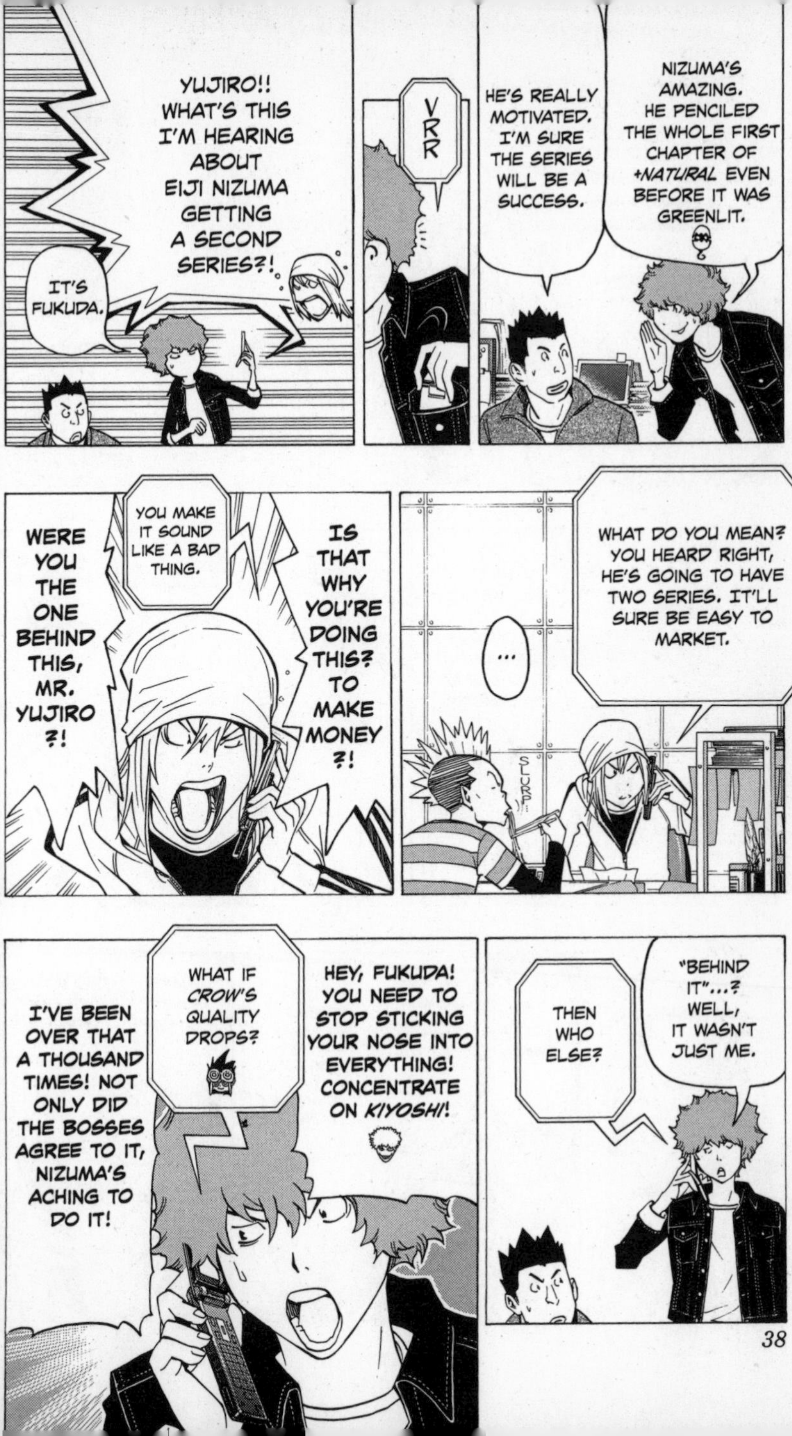
NIZUMA'S AMAZING. HE PENCILED THE WHOLE FIRST CHAPTER OF *+NATURAL* EVEN BEFORE IT WAS GREENLIT.
HE'S REALLY MOTIVATED. I'M SURE THE SERIES WILL BE A SUCCESS.
VRR
YUJIRO!! WHAT'S THIS I'M HEARING ABOUT EIJI NIZUMA GETTING A SECOND SERIES?!
IT'S FUKUDA.
WHAT DO YOU MEAN? YOU HEARD RIGHT, HE'S GOING TO HAVE TWO SERIES. IT'LL SURE BE EASY TO MARKET.
...
SLURP
IS THAT WHY YOU'RE DOING THIS? TO MAKE MONEY?!
YOU MAKE IT SOUND LIKE A BAD THING.
WERE YOU THE ONE BEHIND THIS, MR. YUJIRO?!
"BEHIND IT"...? WELL, IT WASN'T JUST ME.
THEN WHO ELSE?
HEY, FUKUDA! YOU NEED TO STOP STICKING YOUR NOSE INTO EVERYTHING! CONCENTRATE ON *KIYOSHI*!
WHAT IF *CROW'S* QUALITY DROPS?
I'VE BEEN OVER THAT A THOUSAND TIMES! NOT ONLY DID THE BOSSES AGREE TO IT, NIZUMA'S ACHING TO DO IT!

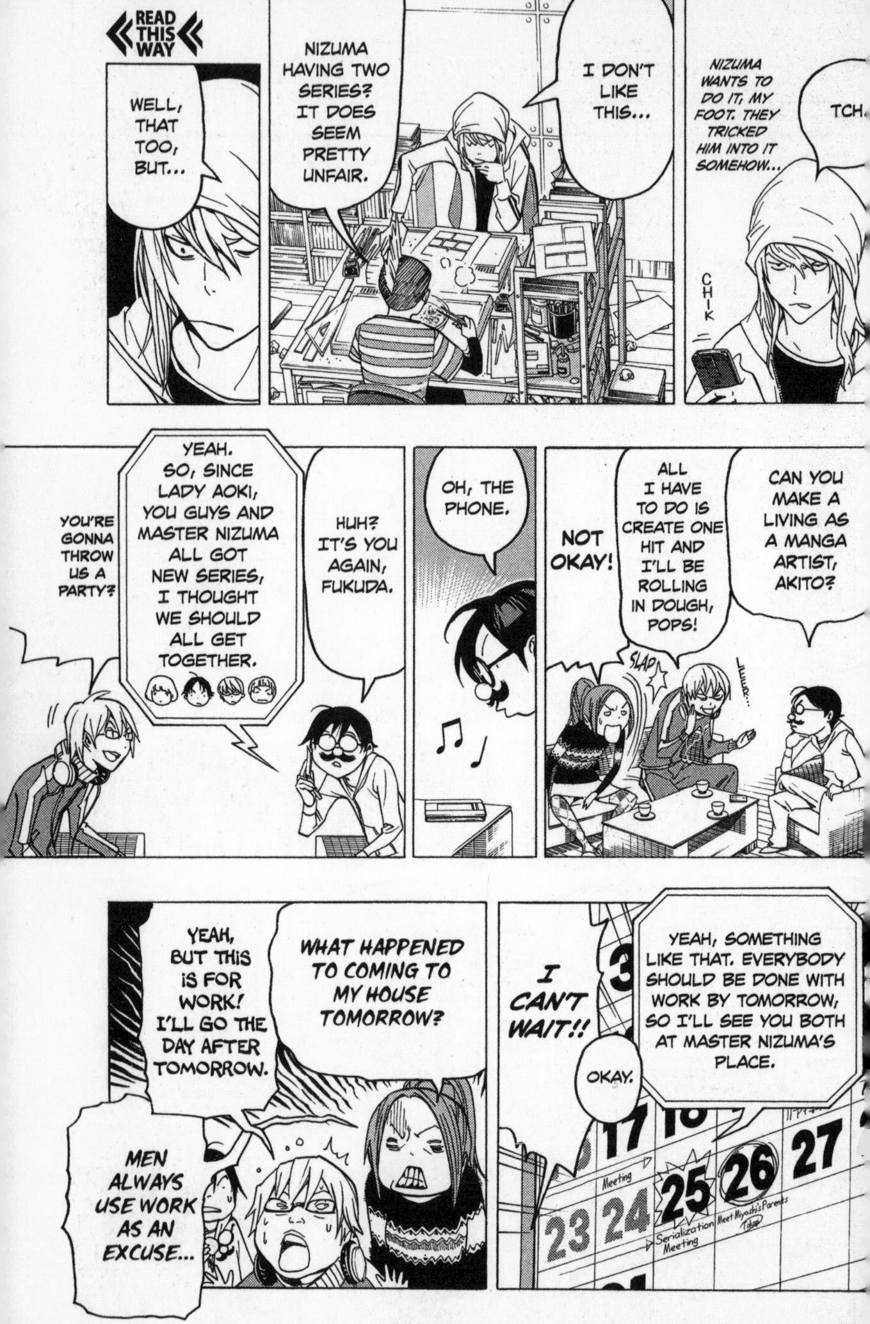
READ THIS WAY
TCH.
NIZUMA WANTS TO DO IT, MY FOOT. THEY TRICKED HIM INTO IT SOMEHOW...
CHIK
I DON'T LIKE THIS...
NIZUMA HAVING TWO SERIES? IT DOES SEEM PRETTY UNFAIR.
WELL, THAT TOO, BUT...
CAN YOU MAKE A LIVING AS A MANGA ARTIST, AKITO?
ALL I HAVE TO DO IS CREATE ONE HIT AND I'LL BE ROLLING IN DOUGH, POPS!
NOT OKAY!
SLAP
LEER...
OH, THE PHONE.
HUH? IT'S YOU AGAIN, FUKUDA.
YEAH. SO, SINCE LADY AOKI, YOU GUYS AND MASTER NIZUMA ALL GOT NEW SERIES, I THOUGHT WE SHOULD ALL GET TOGETHER.
YOU'RE GONNA THROW US A PARTY?
YEAH, SOMETHING LIKE THAT. EVERYBODY SHOULD BE DONE WITH WORK BY TOMORROW, SO I'LL SEE YOU BOTH AT MASTER NIZUMA'S PLACE.
OKAY.
I CAN'T WAIT!!
Meeting
Serialization Meeting
Meet Miyoshi's Parents
WHAT HAPPENED TO COMING TO MY HOUSE TOMORROW?
YEAH, BUT THIS IS FOR WORK! I'LL GO THE DAY AFTER TOMORROW.
MEN ALWAYS USE WORK AS AN EXCUSE...

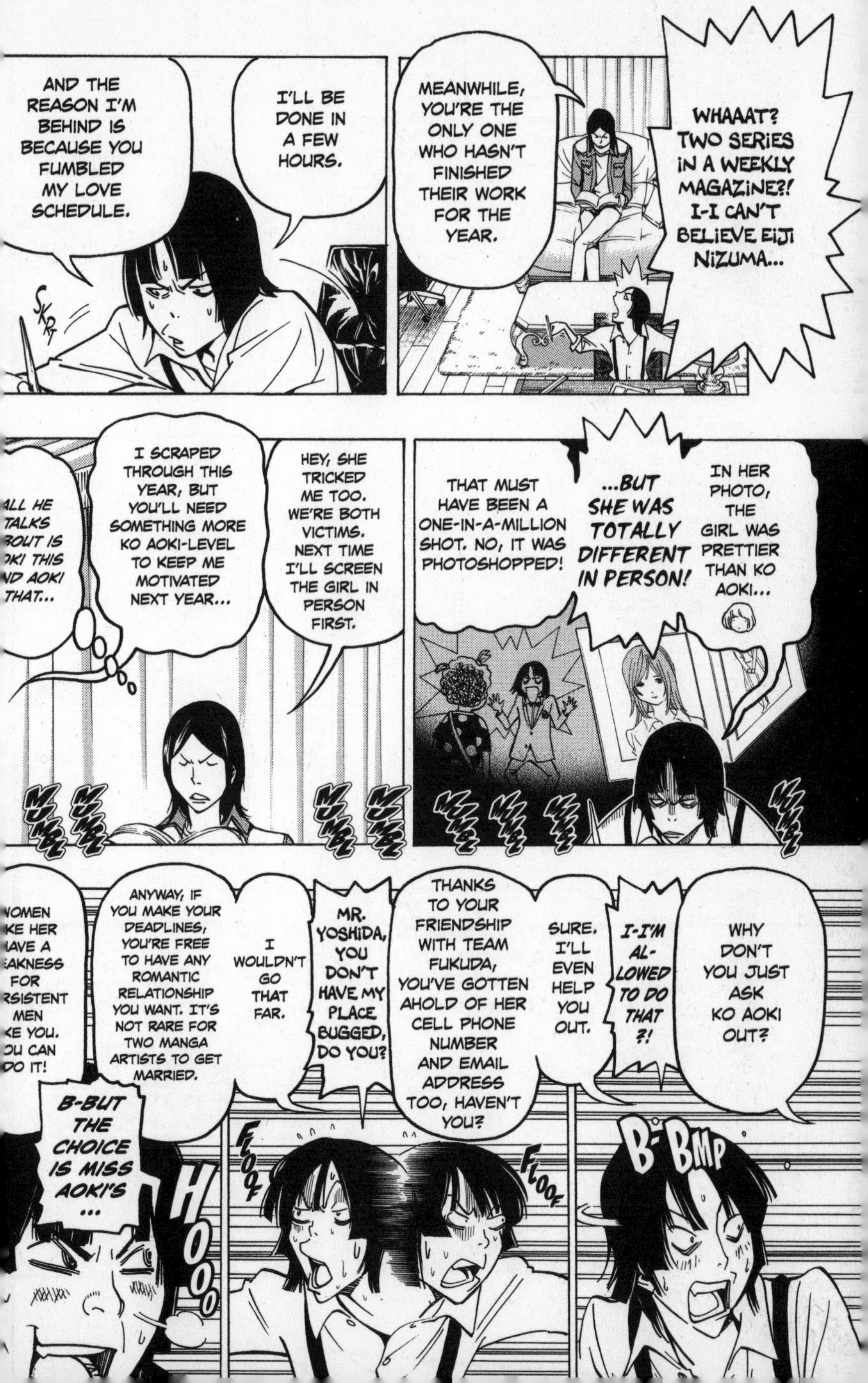
WHAAAT? TWO SERIES IN A WEEKLY MAGAZINE?! I-I CAN'T BELIEVE EIJI NIZUMA...
MEANWHILE, YOU'RE THE ONLY ONE WHO HASN'T FINISHED THEIR WORK FOR THE YEAR.
I'LL BE DONE IN A FEW HOURS.
AND THE REASON I'M BEHIND IS BECAUSE YOU FUMBLED MY LOVE SCHEDULE.
SKRT
IN HER PHOTO, THE GIRL WAS PRETTIER THAN KO AOKI...
...BUT SHE WAS TOTALLY DIFFERENT IN PERSON!
THAT MUST HAVE BEEN A ONE-IN-A-MILLION SHOT. NO, IT WAS PHOTOSHOPPED!
MUMBLE MUMBLE MUMBLE MUMBLE
HEY, SHE TRICKED ME TOO. WE'RE BOTH VICTIMS. NEXT TIME I'LL SCREEN THE GIRL IN PERSON FIRST.
I SCRAPED THROUGH THIS YEAR, BUT YOU'LL NEED SOMETHING MORE KO AOKI-LEVEL TO KEEP ME MOTIVATED NEXT YEAR...
LL HE TALKS BOUT IS OKI THIS ND AOKI THAT...
MUMBLE MUMBLE MUMBLE MUMBLE
WHY DON'T YOU JUST ASK KO AOKI OUT?
B-BMP
I-I'M AL-LOWED TO DO THAT?!
SURE. I'LL EVEN HELP YOU OUT.
THANKS TO YOUR FRIENDSHIP WITH TEAM FUKUDA, YOU'VE GOTTEN AHOLD OF HER CELL PHONE NUMBER AND EMAIL ADDRESS TOO, HAVEN'T YOU?
FLOOF
MR. YOSHIDA, YOU DON'T HAVE MY PLACE BUGGED, DO YOU?
I WOULDN'T GO THAT FAR.
FLOOF
ANYWAY, IF YOU MAKE YOUR DEADLINES, YOU'RE FREE TO HAVE ANY ROMANTIC RELATIONSHIP YOU WANT. IT'S NOT RARE FOR TWO MANGA ARTISTS TO GET MARRIED.
OMEN KE HER AVE A EAKNESS FOR RSISTENT MEN KE YOU. OU CAN DO IT!
HOOO
B-BUT THE CHOICE IS MISS AOKI'S...

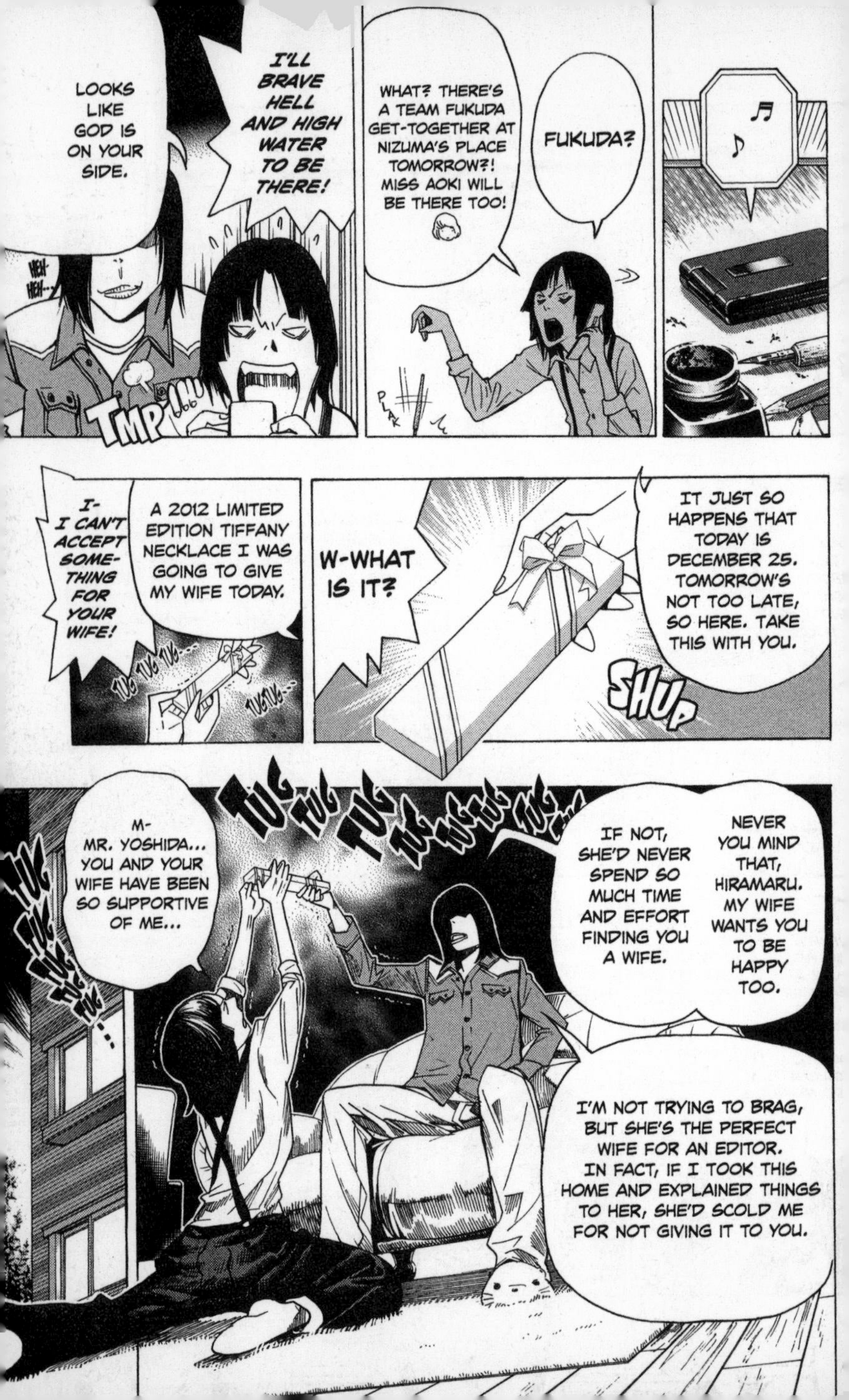
♬ ♪
FUKUDA?
WHAT? THERE'S A TEAM FUKUDA GET-TOGETHER AT NIZUMA'S PLACE TOMORROW?! MISS AOKI WILL BE THERE TOO!
PLAK
I'LL BRAVE HELL AND HIGH WATER TO BE THERE!
TMP
LOOKS LIKE GOD IS ON YOUR SIDE.
HEH-HEH...
IT JUST SO HAPPENS THAT TODAY IS DECEMBER 25. TOMORROW'S NOT TOO LATE, SO HERE. TAKE THIS WITH YOU.
W-WHAT IS IT?
SHUP
A 2012 LIMITED EDITION TIFFANY NECKLACE I WAS GOING TO GIVE MY WIFE TODAY.
I- I CAN'T ACCEPT SOMETHING FOR YOUR WIFE!
TUG TUG TUG...
TUGTUG...
NEVER YOU MIND THAT, HIRAMARU. MY WIFE WANTS YOU TO BE HAPPY TOO.
IF NOT, SHE'D NEVER SPEND SO MUCH TIME AND EFFORT FINDING YOU A WIFE.
TUG TUG TUG TUG TUG TUG...
M- MR. YOSHIDA... YOU AND YOUR WIFE HAVE BEEN SO SUPPORTIVE OF ME...
TUG TUG TUG TUG TUG...
I'M NOT TRYING TO BRAG, BUT SHE'S THE PERFECT WIFE FOR AN EDITOR. IN FACT, IF I TOOK THIS HOME AND EXPLAINED THINGS TO HER, SHE'D SCOLD ME FOR NOT GIVING IT TO YOU.

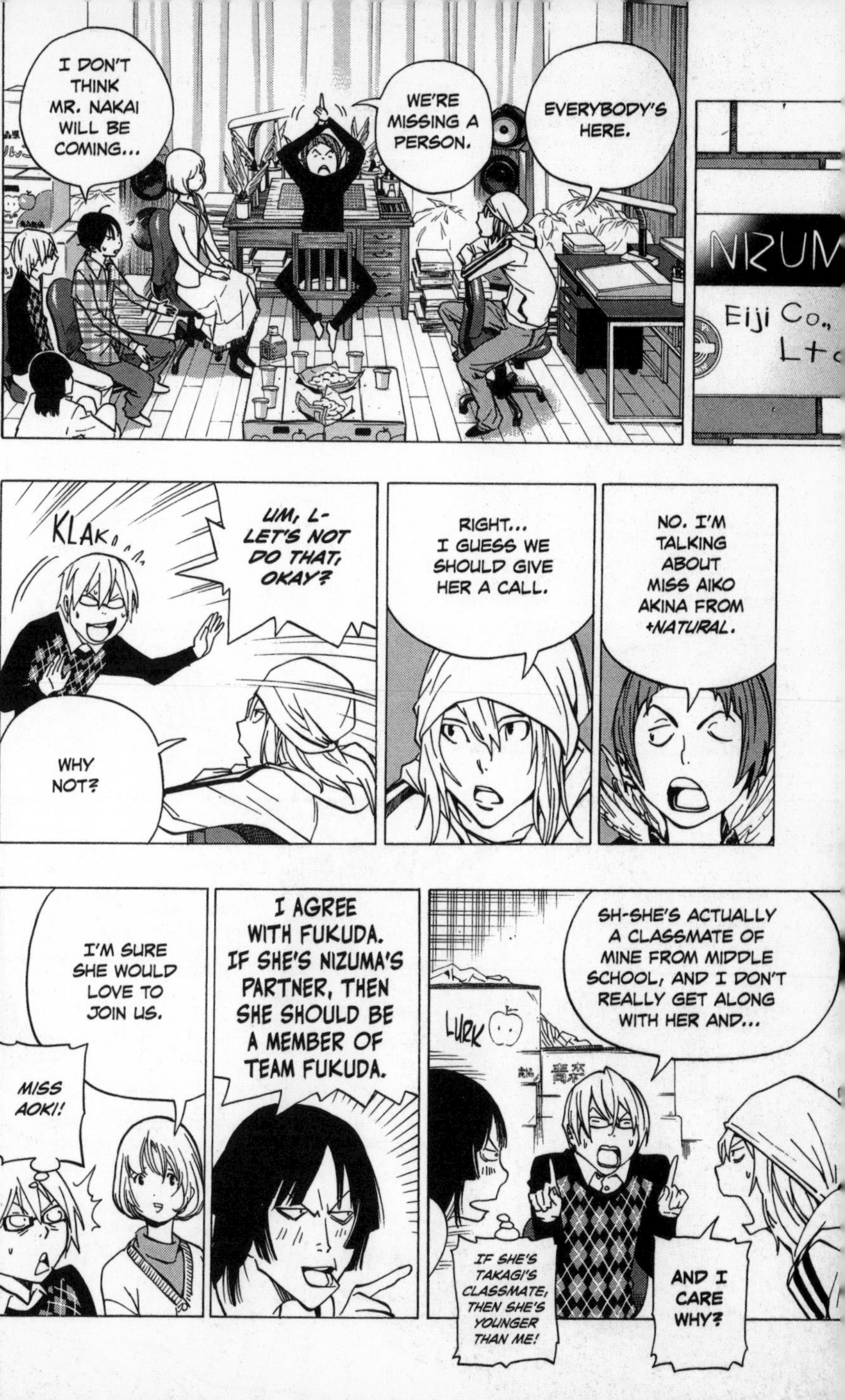
NIZUM
Eiji Co., Lt
EVERYBODY'S HERE.
WE'RE MISSING A PERSON.
I DON'T THINK MR. NAKAI WILL BE COMING...
NO. I'M TALKING ABOUT MISS AIKO AKINA FROM +NATURAL.
RIGHT... I GUESS WE SHOULD GIVE HER A CALL.
UM, L- LET'S NOT DO THAT, OKAY?
KLAK
WHY NOT?
SH-SHE'S ACTUALLY A CLASSMATE OF MINE FROM MIDDLE SCHOOL, AND I DON'T REALLY GET ALONG WITH HER AND...
LURK
AND I CARE WHY?
IF SHE'S TAKAGI'S CLASSMATE, THEN SHE'S YOUNGER THAN ME!
I AGREE WITH FUKUDA. IF SHE'S NIZUMA'S PARTNER, THEN SHE SHOULD BE A MEMBER OF TEAM FUKUDA.
I'M SURE SHE WOULD LOVE TO JOIN US.
MISS AOKI!

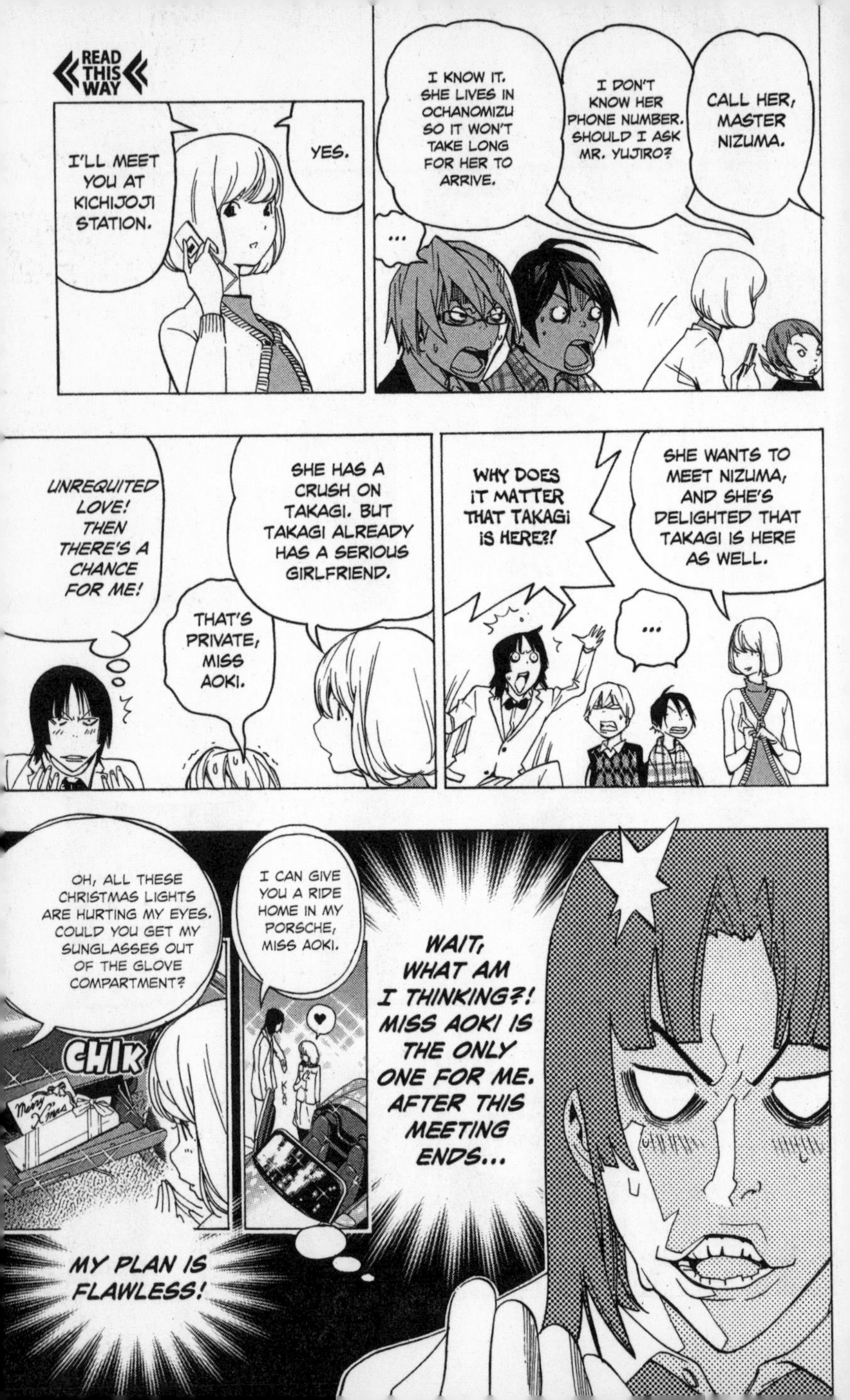
READ THIS WAY
CALL HER, MASTER NIZUMA.
I DON'T KNOW HER PHONE NUMBER. SHOULD I ASK MR. YUJIRO?
I KNOW IT. SHE LIVES IN OCHANOMIZU SO IT WON'T TAKE LONG FOR HER TO ARRIVE.
...
YES.
I'LL MEET YOU AT KICHIJOJI STATION.
SHE WANTS TO MEET NIZUMA, AND SHE'S DELIGHTED THAT TAKAGI IS HERE AS WELL.
WHY DOES IT MATTER THAT TAKAGI IS HERE?!
...
SHE HAS A CRUSH ON TAKAGI. BUT TAKAGI ALREADY HAS A SERIOUS GIRLFRIEND.
THAT'S PRIVATE, MISS AOKI.
UNREQUITED LOVE! THEN THERE'S A CHANCE FOR ME!
I CAN GIVE YOU A RIDE HOME IN MY PORSCHE, MISS AOKI.
OH, ALL THESE CHRISTMAS LIGHTS ARE HURTING MY EYES. COULD YOU GET MY SUNGLASSES OUT OF THE GLOVE COMPARTMENT?
CHIK
Merry X'mas
MY PLAN IS FLAWLESS!
WAIT, WHAT AM I THINKING?! MISS AOKI IS THE ONLY ONE FOR ME. AFTER THIS MEETING ENDS...

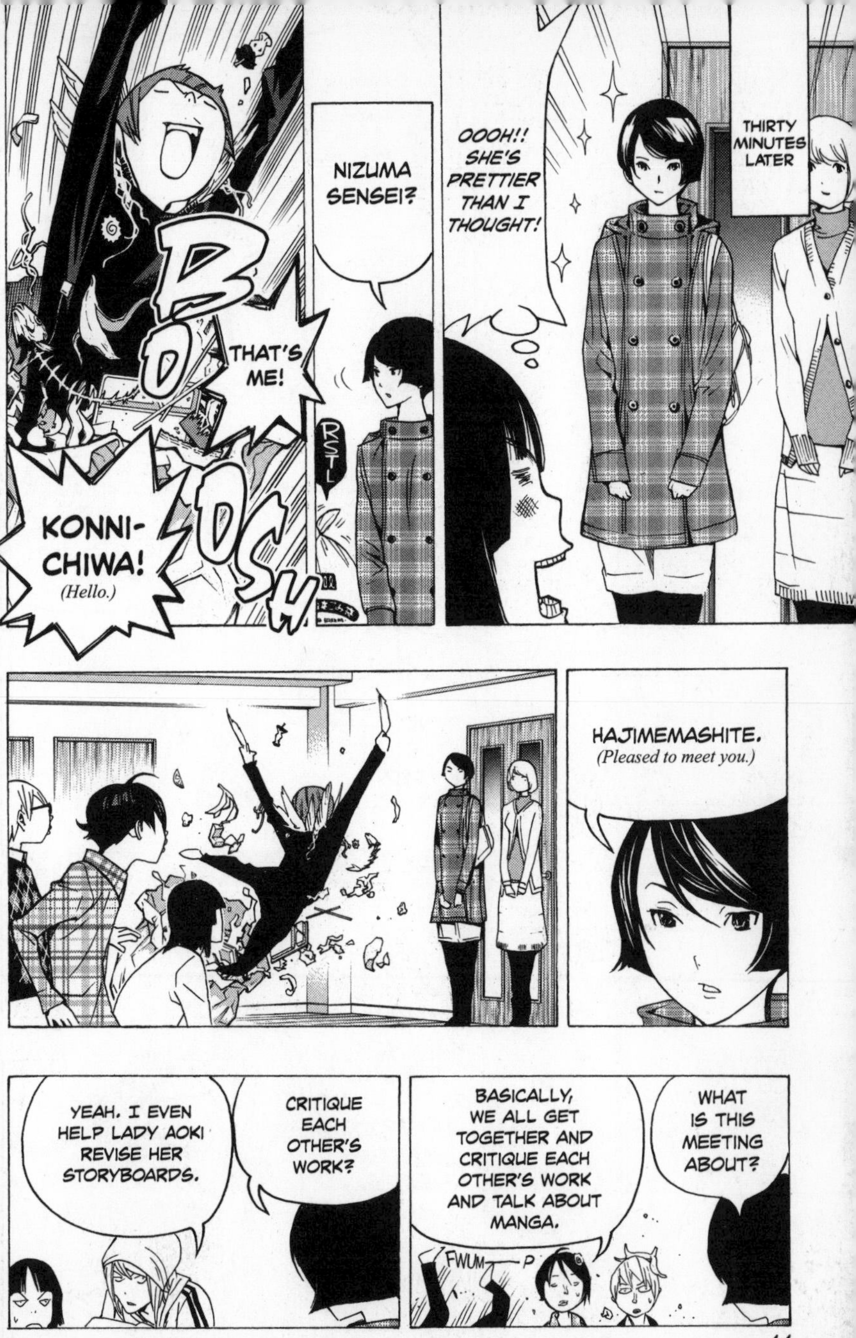
THIRTY MINUTES LATER
OOOH!! SHE'S PRETTIER THAN I THOUGHT!
NIZUMA SENSEI?
RSTL
BOOSH
THAT'S ME!
KONNI-CHIWA!
(Hello.)
HAJIMEMASHITE.
(Pleased to meet you.)
WHAT IS THIS MEETING ABOUT?
BASICALLY, WE ALL GET TOGETHER AND CRITIQUE EACH OTHER'S WORK AND TALK ABOUT MANGA.
FWUMP
CRITIQUE EACH OTHER'S WORK?
YEAH. I EVEN HELP LADY AOKI REVISE HER STORYBOARDS.

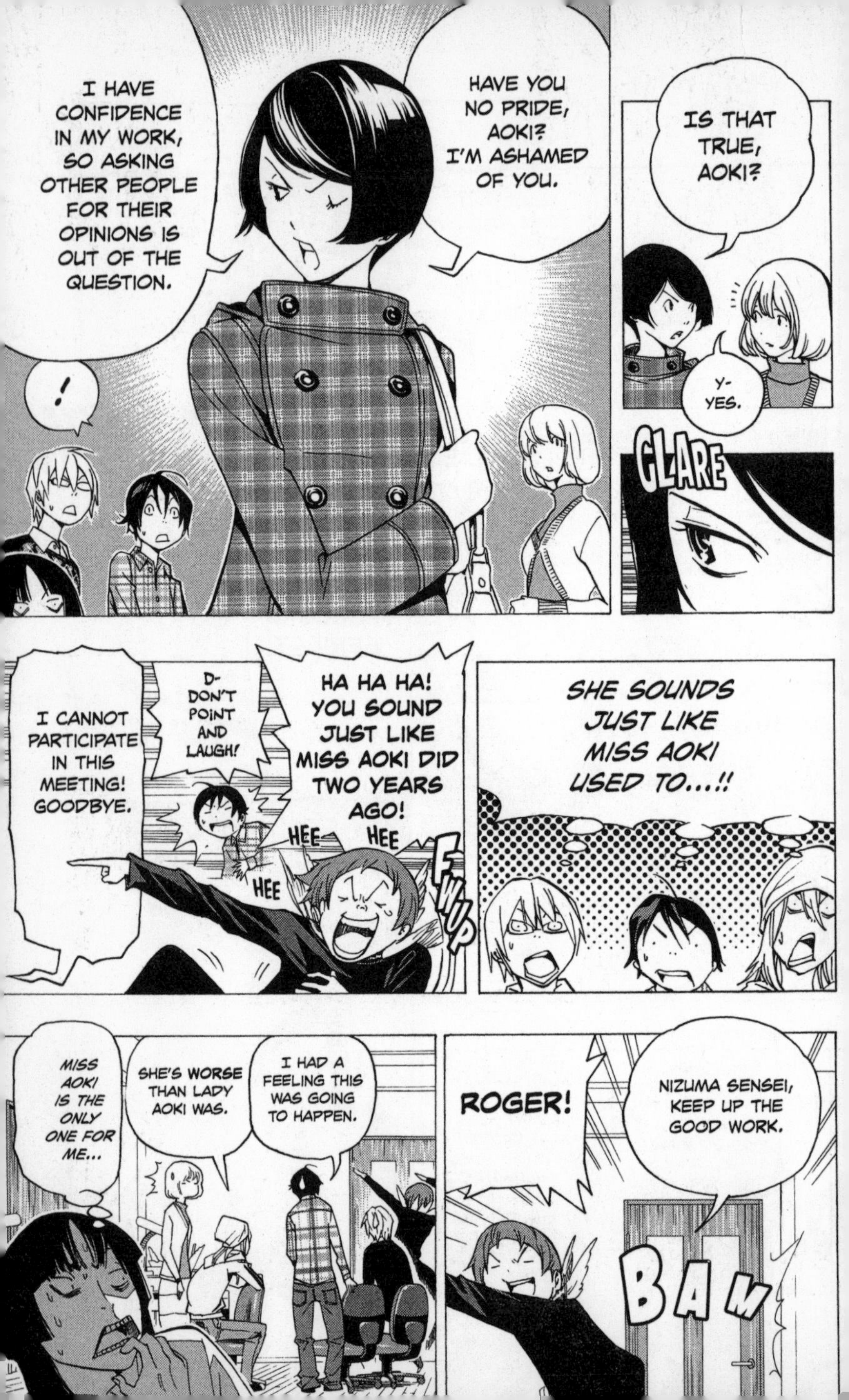
IS THAT TRUE, AOKI?
Y- YES.
GLARE
HAVE YOU NO PRIDE, AOKI? I'M ASHAMED OF YOU.
I HAVE CONFIDENCE IN MY WORK, SO ASKING OTHER PEOPLE FOR THEIR OPINIONS IS OUT OF THE QUESTION.
!
SHE SOUNDS JUST LIKE MISS AOKI USED TO...!!
HA HA HA! YOU SOUND JUST LIKE MISS AOKI DID TWO YEARS AGO!
D- DON'T POINT AND LAUGH!
I CANNOT PARTICIPATE IN THIS MEETING! GOODBYE.
HEE
HEE
HEE
FWUP
NIZUMA SENSEI, KEEP UP THE GOOD WORK.
ROGER!
BAM
I HAD A FEELING THIS WAS GOING TO HAPPEN.
SHE'S WORSE THAN LADY AOKI WAS.
MISS AOKI IS THE ONLY ONE FOR ME...

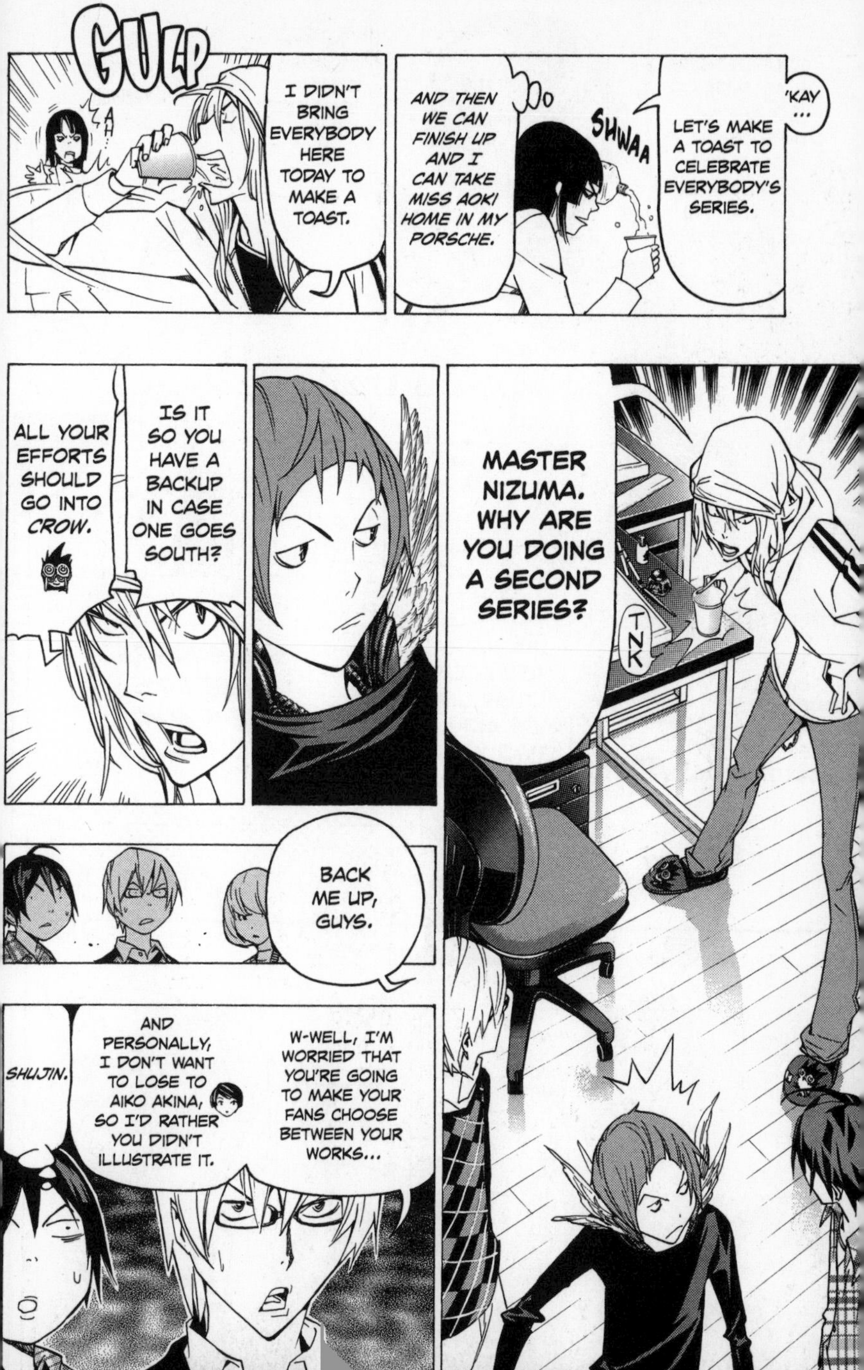
'KAY...
LET'S MAKE A TOAST TO CELEBRATE EVERYBODY'S SERIES.
SHWAA
AND THEN WE CAN FINISH UP AND I CAN TAKE MISS AOKI HOME IN MY PORSCHE.
GULP
I DIDN'T BRING EVERYBODY HERE TODAY TO MAKE A TOAST.
AH
MASTER NIZUMA. WHY ARE YOU DOING A SECOND SERIES?
TNK
IS IT SO YOU HAVE A BACKUP IN CASE ONE GOES SOUTH?
ALL YOUR EFFORTS SHOULD GO INTO *CROW*.
BACK ME UP, GUYS.
W-WELL, I'M WORRIED THAT YOU'RE GOING TO MAKE YOUR FANS CHOOSE BETWEEN YOUR WORKS...
AND PERSONALLY, I DON'T WANT TO LOSE TO AIKO AKINA, SO I'D RATHER YOU DIDN'T ILLUSTRATE IT.
SHUJIN.

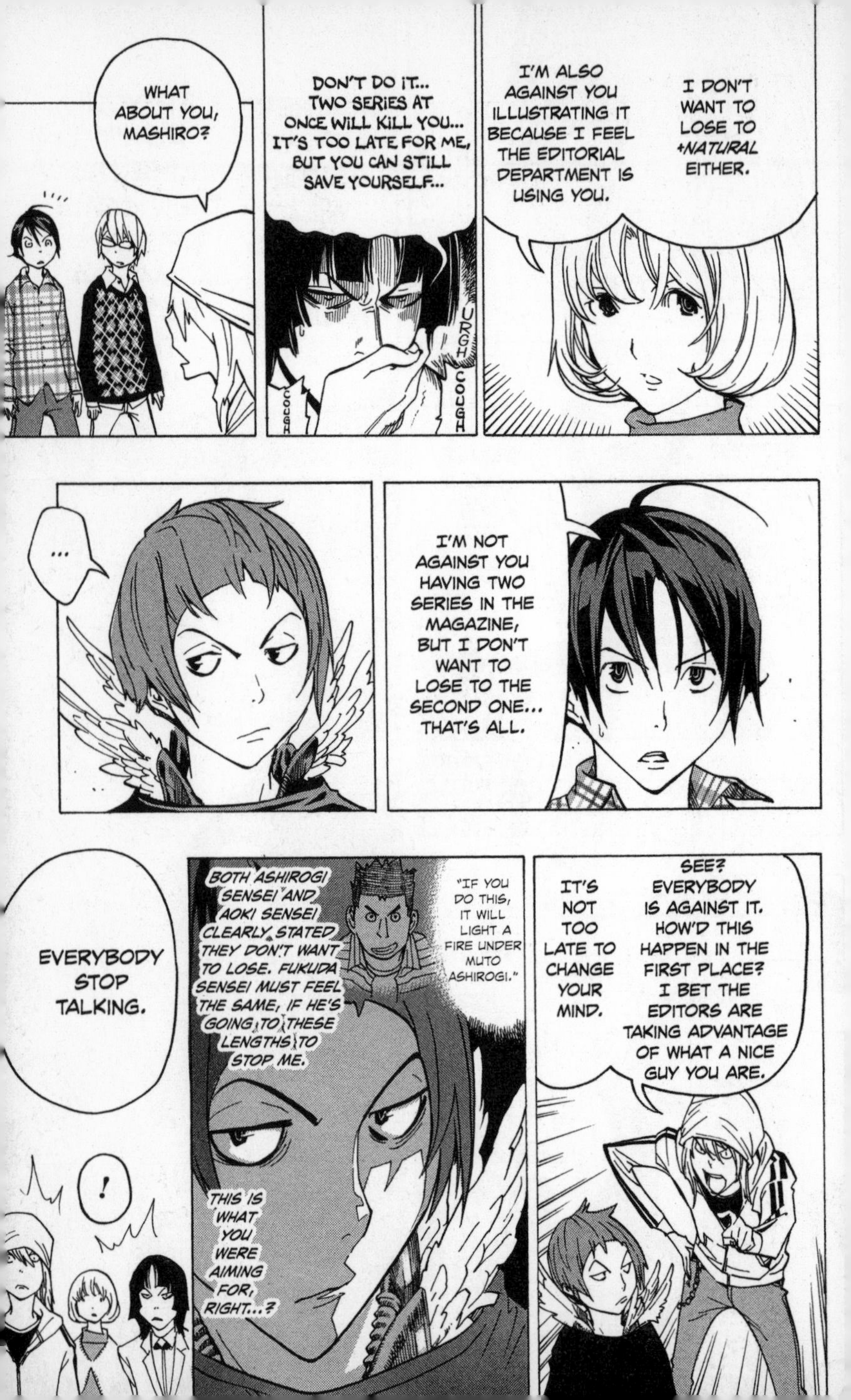
I DON'T WANT TO LOSE TO +NATURAL EITHER.
I'M ALSO AGAINST YOU ILLUSTRATING IT BECAUSE I FEEL THE EDITORIAL DEPARTMENT IS USING YOU.
DON'T DO IT... TWO SERIES AT ONCE WILL KILL YOU... IT'S TOO LATE FOR ME, BUT YOU CAN STILL SAVE YOURSELF...
URGH
COUGH
COUGH
WHAT ABOUT YOU, MASHIRO?
I'M NOT AGAINST YOU HAVING TWO SERIES IN THE MAGAZINE, BUT I DON'T WANT TO LOSE TO THE SECOND ONE... THAT'S ALL.
...
SEE? EVERYBODY IS AGAINST IT. HOW'D THIS HAPPEN IN THE FIRST PLACE? I BET THE EDITORS ARE TAKING ADVANTAGE OF WHAT A NICE GUY YOU ARE.
IT'S NOT TOO LATE TO CHANGE YOUR MIND.
"IF YOU DO THIS, IT WILL LIGHT A FIRE UNDER MUTO ASHIROGI."
BOTH ASHIROGI SENSEI AND AOKI SENSEI CLEARLY STATED THEY DON'T WANT TO LOSE. FUKUDA SENSEI MUST FEEL THE SAME, IF HE'S GOING TO THESE LENGTHS TO STOP ME.
THIS IS WHAT YOU WERE AIMING FOR, RIGHT...?
EVERYBODY STOP TALKING.
!

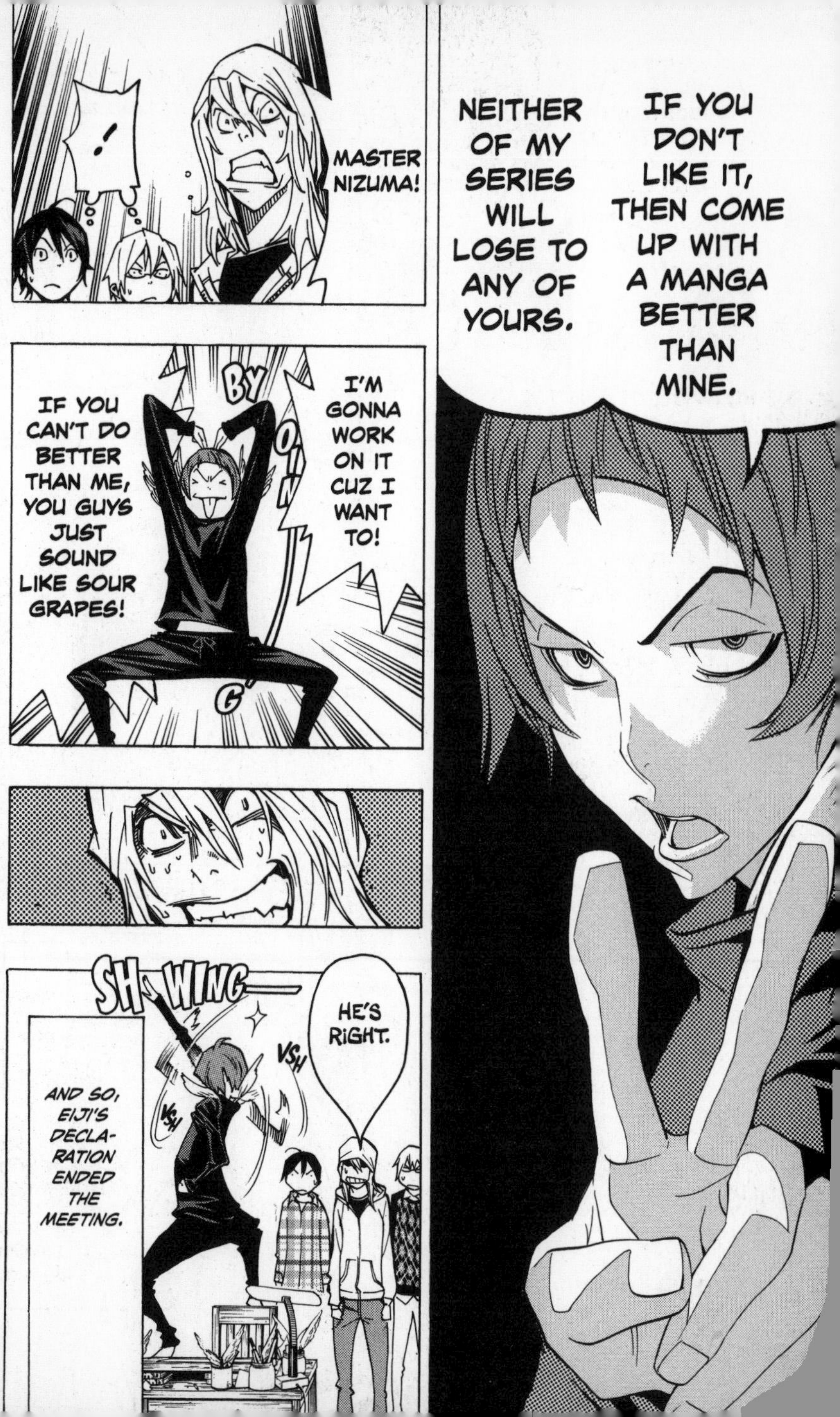
IF YOU DON'T LIKE IT, THEN COME UP WITH A MANGA BETTER THAN MINE.
NEITHER OF MY SERIES WILL LOSE TO ANY OF YOURS.
MASTER NIZUMA!
!
BYOING
I'M GONNA WORK ON IT CUZ I WANT TO!
IF YOU CAN'T DO BETTER THAN ME, YOU GUYS JUST SOUND LIKE SOUR GRAPES!
SHWING—
HE'S RIGHT.
VSH
VSH
AND SO, EIJI'S DECLARATION ENDED THE MEETING.

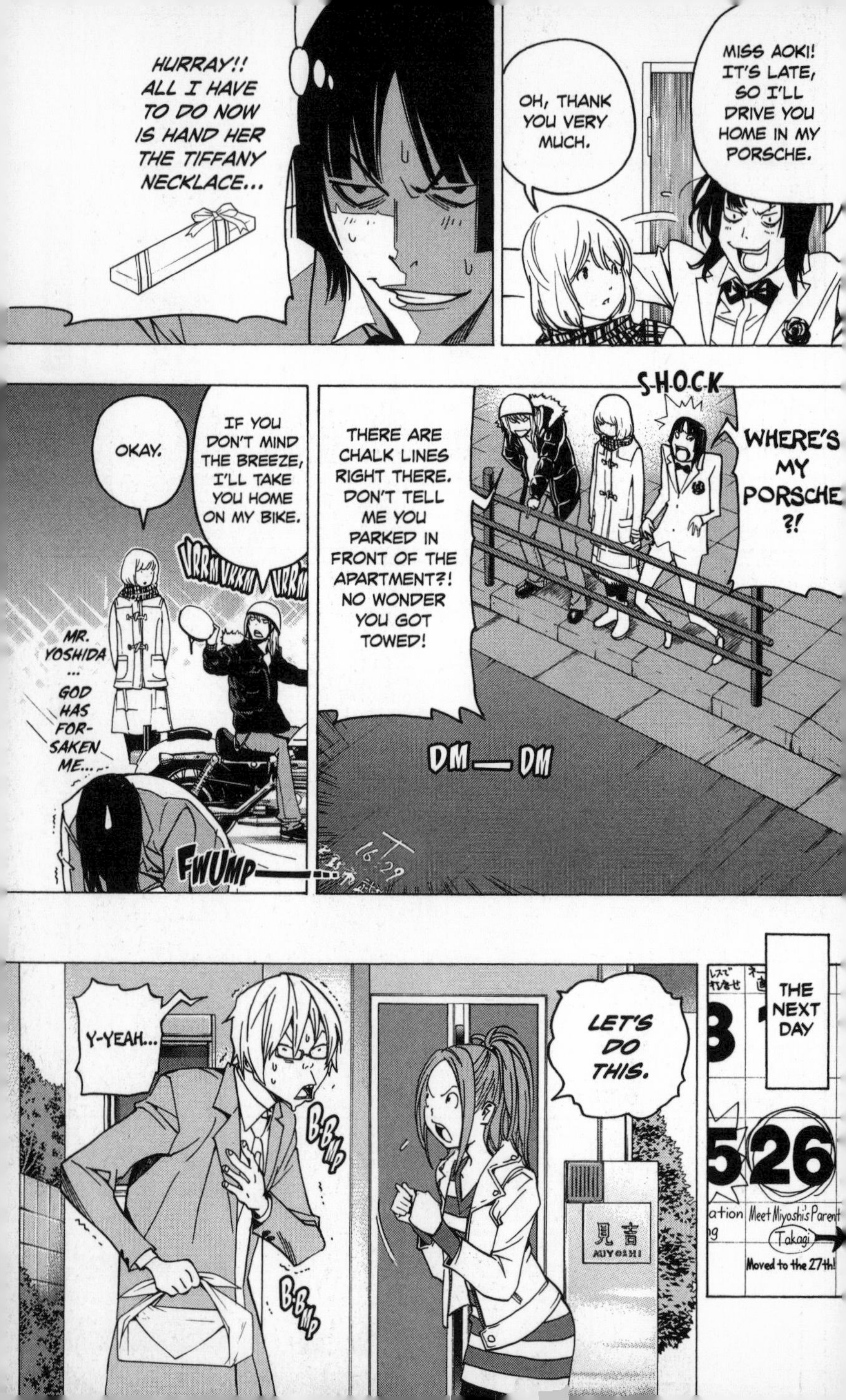
MISS AOKI! IT'S LATE, SO I'LL DRIVE YOU HOME IN MY PORSCHE.
OH, THANK YOU VERY MUCH.
HURRAY!! ALL I HAVE TO DO NOW IS HAND HER THE TIFFANY NECKLACE...
SHOCK
WHERE'S MY PORSCHE?!
THERE ARE CHALK LINES RIGHT THERE. DON'T TELL ME YOU PARKED IN FRONT OF THE APARTMENT?! NO WONDER YOU GOT TOWED!
16:29
DM — DM
IF YOU DON'T MIND THE BREEZE, I'LL TAKE YOU HOME ON MY BIKE.
OKAY.
VRRM VRRM VRRM
MR. YOSHIDA... GOD HAS FORSAKEN ME...
FWUMP
THE NEXT DAY
26
Meet Miyoshi's Parent
Takagi
Moved to the 27th!
LET'S DO THIS.
見吉
Y-YEAH...
B-BMP
B-BMP

OHBA'S STORYBOARD

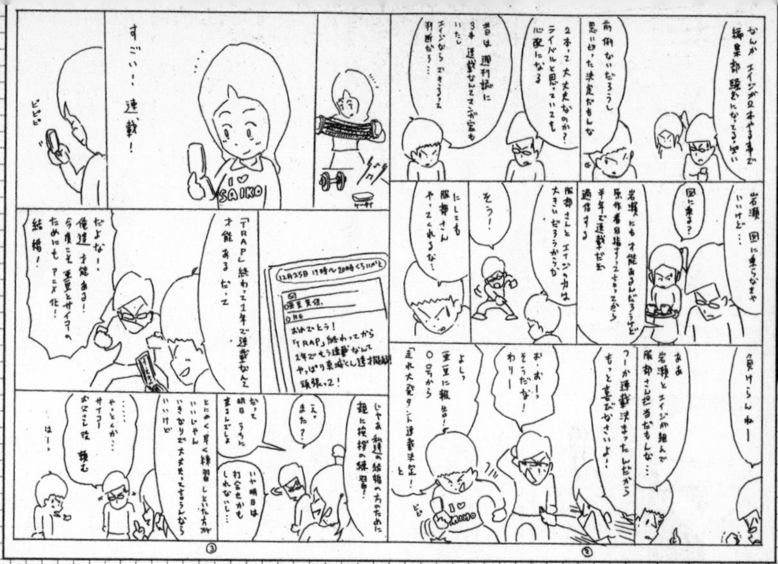
なんか エイジが2本やる事で編集部騒ぎになってるっぽい
前例ないだろうし 思い切った決定かもしんな
2本って大丈夫なのか? ライバルと思っていても心配になる
岩瀬 図に乗らなきゃいいけど…
図に乗る?
服部さんとエイジの力は大きいだろうからな
そう!
にしても服部さん やってくれるな…
負けらんねー
まあ 岩瀬とエイジが組んで服部さん担当だもんな…
つーか連載決まったんだから もっと喜びなさいよ!
わりー
すごい! 連載!
ピピピ
「TRAP」終わって1年で連載なんて 才能あるだって
だよな! 俺達 才能ある! 今度こそ亜豆とサイコーのためにも アニメ化!
結婚!
え、また?
いや明日は 打合せかも しれないし…
は…

OBATA'S STORYBOARD

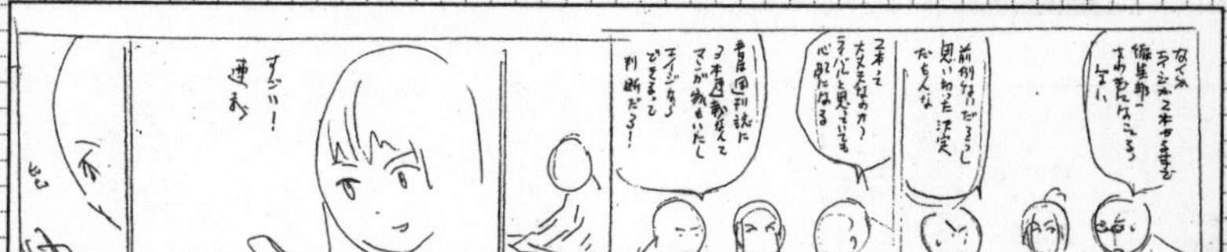

COMPLETE!

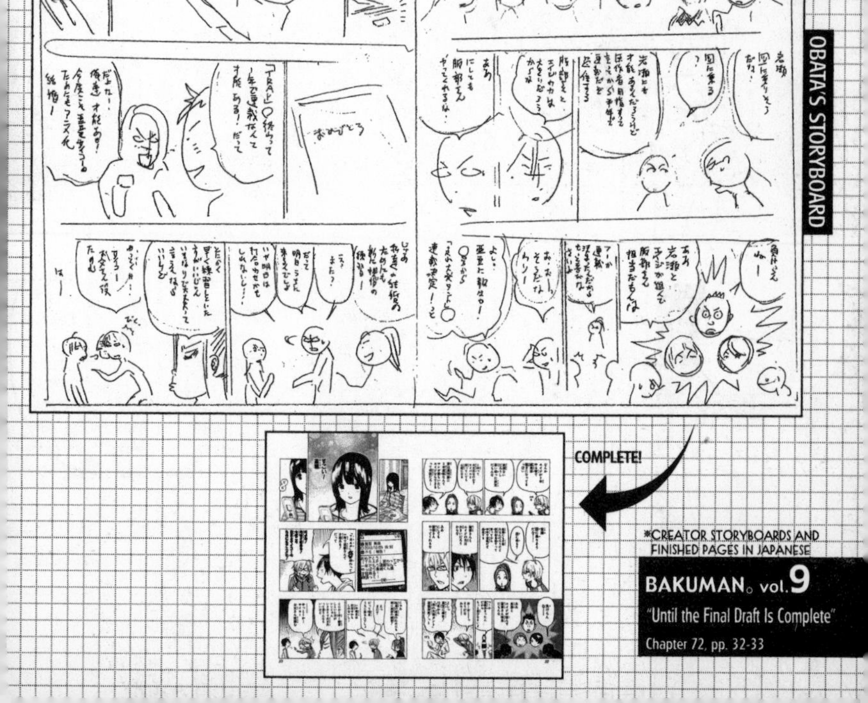

※CREATOR STORYBOARDS AND FINISHED PAGES IN JAPANESE

BAKUMAN。 vol.9

"Until the Final Draft Is Complete"

Chapter 72, pp. 32-33

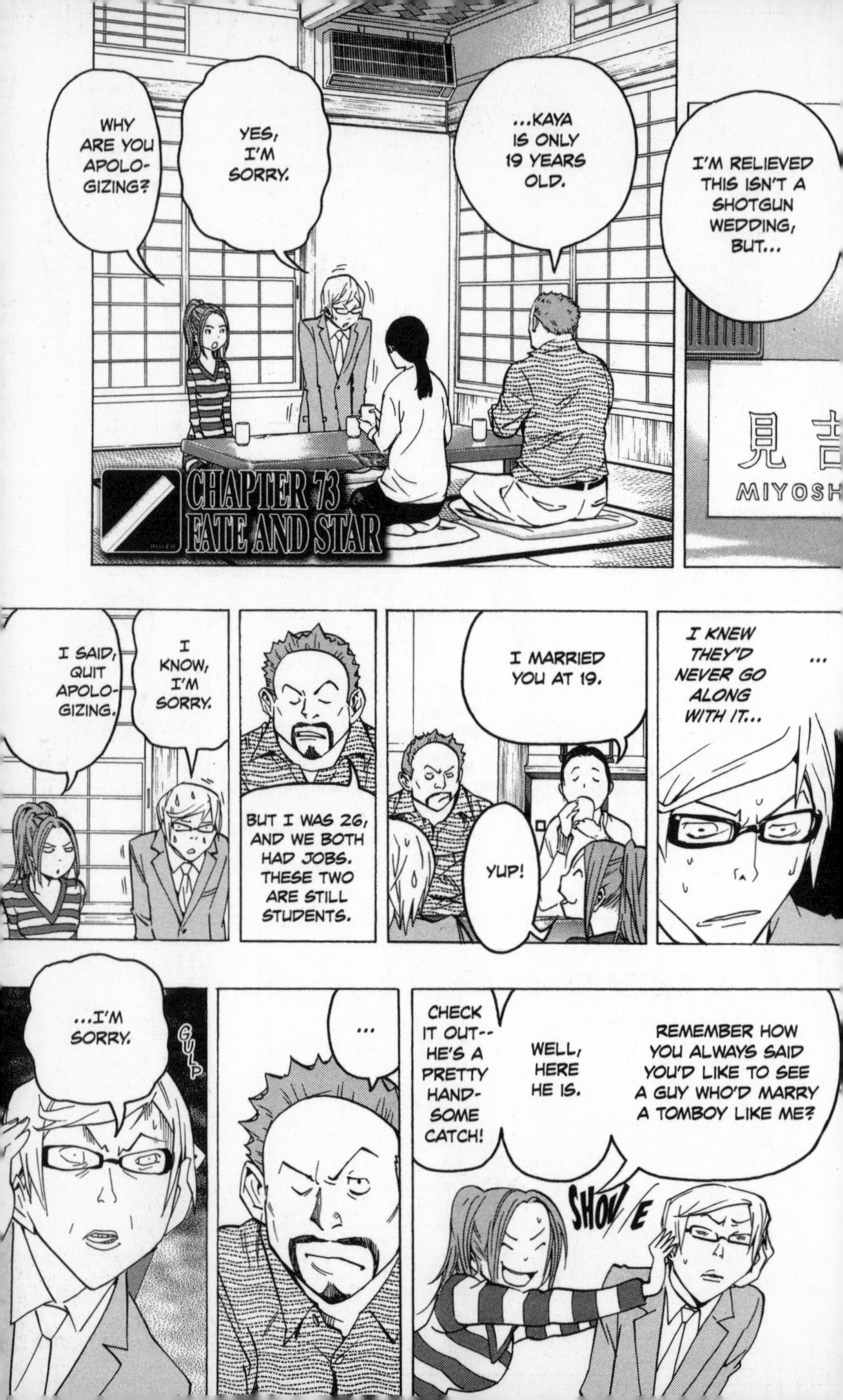
I'M RELIEVED THIS ISN'T A SHOTGUN WEDDING, BUT...
見吉
MIYOSH
...KAYA IS ONLY 19 YEARS OLD.
YES, I'M SORRY.
WHY ARE YOU APOLOGIZING?
CHAPTER 73
FATE AND STAR
I KNEW THEY'D NEVER GO ALONG WITH IT...
...
I MARRIED YOU AT 19.
YUP!
BUT I WAS 26, AND WE BOTH HAD JOBS. THESE TWO ARE STILL STUDENTS.
I KNOW, I'M SORRY.
I SAID, QUIT APOLOGIZING.
REMEMBER HOW YOU ALWAYS SAID YOU'D LIKE TO SEE A GUY WHO'D MARRY A TOMBOY LIKE ME?
WELL, HERE HE IS.
CHECK IT OUT-- HE'S A PRETTY HANDSOME CATCH!
SHOVE
...
...I'M SORRY.
GULP

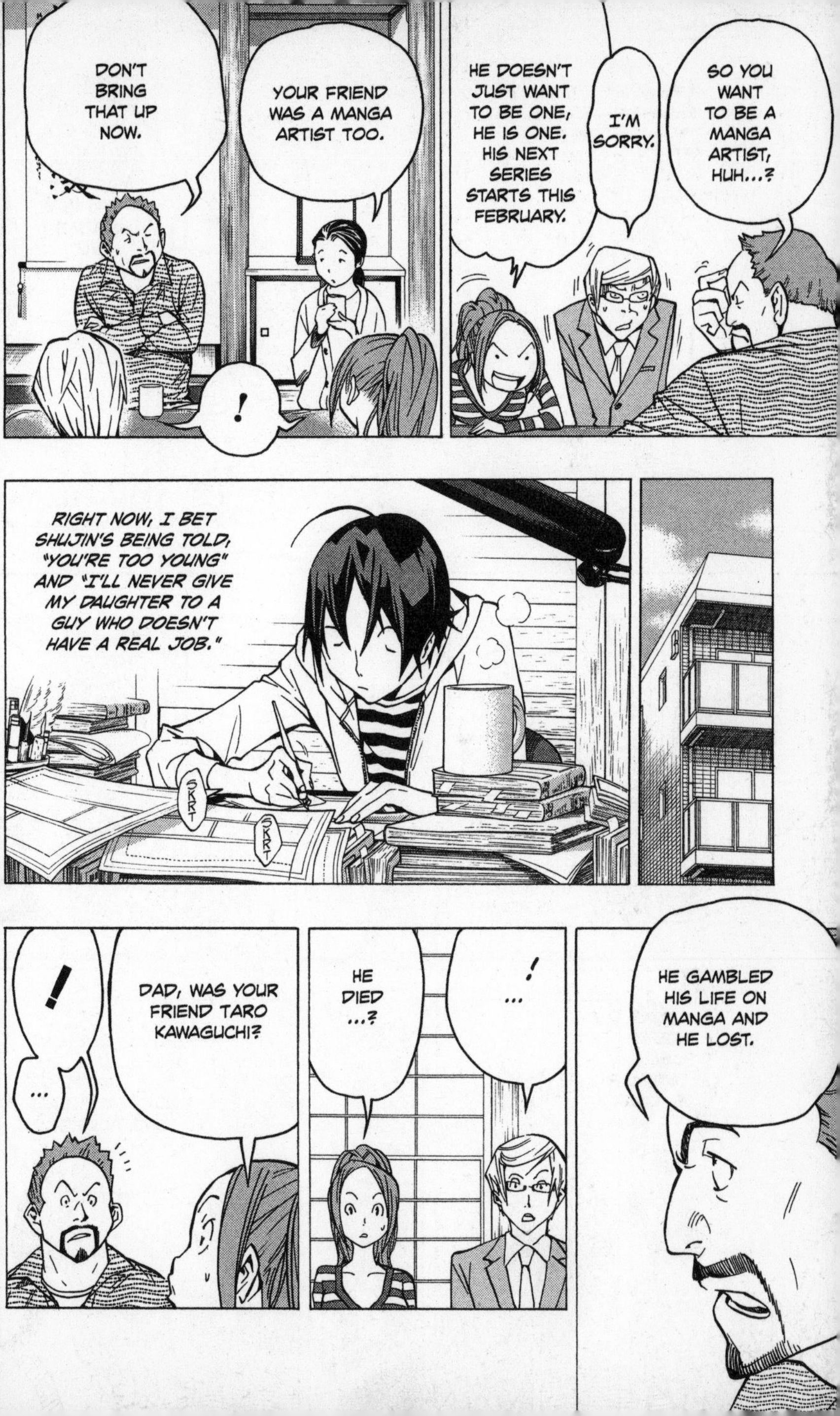
SO YOU WANT TO BE A MANGA ARTIST, HUH...?
I'M SORRY.
HE DOESN'T JUST WANT TO BE ONE, HE IS ONE. HIS NEXT SERIES STARTS THIS FEBRUARY.
YOUR FRIEND WAS A MANGA ARTIST TOO.
DON'T BRING THAT UP NOW.
!
RIGHT NOW, I BET SHUJIN'S BEING TOLD, "YOU'RE TOO YOUNG" AND "I'LL NEVER GIVE MY DAUGHTER TO A GUY WHO DOESN'T HAVE A REAL JOB."
SKRT
SKRT
HE GAMBLED HIS LIFE ON MANGA AND HE LOST.
! ...
HE DIED ...?
DAD, WAS YOUR FRIEND TARO KAWAGUCHI?
! ...

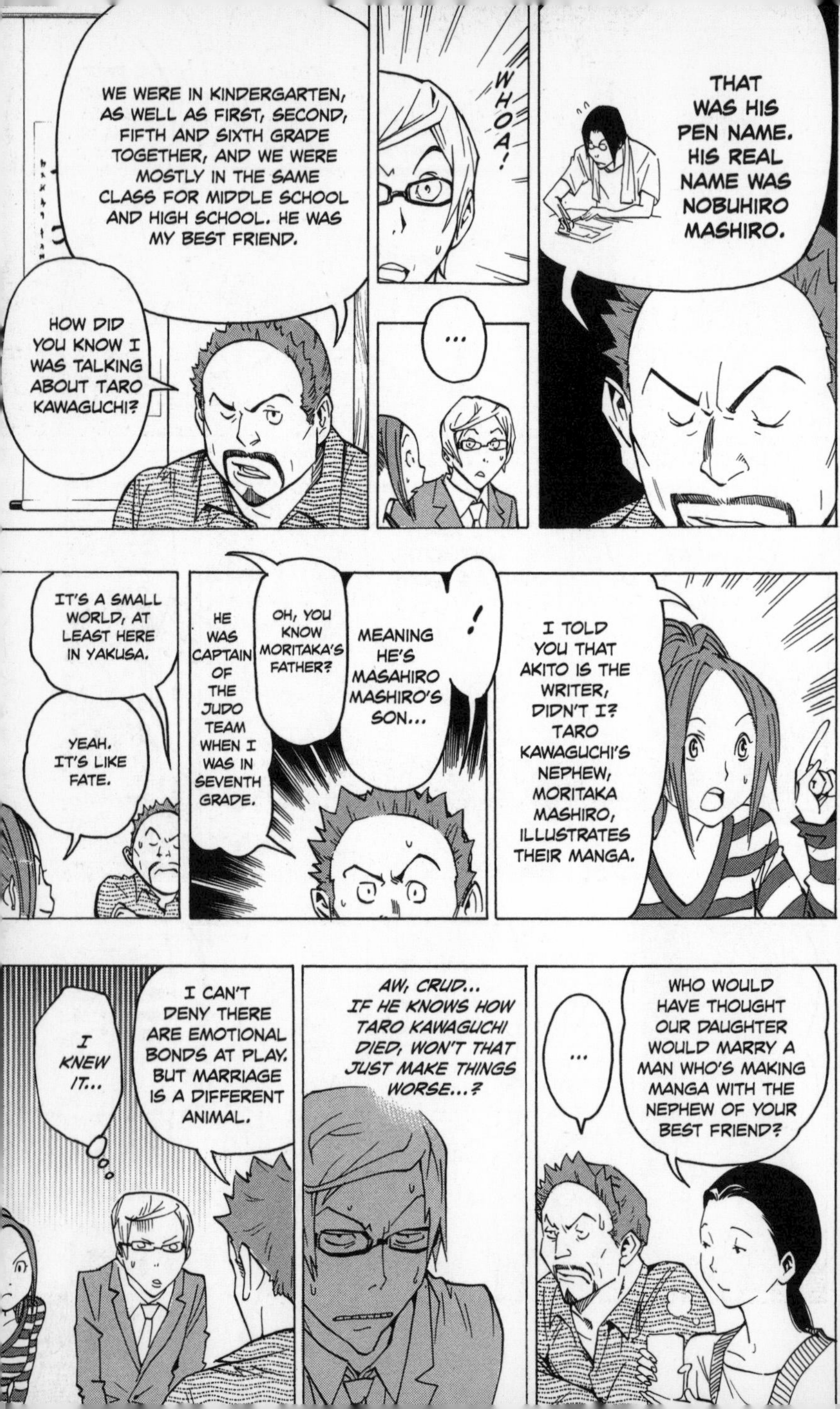
THAT WAS HIS PEN NAME. HIS REAL NAME WAS NOBUHIRO MASHIRO.
WHOA!
...
WE WERE IN KINDERGARTEN, AS WELL AS FIRST, SECOND, FIFTH AND SIXTH GRADE TOGETHER, AND WE WERE MOSTLY IN THE SAME CLASS FOR MIDDLE SCHOOL AND HIGH SCHOOL. HE WAS MY BEST FRIEND.
HOW DID YOU KNOW I WAS TALKING ABOUT TARO KAWAGUCHI?
I TOLD YOU THAT AKITO IS THE WRITER, DIDN'T I? TARO KAWAGUCHI'S NEPHEW, MORITAKA MASHIRO, ILLUSTRATES THEIR MANGA.
!
MEANING HE'S MASAHIRO MASHIRO'S SON...
OH, YOU KNOW MORITAKA'S FATHER?
HE WAS CAPTAIN OF THE JUDO TEAM WHEN I WAS IN SEVENTH GRADE.
IT'S A SMALL WORLD, AT LEAST HERE IN YAKUSA.
YEAH. IT'S LIKE FATE.
WHO WOULD HAVE THOUGHT OUR DAUGHTER WOULD MARRY A MAN WHO'S MAKING MANGA WITH THE NEPHEW OF YOUR BEST FRIEND?
...
AW, CRUD... IF HE KNOWS HOW TARO KAWAGUCHI DIED, WON'T THAT JUST MAKE THINGS WORSE...?
I CAN'T DENY THERE ARE EMOTIONAL BONDS AT PLAY. BUT MARRIAGE IS A DIFFERENT ANIMAL.
I KNEW IT...

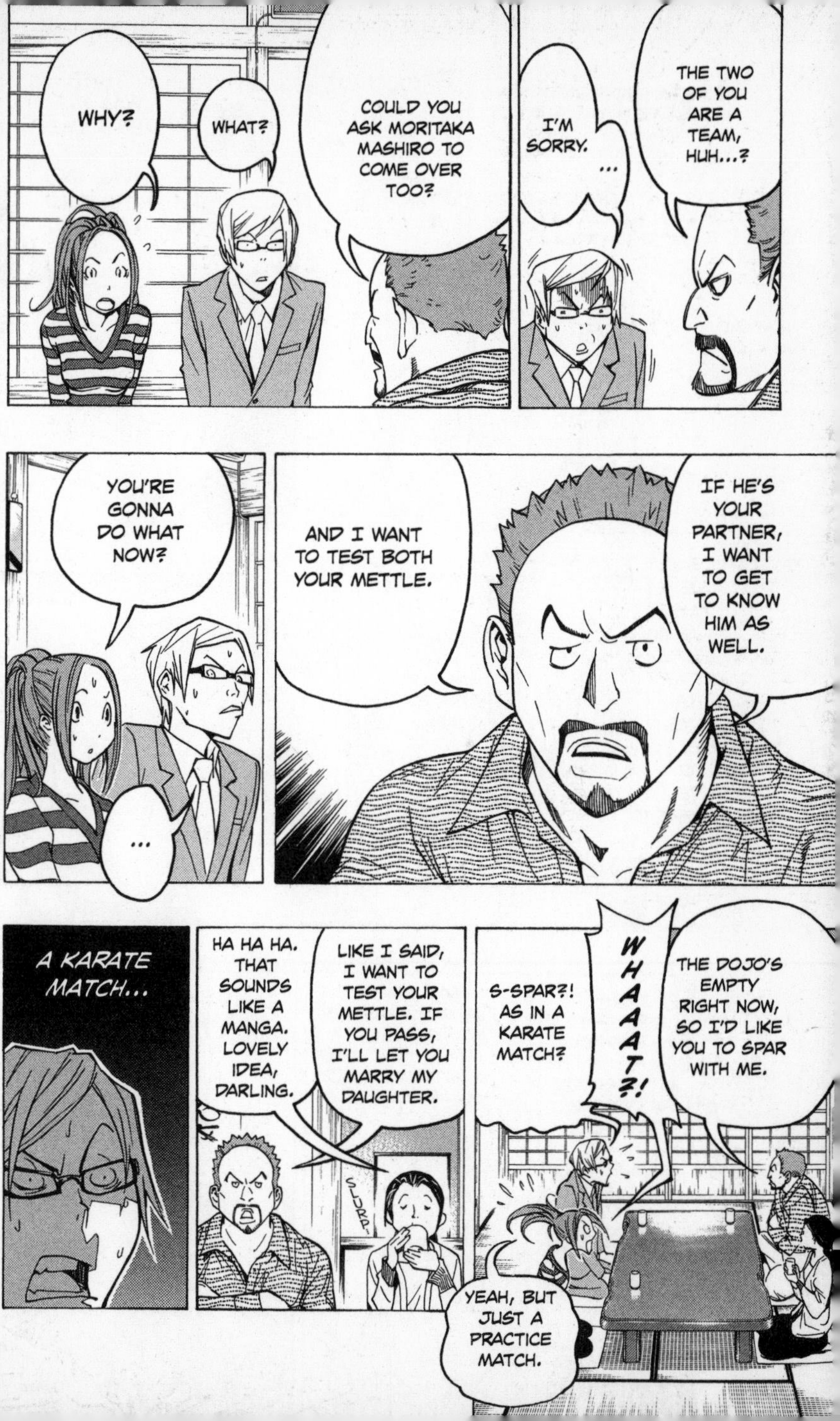
THE TWO OF YOU ARE A TEAM, HUH...?
I'M SORRY.
...
COULD YOU ASK MORITAKA MASHIRO TO COME OVER TOO?
WHAT?
WHY?
IF HE'S YOUR PARTNER, I WANT TO GET TO KNOW HIM AS WELL.
AND I WANT TO TEST BOTH YOUR METTLE.
YOU'RE GONNA DO WHAT NOW?
...
THE DOJO'S EMPTY RIGHT NOW, SO I'D LIKE YOU TO SPAR WITH ME.
WHAAAAT?!
S-SPAR?! AS IN A KARATE MATCH?
YEAH, BUT JUST A PRACTICE MATCH.
LIKE I SAID, I WANT TO TEST YOUR METTLE. IF YOU PASS, I'LL LET YOU MARRY MY DAUGHTER.
HA HA HA. THAT SOUNDS LIKE A MANGA. LOVELY IDEA, DARLING.
SLURP
A KARATE MATCH...

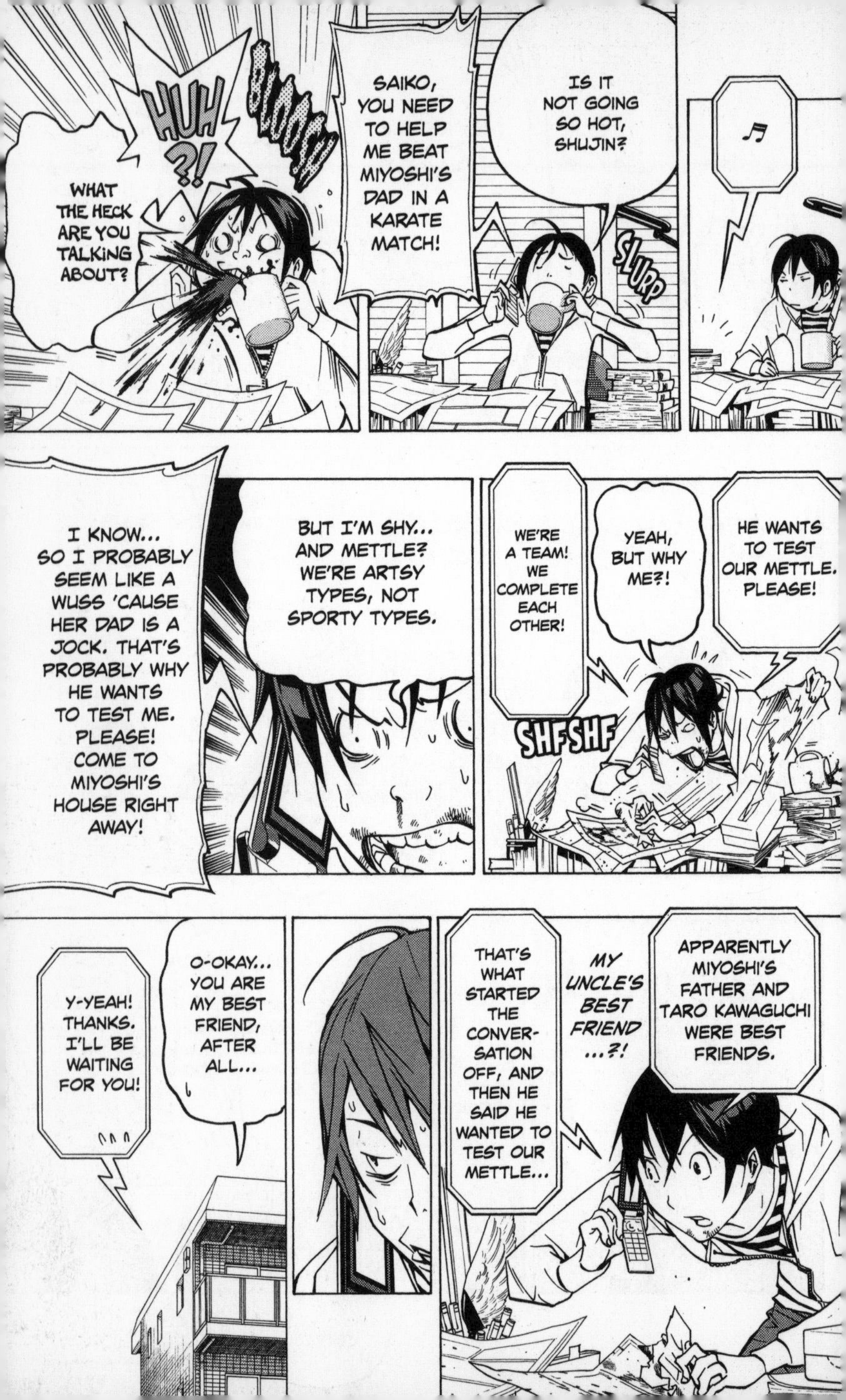
♪
IS IT NOT GOING SO HOT, SHUJIN?
SLURP
SAIKO, YOU NEED TO HELP ME BEAT MIYOSHI'S DAD IN A KARATE MATCH!
HUH ?!
WHAT THE HECK ARE YOU TALKING ABOUT?
HE WANTS TO TEST OUR METTLE. PLEASE!
YEAH, BUT WHY ME?!
WE'RE A TEAM! WE COMPLETE EACH OTHER!
SHF SHF
BUT I'M SHY... AND METTLE? WE'RE ARTSY TYPES, NOT SPORTY TYPES.
I KNOW... SO I PROBABLY SEEM LIKE A WUSS 'CAUSE HER DAD IS A JOCK. THAT'S PROBABLY WHY HE WANTS TO TEST ME. PLEASE! COME TO MIYOSHI'S HOUSE RIGHT AWAY!
APPARENTLY MIYOSHI'S FATHER AND TARO KAWAGUCHI WERE BEST FRIENDS.
MY UNCLE'S BEST FRIEND ...?!
THAT'S WHAT STARTED THE CONVER-SATION OFF, AND THEN HE SAID HE WANTED TO TEST OUR METTLE...
O-OKAY... YOU ARE MY BEST FRIEND, AFTER ALL...
Y-YEAH! THANKS. I'LL BE WAITING FOR YOU!

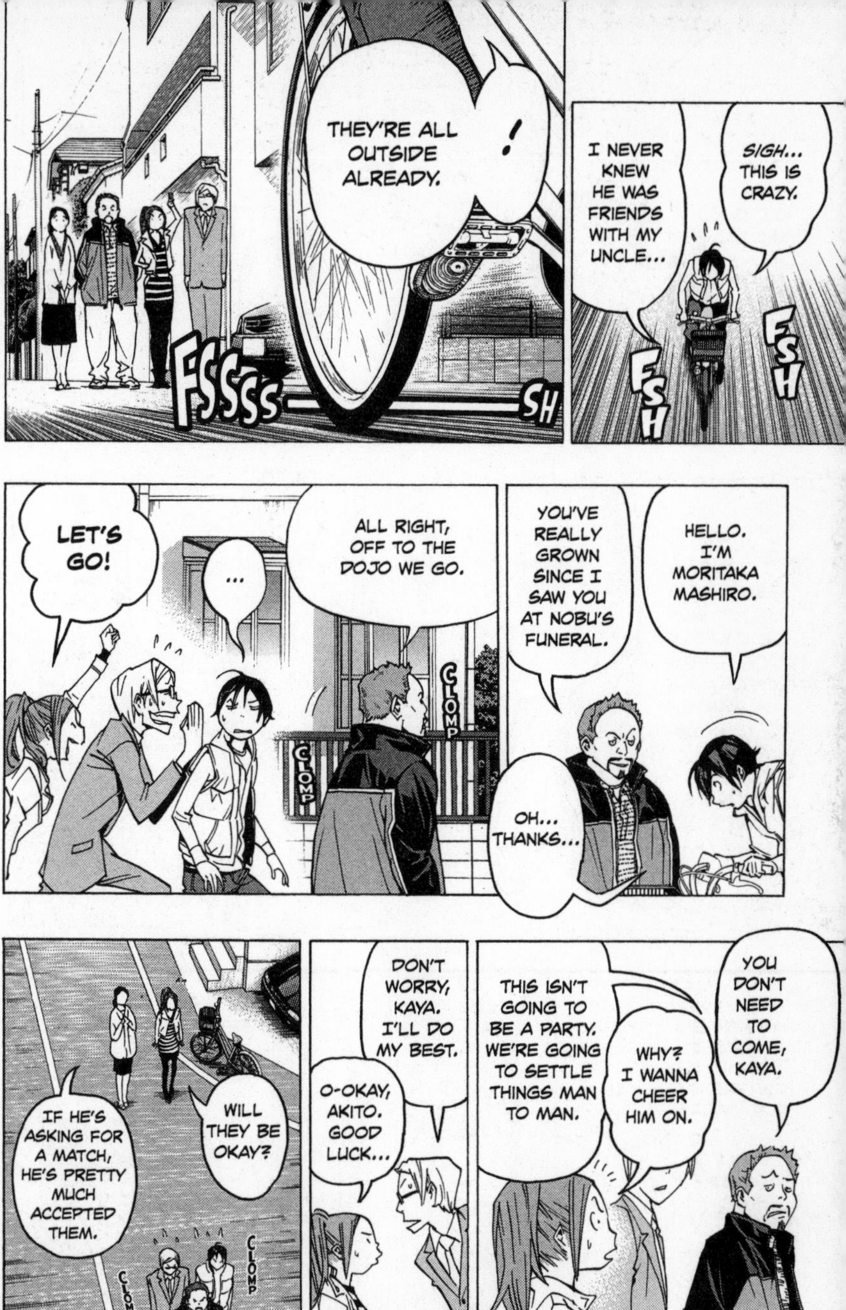
SIGH... THIS IS CRAZY.
I NEVER KNEW HE WAS FRIENDS WITH MY UNCLE...
FSH
FSH
!
THEY'RE ALL OUTSIDE ALREADY.
FSSSS
SH
HELLO. I'M MORITAKA MASHIRO.
YOU'VE REALLY GROWN SINCE I SAW YOU AT NOBU'S FUNERAL.
OH... THANKS...
ALL RIGHT, OFF TO THE DOJO WE GO.
CLOMP
CLOMP
...
LET'S GO!
YOU DON'T NEED TO COME, KAYA.
WHY? I WANNA CHEER HIM ON.
THIS ISN'T GOING TO BE A PARTY. WE'RE GOING TO SETTLE THINGS MAN TO MAN.
DON'T WORRY, KAYA. I'LL DO MY BEST.
O-OKAY, AKITO. GOOD LUCK...
WILL THEY BE OKAY?
IF HE'S ASKING FOR A MATCH, HE'S PRETTY MUCH ACCEPTED THEM.
CLOMP
CLOMP

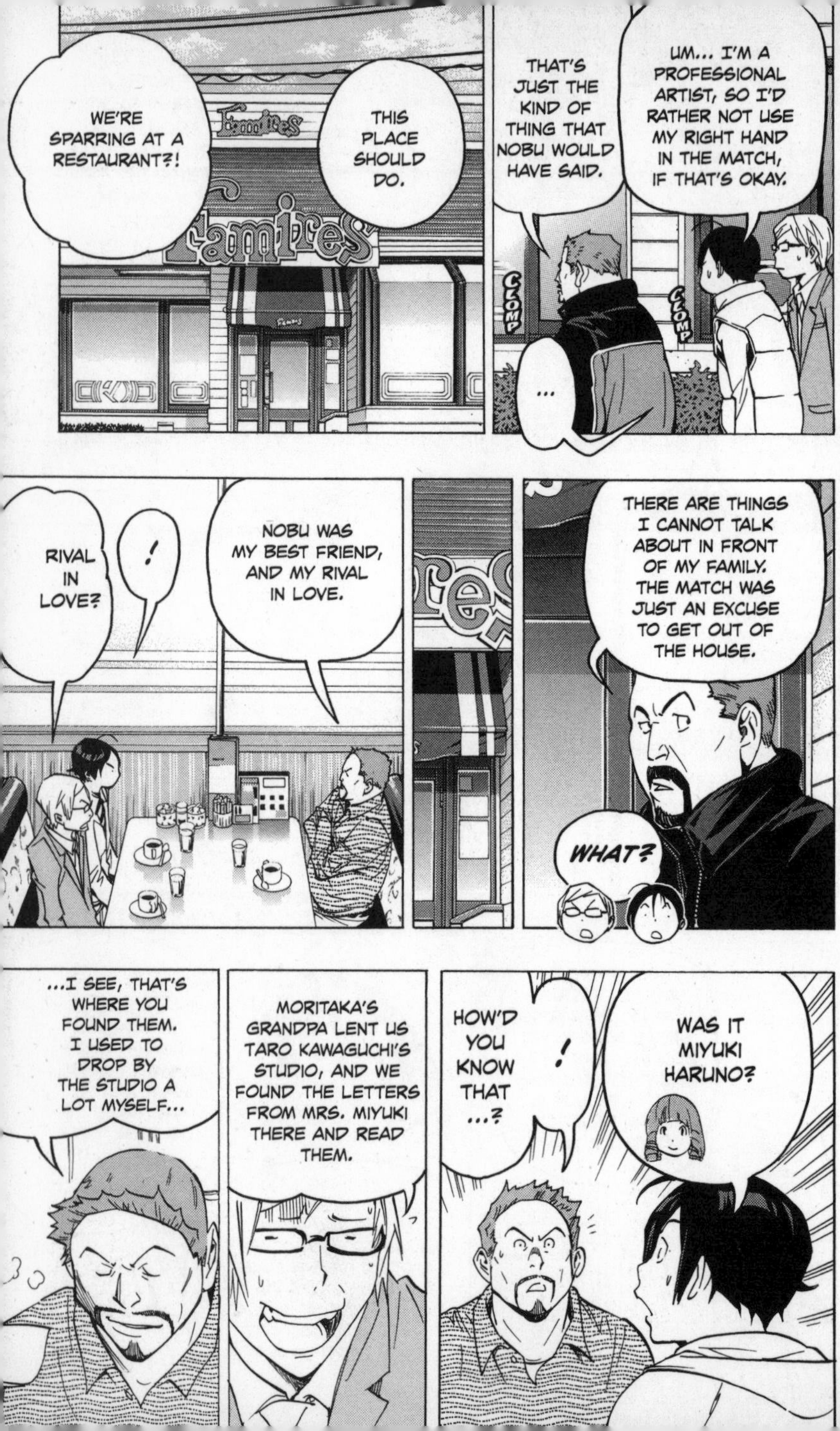
UM... I'M A PROFESSIONAL ARTIST, SO I'D RATHER NOT USE MY RIGHT HAND IN THE MATCH, IF THAT'S OKAY.
THAT'S JUST THE KIND OF THING THAT NOBU WOULD HAVE SAID.
CLOMP
CLOMP
...
THIS PLACE SHOULD DO.
Famires
WE'RE SPARRING AT A RESTAURANT?!
THERE ARE THINGS I CANNOT TALK ABOUT IN FRONT OF MY FAMILY. THE MATCH WAS JUST AN EXCUSE TO GET OUT OF THE HOUSE.
WHAT?
NOBU WAS MY BEST FRIEND, AND MY RIVAL IN LOVE.
!
RIVAL IN LOVE?
WAS IT MIYUKI HARUNO?
!
HOW'D YOU KNOW THAT ...?
MORITAKA'S GRANDPA LENT US TARO KAWAGUCHI'S STUDIO, AND WE FOUND THE LETTERS FROM MRS. MIYUKI THERE AND READ THEM.
...I SEE, THAT'S WHERE YOU FOUND THEM. I USED TO DROP BY THE STUDIO A LOT MYSELF...

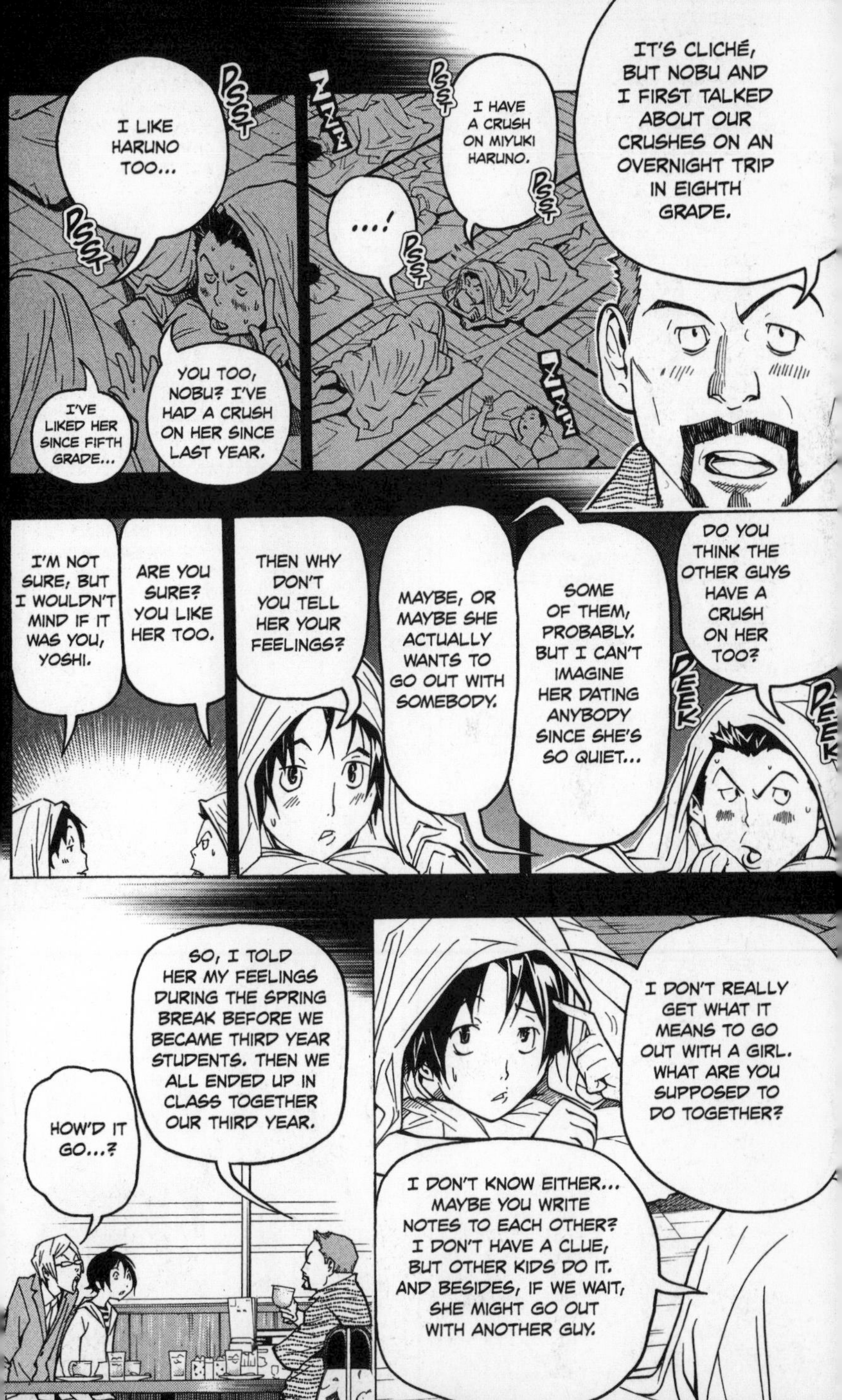
IT'S CLICHÉ, BUT NOBU AND I FIRST TALKED ABOUT OUR CRUSHES ON AN OVERNIGHT TRIP IN EIGHTH GRADE.
PSST
I HAVE A CRUSH ON MIYUKI HARUNO.
PSST
...!
PSST
ZZZ
MMM
PSST
I LIKE HARUNO TOO...
PSSK
YOU TOO, NOBU? I'VE HAD A CRUSH ON HER SINCE LAST YEAR.
I'VE LIKED HER SINCE FIFTH GRADE...
DO YOU THINK THE OTHER GUYS HAVE A CRUSH ON HER TOO?
DEEK
DEEK
SOME OF THEM, PROBABLY. BUT I CAN'T IMAGINE HER DATING ANYBODY SINCE SHE'S SO QUIET...
MAYBE, OR MAYBE SHE ACTUALLY WANTS TO GO OUT WITH SOMEBODY.
THEN WHY DON'T YOU TELL HER YOUR FEELINGS?
ARE YOU SURE? YOU LIKE HER TOO.
I'M NOT SURE, BUT I WOULDN'T MIND IF IT WAS YOU, YOSHI.
I DON'T REALLY GET WHAT IT MEANS TO GO OUT WITH A GIRL. WHAT ARE YOU SUPPOSED TO DO TOGETHER?
I DON'T KNOW EITHER... MAYBE YOU WRITE NOTES TO EACH OTHER? I DON'T HAVE A CLUE, BUT OTHER KIDS DO IT. AND BESIDES, IF WE WAIT, SHE MIGHT GO OUT WITH ANOTHER GUY.
SO, I TOLD HER MY FEELINGS DURING THE SPRING BREAK BEFORE WE BECAME THIRD YEAR STUDENTS. THEN WE ALL ENDED UP IN CLASS TOGETHER OUR THIRD YEAR.
HOW'D IT GO...?

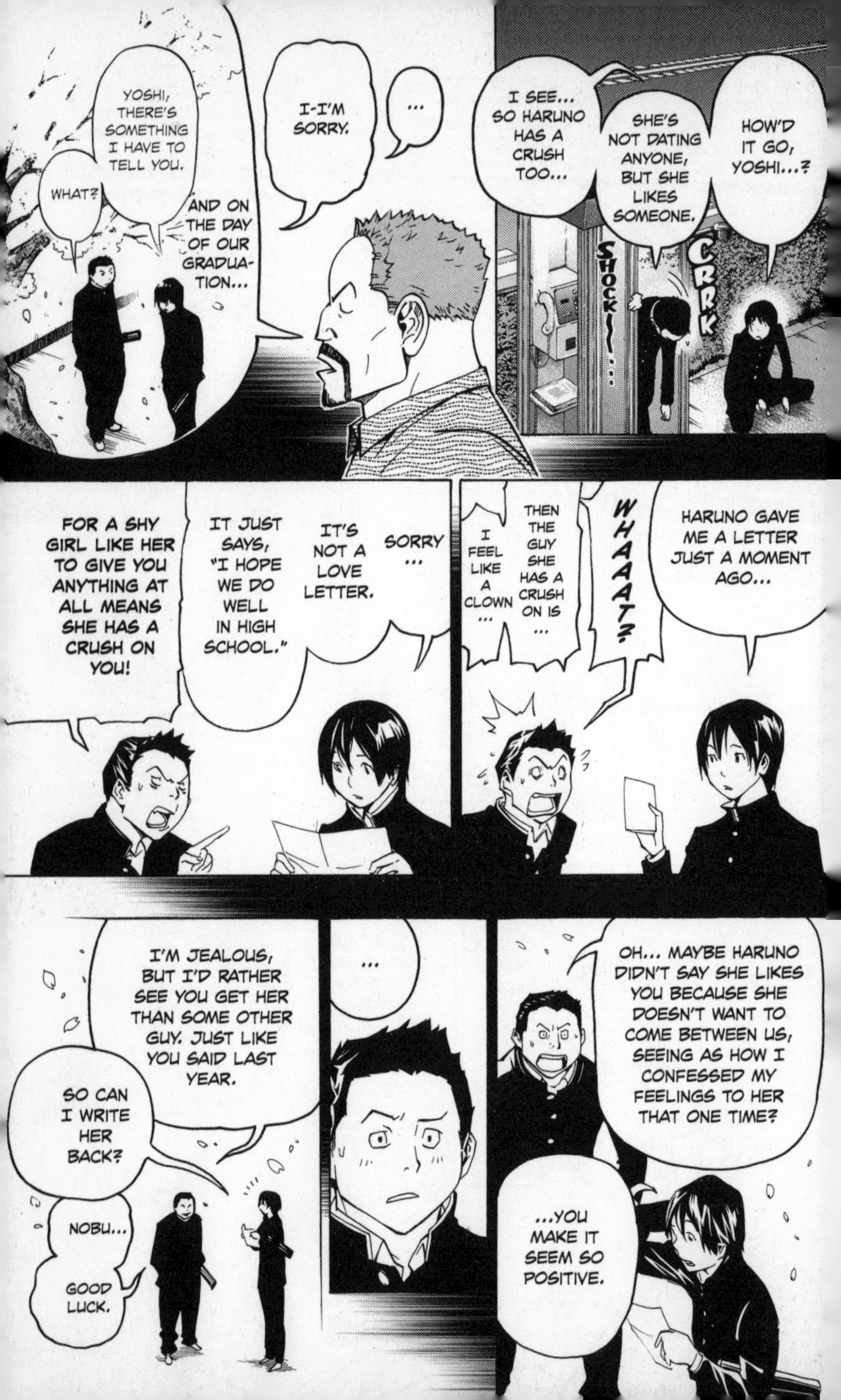
HOW'D IT GO, YOSHI...?
SHE'S NOT DATING ANYONE, BUT SHE LIKES SOMEONE.
CRRK
SHOCK~...
I SEE... SO HARUNO HAS A CRUSH TOO...
...
I-I'M SORRY.
AND ON THE DAY OF OUR GRADUATION...
YOSHI, THERE'S SOMETHING I HAVE TO TELL YOU.
WHAT?
HARUNO GAVE ME A LETTER JUST A MOMENT AGO...
WHAAAAT?
THEN THE GUY SHE HAS A CRUSH ON IS ...
I FEEL LIKE A CLOWN ...
SORRY ...
IT'S NOT A LOVE LETTER.
IT JUST SAYS, "I HOPE WE DO WELL IN HIGH SCHOOL."
FOR A SHY GIRL LIKE HER TO GIVE YOU ANYTHING AT ALL MEANS SHE HAS A CRUSH ON YOU!
OH... MAYBE HARUNO DIDN'T SAY SHE LIKES YOU BECAUSE SHE DOESN'T WANT TO COME BETWEEN US, SEEING AS HOW I CONFESSED MY FEELINGS TO HER THAT ONE TIME?
...YOU MAKE IT SEEM SO POSITIVE.
...
I'M JEALOUS, BUT I'D RATHER SEE YOU GET HER THAN SOME OTHER GUY. JUST LIKE YOU SAID LAST YEAR.
SO CAN I WRITE HER BACK?
NOBU...
GOOD LUCK.

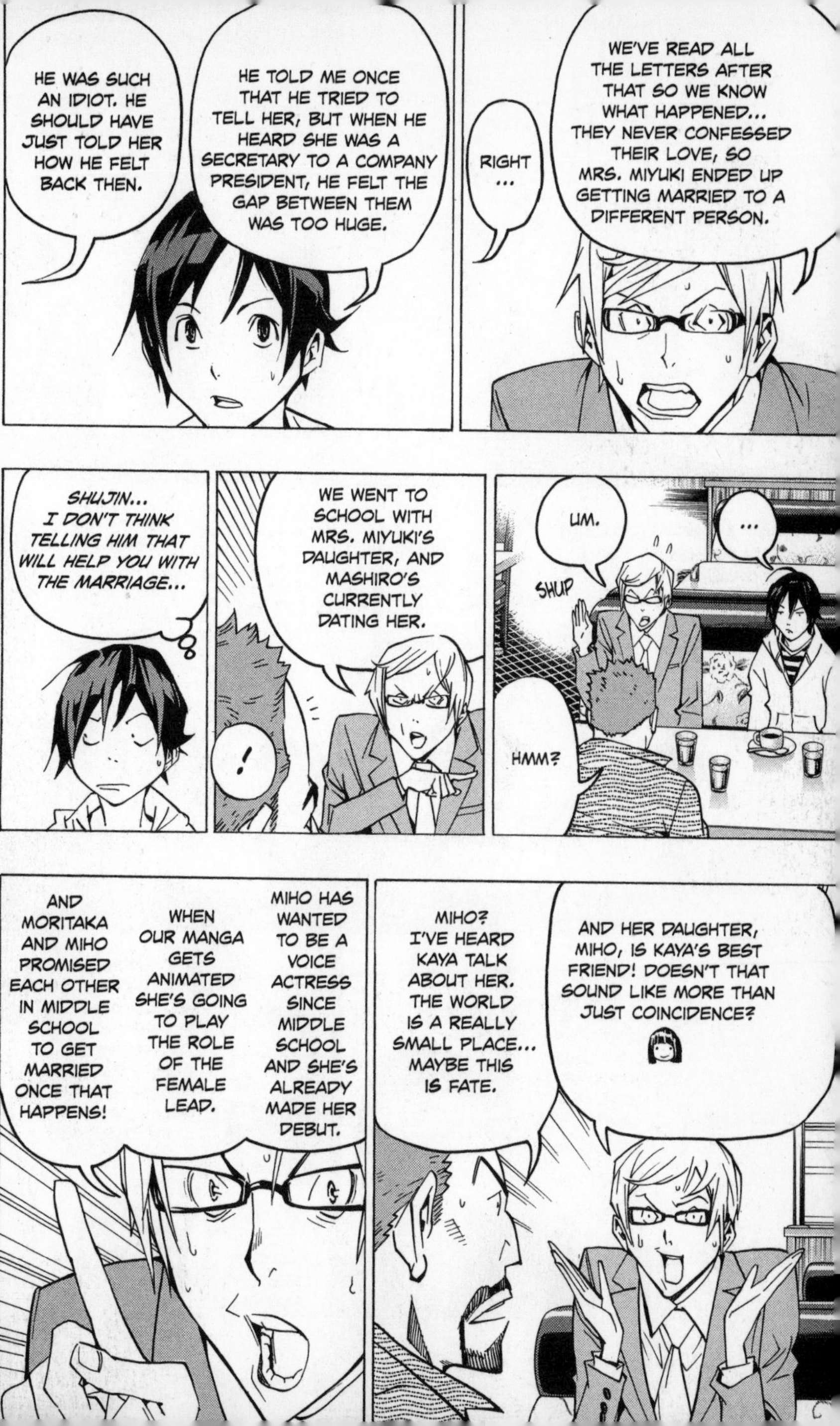
WE'VE READ ALL THE LETTERS AFTER THAT SO WE KNOW WHAT HAPPENED... THEY NEVER CONFESSED THEIR LOVE, SO MRS. MIYUKI ENDED UP GETTING MARRIED TO A DIFFERENT PERSON.
RIGHT...
HE TOLD ME ONCE THAT HE TRIED TO TELL HER, BUT WHEN HE HEARD SHE WAS A SECRETARY TO A COMPANY PRESIDENT, HE FELT THE GAP BETWEEN THEM WAS TOO HUGE.
HE WAS SUCH AN IDIOT. HE SHOULD HAVE JUST TOLD HER HOW HE FELT BACK THEN.
UM.
...
SHUP
HMM?
WE WENT TO SCHOOL WITH MRS. MIYUKI'S DAUGHTER, AND MASHIRO'S CURRENTLY DATING HER.
!
SHUJIN... I DON'T THINK TELLING HIM THAT WILL HELP YOU WITH THE MARRIAGE...
AND HER DAUGHTER, MIHO, IS KAYA'S BEST FRIEND! DOESN'T THAT SOUND LIKE MORE THAN JUST COINCIDENCE?
MIHO? I'VE HEARD KAYA TALK ABOUT HER. THE WORLD IS A REALLY SMALL PLACE... MAYBE THIS IS FATE.
MIHO HAS WANTED TO BE A VOICE ACTRESS SINCE MIDDLE SCHOOL AND SHE'S ALREADY MADE HER DEBUT.
WHEN OUR MANGA GETS ANIMATED SHE'S GOING TO PLAY THE ROLE OF THE FEMALE LEAD.
AND MORITAKA AND MIHO PROMISED EACH OTHER IN MIDDLE SCHOOL TO GET MARRIED ONCE THAT HAPPENS!

READ THIS WAY

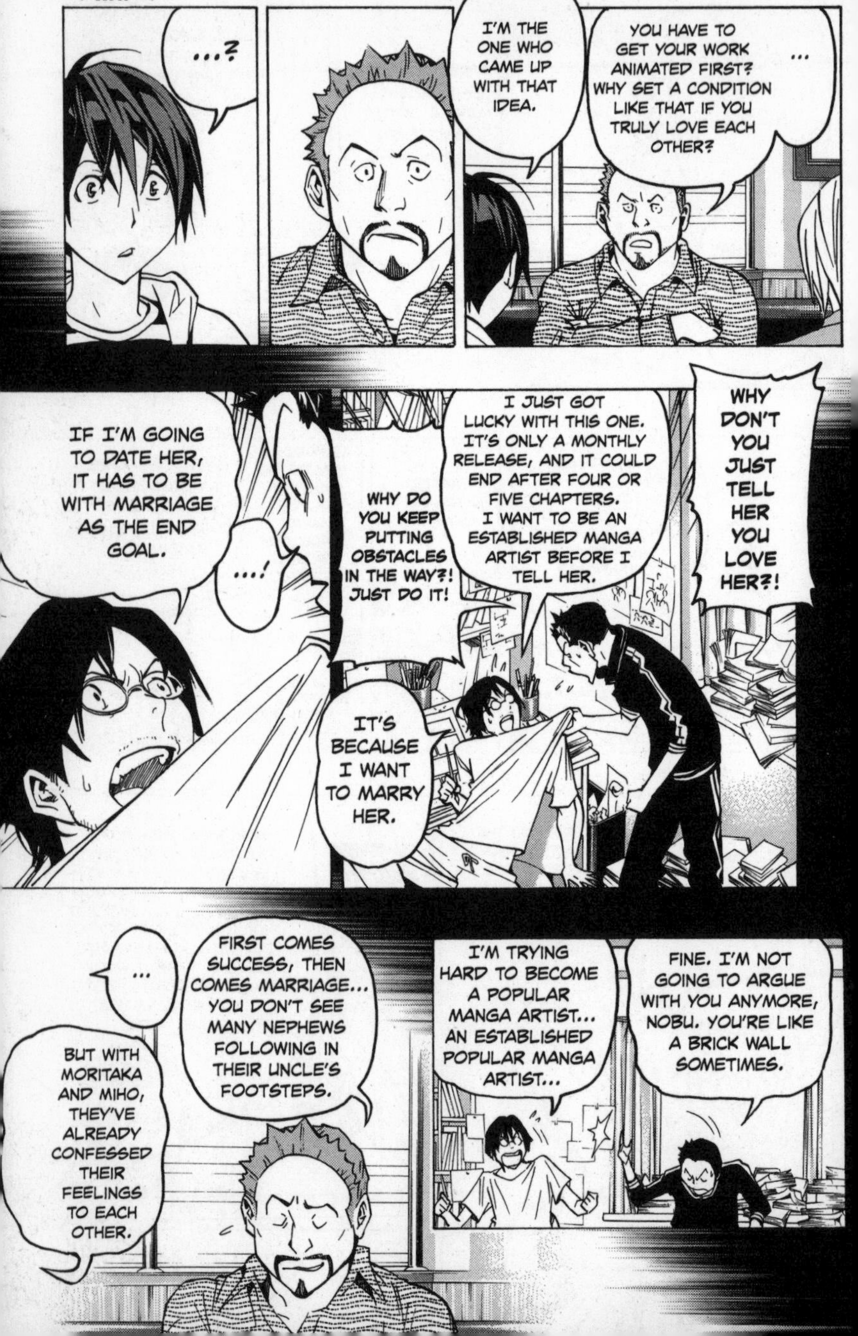

...
YOU HAVE TO GET YOUR WORK ANIMATED FIRST? WHY SET A CONDITION LIKE THAT IF YOU TRULY LOVE EACH OTHER?
I'M THE ONE WHO CAME UP WITH THAT IDEA.
...?
WHY DON'T YOU JUST TELL HER YOU LOVE HER?!
I JUST GOT LUCKY WITH THIS ONE. IT'S ONLY A MONTHLY RELEASE, AND IT COULD END AFTER FOUR OR FIVE CHAPTERS. I WANT TO BE AN ESTABLISHED MANGA ARTIST BEFORE I TELL HER.
WHY DO YOU KEEP PUTTING OBSTACLES IN THE WAY?! JUST DO IT!
IT'S BECAUSE I WANT TO MARRY HER.
...!
IF I'M GOING TO DATE HER, IT HAS TO BE WITH MARRIAGE AS THE END GOAL.
FINE. I'M NOT GOING TO ARGUE WITH YOU ANYMORE, NOBU. YOU'RE LIKE A BRICK WALL SOMETIMES.
I'M TRYING HARD TO BECOME A POPULAR MANGA ARTIST... AN ESTABLISHED POPULAR MANGA ARTIST...
FIRST COMES SUCCESS, THEN COMES MARRIAGE... YOU DON'T SEE MANY NEPHEWS FOLLOWING IN THEIR UNCLE'S FOOTSTEPS.
...
BUT WITH MORITAKA AND MIHO, THEY'VE ALREADY CONFESSED THEIR FEELINGS TO EACH OTHER.

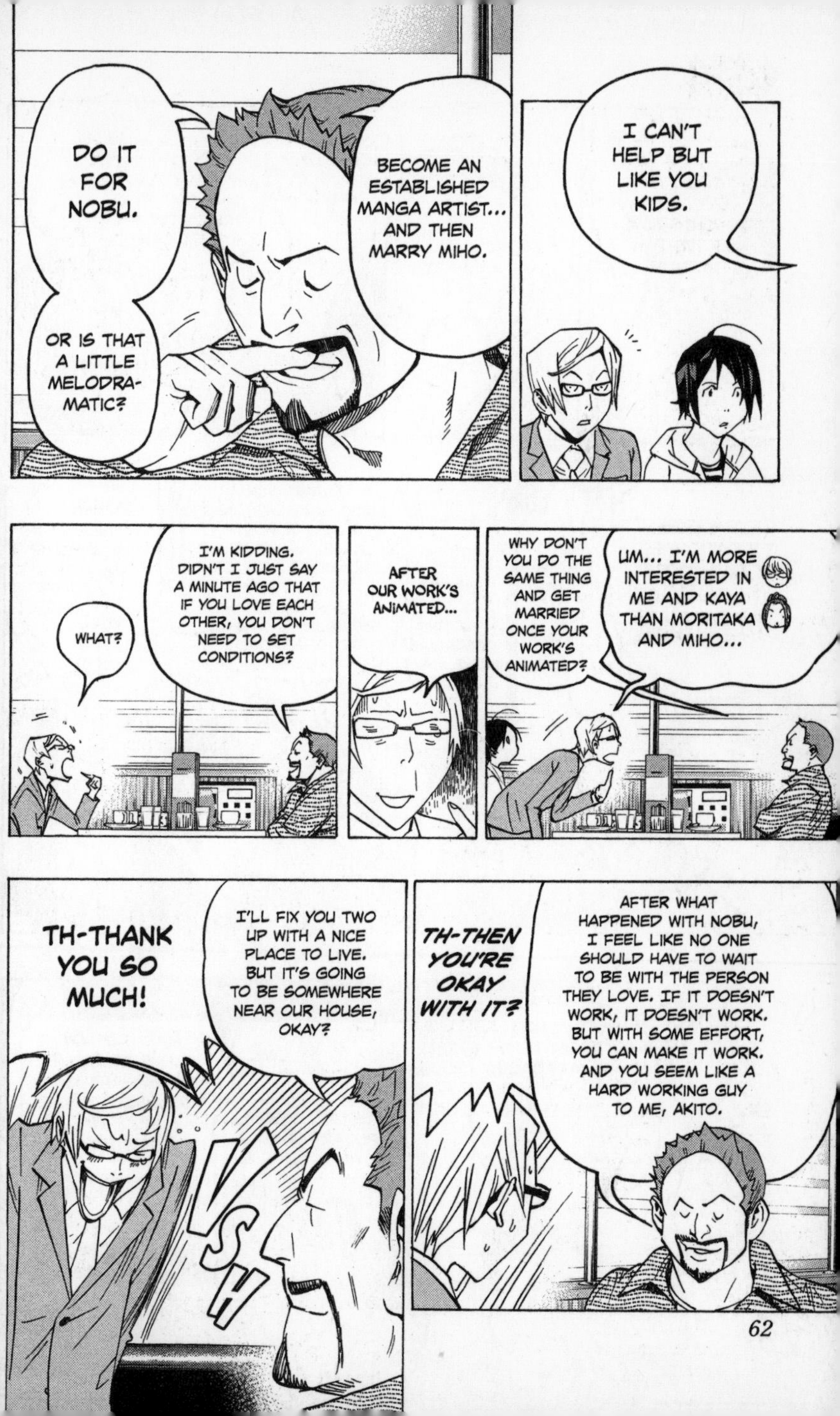
I CAN'T HELP BUT LIKE YOU KIDS.
BECOME AN ESTABLISHED MANGA ARTIST... AND THEN MARRY MIHO.
DO IT FOR NOBU.
OR IS THAT A LITTLE MELODRAMATIC?
WHY DON'T YOU DO THE SAME THING AND GET MARRIED ONCE YOUR WORK'S ANIMATED?
UM... I'M MORE INTERESTED IN ME AND KAYA THAN MORITAKA AND MIHO...
AFTER OUR WORK'S ANIMATED...
I'M KIDDING. DIDN'T I JUST SAY A MINUTE AGO THAT IF YOU LOVE EACH OTHER, YOU DON'T NEED TO SET CONDITIONS?
WHAT?
AFTER WHAT HAPPENED WITH NOBU, I FEEL LIKE NO ONE SHOULD HAVE TO WAIT TO BE WITH THE PERSON THEY LOVE. IF IT DOESN'T WORK, IT DOESN'T WORK. BUT WITH SOME EFFORT, YOU CAN MAKE IT WORK. AND YOU SEEM LIKE A HARD WORKING GUY TO ME, AKITO.
TH-THEN YOU'RE OKAY WITH IT?
I'LL FIX YOU TWO UP WITH A NICE PLACE TO LIVE. BUT IT'S GOING TO BE SOMEWHERE NEAR OUR HOUSE, OKAY?
TH-THANK YOU SO MUCH!
VSH

READ THIS WAY

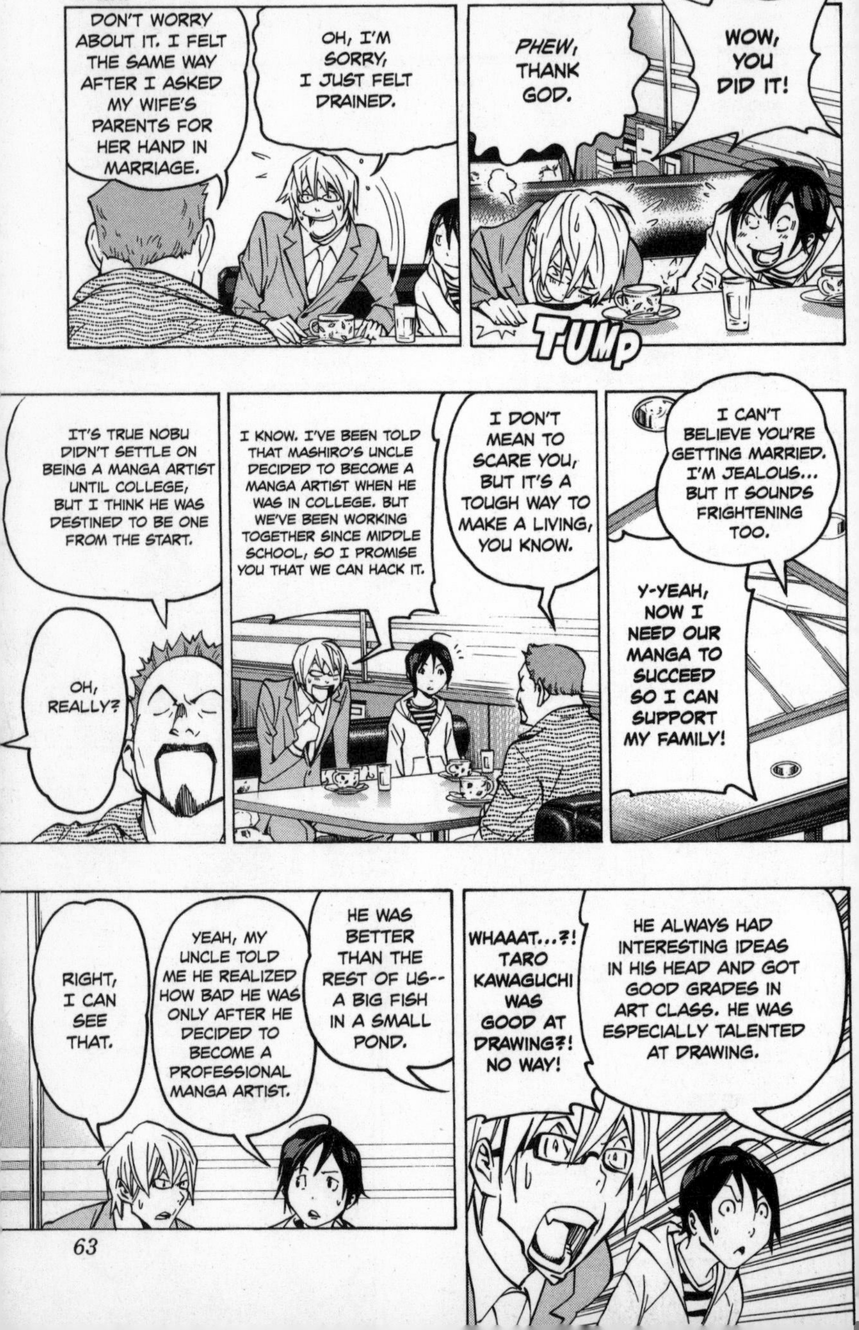

WOW, YOU DID IT!
PHEW, THANK GOD.
TUMP
OH, I'M SORRY, I JUST FELT DRAINED.
DON'T WORRY ABOUT IT. I FELT THE SAME WAY AFTER I ASKED MY WIFE'S PARENTS FOR HER HAND IN MARRIAGE.
I CAN'T BELIEVE YOU'RE GETTING MARRIED. I'M JEALOUS... BUT IT SOUNDS FRIGHTENING TOO.
Y-YEAH, NOW I NEED OUR MANGA TO SUCCEED SO I CAN SUPPORT MY FAMILY!
I DON'T MEAN TO SCARE YOU, BUT IT'S A TOUGH WAY TO MAKE A LIVING, YOU KNOW.
I KNOW. I'VE BEEN TOLD THAT MASHIRO'S UNCLE DECIDED TO BECOME A MANGA ARTIST WHEN HE WAS IN COLLEGE. BUT WE'VE BEEN WORKING TOGETHER SINCE MIDDLE SCHOOL, SO I PROMISE YOU THAT WE CAN HACK IT.
IT'S TRUE NOBU DIDN'T SETTLE ON BEING A MANGA ARTIST UNTIL COLLEGE, BUT I THINK HE WAS DESTINED TO BE ONE FROM THE START.
OH, REALLY?
HE ALWAYS HAD INTERESTING IDEAS IN HIS HEAD AND GOT GOOD GRADES IN ART CLASS. HE WAS ESPECIALLY TALENTED AT DRAWING.
WHAAAT...?! TARO KAWAGUCHI WAS GOOD AT DRAWING?! NO WAY!
HE WAS BETTER THAN THE REST OF US-- A BIG FISH IN A SMALL POND.
YEAH, MY UNCLE TOLD ME HE REALIZED HOW BAD HE WAS ONLY AFTER HE DECIDED TO BECOME A PROFESSIONAL MANGA ARTIST.
RIGHT, I CAN SEE THAT.

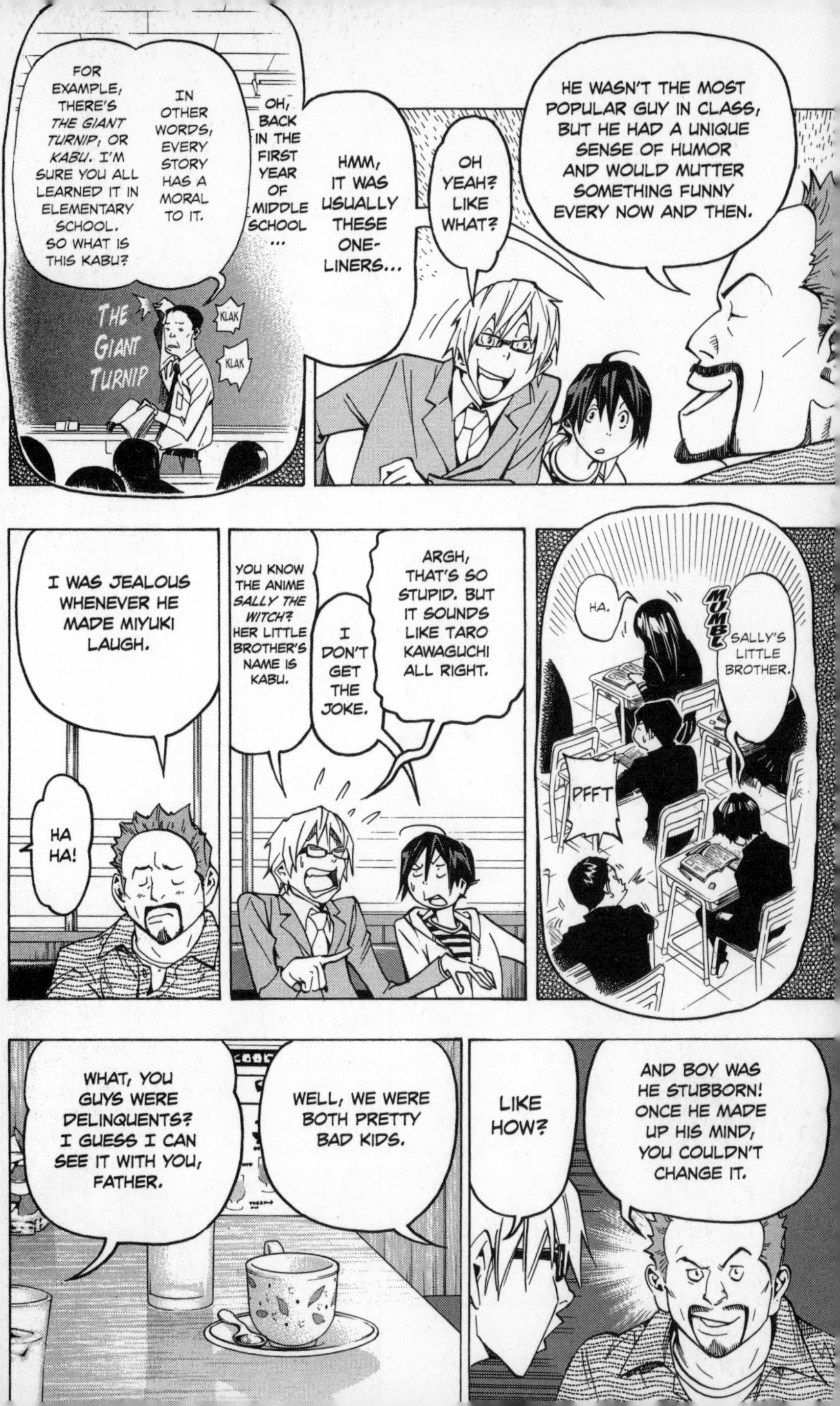
HE WASN'T THE MOST POPULAR GUY IN CLASS, BUT HE HAD A UNIQUE SENSE OF HUMOR AND WOULD MUTTER SOMETHING FUNNY EVERY NOW AND THEN.
OH YEAH? LIKE WHAT?
HMM, IT WAS USUALLY THESE ONE-LINERS...
OH, BACK IN THE FIRST YEAR OF MIDDLE SCHOOL...
IN OTHER WORDS, EVERY STORY HAS A MORAL TO IT.
FOR EXAMPLE, THERE'S *THE GIANT TURNIP*, OR *KABU*. I'M SURE YOU ALL LEARNED IT IN ELEMENTARY SCHOOL. SO WHAT IS THIS KABU?
KLAK
KLAK
THE GIANT TURNIP
MUMBL
SALLY'S LITTLE BROTHER.
HA.
PFFT
ARGH, THAT'S SO STUPID. BUT IT SOUNDS LIKE TARO KAWAGUCHI ALL RIGHT.
I DON'T GET THE JOKE.
YOU KNOW THE ANIME *SALLY THE WITCH*? HER LITTLE BROTHER'S NAME IS KABU.
I WAS JEALOUS WHENEVER HE MADE MIYUKI LAUGH.
HA HA!
AND BOY WAS HE STUBBORN! ONCE HE MADE UP HIS MIND, YOU COULDN'T CHANGE IT.
LIKE HOW?
WELL, WE WERE BOTH PRETTY BAD KIDS.
WHAT, YOU GUYS WERE DELINQUENTS? I GUESS I CAN SEE IT WITH YOU, FATHER.

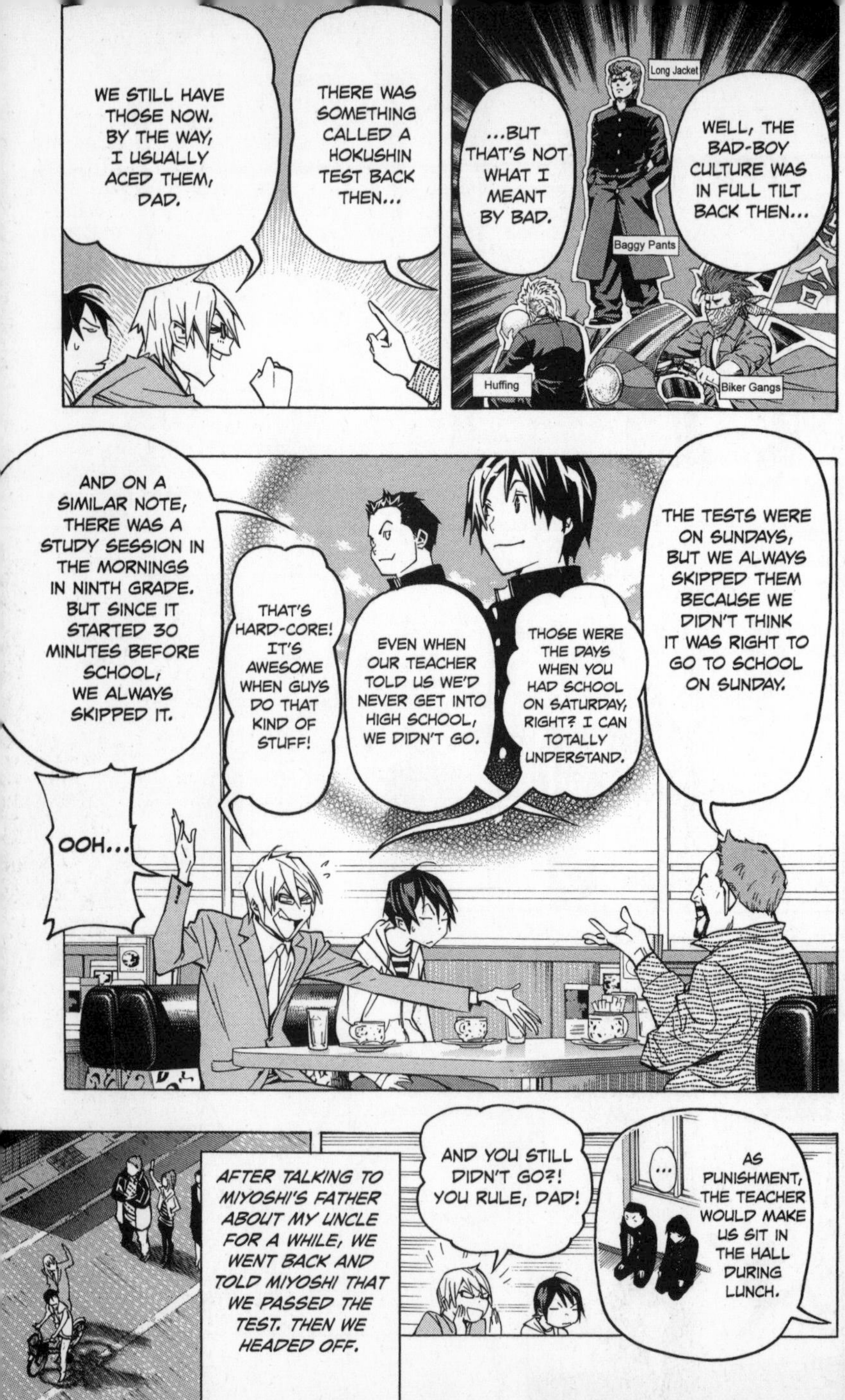
WELL, THE BAD-BOY CULTURE WAS IN FULL TILT BACK THEN...
Long Jacket
...BUT THAT'S NOT WHAT I MEANT BY BAD.
Baggy Pants
Biker Gangs
Huffing
THERE WAS SOMETHING CALLED A HOKUSHIN TEST BACK THEN...
WE STILL HAVE THOSE NOW. BY THE WAY, I USUALLY ACED THEM, DAD.
THE TESTS WERE ON SUNDAYS, BUT WE ALWAYS SKIPPED THEM BECAUSE WE DIDN'T THINK IT WAS RIGHT TO GO TO SCHOOL ON SUNDAY.
THOSE WERE THE DAYS WHEN YOU HAD SCHOOL ON SATURDAY, RIGHT? I CAN TOTALLY UNDERSTAND.
EVEN WHEN OUR TEACHER TOLD US WE'D NEVER GET INTO HIGH SCHOOL, WE DIDN'T GO.
THAT'S HARD-CORE! IT'S AWESOME WHEN GUYS DO THAT KIND OF STUFF!
AND ON A SIMILAR NOTE, THERE WAS A STUDY SESSION IN THE MORNINGS IN NINTH GRADE. BUT SINCE IT STARTED 30 MINUTES BEFORE SCHOOL, WE ALWAYS SKIPPED IT.
OOH...
AS PUNISHMENT, THE TEACHER WOULD MAKE US SIT IN THE HALL DURING LUNCH.
...
AND YOU STILL DIDN'T GO?! YOU RULE, DAD!
AFTER TALKING TO MIYOSHI'S FATHER ABOUT MY UNCLE FOR A WHILE, WE WENT BACK AND TOLD MIYOSHI THAT WE PASSED THE TEST. THEN WE HEADED OFF.

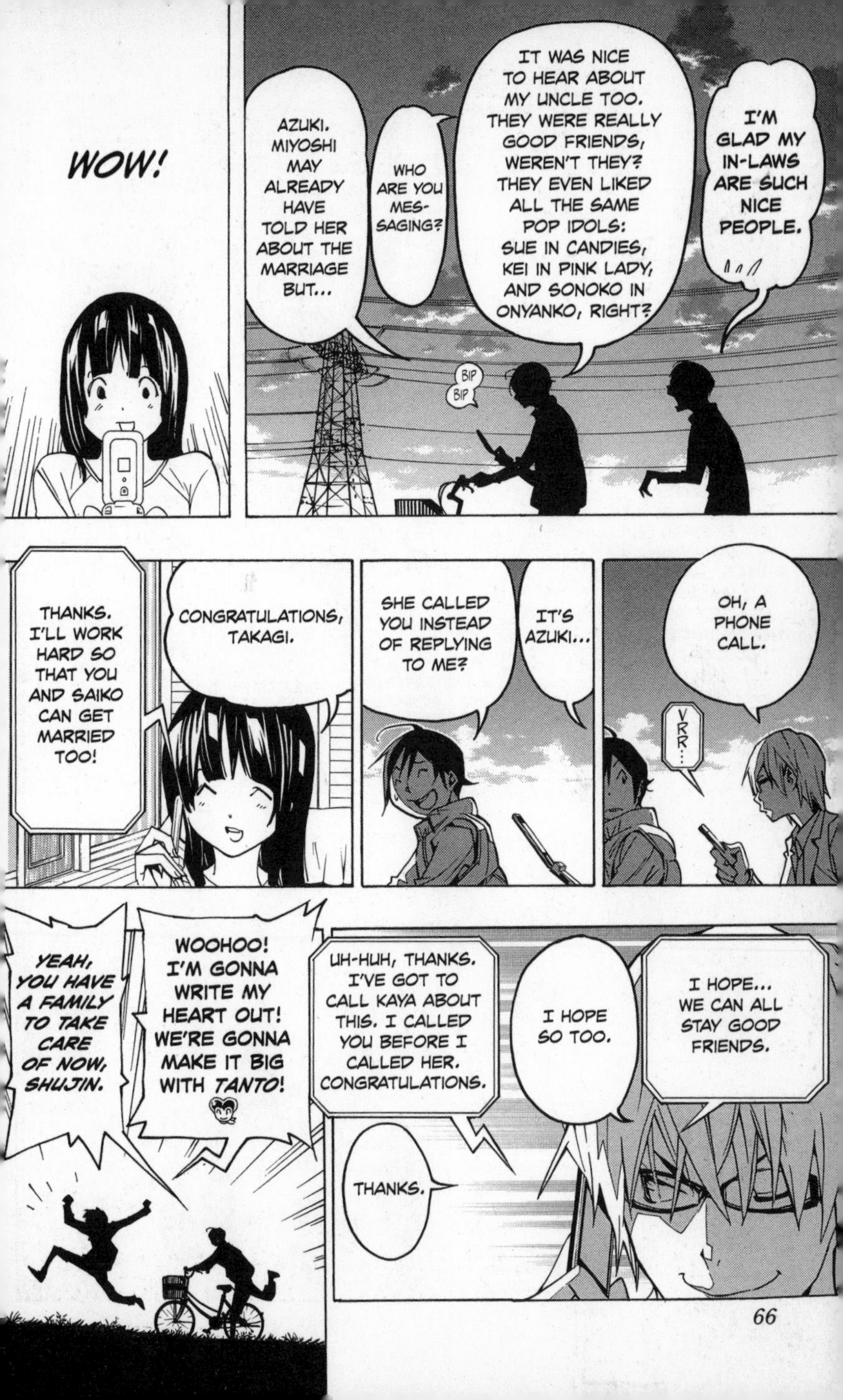
I'M GLAD MY IN-LAWS ARE SUCH NICE PEOPLE.
IT WAS NICE TO HEAR ABOUT MY UNCLE TOO. THEY WERE REALLY GOOD FRIENDS, WEREN'T THEY? THEY EVEN LIKED ALL THE SAME POP IDOLS: SUE IN CANDIES, KEI IN PINK LADY, AND SONOKO IN ONYANKO, RIGHT?
BIP BIP
WHO ARE YOU MES-SAGING?
AZUKI. MIYOSHI MAY ALREADY HAVE TOLD HER ABOUT THE MARRIAGE BUT...
WOW!
OH, A PHONE CALL.
VRR...
IT'S AZUKI...
SHE CALLED YOU INSTEAD OF REPLYING TO ME?
CONGRATULATIONS, TAKAGI.
THANKS. I'LL WORK HARD SO THAT YOU AND SAIKO CAN GET MARRIED TOO!
I HOPE... WE CAN ALL STAY GOOD FRIENDS.
I HOPE SO TOO.
UH-HUH, THANKS. I'VE GOT TO CALL KAYA ABOUT THIS. I CALLED YOU BEFORE I CALLED HER. CONGRATULATIONS.
THANKS.
WOOHOO! I'M GONNA WRITE MY HEART OUT! WE'RE GONNA MAKE IT BIG WITH *TANTO*!
YEAH, YOU HAVE A FAMILY TO TAKE CARE OF NOW, SHUJIN.

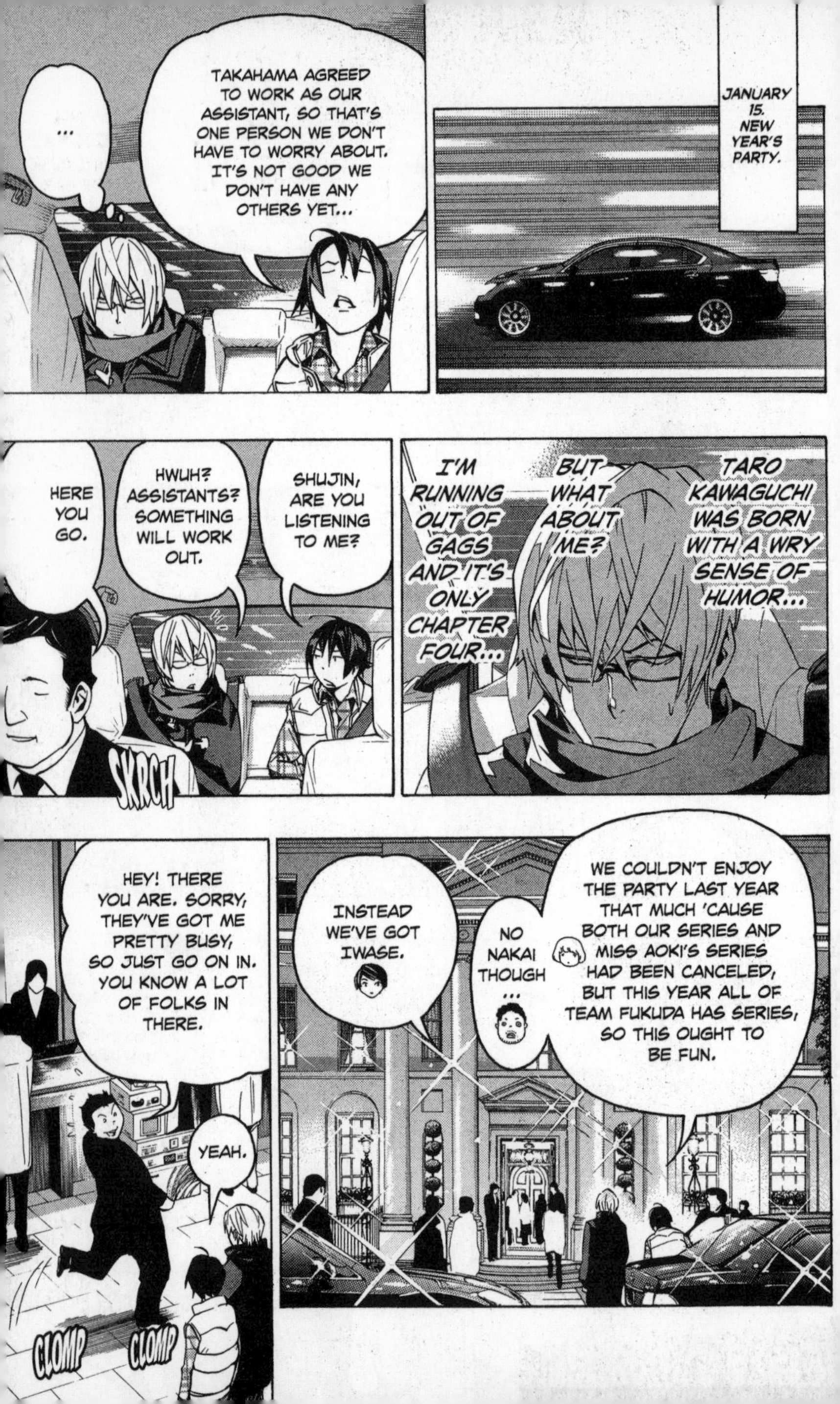
JANUARY 15. NEW YEAR'S PARTY.
TAKAHAMA AGREED TO WORK AS OUR ASSISTANT, SO THAT'S ONE PERSON WE DON'T HAVE TO WORRY ABOUT. IT'S NOT GOOD WE DON'T HAVE ANY OTHERS YET...
...
TARO KAWAGUCHI WAS BORN WITH A WRY SENSE OF HUMOR...
BUT WHAT ABOUT ME?
I'M RUNNING OUT OF GAGS AND IT'S ONLY CHAPTER FOUR...
SHUJIN, ARE YOU LISTENING TO ME?
HWUH? ASSISTANTS? SOMETHING WILL WORK OUT.
HERE YOU GO.
SKRCH
WE COULDN'T ENJOY THE PARTY LAST YEAR THAT MUCH 'CAUSE BOTH OUR SERIES AND MISS AOKI'S SERIES HAD BEEN CANCELED, BUT THIS YEAR ALL OF TEAM FUKUDA HAS SERIES, SO THIS OUGHT TO BE FUN.
NO NAKAI THOUGH...
INSTEAD WE'VE GOT IWASE.
HEY! THERE YOU ARE. SORRY, THEY'VE GOT ME PRETTY BUSY, SO JUST GO ON IN. YOU KNOW A LOT OF FOLKS IN THERE.
YEAH.
CLOMP
CLOMP

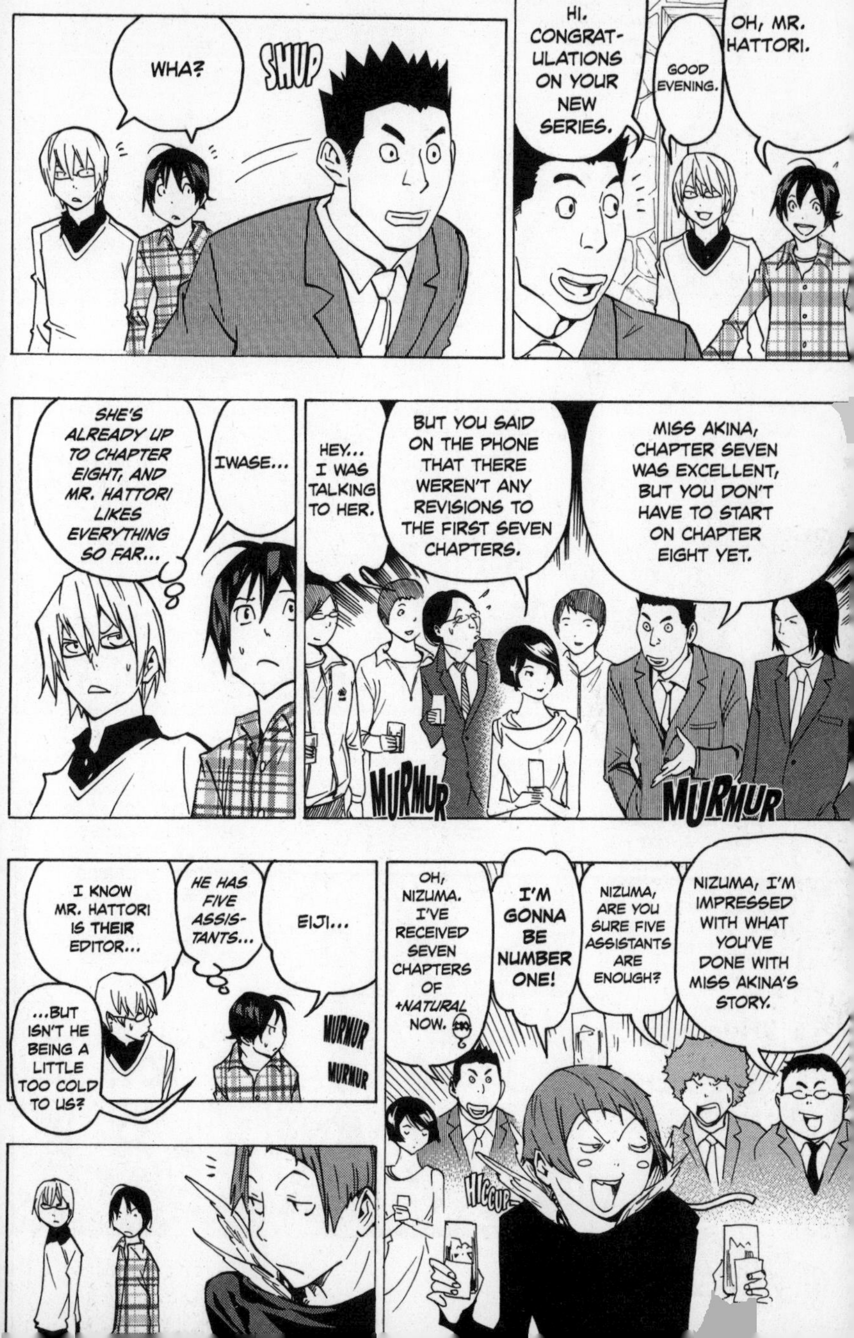
OH, MR. HATTORI.
GOOD EVENING.
HI. CONGRAT-ULATIONS ON YOUR NEW SERIES.
SHUP
WHA?
MISS AKINA, CHAPTER SEVEN WAS EXCELLENT, BUT YOU DON'T HAVE TO START ON CHAPTER EIGHT YET.
BUT YOU SAID ON THE PHONE THAT THERE WEREN'T ANY REVISIONS TO THE FIRST SEVEN CHAPTERS.
HEY... I WAS TALKING TO HER.
MURMUR
MURMUR
IWASE...
SHE'S ALREADY UP TO CHAPTER EIGHT, AND MR. HATTORI LIKES EVERYTHING SO FAR...
NIZUMA, I'M IMPRESSED WITH WHAT YOU'VE DONE WITH MISS AKINA'S STORY.
NIZUMA, ARE YOU SURE FIVE ASSISTANTS ARE ENOUGH?
I'M GONNA BE NUMBER ONE!
OH, NIZUMA. I'VE RECEIVED SEVEN CHAPTERS OF +NATURAL NOW.
HICCUP
EIJI...
HE HAS FIVE ASSIS-TANTS...
I KNOW MR. HATTORI IS THEIR EDITOR...
MURMUR
MURMUR
...BUT ISN'T HE BEING A LITTLE TOO COLD TO US?

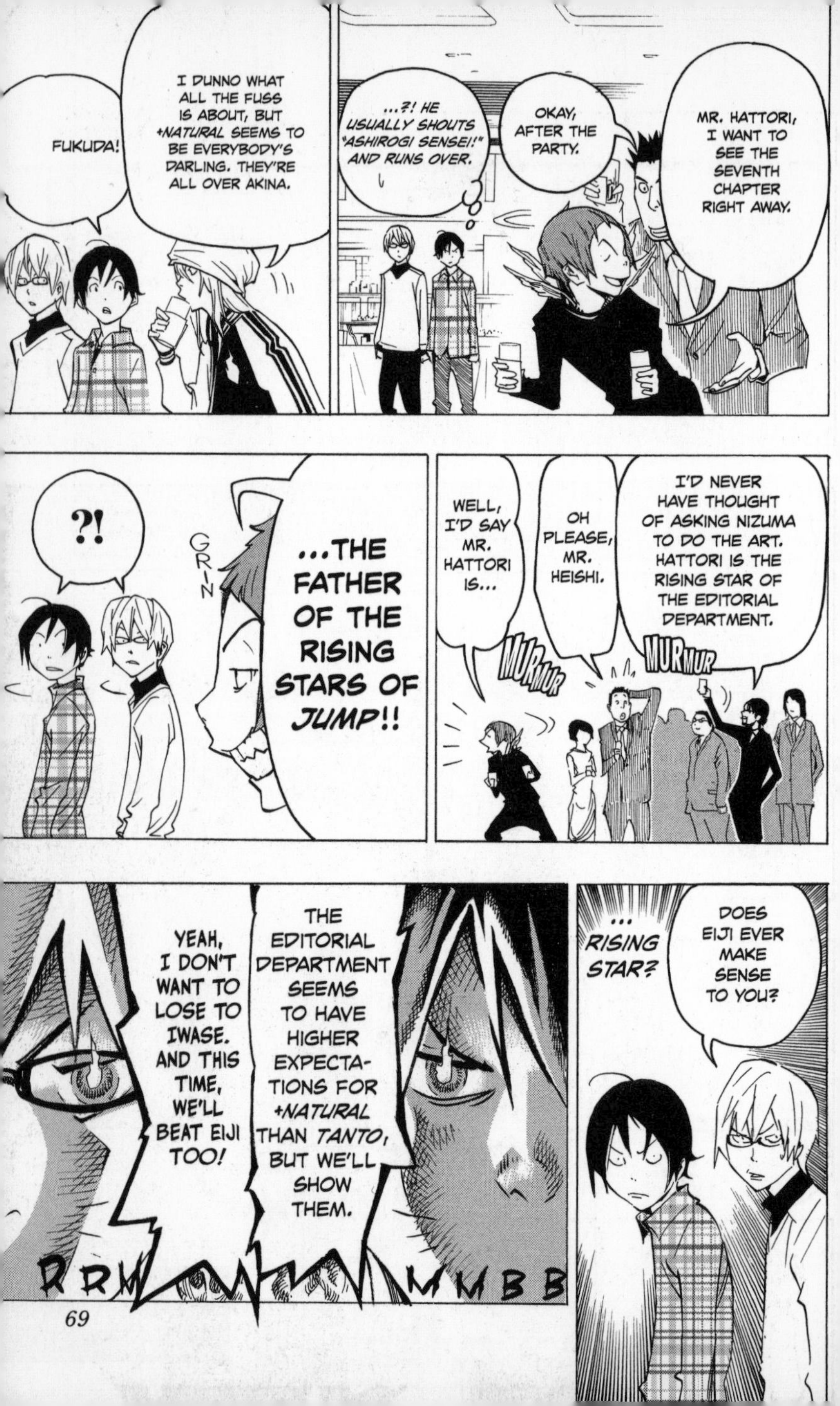
MR. HATTORI, I WANT TO SEE THE SEVENTH CHAPTER RIGHT AWAY.
OKAY, AFTER THE PARTY.
...?! HE USUALLY SHOUTS "ASHIROGI SENSEI!" AND RUNS OVER.
I DUNNO WHAT ALL THE FUSS IS ABOUT, BUT +NATURAL SEEMS TO BE EVERYBODY'S DARLING. THEY'RE ALL OVER AKINA.
FUKUDA!
I'D NEVER HAVE THOUGHT OF ASKING NIZUMA TO DO THE ART. HATTORI IS THE RISING STAR OF THE EDITORIAL DEPARTMENT.
MURMUR
OH PLEASE, MR. HEISHI.
MURMUR
WELL, I'D SAY MR. HATTORI IS...
...THE FATHER OF THE RISING STARS OF JUMP!!
GRIN
?!
DOES EIJI EVER MAKE SENSE TO YOU?
...RISING STAR?
THE EDITORIAL DEPARTMENT SEEMS TO HAVE HIGHER EXPECTATIONS FOR +NATURAL THAN TANTO, BUT WE'LL SHOW THEM.
YEAH, I DON'T WANT TO LOSE TO IWASE. AND THIS TIME, WE'LL BEAT EIJI TOO!
DRRMMMBB

OHBA'S STORYBOARD

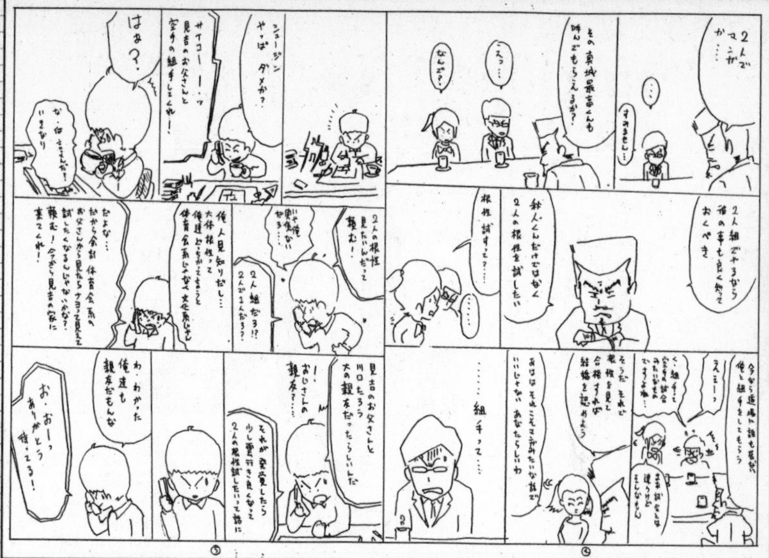
2人でマンガか……
…
すみません…
その真城最高くんも呼んでもらえるか？
えっ…
なんで？
2人組でやるなら彼の事も良く知っておくべき
秋人くんだけではなく2人の根性を試したい
根性試すって…
……
今なら道場に誰も居ないし俺と組手をしてもらう
えぇーっ
く、組手って空手の試合みたいなものですよね…
まあ試合とは違うけどそんなもん
そうだ それで根性を見て合格すれば結婚を認めよう
あはは それこそマンガみたいな話でいいじゃない あなたらしいわ
……組手って……
シュージン やっぱダメか？
サイコー！ッ 見吉のお父さんと空手の組手してくれ！
はぁ？
な、何言ってんだ！ いきなり
2人の根性見たいんだって 頼む！
いや俺実際ないだろ…
2人組だろ!? 2人で1人だろ？
俺人見知りだし… 大体根性って 俺達どう考えても体育会系じゃなく文化系じゃん
だよな… だから余計 体育会系のお父さんから見たらナヨって見えて試したくなるんじゃないかな？ 頼む！今から見吉の家に来てくれ！
見吉のお父さんと川口たろう 大の親友だったらしいんだ
！ おじさんの親友…
それが発覚したら少し雲行き良くなって2人の根性試したいって話に
わ、わかった 俺達も親友だもんな
お、おーっ ありがとう 待ってる！

OBATA'S STORYBOARD

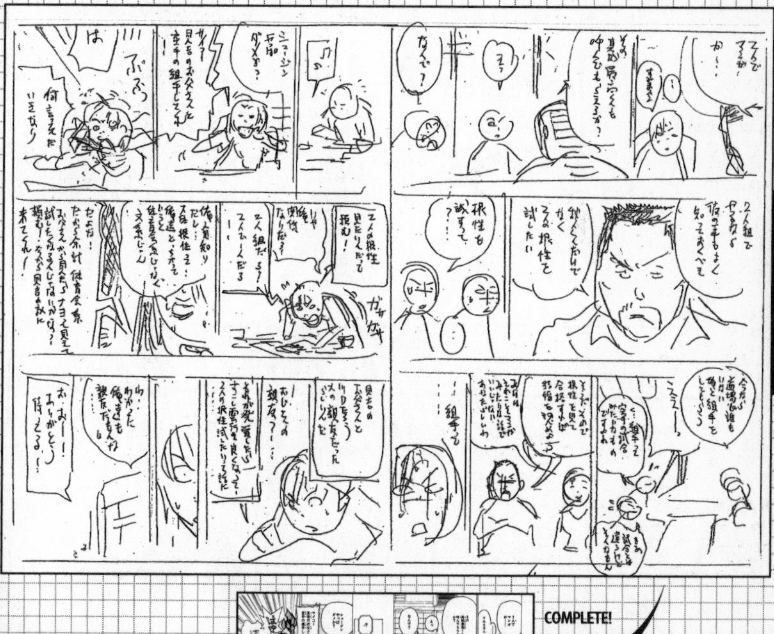

COMPLETE!

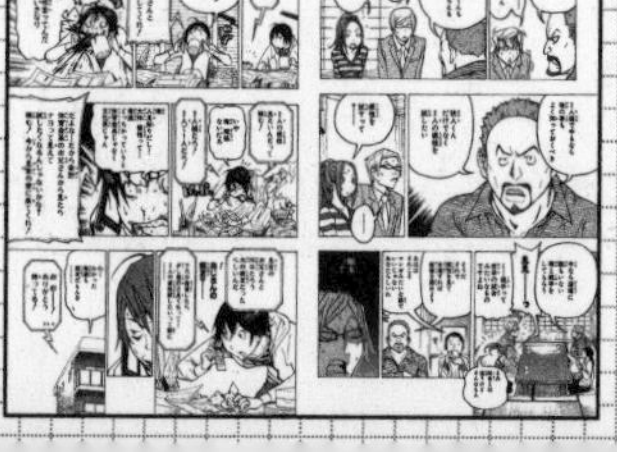

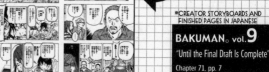

※CREATOR STORYBOARDS AND FINISHED PAGES IN JAPANESE

BAKUMAN。 vol.9

"Until the Final Draft Is Complete"

Chapter 71, pp. 7

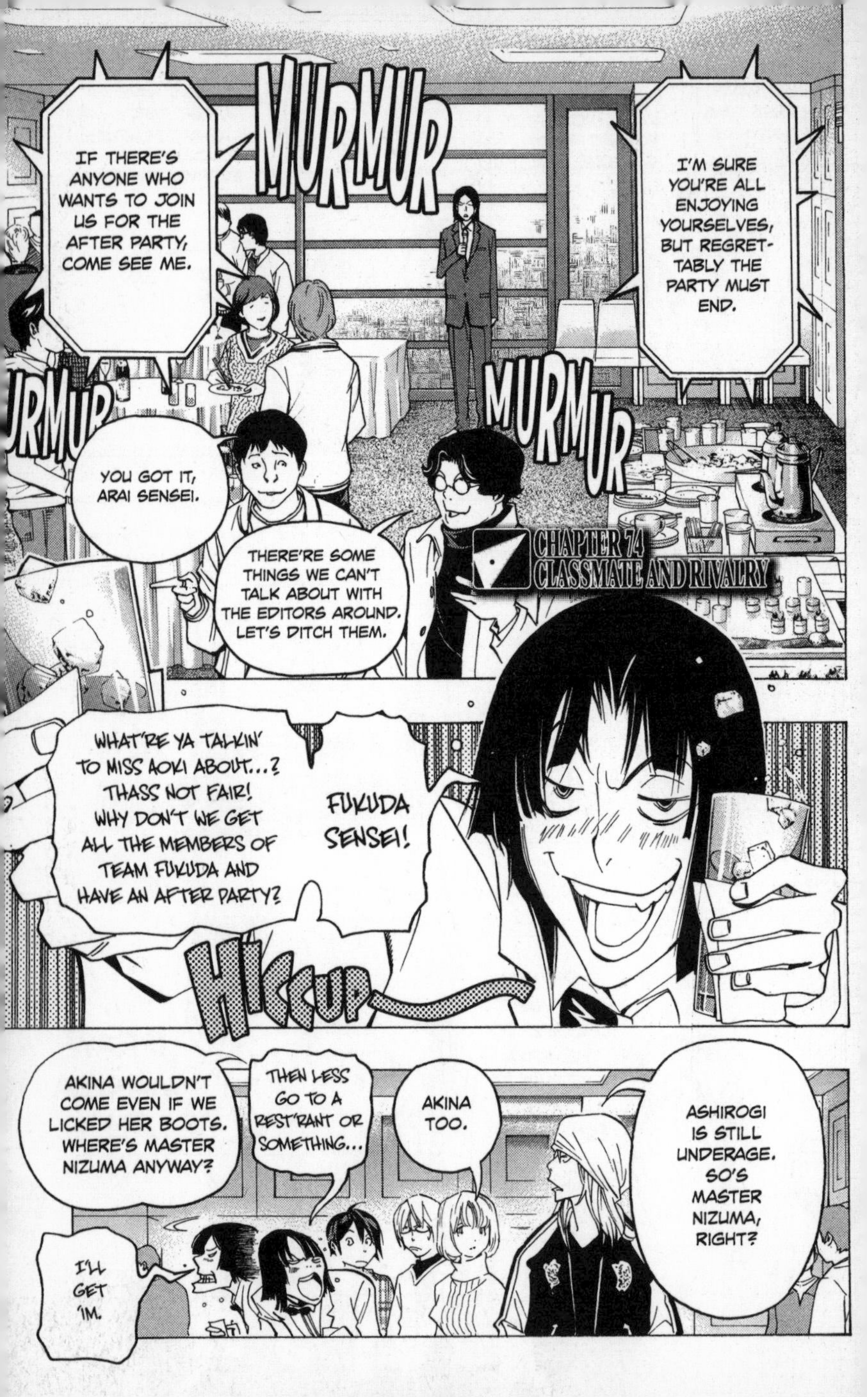
I'M SURE YOU'RE ALL ENJOYING YOURSELVES, BUT REGRET-TABLY THE PARTY MUST END.
MURMUR
MURMUR
IF THERE'S ANYONE WHO WANTS TO JOIN US FOR THE AFTER PARTY, COME SEE ME.
URMUR
THERE'RE SOME THINGS WE CAN'T TALK ABOUT WITH THE EDITORS AROUND. LET'S DITCH THEM.
YOU GOT IT, ARAI SENSEI.
CHAPTER 74 CLASSMATE AND RIVALRY
FUKUDA SENSEI!
WHAT'RE YA TALKIN' TO MISS AOKI ABOUT...? THASS NOT FAIR! WHY DON'T WE GET ALL THE MEMBERS OF TEAM FUKUDA AND HAVE AN AFTER PARTY?
HICCUP
ASHIROGI IS STILL UNDERAGE. SO'S MASTER NIZUMA, RIGHT?
AKINA TOO.
THEN LESS GO TO A REST'RANT OR SOMETHING...
AKINA WOULDN'T COME EVEN IF WE LICKED HER BOOTS. WHERE'S MASTER NIZUMA ANYWAY?
I'LL GET 'IM.

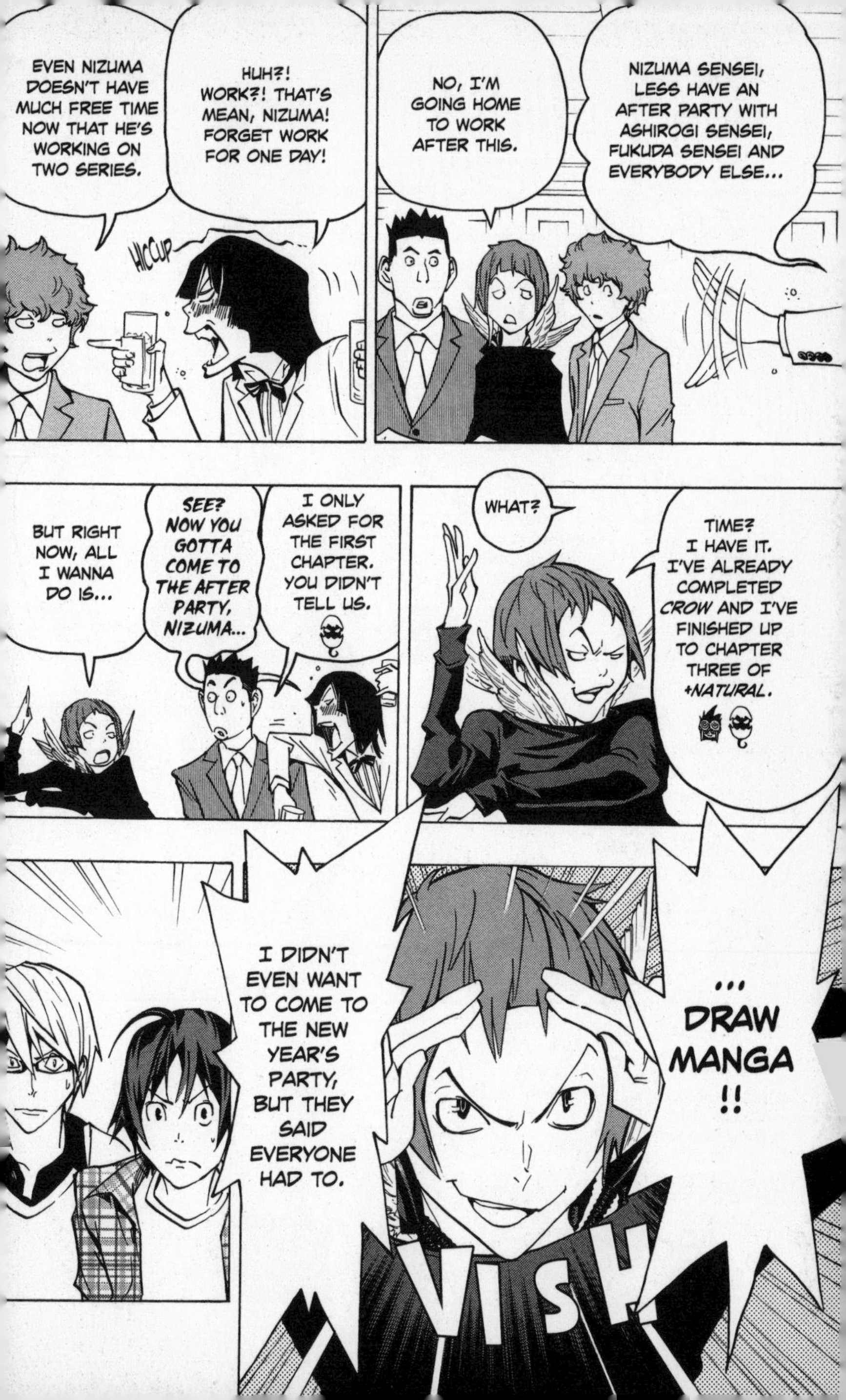
NIZUMA SENSEI, LESS HAVE AN AFTER PARTY WITH ASHIROGI SENSEI, FUKUDA SENSEI AND EVERYBODY ELSE...
NO, I'M GOING HOME TO WORK AFTER THIS.
HUH?! WORK?! THAT'S MEAN, NIZUMA! FORGET WORK FOR ONE DAY!
HICCUP
EVEN NIZUMA DOESN'T HAVE MUCH FREE TIME NOW THAT HE'S WORKING ON TWO SERIES.
WHAT?
TIME? I HAVE IT. I'VE ALREADY COMPLETED *CROW* AND I'VE FINISHED UP TO CHAPTER THREE OF *+NATURAL*.
I ONLY ASKED FOR THE FIRST CHAPTER. YOU DIDN'T TELL US.
SEE? NOW YOU GOTTA COME TO THE AFTER PARTY, NIZUMA...
BUT RIGHT NOW, ALL I WANNA DO IS...
...DRAW MANGA!!
VISH
I DIDN'T EVEN WANT TO COME TO THE NEW YEAR'S PARTY, BUT THEY SAID EVERYONE HAD TO.

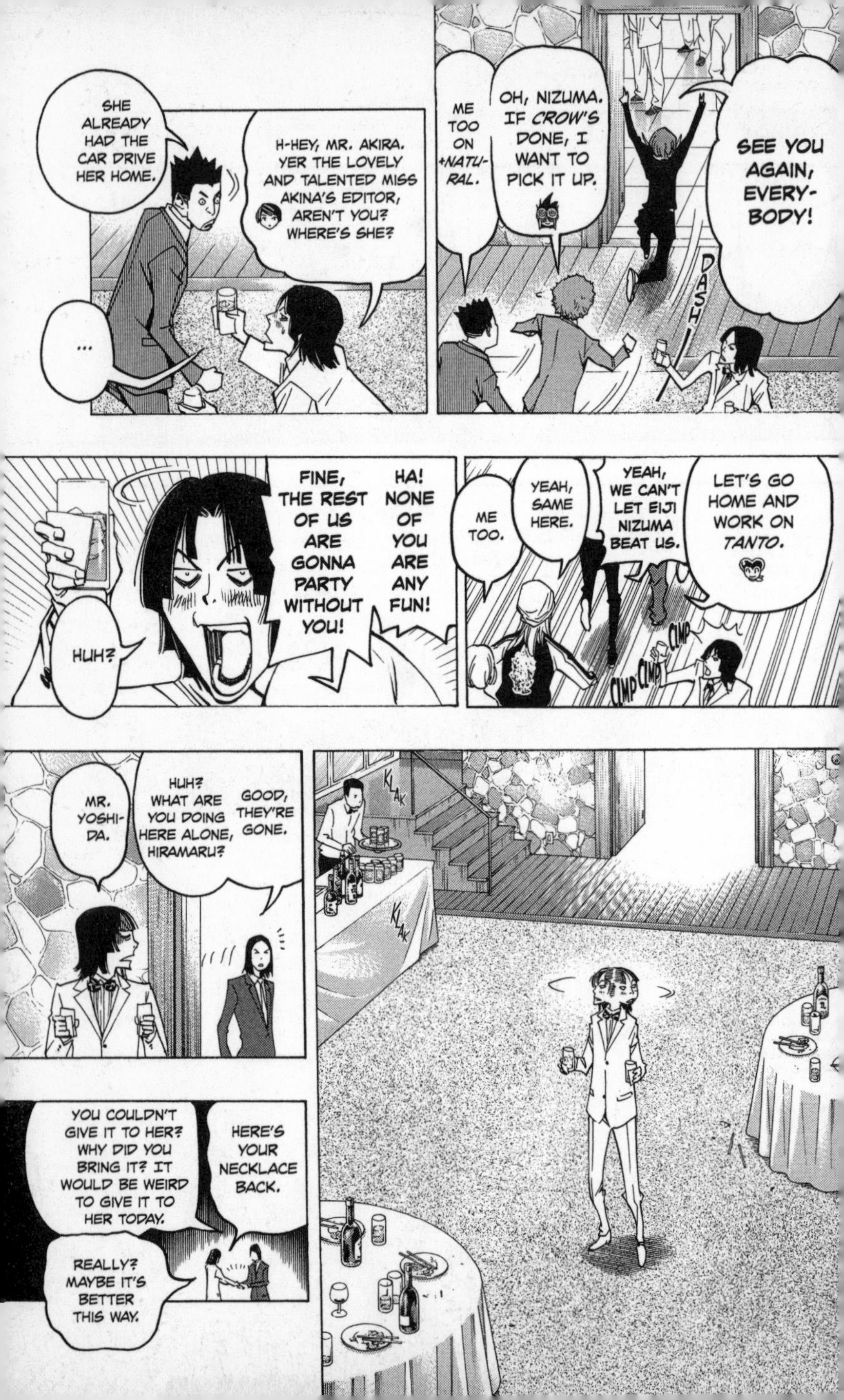
SEE YOU AGAIN, EVERYBODY!
DASH
OH, NIZUMA. IF *CROW'S* DONE, I WANT TO PICK IT UP.
ME TOO ON *+NATURAL*.
H-HEY, MR. AKIRA. YER THE LOVELY AND TALENTED MISS AKINA'S EDITOR, AREN'T YOU? WHERE'S SHE?
SHE ALREADY HAD THE CAR DRIVE HER HOME.
...
LET'S GO HOME AND WORK ON *TANTO*.
YEAH, WE CAN'T LET EIJI NIZUMA BEAT US.
YEAH, SAME HERE.
ME TOO.
CLIMP CLIMP CLIMP CLIMP
HA! NONE OF YOU ARE ANY FUN!
FINE, THE REST OF US ARE GONNA PARTY WITHOUT YOU!
HUH?
KLAK
KLAK
GOOD, THEY'RE GONE.
HUH? WHAT ARE YOU DOING HERE ALONE, HIRAMARU?
MR. YOSHIDA.
HERE'S YOUR NECKLACE BACK.
YOU COULDN'T GIVE IT TO HER? WHY DID YOU BRING IT? IT WOULD BE WEIRD TO GIVE IT TO HER TODAY.
REALLY? MAYBE IT'S BETTER THIS WAY.

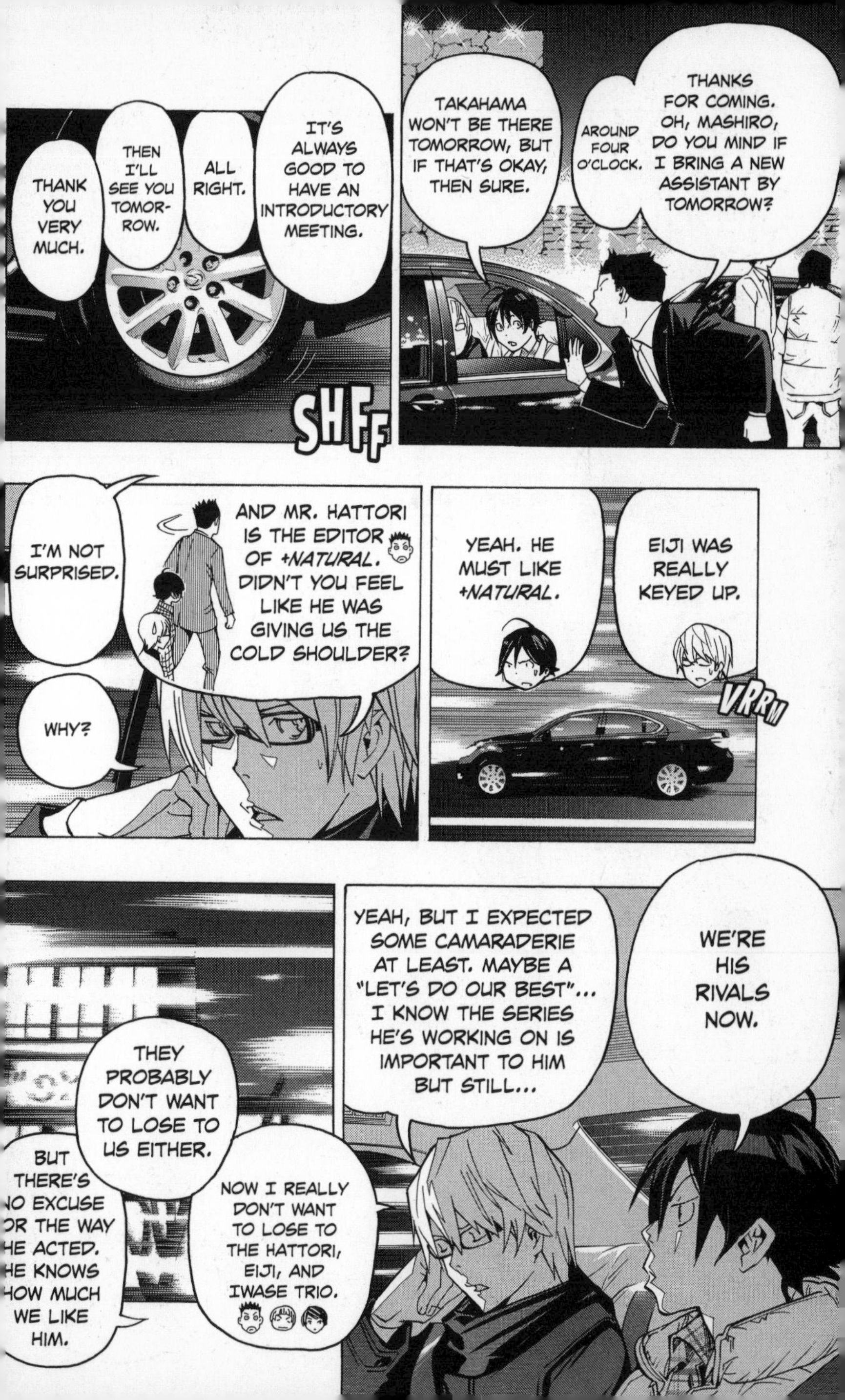
THANKS FOR COMING. OH, MASHIRO, DO YOU MIND IF I BRING A NEW ASSISTANT BY TOMORROW?
AROUND FOUR O'CLOCK.
TAKAHAMA WON'T BE THERE TOMORROW, BUT IF THAT'S OKAY, THEN SURE.
IT'S ALWAYS GOOD TO HAVE AN INTRODUCTORY MEETING.
ALL RIGHT.
THEN I'LL SEE YOU TOMORROW.
THANK YOU VERY MUCH.
SHFF
EIJI WAS REALLY KEYED UP.
YEAH. HE MUST LIKE +NATURAL.
VRRM
AND MR. HATTORI IS THE EDITOR OF +NATURAL. DIDN'T YOU FEEL LIKE HE WAS GIVING US THE COLD SHOULDER?
I'M NOT SURPRISED.
WHY?
WE'RE HIS RIVALS NOW.
YEAH, BUT I EXPECTED SOME CAMARADERIE AT LEAST. MAYBE A "LET'S DO OUR BEST"... I KNOW THE SERIES HE'S WORKING ON IS IMPORTANT TO HIM BUT STILL...
THEY PROBABLY DON'T WANT TO LOSE TO US EITHER.
NOW I REALLY DON'T WANT TO LOSE TO THE HATTORI, EIJI, AND IWASE TRIO.
BUT THERE'S NO EXCUSE FOR THE WAY HE ACTED. HE KNOWS HOW MUCH WE LIKE HIM.

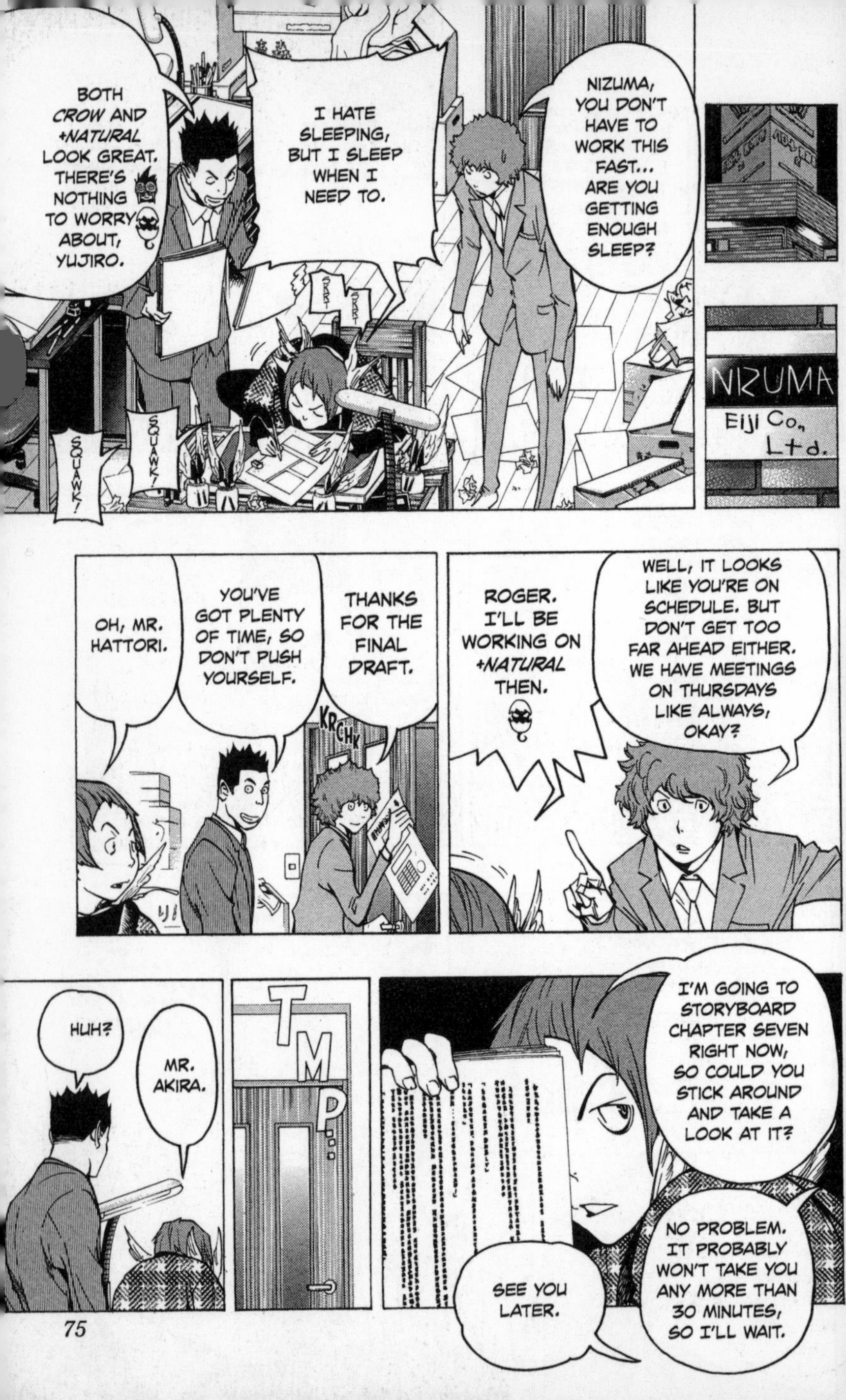
NIZUMA
Eiji Co., Ltd.
NIZUMA, YOU DON'T HAVE TO WORK THIS FAST... ARE YOU GETTING ENOUGH SLEEP?
I HATE SLEEPING, BUT I SLEEP WHEN I NEED TO.
BOTH CROW AND +NATURAL LOOK GREAT. THERE'S NOTHING TO WORRY ABOUT, YUJIRO.
SKRT
SKRT
SQUAWK!
SQUAWK!
WELL, IT LOOKS LIKE YOU'RE ON SCHEDULE. BUT DON'T GET TOO FAR AHEAD EITHER. WE HAVE MEETINGS ON THURSDAYS LIKE ALWAYS, OKAY?
ROGER. I'LL BE WORKING ON +NATURAL THEN.
THANKS FOR THE FINAL DRAFT.
KRCHK
YOU'VE GOT PLENTY OF TIME, SO DON'T PUSH YOURSELF.
OH, MR. HATTORI.
I'M GOING TO STORYBOARD CHAPTER SEVEN RIGHT NOW, SO COULD YOU STICK AROUND AND TAKE A LOOK AT IT?
NO PROBLEM. IT PROBABLY WON'T TAKE YOU ANY MORE THAN 30 MINUTES, SO I'LL WAIT.
SEE YOU LATER.
TMP
MR. AKIRA.
HUH?

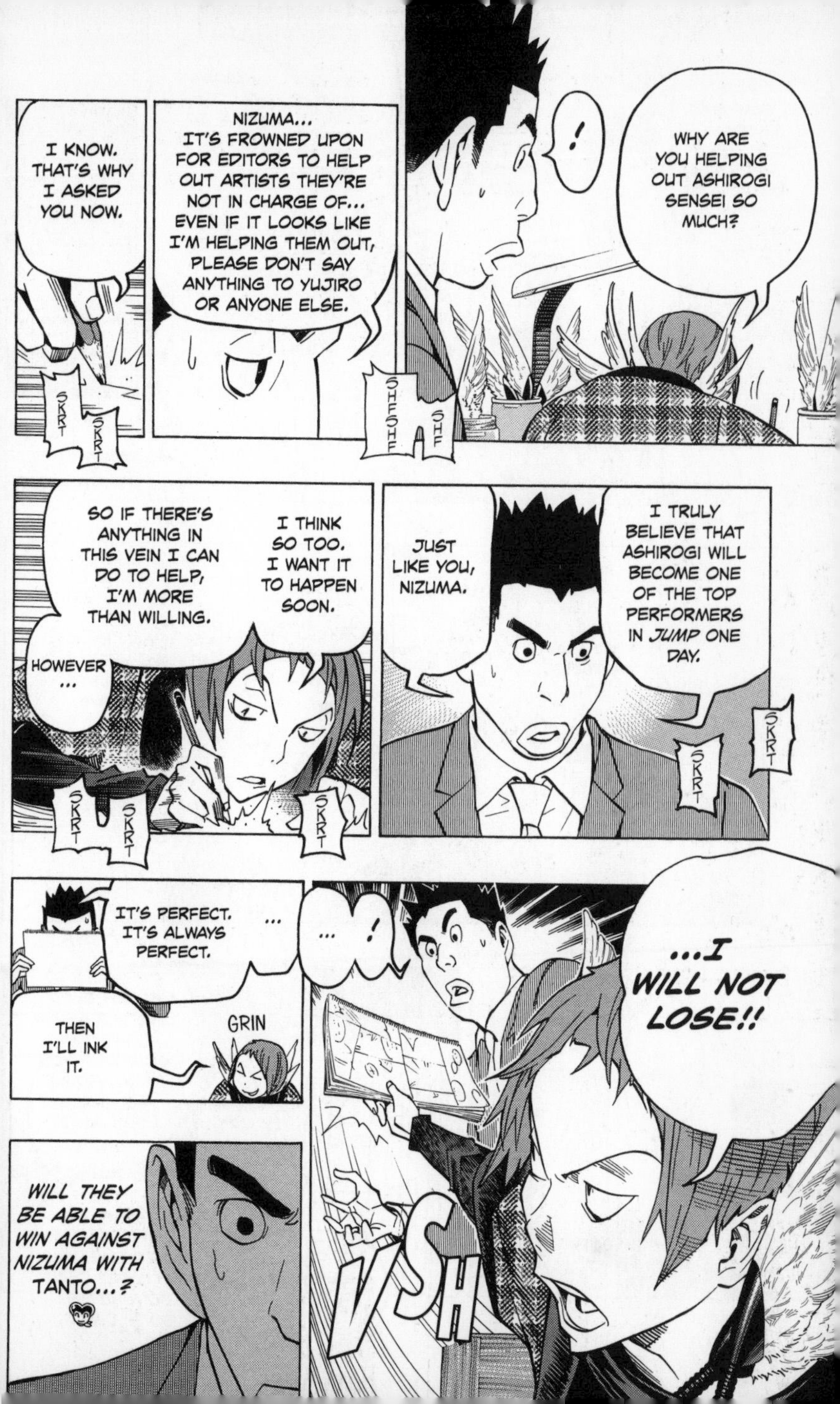
!
WHY ARE YOU HELPING OUT ASHIROGI SENSEI SO MUCH?
SHF
SHFSHF
NIZUMA... IT'S FROWNED UPON FOR EDITORS TO HELP OUT ARTISTS THEY'RE NOT IN CHARGE OF... EVEN IF IT LOOKS LIKE I'M HELPING THEM OUT, PLEASE DON'T SAY ANYTHING TO YUJIRO OR ANYONE ELSE.
I KNOW. THAT'S WHY I ASKED YOU NOW.
SKRT
SKRT
I TRULY BELIEVE THAT ASHIROGI WILL BECOME ONE OF THE TOP PERFORMERS IN *JUMP* ONE DAY.
JUST LIKE YOU, NIZUMA.
SKRT
SKRT
I THINK SO TOO. I WANT IT TO HAPPEN SOON.
SO IF THERE'S ANYTHING IN THIS VEIN I CAN DO TO HELP, I'M MORE THAN WILLING.
HOWEVER...
SKRT
SKRT
SKRT
...I WILL NOT LOSE!!
...!
VSH
IT'S PERFECT. IT'S ALWAYS PERFECT.
...
THEN I'LL INK IT.
GRIN
WILL THEY BE ABLE TO WIN AGAINST NIZUMA WITH TANTO...?

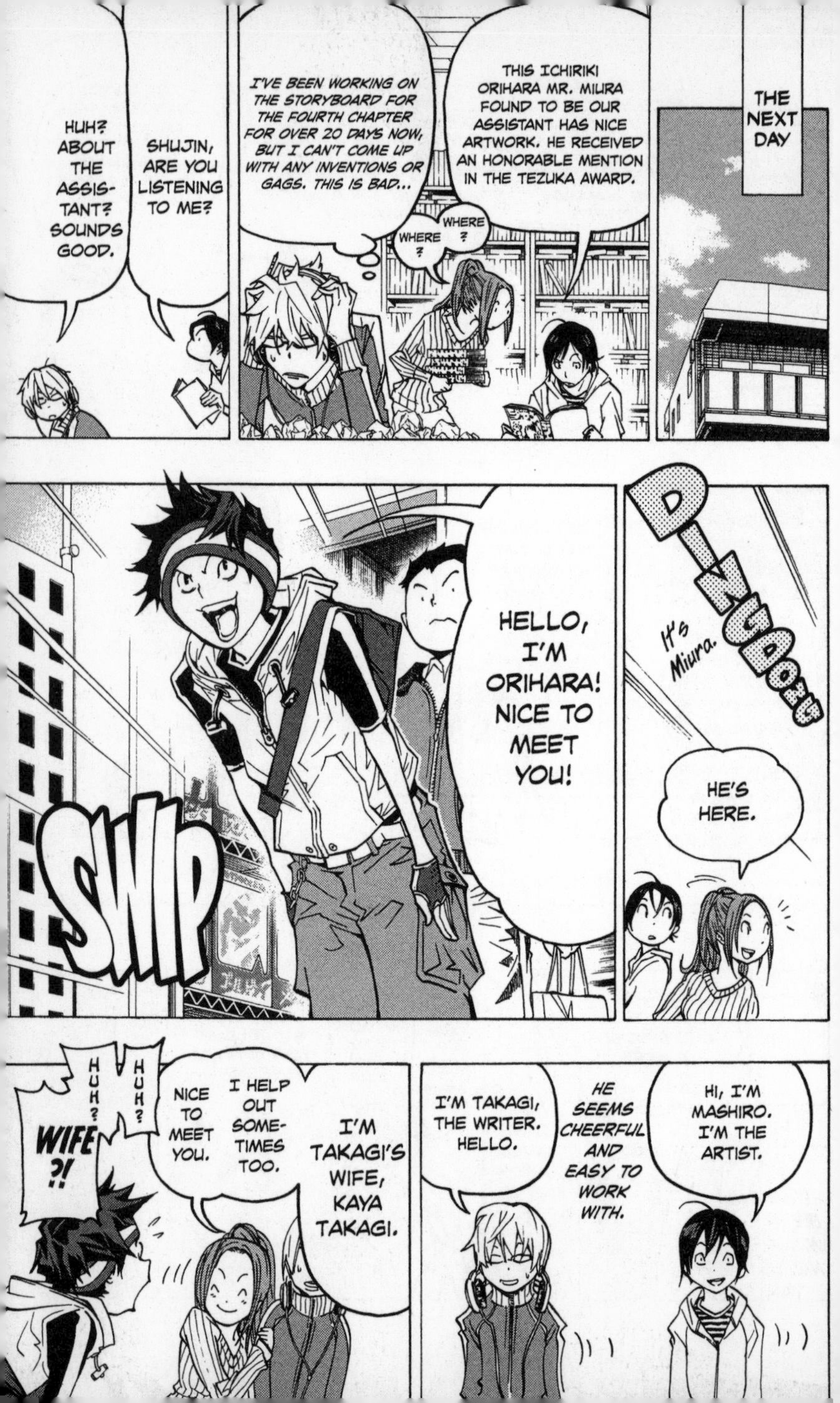
THE NEXT DAY
THIS ICHIRIKI ORIHARA MR. MIURA FOUND TO BE OUR ASSISTANT HAS NICE ARTWORK. HE RECEIVED AN HONORABLE MENTION IN THE TEZUKA AWARD.
WHERE?
WHERE?
I'VE BEEN WORKING ON THE STORYBOARD FOR THE FOURTH CHAPTER FOR OVER 20 DAYS NOW, BUT I CAN'T COME UP WITH ANY INVENTIONS OR GAGS. THIS IS BAD...
SHUJIN, ARE YOU LISTENING TO ME?
HUH? ABOUT THE ASSISTANT? SOUNDS GOOD.
DINGDONG
It's Miura.
HE'S HERE.
HELLO, I'M ORIHARA! NICE TO MEET YOU!
SWIP
HI, I'M MASHIRO. I'M THE ARTIST.
HE SEEMS CHEERFUL AND EASY TO WORK WITH.
I'M TAKAGI, THE WRITER. HELLO.
I'M TAKAGI'S WIFE, KAYA TAKAGI.
I HELP OUT SOME-TIMES TOO.
NICE TO MEET YOU.
HUH?
HUH?
WIFE?!

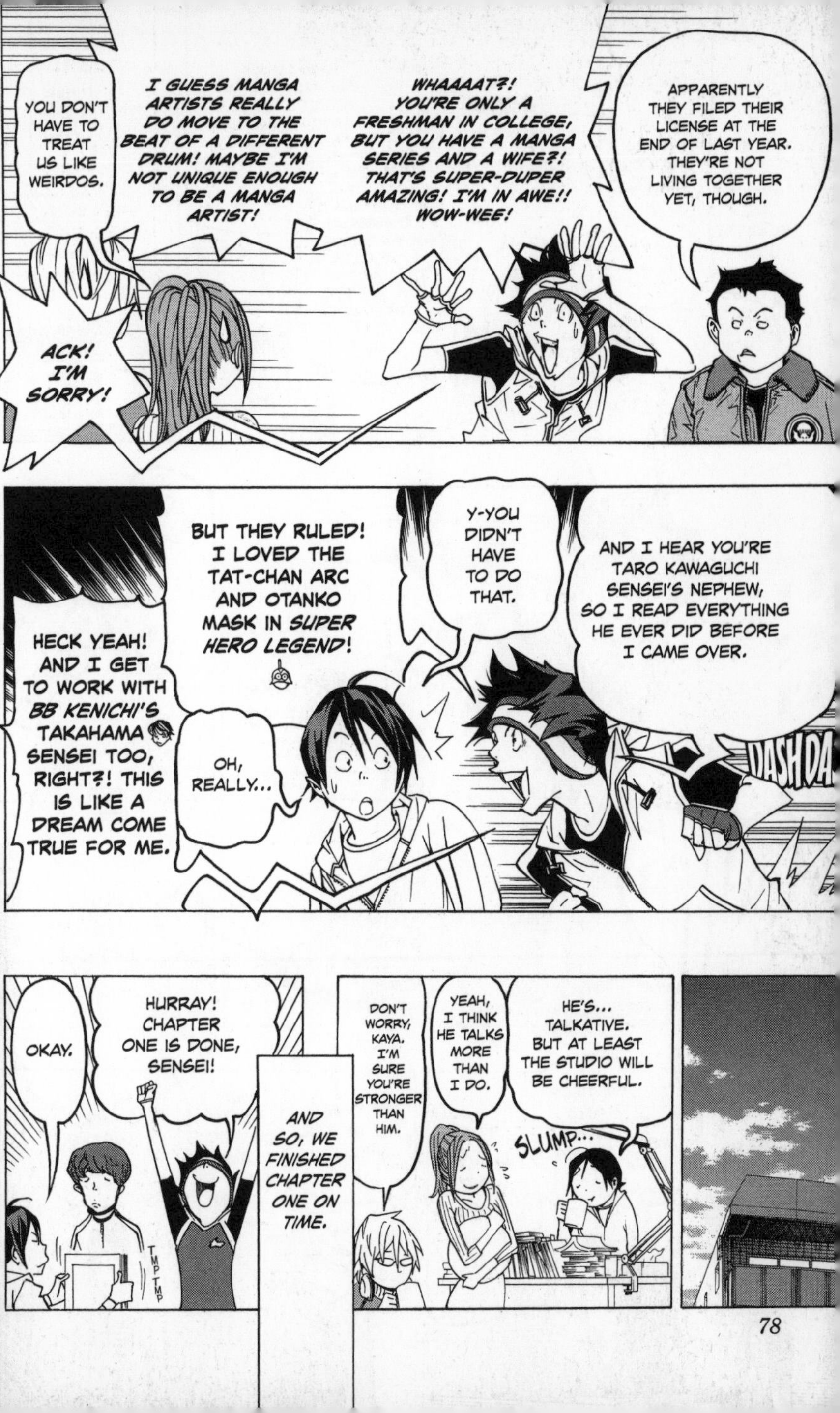
APPARENTLY THEY FILED THEIR LICENSE AT THE END OF LAST YEAR. THEY'RE NOT LIVING TOGETHER YET, THOUGH.
WHAAAAT?! YOU'RE ONLY A FRESHMAN IN COLLEGE, BUT YOU HAVE A MANGA SERIES AND A WIFE?! THAT'S SUPER-DUPER AMAZING! I'M IN AWE!! WOW-WEE!
I GUESS MANGA ARTISTS REALLY DO MOVE TO THE BEAT OF A DIFFERENT DRUM! MAYBE I'M NOT UNIQUE ENOUGH TO BE A MANGA ARTIST!
YOU DON'T HAVE TO TREAT US LIKE WEIRDOS.
ACK! I'M SORRY!
AND I HEAR YOU'RE TARO KAWAGUCHI SENSEI'S NEPHEW, SO I READ EVERYTHING HE EVER DID BEFORE I CAME OVER.
DASHDA
Y-YOU DIDN'T HAVE TO DO THAT.
BUT THEY RULED! I LOVED THE TAT-CHAN ARC AND OTANKO MASK IN SUPER HERO LEGEND!
HECK YEAH! AND I GET TO WORK WITH BB KENICHI'S TAKAHAMA SENSEI TOO, RIGHT?! THIS IS LIKE A DREAM COME TRUE FOR ME.
OH, REALLY...
HE'S... TALKATIVE. BUT AT LEAST THE STUDIO WILL BE CHEERFUL.
SLUMP...
YEAH, I THINK HE TALKS MORE THAN I DO.
DON'T WORRY, KAYA. I'M SURE YOU'RE STRONGER THAN HIM.
AND SO, WE FINISHED CHAPTER ONE ON TIME.
HURRAY! CHAPTER ONE IS DONE, SENSEI!
OKAY.
TMP TMP

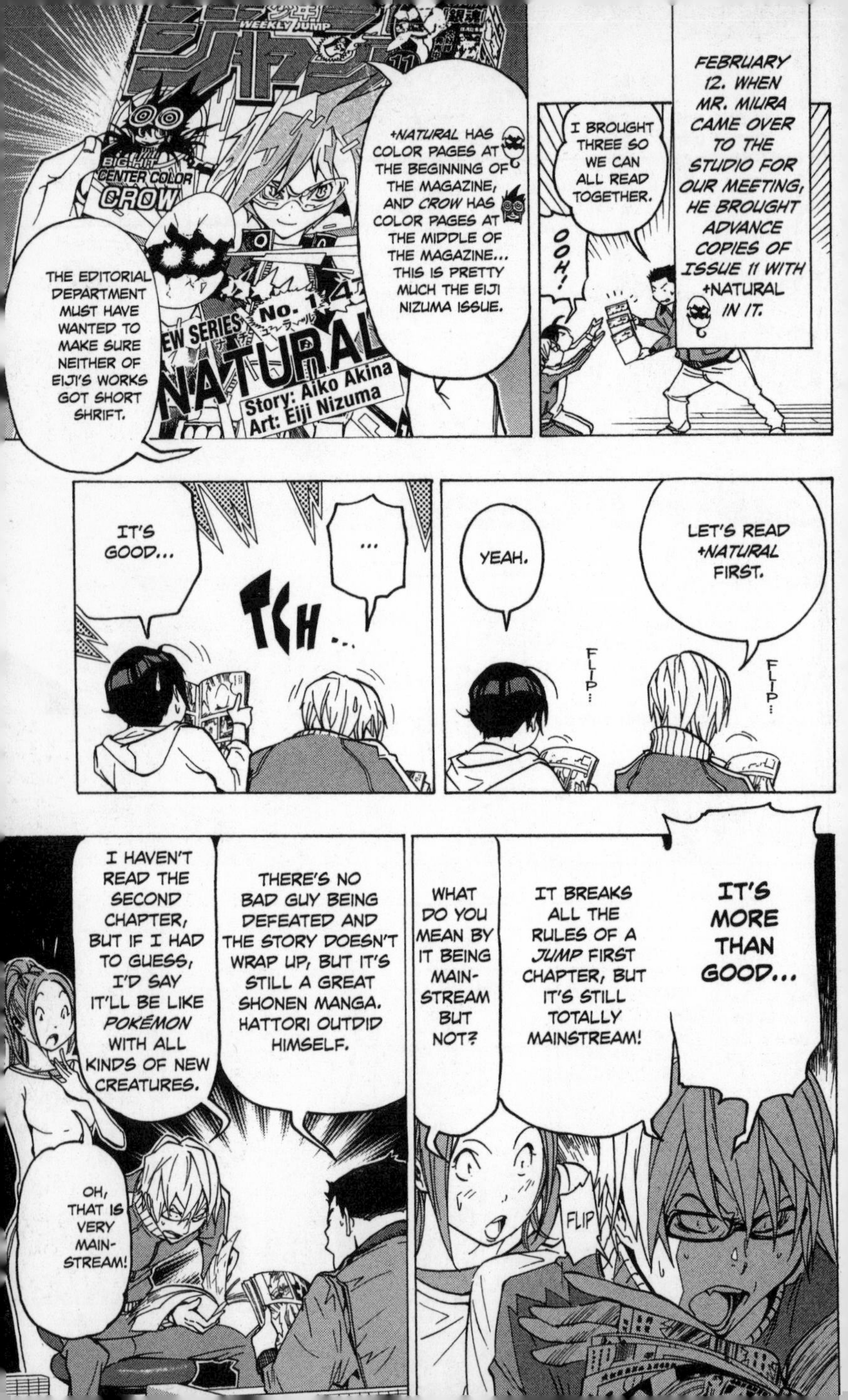
FEBRUARY 12. WHEN MR. MIURA CAME OVER TO THE STUDIO FOR OUR MEETING, HE BROUGHT ADVANCE COPIES OF ISSUE 11 WITH +NATURAL IN IT.
I BROUGHT THREE SO WE CAN ALL READ TOGETHER.
OOH!
WEEKLY JUMP
11
BIG HIT CENTER COLOR
CROW
EW SERIES
No. 1
NATURAL
Story: Aiko Akina
Art: Eiji Nizuma
+NATURAL HAS COLOR PAGES AT THE BEGINNING OF THE MAGAZINE, AND CROW HAS COLOR PAGES AT THE MIDDLE OF THE MAGAZINE... THIS IS PRETTY MUCH THE EIJI NIZUMA ISSUE.
THE EDITORIAL DEPARTMENT MUST HAVE WANTED TO MAKE SURE NEITHER OF EIJI'S WORKS GOT SHORT SHRIFT.
LET'S READ +NATURAL FIRST.
FLIP...
YEAH.
FLIP...
...
TCH...
IT'S GOOD...
IT'S MORE THAN GOOD...
IT BREAKS ALL THE RULES OF A JUMP FIRST CHAPTER, BUT IT'S STILL TOTALLY MAINSTREAM!
WHAT DO YOU MEAN BY IT BEING MAIN-STREAM BUT NOT?
FLIP
THERE'S NO BAD GUY BEING DEFEATED AND THE STORY DOESN'T WRAP UP, BUT IT'S STILL A GREAT SHONEN MANGA. HATTORI OUTDID HIMSELF.
I HAVEN'T READ THE SECOND CHAPTER, BUT IF I HAD TO GUESS, I'D SAY IT'LL BE LIKE POKÉMON WITH ALL KINDS OF NEW CREATURES.
OH, THAT IS VERY MAIN-STREAM!

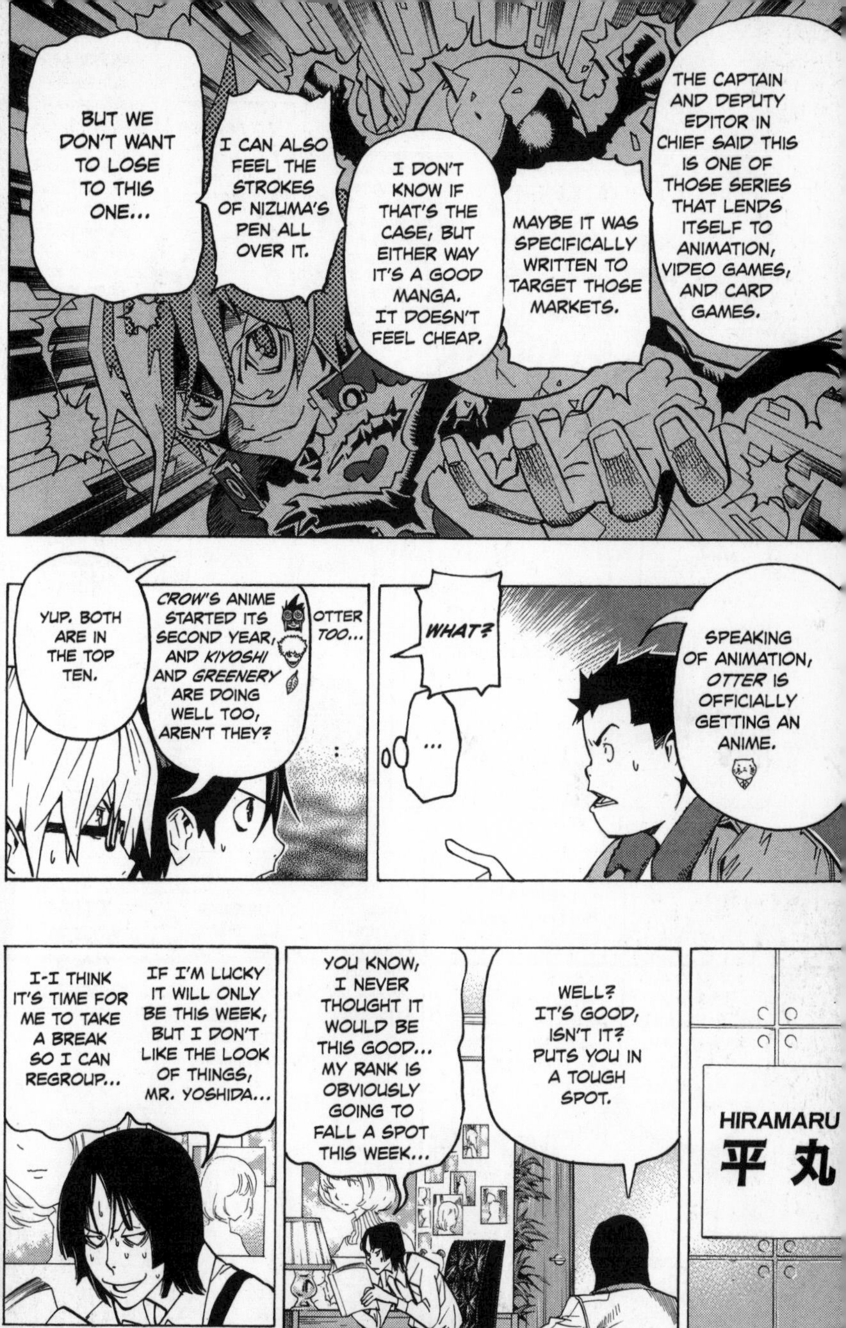
THE CAPTAIN AND DEPUTY EDITOR IN CHIEF SAID THIS IS ONE OF THOSE SERIES THAT LENDS ITSELF TO ANIMATION, VIDEO GAMES, AND CARD GAMES.
MAYBE IT WAS SPECIFICALLY WRITTEN TO TARGET THOSE MARKETS.
I DON'T KNOW IF THAT'S THE CASE, BUT EITHER WAY IT'S A GOOD MANGA. IT DOESN'T FEEL CHEAP.
I CAN ALSO FEEL THE STROKES OF NIZUMA'S PEN ALL OVER IT.
BUT WE DON'T WANT TO LOSE TO THIS ONE...
SPEAKING OF ANIMATION, OTTER IS OFFICIALLY GETTING AN ANIME.
WHAT?
...
OTTER TOO...
CROW'S ANIME STARTED ITS SECOND YEAR, AND KIYOSHI AND GREENERY ARE DOING WELL TOO, AREN'T THEY?
YUP. BOTH ARE IN THE TOP TEN.
HIRAMARU
平丸
WELL? IT'S GOOD, ISN'T IT? PUTS YOU IN A TOUGH SPOT.
YOU KNOW, I NEVER THOUGHT IT WOULD BE THIS GOOD... MY RANK IS OBVIOUSLY GOING TO FALL A SPOT THIS WEEK...
IF I'M LUCKY IT WILL ONLY BE THIS WEEK, BUT I DON'T LIKE THE LOOK OF THINGS, MR. YOSHIDA...
I-I THINK IT'S TIME FOR ME TO TAKE A BREAK SO I CAN REGROUP...

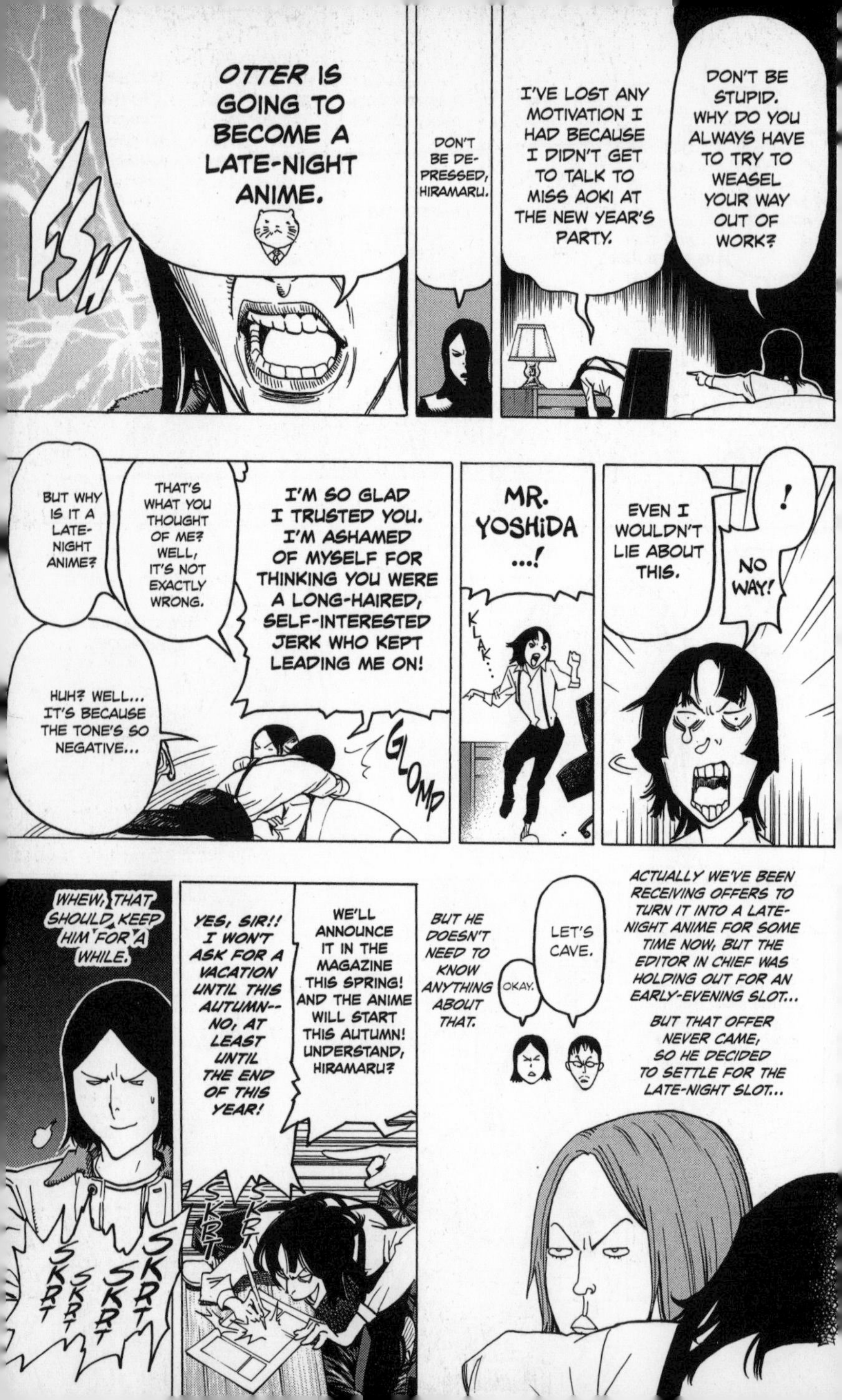

DON'T BE STUPID. WHY DO YOU ALWAYS HAVE TO TRY TO WEASEL YOUR WAY OUT OF WORK?
I'VE LOST ANY MOTIVATION I HAD BECAUSE I DIDN'T GET TO TALK TO MISS AOKI AT THE NEW YEAR'S PARTY.
DON'T BE DE-PRESSED, HIRAMARU.
OTTER IS GOING TO BECOME A LATE-NIGHT ANIME.
FSH
!
EVEN I WOULDN'T LIE ABOUT THIS.
NO WAY!
MR. YOSHIDA ...!
KLAK...
I'M SO GLAD I TRUSTED YOU. I'M ASHAMED OF MYSELF FOR THINKING YOU WERE A LONG-HAIRED, SELF-INTERESTED JERK WHO KEPT LEADING ME ON!
GLOMP
THAT'S WHAT YOU THOUGHT OF ME? WELL, IT'S NOT EXACTLY WRONG.
BUT WHY IS IT A LATE-NIGHT ANIME?
HUH? WELL... IT'S BECAUSE THE TONE'S SO NEGATIVE...
ACTUALLY WE'VE BEEN RECEIVING OFFERS TO TURN IT INTO A LATE-NIGHT ANIME FOR SOME TIME NOW, BUT THE EDITOR IN CHIEF WAS HOLDING OUT FOR AN EARLY-EVENING SLOT...
BUT THAT OFFER NEVER CAME, SO HE DECIDED TO SETTLE FOR THE LATE-NIGHT SLOT...
LET'S CAVE.
OKAY.
BUT HE DOESN'T NEED TO KNOW ANYTHING ABOUT THAT.
WE'LL ANNOUNCE IT IN THE MAGAZINE THIS SPRING! AND THE ANIME WILL START THIS AUTUMN! UNDERSTAND, HIRAMARU?
YES, SIR!! I WON'T ASK FOR A VACATION UNTIL THIS AUTUMN-- NO, AT LEAST UNTIL THE END OF THIS YEAR!
SKRT SKRT
WHEW, THAT SHOULD KEEP HIM FOR A WHILE.
SKRT SKRT SKRT SKRT

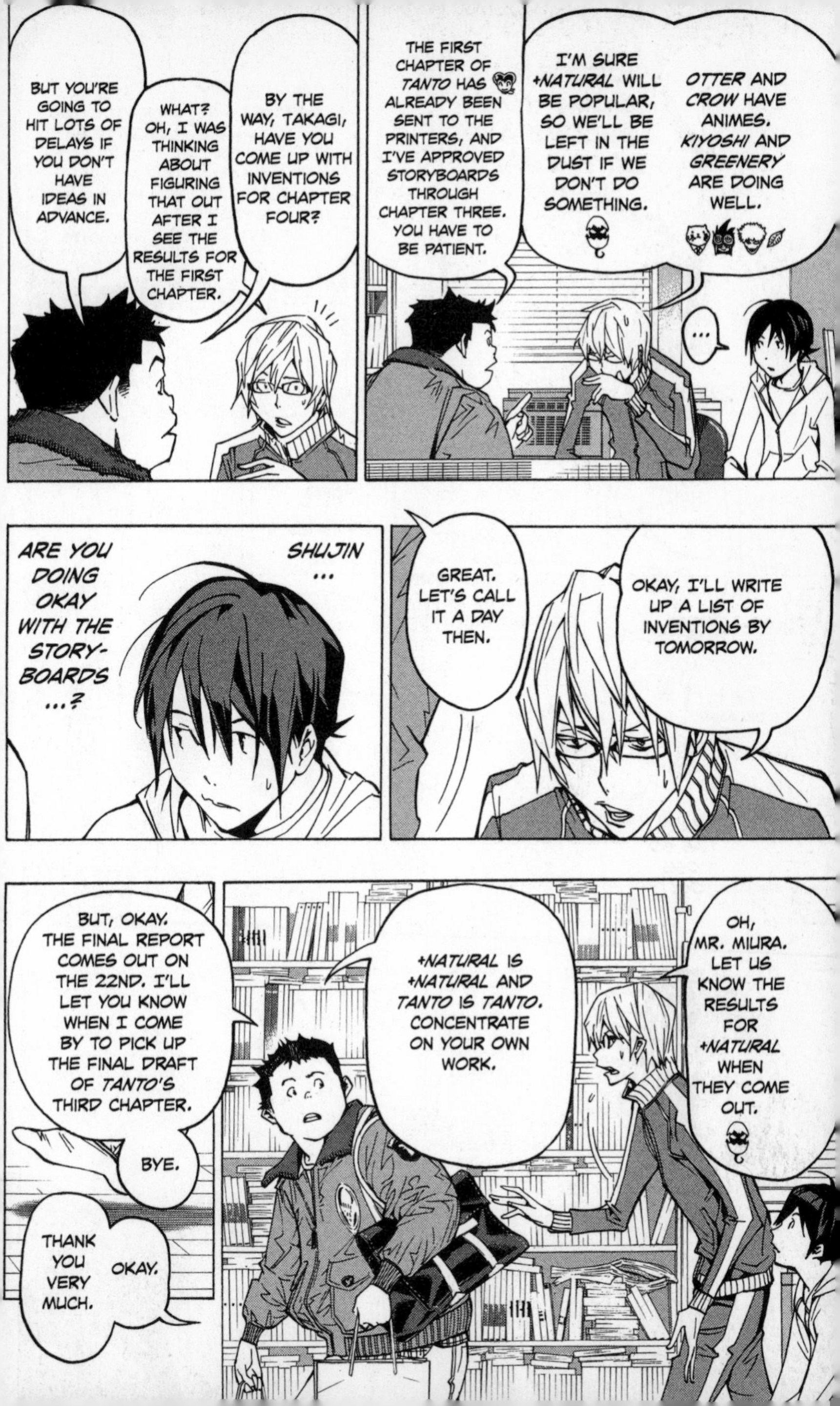

OTTER AND CROW HAVE ANIMES. KIYOSHI AND GREENERY ARE DOING WELL.
I'M SURE +NATURAL WILL BE POPULAR, SO WE'LL BE LEFT IN THE DUST IF WE DON'T DO SOMETHING.
THE FIRST CHAPTER OF TANTO HAS ALREADY BEEN SENT TO THE PRINTERS, AND I'VE APPROVED STORYBOARDS THROUGH CHAPTER THREE. YOU HAVE TO BE PATIENT.
...
BY THE WAY, TAKAGI, HAVE YOU COME UP WITH INVENTIONS FOR CHAPTER FOUR?
WHAT? OH, I WAS THINKING ABOUT FIGURING THAT OUT AFTER I SEE THE RESULTS FOR THE FIRST CHAPTER.
BUT YOU'RE GOING TO HIT LOTS OF DELAYS IF YOU DON'T HAVE IDEAS IN ADVANCE.
OKAY, I'LL WRITE UP A LIST OF INVENTIONS BY TOMORROW.
GREAT. LET'S CALL IT A DAY THEN.
SHUJIN ...
ARE YOU DOING OKAY WITH THE STORY-BOARDS ...?
OH, MR. MIURA. LET US KNOW THE RESULTS FOR +NATURAL WHEN THEY COME OUT.
+NATURAL IS +NATURAL AND TANTO IS TANTO. CONCENTRATE ON YOUR OWN WORK.
BUT, OKAY. THE FINAL REPORT COMES OUT ON THE 22ND. I'LL LET YOU KNOW WHEN I COME BY TO PICK UP THE FINAL DRAFT OF TANTO'S THIRD CHAPTER.
BYE.
OKAY.
THANK YOU VERY MUCH.

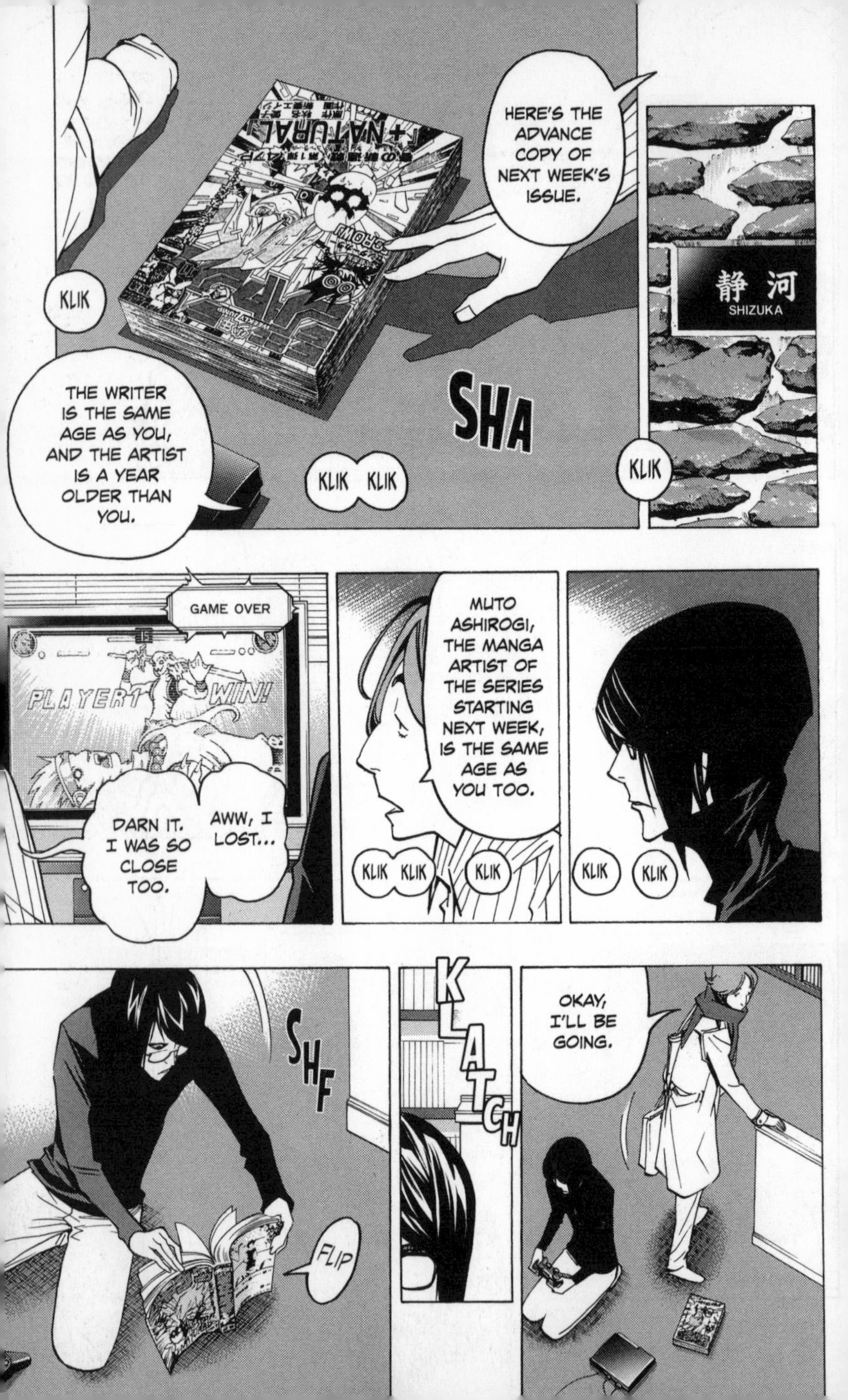
静河
SHIZUKA
KLIK
HERE'S THE ADVANCE COPY OF NEXT WEEK'S ISSUE.
KLIK
SHA
THE WRITER IS THE SAME AGE AS YOU, AND THE ARTIST IS A YEAR OLDER THAN YOU.
KLIK KLIK
KLIK
KLIK
MUTO ASHIROGI, THE MANGA ARTIST OF THE SERIES STARTING NEXT WEEK, IS THE SAME AGE AS YOU TOO.
KLIK
KLIK KLIK
GAME OVER
PLAYER1 WIN!
AWW, I LOST...
DARN IT. I WAS SO CLOSE TOO.
OKAY, I'LL BE GOING.
KLATCH
SHF
FLIP

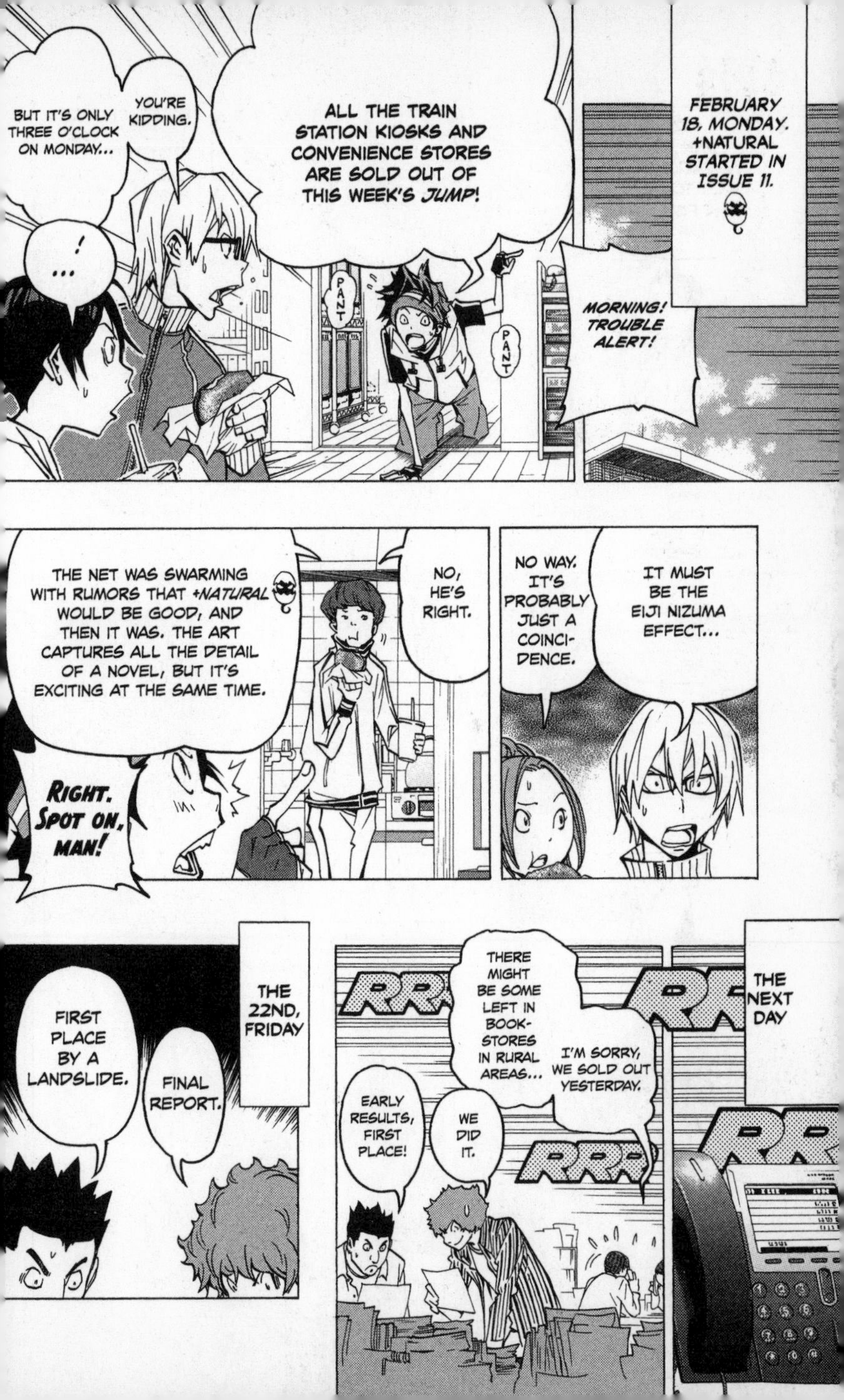
FEBRUARY 18, MONDAY. +NATURAL STARTED IN ISSUE 11.
MORNING! TROUBLE ALERT!
PANT
PANT
ALL THE TRAIN STATION KIOSKS AND CONVENIENCE STORES ARE SOLD OUT OF THIS WEEK'S *JUMP*!
YOU'RE KIDDING.
BUT IT'S ONLY THREE O'CLOCK ON MONDAY...
! ...
IT MUST BE THE EIJI NIZUMA EFFECT...
NO WAY. IT'S PROBABLY JUST A COINCIDENCE.
NO, HE'S RIGHT.
THE NET WAS SWARMING WITH RUMORS THAT *+NATURAL* WOULD BE GOOD, AND THEN IT WAS. THE ART CAPTURES ALL THE DETAIL OF A NOVEL, BUT IT'S EXCITING AT THE SAME TIME.
RIGHT. SPOT ON, MAN!
THE NEXT DAY
RRR
THERE MIGHT BE SOME LEFT IN BOOKSTORES IN RURAL AREAS...
I'M SORRY, WE SOLD OUT YESTERDAY.
RRR
RRR
WE DID IT.
EARLY RESULTS, FIRST PLACE!
THE 22ND, FRIDAY
FINAL REPORT.
FIRST PLACE BY A LANDSLIDE.

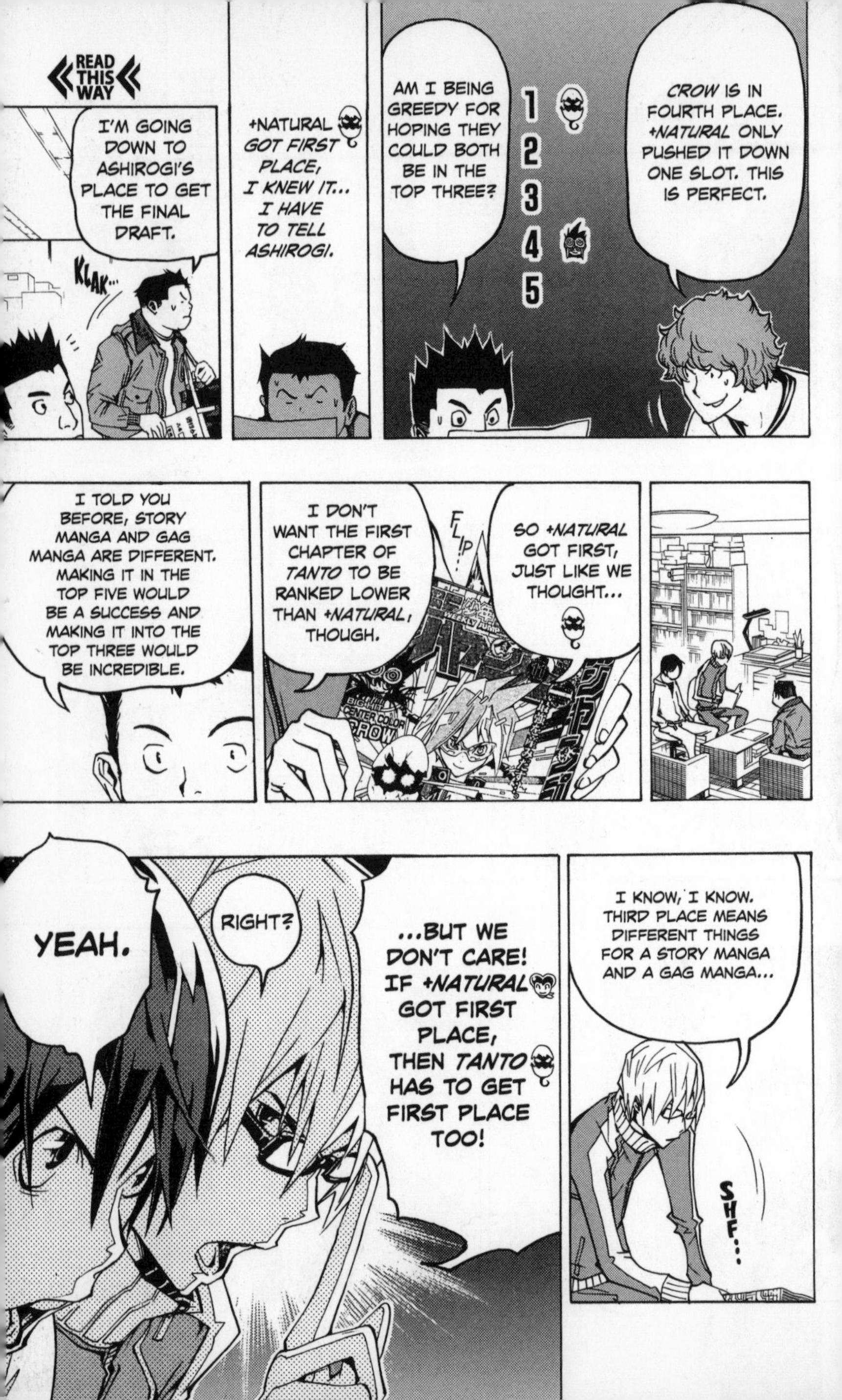
READ THIS WAY
CROW IS IN FOURTH PLACE. +NATURAL ONLY PUSHED IT DOWN ONE SLOT. THIS IS PERFECT.
1 2 3 4 5
AM I BEING GREEDY FOR HOPING THEY COULD BOTH BE IN THE TOP THREE?
+NATURAL GOT FIRST PLACE, I KNEW IT... I HAVE TO TELL ASHIROGI.
I'M GOING DOWN TO ASHIROGI'S PLACE TO GET THE FINAL DRAFT.
KLAK...
SO +NATURAL GOT FIRST, JUST LIKE WE THOUGHT...
FLIP
I DON'T WANT THE FIRST CHAPTER OF TANTO TO BE RANKED LOWER THAN +NATURAL, THOUGH.
I TOLD YOU BEFORE, STORY MANGA AND GAG MANGA ARE DIFFERENT. MAKING IT IN THE TOP FIVE WOULD BE A SUCCESS AND MAKING IT INTO THE TOP THREE WOULD BE INCREDIBLE.
I KNOW, I KNOW. THIRD PLACE MEANS DIFFERENT THINGS FOR A STORY MANGA AND A GAG MANGA...
SHF...
...BUT WE DON'T CARE! IF +NATURAL GOT FIRST PLACE, THEN TANTO HAS TO GET FIRST PLACE TOO!
RIGHT?
YEAH.

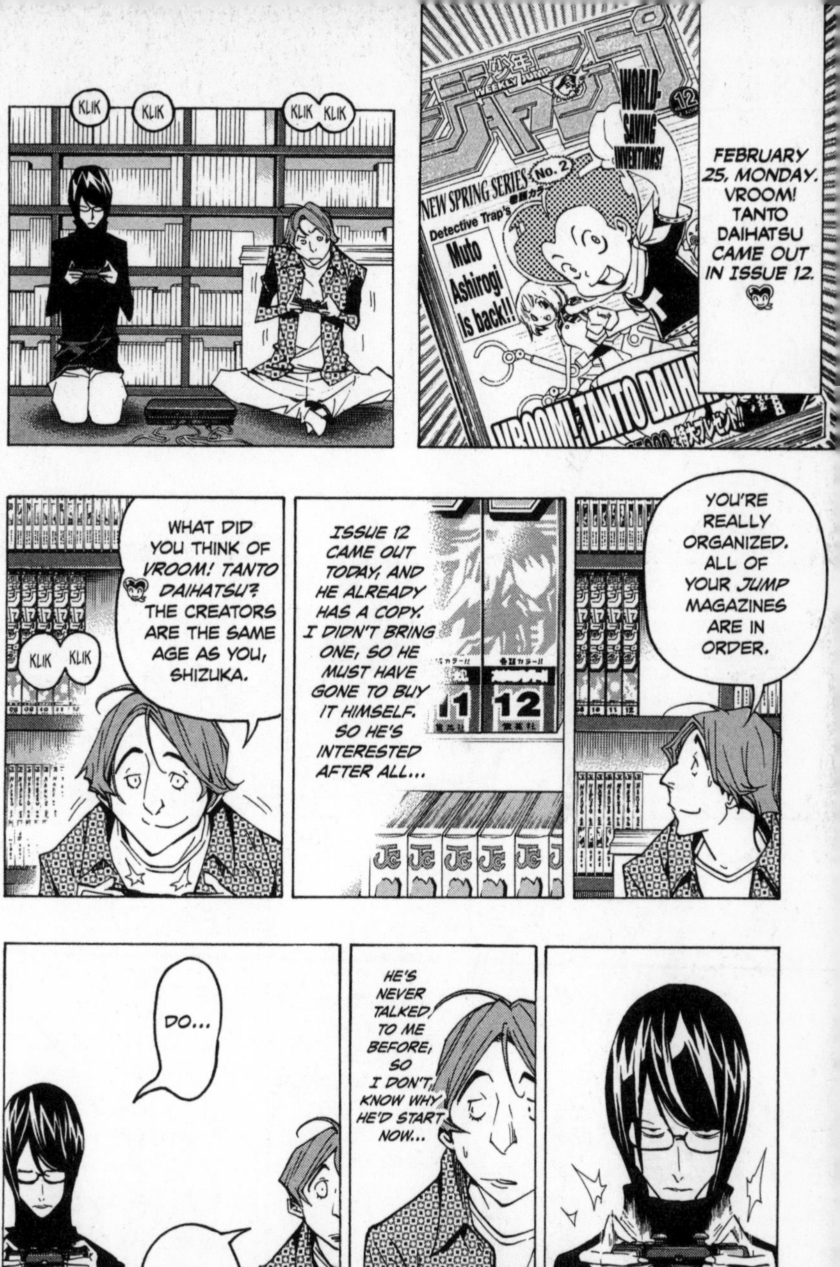
WEEKLY JUMP
12
WORLD-SAVING INVENTIONS!
NEW SPRING SERIES No. 2
Detective Trap's
Muto Ashirogi Is back!!
FEBRUARY 25, MONDAY. VROOM! TANTO DAIHATSU CAME OUT IN ISSUE 12.
KLIK KLIK
KLIK KLIK
YOU'RE REALLY ORGANIZED. ALL OF YOUR JUMP MAGAZINES ARE IN ORDER.
12
ISSUE 12 CAME OUT TODAY, AND HE ALREADY HAS A COPY. I DIDN'T BRING ONE, SO HE MUST HAVE GONE TO BUY IT HIMSELF. SO HE'S INTERESTED AFTER ALL...
WHAT DID YOU THINK OF VROOM! TANTO DAIHATSU? THE CREATORS ARE THE SAME AGE AS YOU, SHIZUKA.
KLIK KLIK
KLIK KLIK
HE'S NEVER TALKED TO ME BEFORE, SO I DON'T KNOW WHY HE'D START NOW...
DO...
WHAT?

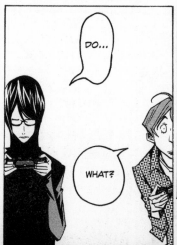

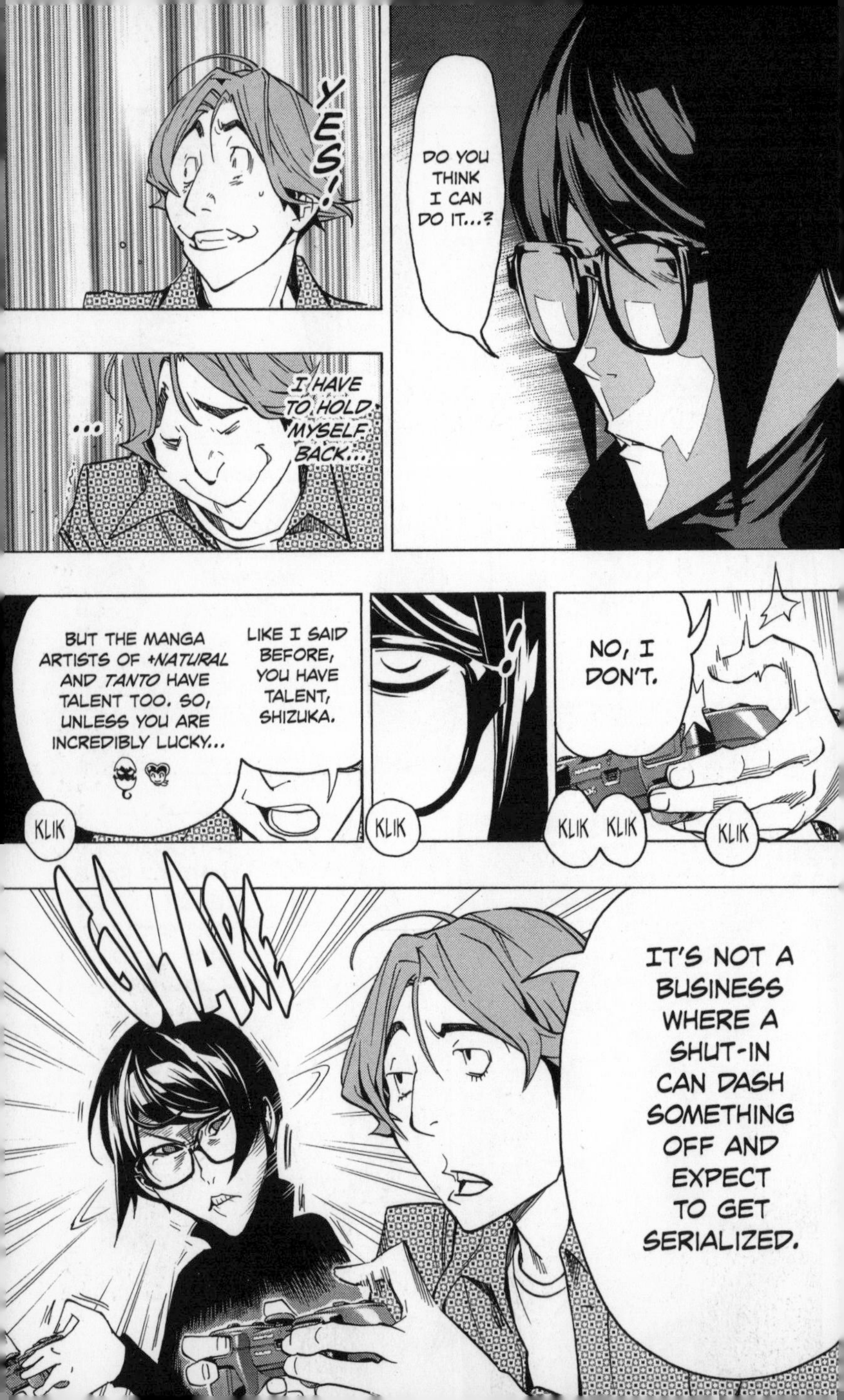
DO YOU THINK I CAN DO IT...?
YES!
I HAVE TO HOLD MYSELF BACK...
...
NO, I DON'T.
KLIK
KLIK KLIK
KLIK
LIKE I SAID BEFORE, YOU HAVE TALENT, SHIZUKA.
BUT THE MANGA ARTISTS OF *+NATURAL* AND *TANTO* HAVE TALENT TOO. SO, UNLESS YOU ARE INCREDIBLY LUCKY...
KLIK
IT'S NOT A BUSINESS WHERE A SHUT-IN CAN DASH SOMETHING OFF AND EXPECT TO GET SERIALIZED.

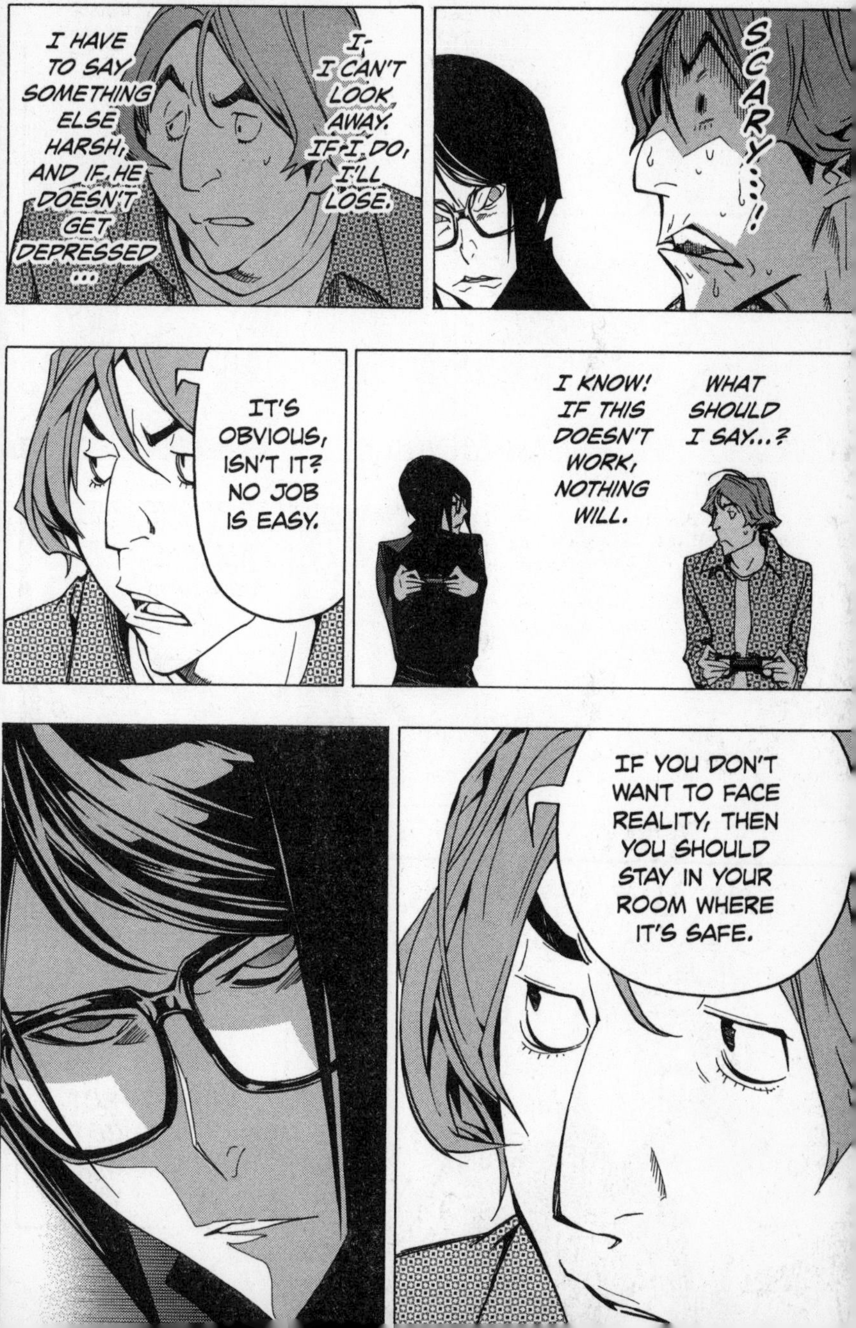
SCARY...!
I- I CAN'T LOOK AWAY. IF I DO, I'LL LOSE.
I HAVE TO SAY SOMETHING ELSE HARSH, AND IF HE DOESN'T GET DEPRESSED...
WHAT SHOULD I SAY...?
I KNOW! IF THIS DOESN'T WORK, NOTHING WILL.
IT'S OBVIOUS, ISN'T IT? NO JOB IS EASY.
IF YOU DON'T WANT TO FACE REALITY, THEN YOU SHOULD STAY IN YOUR ROOM WHERE IT'S SAFE.

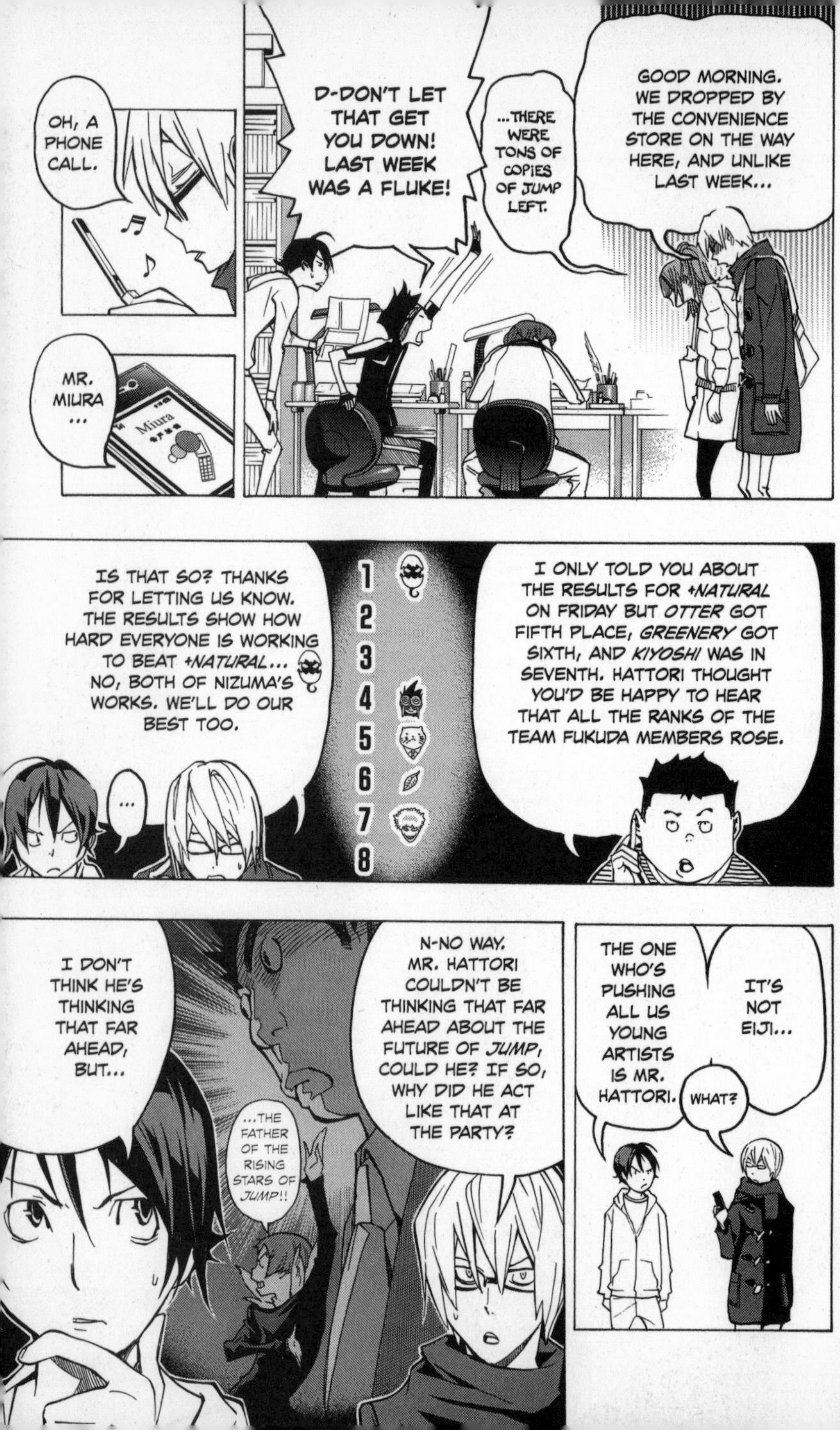

GOOD MORNING. WE DROPPED BY THE CONVENIENCE STORE ON THE WAY HERE, AND UNLIKE LAST WEEK...
...THERE WERE TONS OF COPIES OF JUMP LEFT.
D-DON'T LET THAT GET YOU DOWN! LAST WEEK WAS A FLUKE!
OH, A PHONE CALL.
MR. MIURA ...
Miura
I ONLY TOLD YOU ABOUT THE RESULTS FOR +NATURAL ON FRIDAY BUT OTTER GOT FIFTH PLACE, GREENERY GOT SIXTH, AND KIYOSHI WAS IN SEVENTH. HATTORI THOUGHT YOU'D BE HAPPY TO HEAR THAT ALL THE RANKS OF THE TEAM FUKUDA MEMBERS ROSE.
1
2
3
4
5
6
7
8
IS THAT SO? THANKS FOR LETTING US KNOW. THE RESULTS SHOW HOW HARD EVERYONE IS WORKING TO BEAT +NATURAL... NO, BOTH OF NIZUMA'S WORKS. WE'LL DO OUR BEST TOO.
...
IT'S NOT EIJI...
THE ONE WHO'S PUSHING ALL US YOUNG ARTISTS IS MR. HATTORI.
WHAT?
N-NO WAY. MR. HATTORI COULDN'T BE THINKING THAT FAR AHEAD ABOUT THE FUTURE OF JUMP, COULD HE? IF SO, WHY DID HE ACT LIKE THAT AT THE PARTY?
I DON'T THINK HE'S THINKING THAT FAR AHEAD, BUT...
...THE FATHER OF THE RISING STARS OF JUMP!!

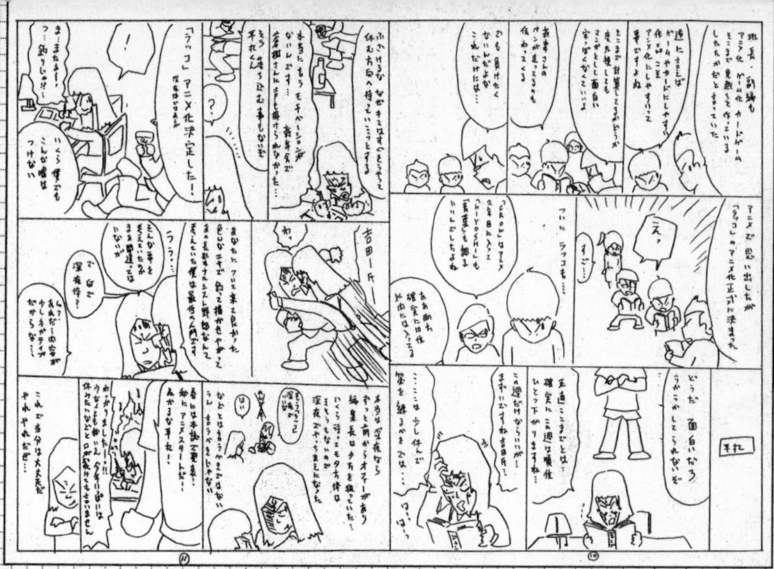

OHBA'S STORYBOARD
班長・副編もアニメ化 ゲーム化 カードゲームのところまで見越して作っている
したたかだと言っていた
ゲームやカードにしやすい作品ってアニメ化にしやすいって事ですよね
でも負けたくないんだよな これだけには…
アニメで思い出したが「ラッコ」のアニメ化正式に決まった
え
すご…
ついにラッコも…
ああ 確実に10位以内には入ってる
平丸
どうだ 面白いだろう うかうかしてられないぞ
この週だけならいいが まずいですね吉田氏…
ここは少し休んで策を練るべきでは…
は…は…
ふざけるな なぜキミはすぐそうやって休む方向へ持っていこうとする
?
「ラッコ」アニメ化決定した!
!
いくら僕でもこんな嘘はつけない
吉田ー氏ー!
わ
ラ、ラ…
で…でも深夜枠?
はい
これで当分は大丈夫だ やれやれだぜ…

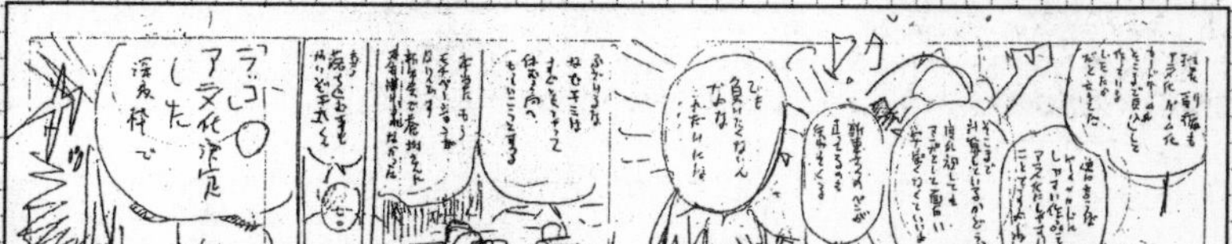

OBATA'S STORYBOARD

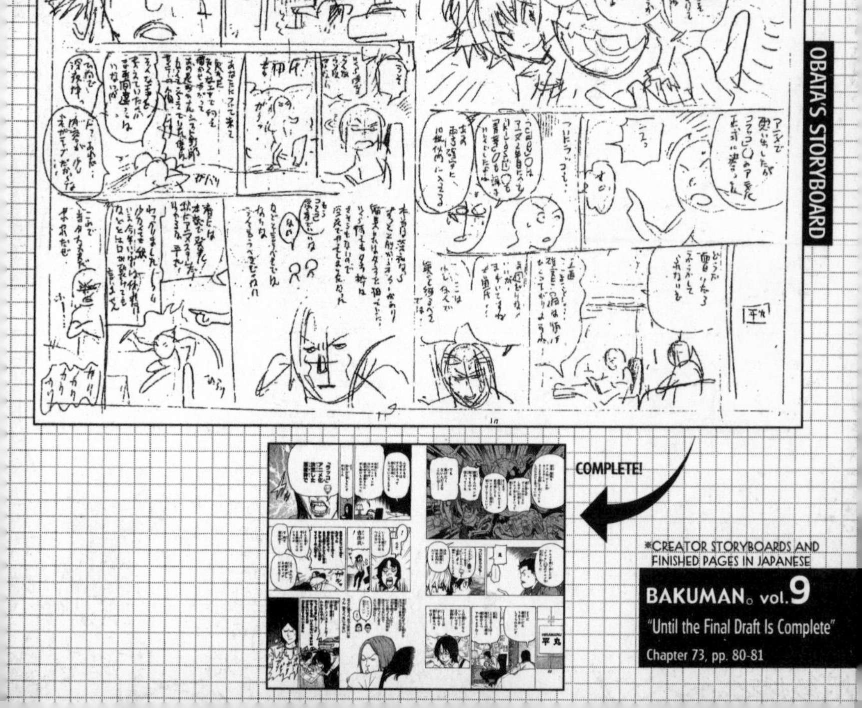

COMPLETE!

*CREATOR STORYBOARDS AND FINISHED PAGES IN JAPANESE

BAKUMAN。vol.9

"Until the Final Draft Is Complete"

Chapter 73, pp. 80-81

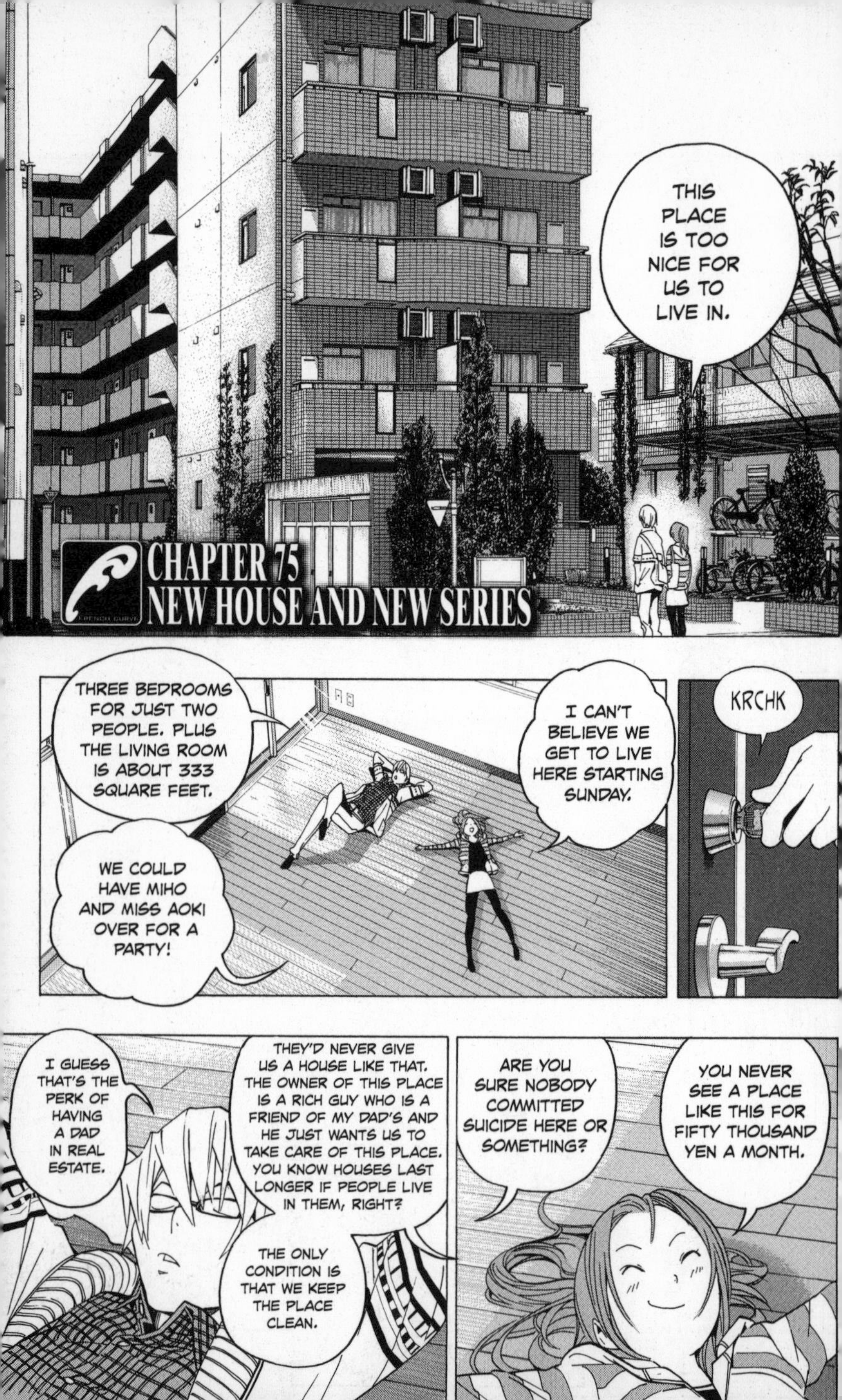
THIS PLACE IS TOO NICE FOR US TO LIVE IN.
CHAPTER 75
NEW HOUSE AND NEW SERIES
KRCHK
I CAN'T BELIEVE WE GET TO LIVE HERE STARTING SUNDAY.
THREE BEDROOMS FOR JUST TWO PEOPLE. PLUS THE LIVING ROOM IS ABOUT 333 SQUARE FEET.
WE COULD HAVE MIHO AND MISS AOKI OVER FOR A PARTY!
YOU NEVER SEE A PLACE LIKE THIS FOR FIFTY THOUSAND YEN A MONTH.
ARE YOU SURE NOBODY COMMITTED SUICIDE HERE OR SOMETHING?
THEY'D NEVER GIVE US A HOUSE LIKE THAT. THE OWNER OF THIS PLACE IS A RICH GUY WHO IS A FRIEND OF MY DAD'S AND HE JUST WANTS US TO TAKE CARE OF THIS PLACE. YOU KNOW HOUSES LAST LONGER IF PEOPLE LIVE IN THEM, RIGHT?
I GUESS THAT'S THE PERK OF HAVING A DAD IN REAL ESTATE.
THE ONLY CONDITION IS THAT WE KEEP THE PLACE CLEAN.

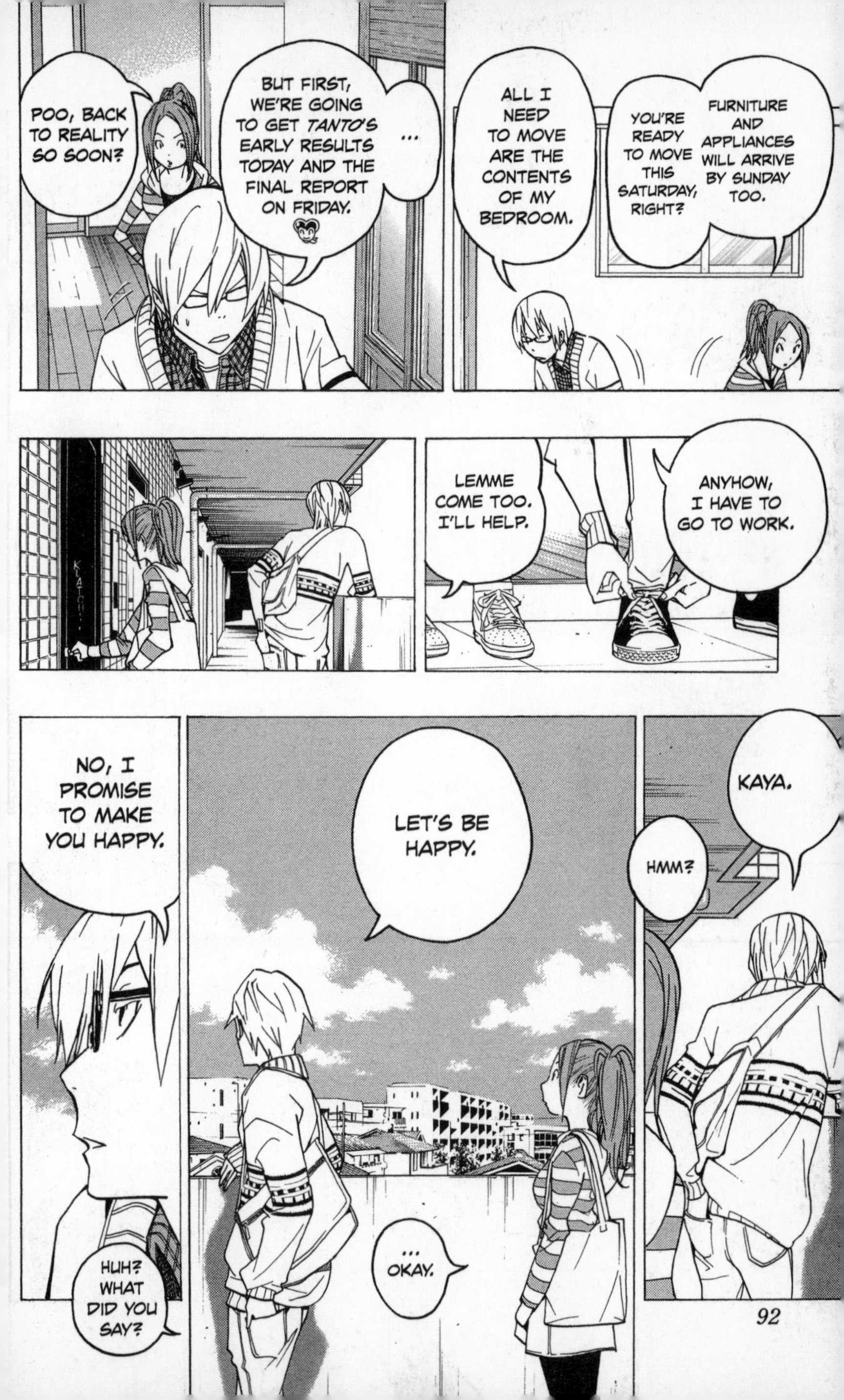
FURNITURE AND APPLIANCES WILL ARRIVE BY SUNDAY TOO.
YOU'RE READY TO MOVE THIS SATURDAY, RIGHT?
ALL I NEED TO MOVE ARE THE CONTENTS OF MY BEDROOM.
...
BUT FIRST, WE'RE GOING TO GET *TANTO'S* EARLY RESULTS TODAY AND THE FINAL REPORT ON FRIDAY.
POO, BACK TO REALITY SO SOON?
ANYHOW, I HAVE TO GO TO WORK.
LEMME COME TOO. I'LL HELP.
KLATCH
KAYA.
HMM?
LET'S BE HAPPY.
... OKAY.
NO, I PROMISE TO MAKE YOU HAPPY.
HUH? WHAT DID YOU SAY?

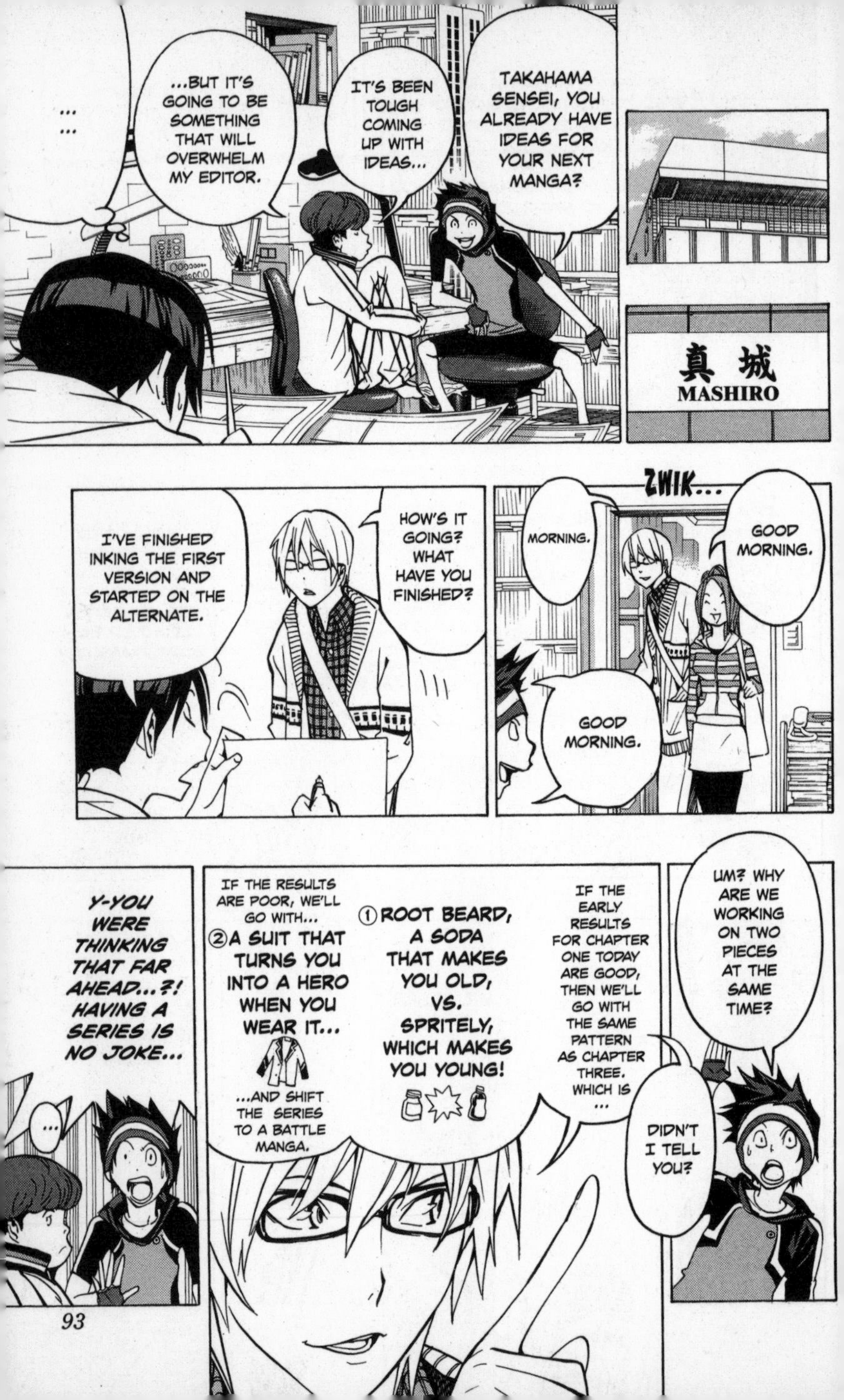
真城
MASHIRO
TAKAHAMA SENSEI, YOU ALREADY HAVE IDEAS FOR YOUR NEXT MANGA?
IT'S BEEN TOUGH COMING UP WITH IDEAS...
...BUT IT'S GOING TO BE SOMETHING THAT WILL OVERWHELM MY EDITOR.
... ...
ZWIK...
GOOD MORNING.
MORNING.
GOOD MORNING.
HOW'S IT GOING? WHAT HAVE YOU FINISHED?
I'VE FINISHED INKING THE FIRST VERSION AND STARTED ON THE ALTERNATE.
UM? WHY ARE WE WORKING ON TWO PIECES AT THE SAME TIME?
DIDN'T I TELL YOU?
IF THE EARLY RESULTS FOR CHAPTER ONE TODAY ARE GOOD, THEN WE'LL GO WITH THE SAME PATTERN AS CHAPTER THREE. WHICH IS ...
① ROOT BEARD, A SODA THAT MAKES YOU OLD, VS. SPRITELY, WHICH MAKES YOU YOUNG!
IF THE RESULTS ARE POOR, WE'LL GO WITH...
② A SUIT THAT TURNS YOU INTO A HERO WHEN YOU WEAR IT...
...AND SHIFT THE SERIES TO A BATTLE MANGA.
Y-YOU WERE THINKING THAT FAR AHEAD...?! HAVING A SERIES IS NO JOKE...
...

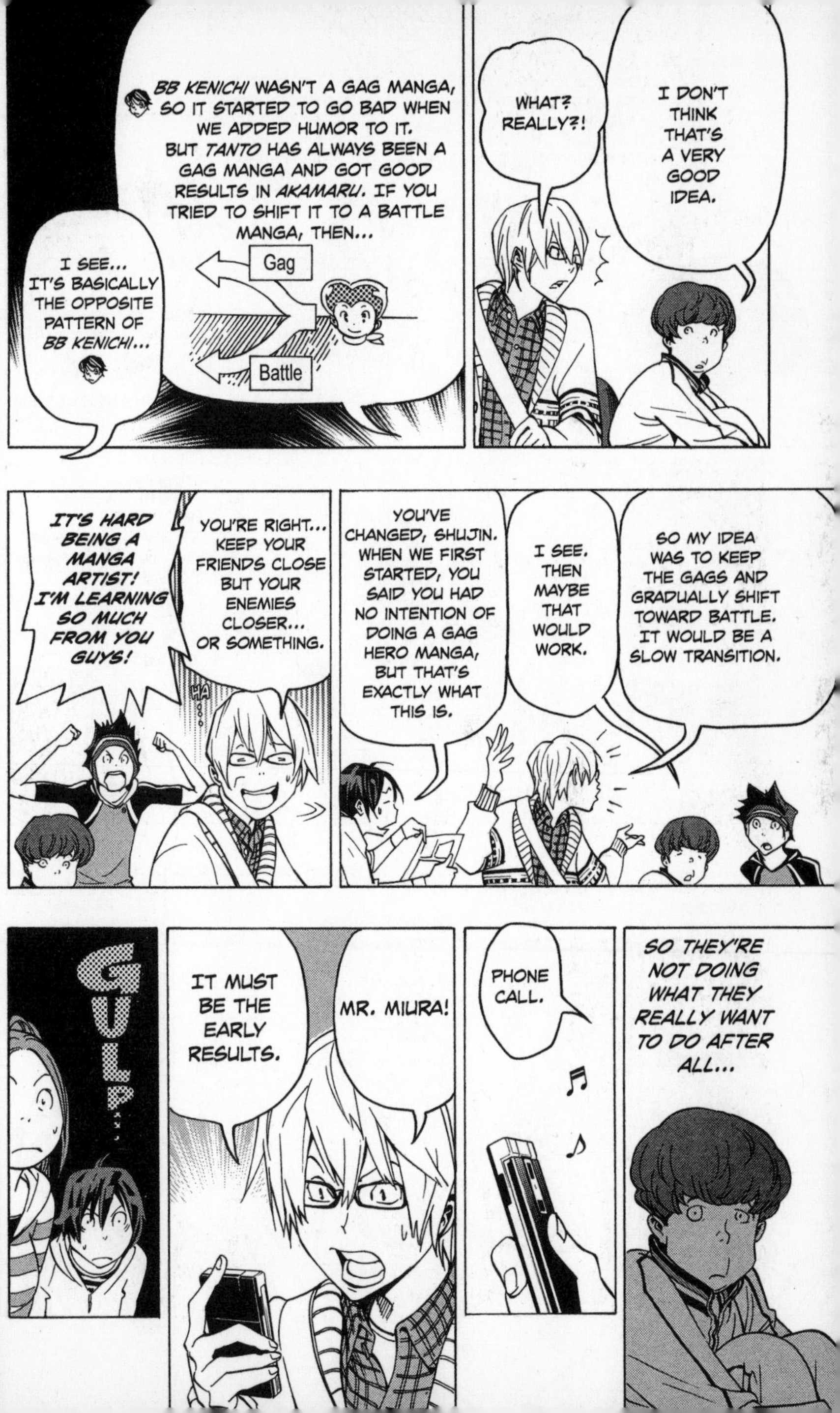
I DON'T THINK THAT'S A VERY GOOD IDEA.
WHAT? REALLY?!
BB KENICHI WASN'T A GAG MANGA, SO IT STARTED TO GO BAD WHEN WE ADDED HUMOR TO IT. BUT TANTO HAS ALWAYS BEEN A GAG MANGA AND GOT GOOD RESULTS IN AKAMARU. IF YOU TRIED TO SHIFT IT TO A BATTLE MANGA, THEN...
Gag
Battle
I SEE... IT'S BASICALLY THE OPPOSITE PATTERN OF BB KENICHI...
SO MY IDEA WAS TO KEEP THE GAGS AND GRADUALLY SHIFT TOWARD BATTLE. IT WOULD BE A SLOW TRANSITION.
I SEE. THEN MAYBE THAT WOULD WORK.
YOU'VE CHANGED, SHUJIN. WHEN WE FIRST STARTED, YOU SAID YOU HAD NO INTENTION OF DOING A GAG HERO MANGA, BUT THAT'S EXACTLY WHAT THIS IS.
YOU'RE RIGHT... KEEP YOUR FRIENDS CLOSE BUT YOUR ENEMIES CLOSER... OR SOMETHING.
HA
IT'S HARD BEING A MANGA ARTIST! I'M LEARNING SO MUCH FROM YOU GUYS!
SO THEY'RE NOT DOING WHAT THEY REALLY WANT TO DO AFTER ALL...
PHONE CALL.
MR. MIURA!
IT MUST BE THE EARLY RESULTS.
GULP

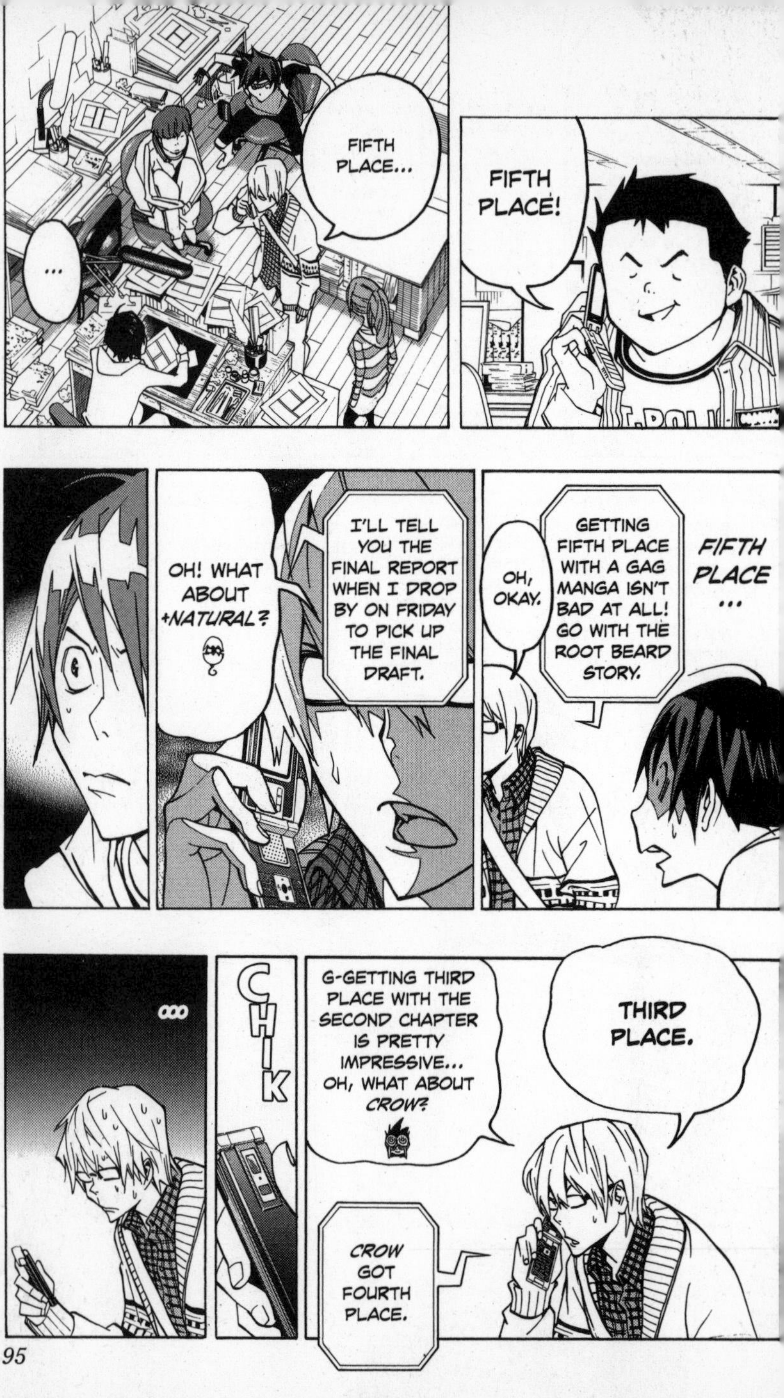
FIFTH PLACE!
FIFTH PLACE...
...
FIFTH PLACE ...
GETTING FIFTH PLACE WITH A GAG MANGA ISN'T BAD AT ALL! GO WITH THE ROOT BEARD STORY.
OH, OKAY.
I'LL TELL YOU THE FINAL REPORT WHEN I DROP BY ON FRIDAY TO PICK UP THE FINAL DRAFT.
OH! WHAT ABOUT +NATURAL?
THIRD PLACE.
G-GETTING THIRD PLACE WITH THE SECOND CHAPTER IS PRETTY IMPRESSIVE... OH, WHAT ABOUT CROW?
CROW GOT FOURTH PLACE.
CHIK

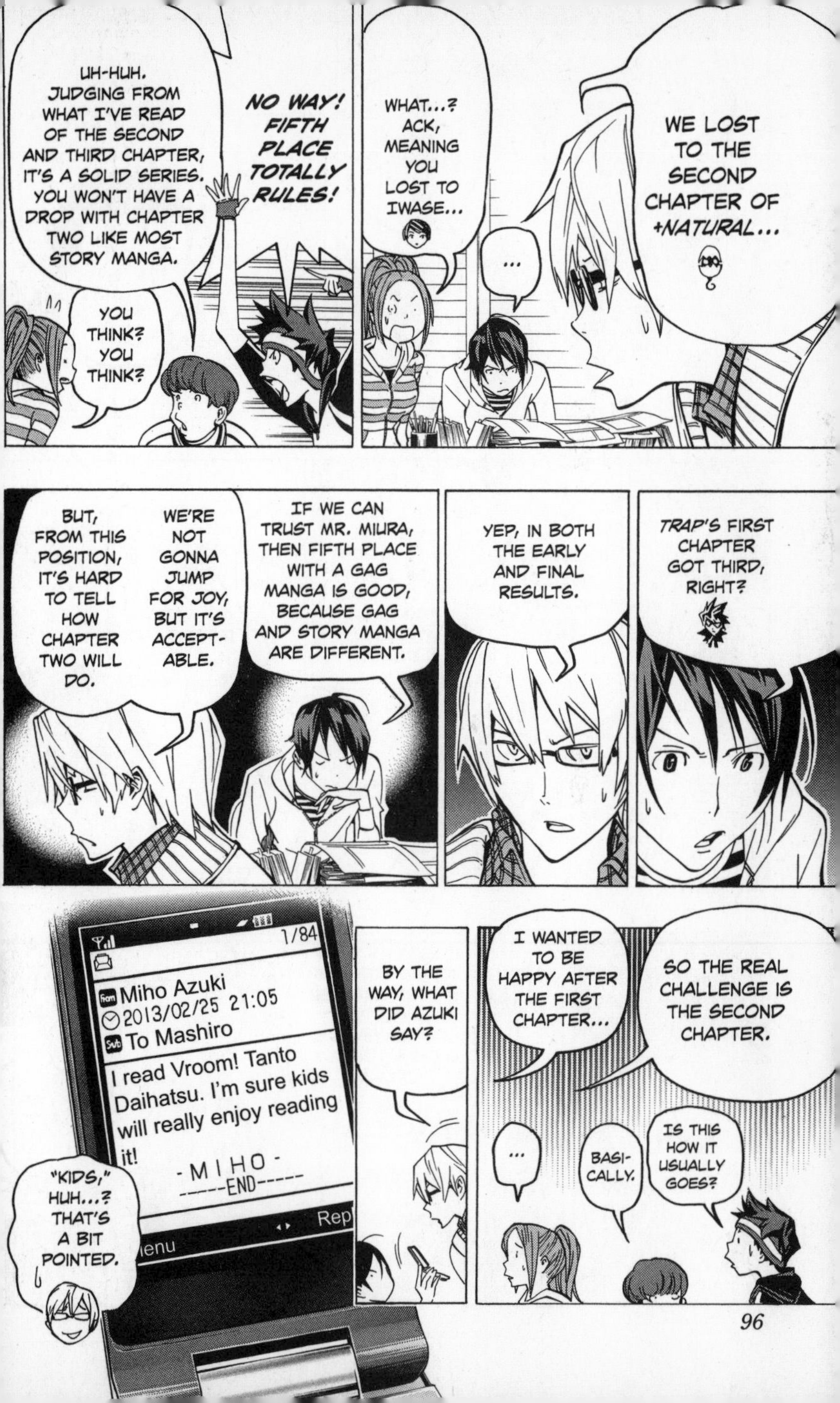
WE LOST TO THE SECOND CHAPTER OF +NATURAL...
...
WHAT...? ACK, MEANING YOU LOST TO IWASE...
NO WAY! FIFTH PLACE TOTALLY RULES!
UH-HUH. JUDGING FROM WHAT I'VE READ OF THE SECOND AND THIRD CHAPTER, IT'S A SOLID SERIES. YOU WON'T HAVE A DROP WITH CHAPTER TWO LIKE MOST STORY MANGA.
YOU THINK? YOU THINK?
TRAP'S FIRST CHAPTER GOT THIRD, RIGHT?
YEP, IN BOTH THE EARLY AND FINAL RESULTS.
IF WE CAN TRUST MR. MIURA, THEN FIFTH PLACE WITH A GAG MANGA IS GOOD, BECAUSE GAG AND STORY MANGA ARE DIFFERENT.
WE'RE NOT GONNA JUMP FOR JOY, BUT IT'S ACCEPTABLE.
BUT, FROM THIS POSITION, IT'S HARD TO TELL HOW CHAPTER TWO WILL DO.
SO THE REAL CHALLENGE IS THE SECOND CHAPTER.
I WANTED TO BE HAPPY AFTER THE FIRST CHAPTER...
IS THIS HOW IT USUALLY GOES?
BASICALLY.
...
BY THE WAY, WHAT DID AZUKI SAY?
1/84
From Miho Azuki
2013/02/25 21:05
Sub To Mashiro
I read Vroom! Tanto Daihatsu. I'm sure kids will really enjoy reading it!
-MIHO-
-----END-----
Rep
Menu
"KIDS," HUH...? THAT'S A BIT POINTED.

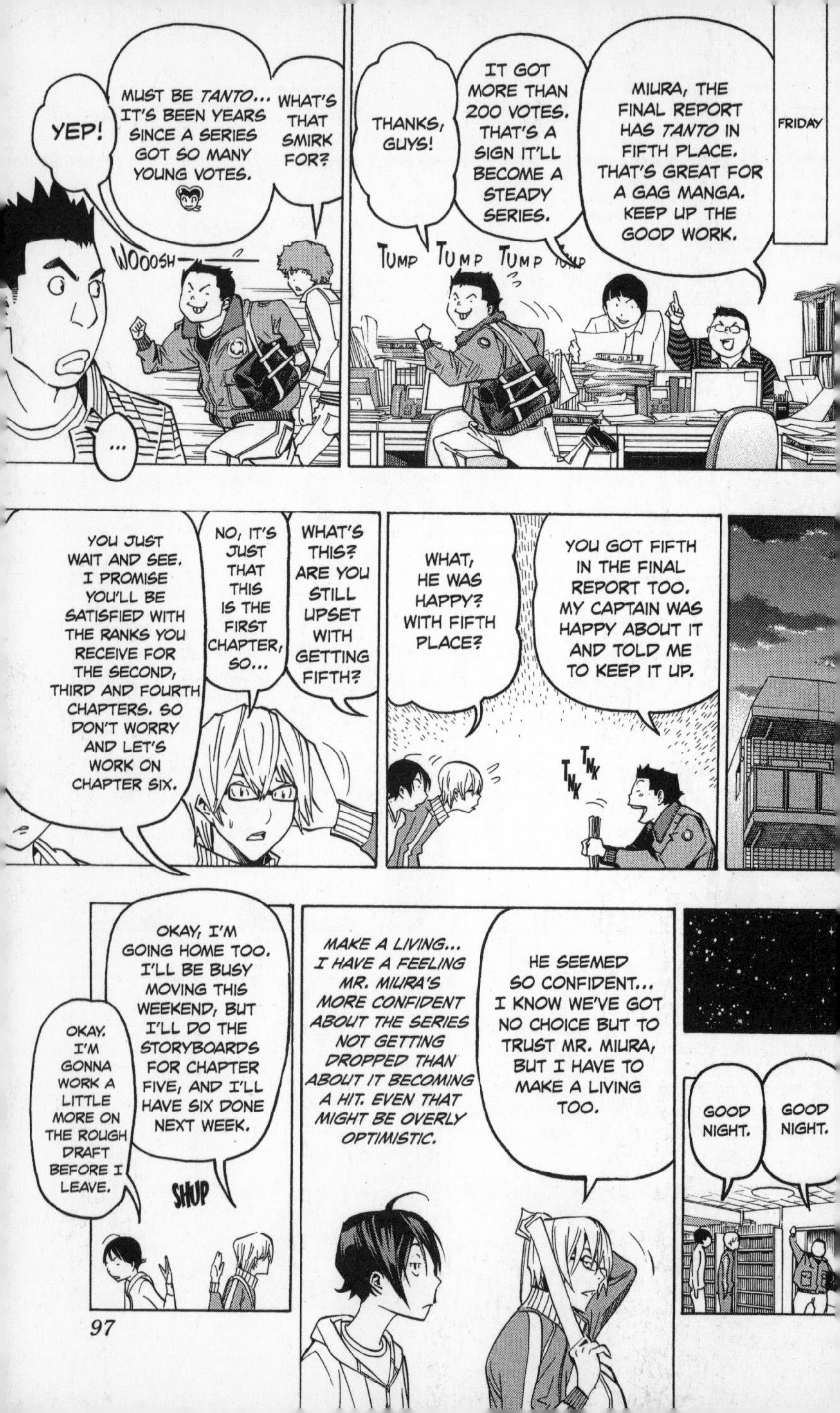
FRIDAY
MIURA, THE FINAL REPORT HAS *TANTO* IN FIFTH PLACE. THAT'S GREAT FOR A GAG MANGA. KEEP UP THE GOOD WORK.
IT GOT MORE THAN 200 VOTES. THAT'S A SIGN IT'LL BECOME A STEADY SERIES.
THANKS, GUYS!
TUMP TUMP TUMP
WHAT'S THAT SMIRK FOR?
MUST BE *TANTO*... IT'S BEEN YEARS SINCE A SERIES GOT SO MANY YOUNG VOTES.
YEP!
WOOOSH
...
YOU GOT FIFTH IN THE FINAL REPORT TOO. MY CAPTAIN WAS HAPPY ABOUT IT AND TOLD ME TO KEEP IT UP.
WHAT, HE WAS HAPPY? WITH FIFTH PLACE?
TNK TNK
WHAT'S THIS? ARE YOU STILL UPSET WITH GETTING FIFTH?
NO, IT'S JUST THAT THIS IS THE FIRST CHAPTER, SO...
YOU JUST WAIT AND SEE. I PROMISE YOU'LL BE SATISFIED WITH THE RANKS YOU RECEIVE FOR THE SECOND, THIRD AND FOURTH CHAPTERS. SO DON'T WORRY AND LET'S WORK ON CHAPTER SIX.
GOOD NIGHT.
GOOD NIGHT.
HE SEEMED SO CONFIDENT... I KNOW WE'VE GOT NO CHOICE BUT TO TRUST MR. MIURA, BUT I HAVE TO MAKE A LIVING TOO.
MAKE A LIVING... I HAVE A FEELING MR. MIURA'S MORE CONFIDENT ABOUT THE SERIES NOT GETTING DROPPED THAN ABOUT IT BECOMING A HIT. EVEN THAT MIGHT BE OVERLY OPTIMISTIC.
OKAY, I'M GOING HOME TOO. I'LL BE BUSY MOVING THIS WEEKEND, BUT I'LL DO THE STORYBOARDS FOR CHAPTER FIVE, AND I'LL HAVE SIX DONE NEXT WEEK.
OKAY. I'M GONNA WORK A LITTLE MORE ON THE ROUGH DRAFT BEFORE I LEAVE.
SHUP

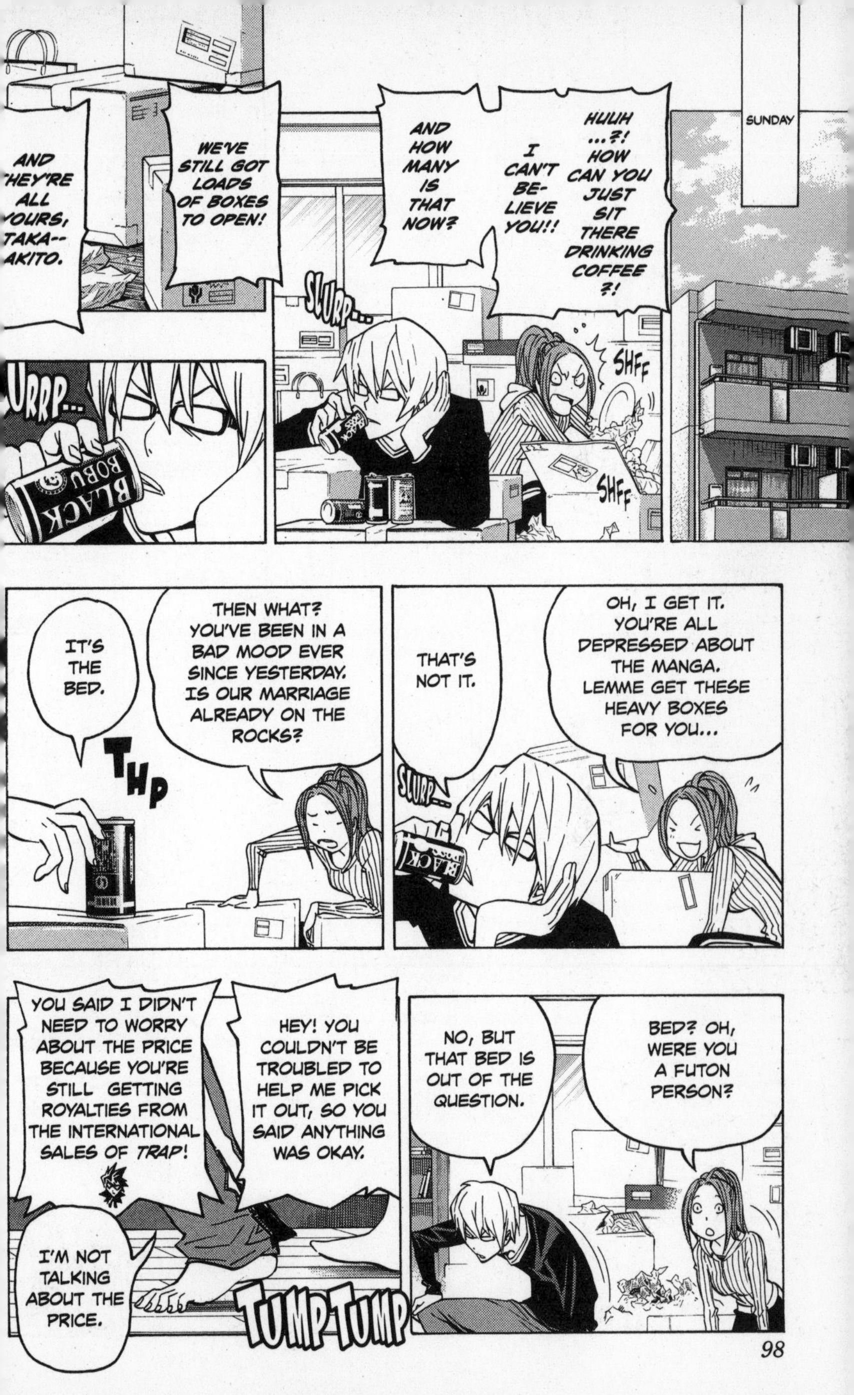
SUNDAY
HUUH ...?! HOW CAN YOU JUST SIT THERE DRINKING COFFEE ?!
I CAN'T BE-LIEVE YOU!!
AND HOW MANY IS THAT NOW?
SLURP...
SHFF
SHFF
WE'VE STILL GOT LOADS OF BOXES TO OPEN!
AND THEY'RE ALL YOURS, TAKA--AKITO.
URRP...
OH, I GET IT. YOU'RE ALL DEPRESSED ABOUT THE MANGA. LEMME GET THESE HEAVY BOXES FOR YOU...
THAT'S NOT IT.
SLURP...
THEN WHAT? YOU'VE BEEN IN A BAD MOOD EVER SINCE YESTERDAY. IS OUR MARRIAGE ALREADY ON THE ROCKS?
IT'S THE BED.
THP
BED? OH, WERE YOU A FUTON PERSON?
NO, BUT THAT BED IS OUT OF THE QUESTION.
HEY! YOU COULDN'T BE TROUBLED TO HELP ME PICK IT OUT, SO YOU SAID ANYTHING WAS OKAY.
YOU SAID I DIDN'T NEED TO WORRY ABOUT THE PRICE BECAUSE YOU'RE STILL GETTING ROYALTIES FROM THE INTERNATIONAL SALES OF *TRAP*!
I'M NOT TALKING ABOUT THE PRICE.
TUMP TUMP

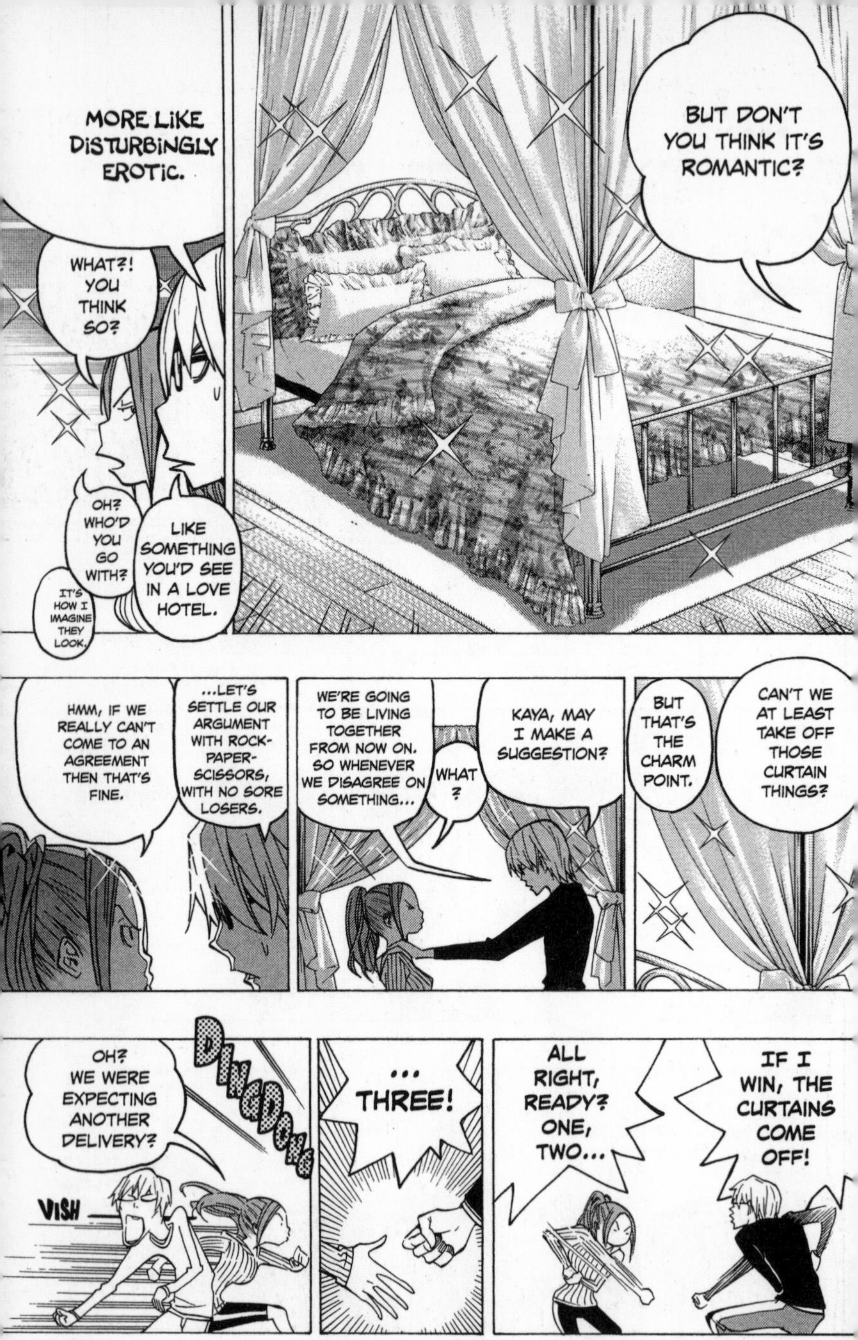

BUT DON'T YOU THINK IT'S ROMANTIC?
MORE LIKE DISTURBINGLY EROTIC.
WHAT?! YOU THINK SO?
LIKE SOMETHING YOU'D SEE IN A LOVE HOTEL.
OH? WHO'D YOU GO WITH?
IT'S HOW I IMAGINE THEY LOOK.
CAN'T WE AT LEAST TAKE OFF THOSE CURTAIN THINGS?
BUT THAT'S THE CHARM POINT.
KAYA, MAY I MAKE A SUGGESTION?
WHAT?
WE'RE GOING TO BE LIVING TOGETHER FROM NOW ON. SO WHENEVER WE DISAGREE ON SOMETHING...
...LET'S SETTLE OUR ARGUMENT WITH ROCK-PAPER-SCISSORS, WITH NO SORE LOSERS.
HMM, IF WE REALLY CAN'T COME TO AN AGREEMENT THEN THAT'S FINE.
IF I WIN, THE CURTAINS COME OFF!
ALL RIGHT, READY? ONE, TWO...
...THREE!
DING DONG
OH? WE WERE EXPECTING ANOTHER DELIVERY?
VISH

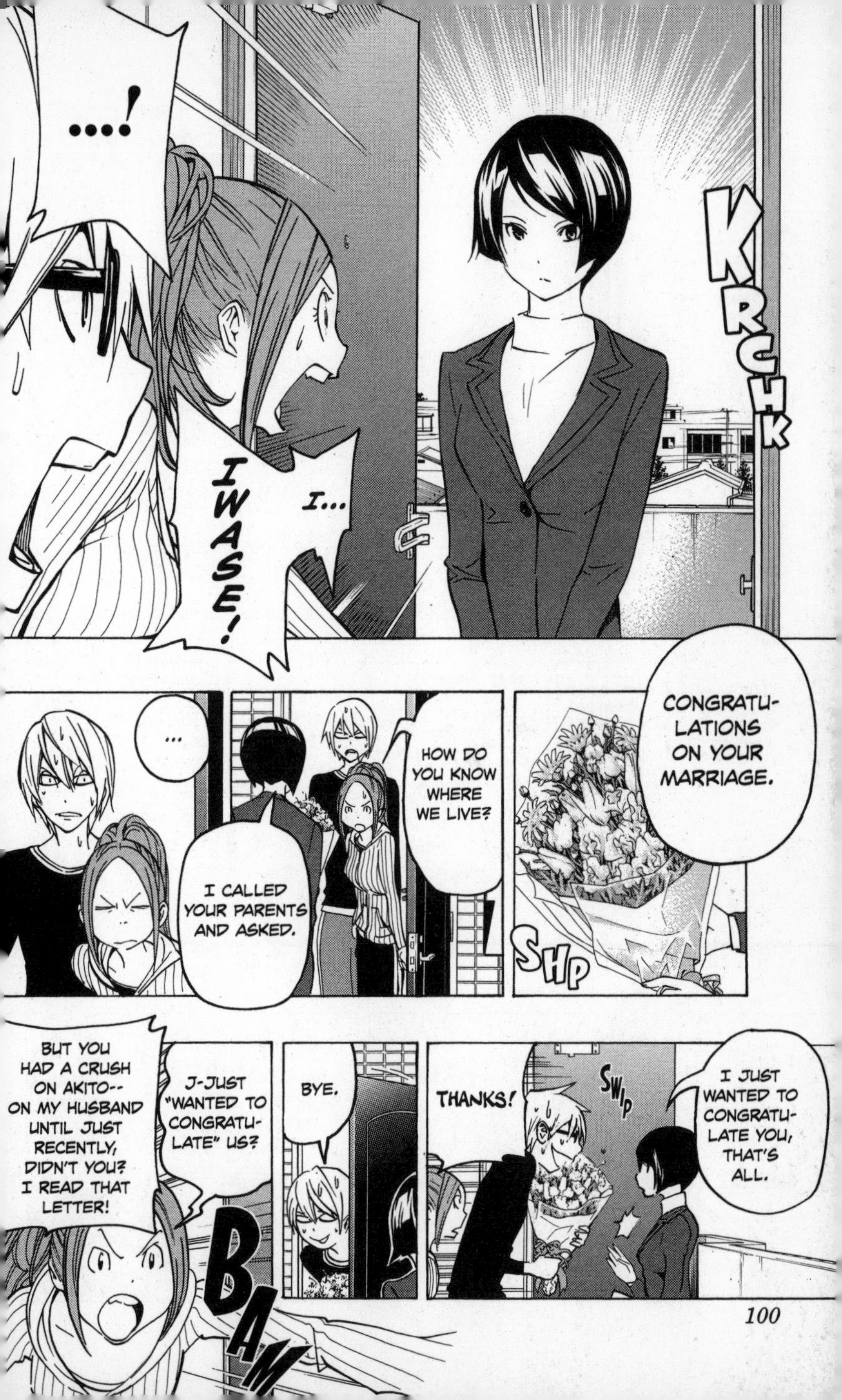
KRCHK
....!
I...
IWASE!
CONGRATULATIONS ON YOUR MARRIAGE.
SHP
HOW DO YOU KNOW WHERE WE LIVE?
I CALLED YOUR PARENTS AND ASKED.
...
I JUST WANTED TO CONGRATULATE YOU, THAT'S ALL.
SWIP
THANKS!
BYE.
J-JUST "WANTED TO CONGRATULATE" US?
BUT YOU HAD A CRUSH ON AKITO-- ON MY HUSBAND UNTIL JUST RECENTLY, DIDN'T YOU? I READ THAT LETTER!
BAM

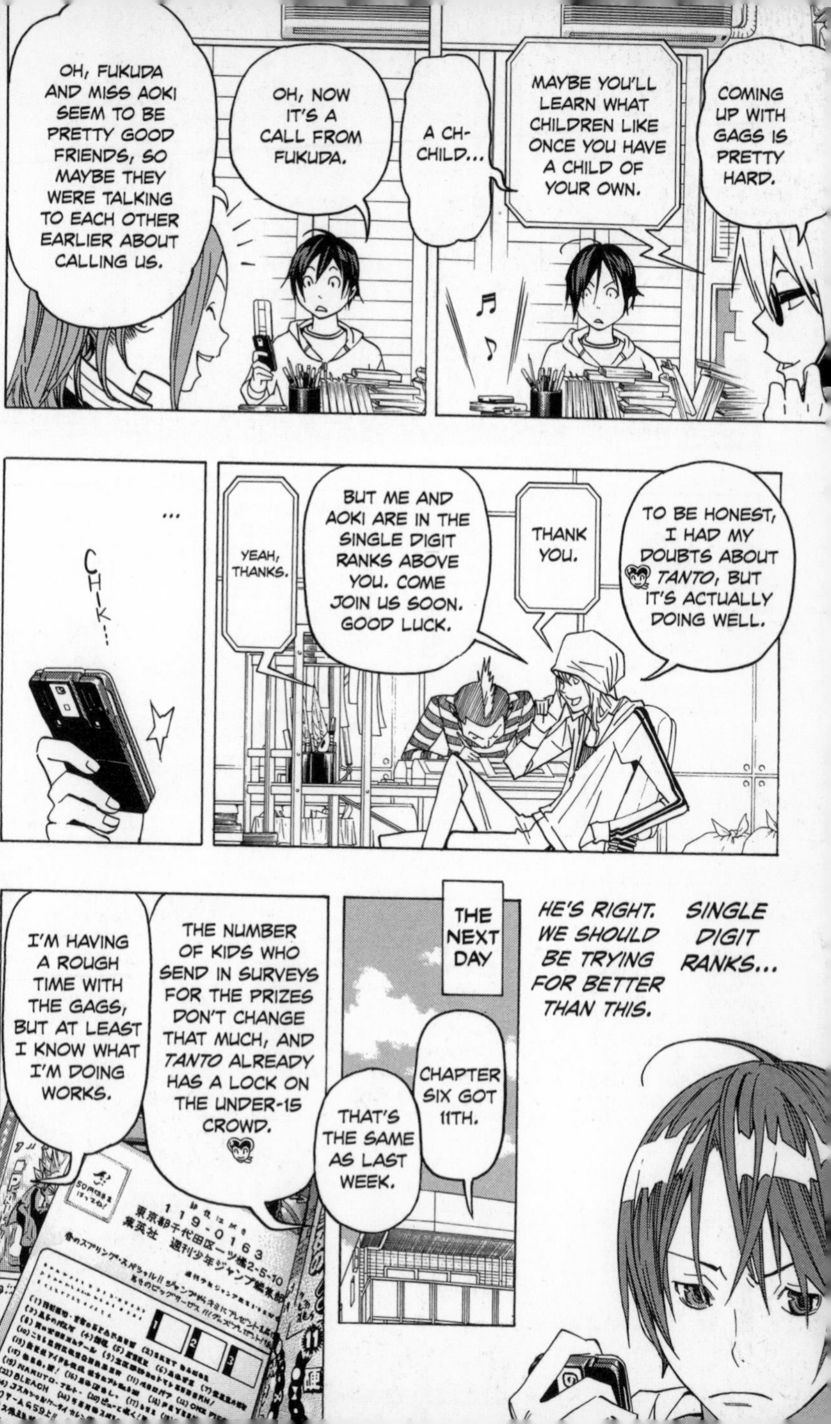
COMING UP WITH GAGS IS PRETTY HARD.
MAYBE YOU'LL LEARN WHAT CHILDREN LIKE ONCE YOU HAVE A CHILD OF YOUR OWN.
A CH- CHILD...
OH, NOW IT'S A CALL FROM FUKUDA.
OH, FUKUDA AND MISS AOKI SEEM TO BE PRETTY GOOD FRIENDS, SO MAYBE THEY WERE TALKING TO EACH OTHER EARLIER ABOUT CALLING US.
TO BE HONEST, I HAD MY DOUBTS ABOUT *TANTO*, BUT IT'S ACTUALLY DOING WELL.
THANK YOU.
BUT ME AND AOKI ARE IN THE SINGLE DIGIT RANKS ABOVE YOU. COME JOIN US SOON. GOOD LUCK.
YEAH, THANKS.
...
CHIK...
SINGLE DIGIT RANKS...
HE'S RIGHT. WE SHOULD BE TRYING FOR BETTER THAN THIS.
THE NEXT DAY
CHAPTER SIX GOT 11TH.
THAT'S THE SAME AS LAST WEEK.
THE NUMBER OF KIDS WHO SEND IN SURVEYS FOR THE PRIZES DON'T CHANGE THAT MUCH, AND *TANTO* ALREADY HAS A LOCK ON THE UNDER-15 CROWD.
I'M HAVING A ROUGH TIME WITH THE GAGS, BUT AT LEAST I KNOW WHAT I'M DOING WORKS.
119-0163
東京都千代田区一ツ橋2-5-10
集英社 週刊少年ジャンプ編集部

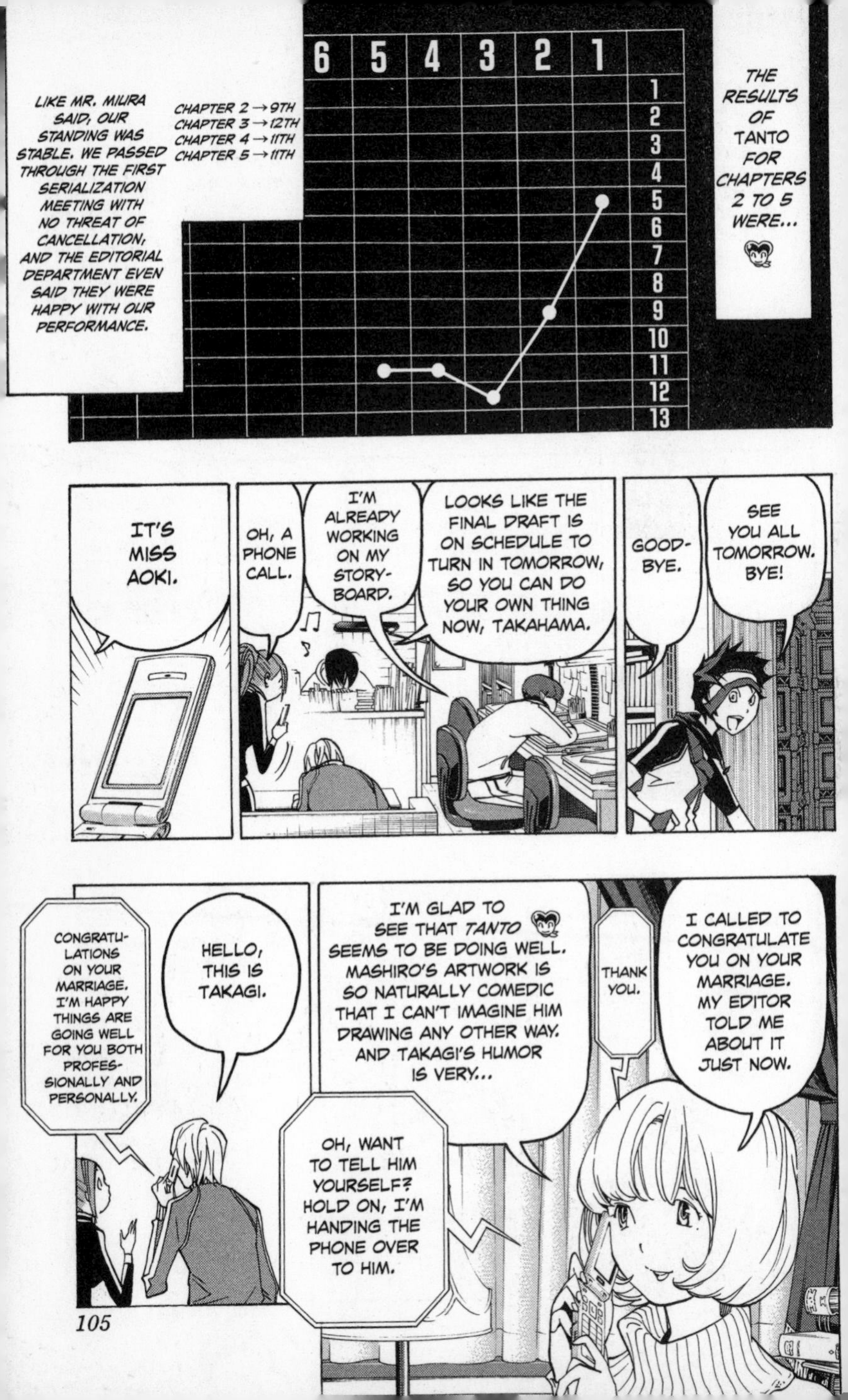
THE RESULTS OF TANTO FOR CHAPTERS 2 TO 5 WERE...
6 5 4 3 2 1
1 2 3 4 5 6 7 8 9 10 11 12 13
CHAPTER 2 → 9TH
CHAPTER 3 → 12TH
CHAPTER 4 → 11TH
CHAPTER 5 → 11TH
LIKE MR. MIURA SAID, OUR STANDING WAS STABLE. WE PASSED THROUGH THE FIRST SERIALIZATION MEETING WITH NO THREAT OF CANCELLATION, AND THE EDITORIAL DEPARTMENT EVEN SAID THEY WERE HAPPY WITH OUR PERFORMANCE.
SEE YOU ALL TOMORROW. BYE!
GOOD-BYE.
LOOKS LIKE THE FINAL DRAFT IS ON SCHEDULE TO TURN IN TOMORROW, SO YOU CAN DO YOUR OWN THING NOW, TAKAHAMA.
I'M ALREADY WORKING ON MY STORYBOARD.
OH, A PHONE CALL.
IT'S MISS AOKI.
I CALLED TO CONGRATULATE YOU ON YOUR MARRIAGE. MY EDITOR TOLD ME ABOUT IT JUST NOW.
THANK YOU.
I'M GLAD TO SEE THAT *TANTO* SEEMS TO BE DOING WELL. MASHIRO'S ARTWORK IS SO NATURALLY COMEDIC THAT I CAN'T IMAGINE HIM DRAWING ANY OTHER WAY. AND TAKAGI'S HUMOR IS VERY...
OH, WANT TO TELL HIM YOURSELF? HOLD ON, I'M HANDING THE PHONE OVER TO HIM.
HELLO, THIS IS TAKAGI.
CONGRATULATIONS ON YOUR MARRIAGE. I'M HAPPY THINGS ARE GOING WELL FOR YOU BOTH PROFESSIONALLY AND PERSONALLY.

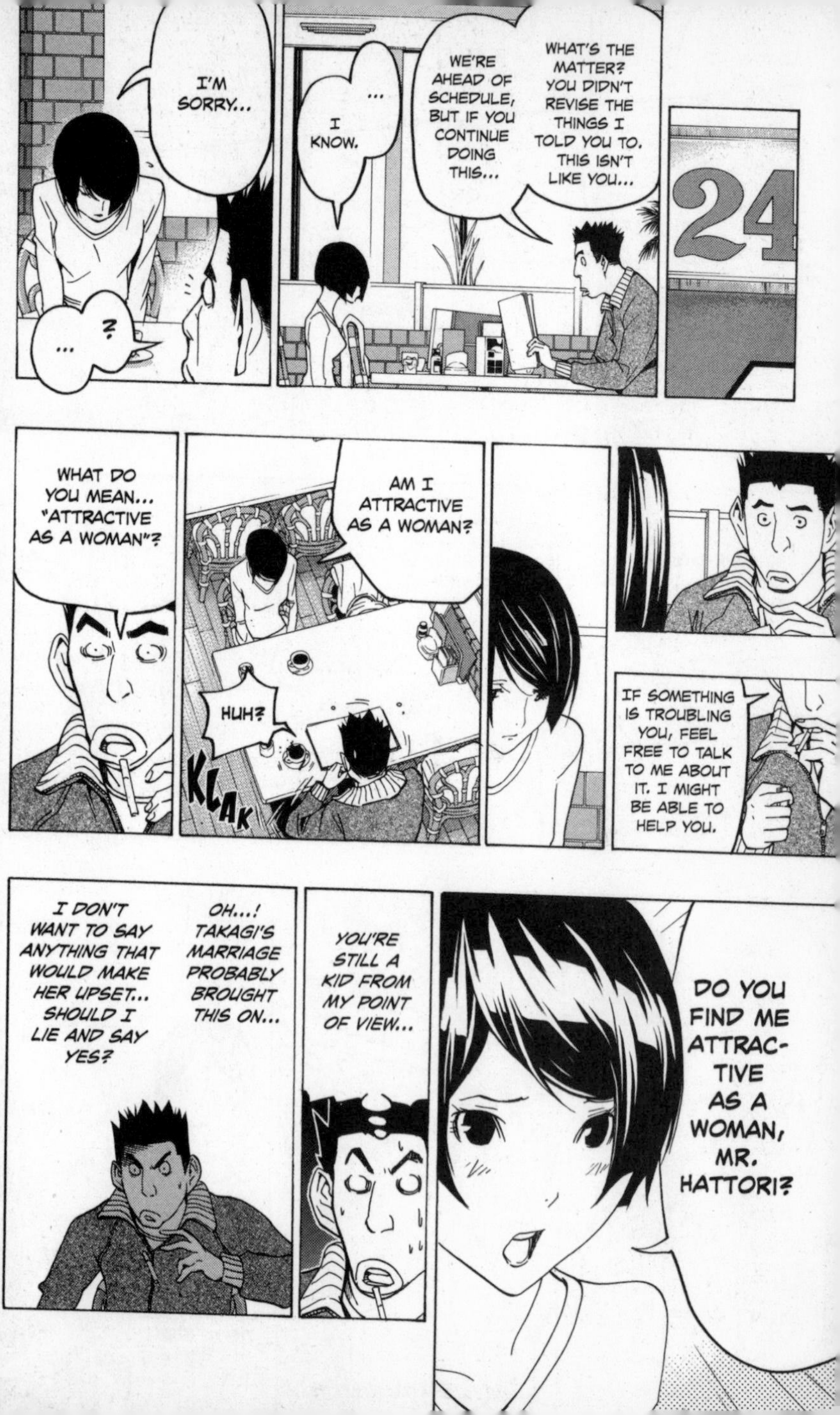
24
WHAT'S THE MATTER? YOU DIDN'T REVISE THE THINGS I TOLD YOU TO. THIS ISN'T LIKE YOU...
WE'RE AHEAD OF SCHEDULE, BUT IF YOU CONTINUE DOING THIS...
...
I KNOW.
I'M SORRY...
...?
IF SOMETHING IS TROUBLING YOU, FEEL FREE TO TALK TO ME ABOUT IT. I MIGHT BE ABLE TO HELP YOU.
AM I ATTRACTIVE AS A WOMAN?
HUH?
KLAK
WHAT DO YOU MEAN... "ATTRACTIVE AS A WOMAN"?
DO YOU FIND ME ATTRAC-TIVE AS A WOMAN, MR. HATTORI?
YOU'RE STILL A KID FROM MY POINT OF VIEW...
OH...! TAKAGI'S MARRIAGE PROBABLY BROUGHT THIS ON...
I DON'T WANT TO SAY ANYTHING THAT WOULD MAKE HER UPSET... SHOULD I LIE AND SAY YES?

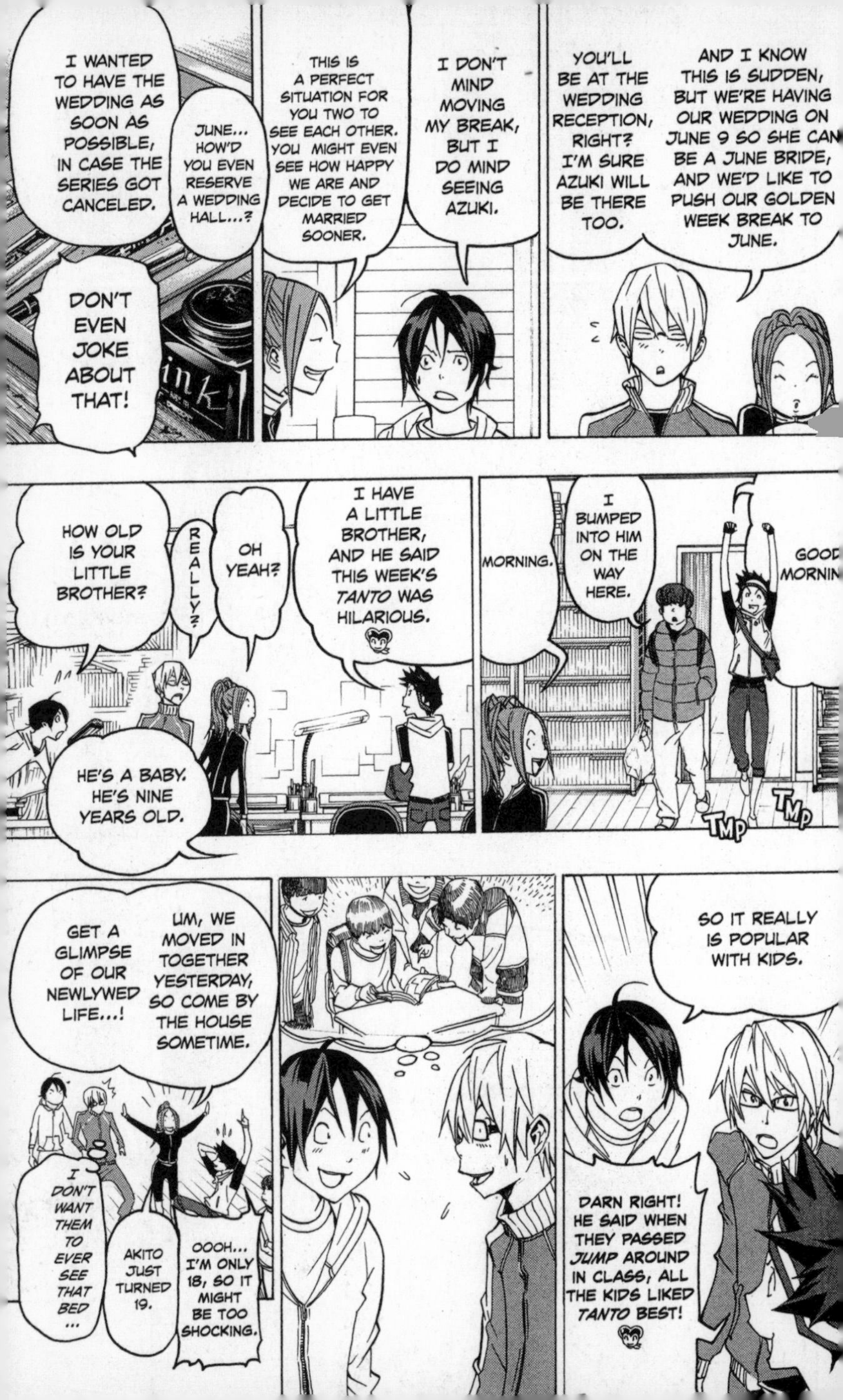
AND I KNOW THIS IS SUDDEN, BUT WE'RE HAVING OUR WEDDING ON JUNE 9 SO SHE CAN BE A JUNE BRIDE, AND WE'D LIKE TO PUSH OUR GOLDEN WEEK BREAK TO JUNE.
YOU'LL BE AT THE WEDDING RECEPTION, RIGHT? I'M SURE AZUKI WILL BE THERE TOO.
I DON'T MIND MOVING MY BREAK, BUT I DO MIND SEEING AZUKI.
THIS IS A PERFECT SITUATION FOR YOU TWO TO SEE EACH OTHER. YOU MIGHT EVEN SEE HOW HAPPY WE ARE AND DECIDE TO GET MARRIED SOONER.
JUNE... HOW'D YOU EVEN RESERVE A WEDDING HALL...?
I WANTED TO HAVE THE WEDDING AS SOON AS POSSIBLE, IN CASE THE SERIES GOT CANCELED.
DON'T EVEN JOKE ABOUT THAT!
GOOD MORNIN
TMP
TMP
I BUMPED INTO HIM ON THE WAY HERE.
MORNING.
I HAVE A LITTLE BROTHER, AND HE SAID THIS WEEK'S *TANTO* WAS HILARIOUS.
OH YEAH?
REALLY?
HOW OLD IS YOUR LITTLE BROTHER?
HE'S A BABY. HE'S NINE YEARS OLD.
SO IT REALLY IS POPULAR WITH KIDS.
DARN RIGHT! HE SAID WHEN THEY PASSED *JUMP* AROUND IN CLASS, ALL THE KIDS LIKED *TANTO* BEST!
UM, WE MOVED IN TOGETHER YESTERDAY, SO COME BY THE HOUSE SOMETIME.
GET A GLIMPSE OF OUR NEWLYWED LIFE...!
OOOH... I'M ONLY 18, SO IT MIGHT BE TOO SHOCKING.
AKITO JUST TURNED 19.
I DON'T WANT THEM TO EVER SEE THAT BED...

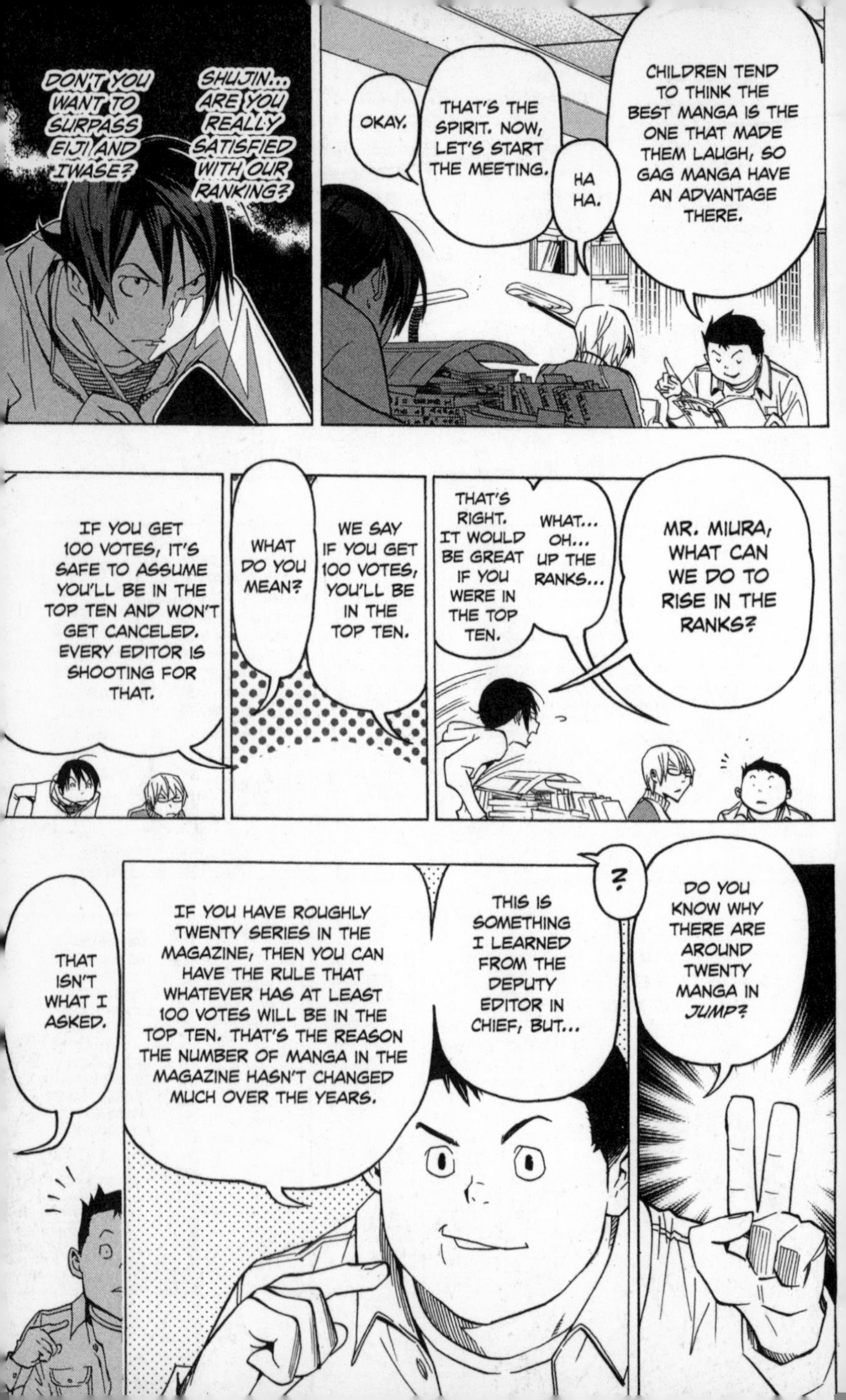
CHILDREN TEND TO THINK THE BEST MANGA IS THE ONE THAT MADE THEM LAUGH, SO GAG MANGA HAVE AN ADVANTAGE THERE.
HA HA.
THAT'S THE SPIRIT. NOW, LET'S START THE MEETING.
OKAY.
SHUJIN... ARE YOU REALLY SATISFIED WITH OUR RANKING?
DON'T YOU WANT TO SURPASS EIJI AND IWASE?
MR. MIURA, WHAT CAN WE DO TO RISE IN THE RANKS?
WHAT... OH... UP THE RANKS...
THAT'S RIGHT. IT WOULD BE GREAT IF YOU WERE IN THE TOP TEN.
WE SAY IF YOU GET 100 VOTES, YOU'LL BE IN THE TOP TEN.
WHAT DO YOU MEAN?
IF YOU GET 100 VOTES, IT'S SAFE TO ASSUME YOU'LL BE IN THE TOP TEN AND WON'T GET CANCELED. EVERY EDITOR IS SHOOTING FOR THAT.
DO YOU KNOW WHY THERE ARE AROUND TWENTY MANGA IN *JUMP*?
?
THIS IS SOMETHING I LEARNED FROM THE DEPUTY EDITOR IN CHIEF, BUT...
IF YOU HAVE ROUGHLY TWENTY SERIES IN THE MAGAZINE, THEN YOU CAN HAVE THE RULE THAT WHATEVER HAS AT LEAST 100 VOTES WILL BE IN THE TOP TEN. THAT'S THE REASON THE NUMBER OF MANGA IN THE MAGAZINE HASN'T CHANGED MUCH OVER THE YEARS.
THAT ISN'T WHAT I ASKED.

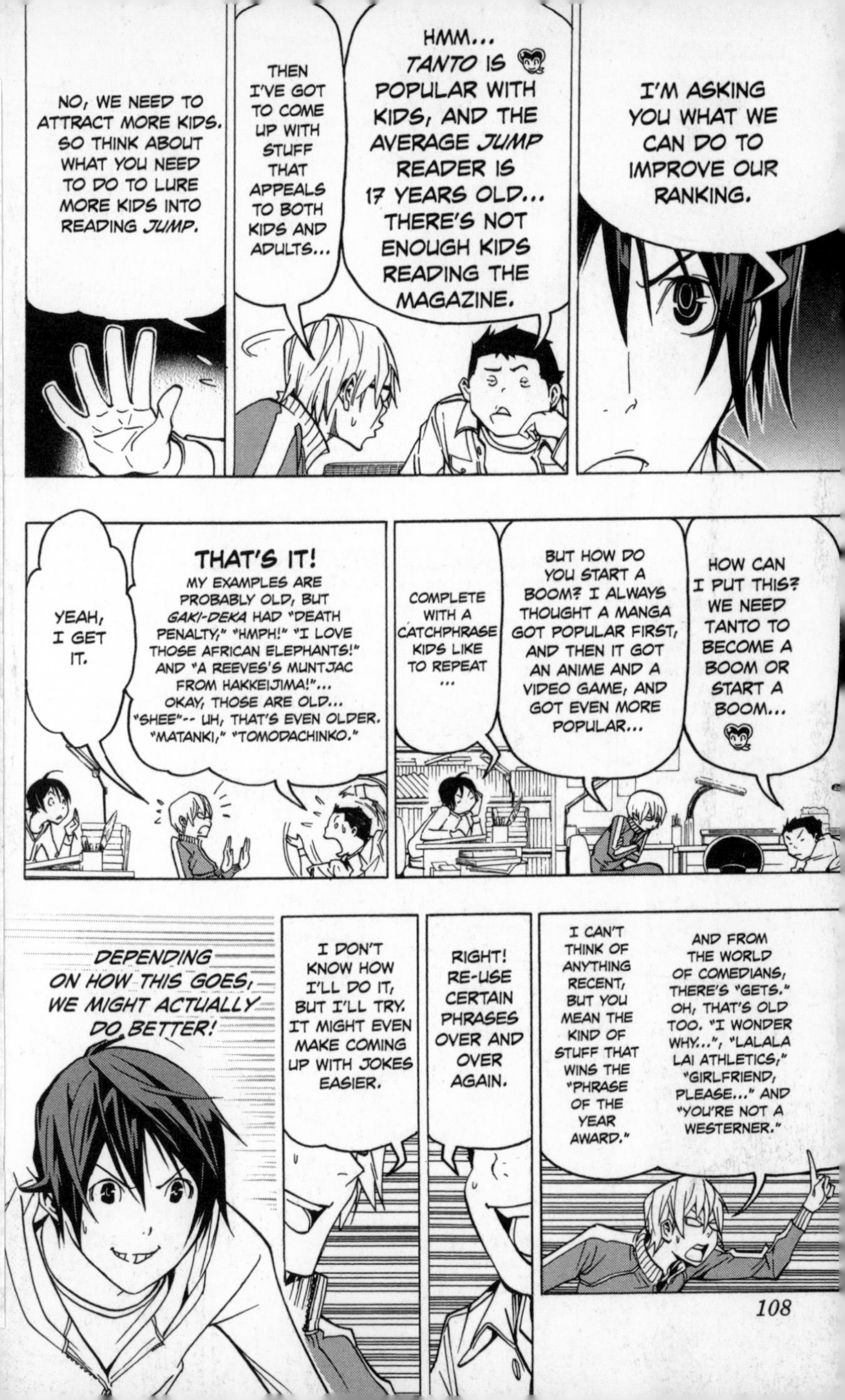
I'M ASKING YOU WHAT WE CAN DO TO IMPROVE OUR RANKING.
HMM... *TANTO* IS POPULAR WITH KIDS, AND THE AVERAGE *JUMP* READER IS 17 YEARS OLD... THERE'S NOT ENOUGH KIDS READING THE MAGAZINE.
THEN I'VE GOT TO COME UP WITH STUFF THAT APPEALS TO BOTH KIDS AND ADULTS...
NO, WE NEED TO ATTRACT MORE KIDS. SO THINK ABOUT WHAT YOU NEED TO DO TO LURE MORE KIDS INTO READING *JUMP*.
HOW CAN I PUT THIS? WE NEED TANTO TO BECOME A BOOM OR START A BOOM...
BUT HOW DO YOU START A BOOM? I ALWAYS THOUGHT A MANGA GOT POPULAR FIRST, AND THEN IT GOT AN ANIME AND A VIDEO GAME, AND GOT EVEN MORE POPULAR...
COMPLETE WITH A CATCHPHRASE KIDS LIKE TO REPEAT ...
THAT'S IT! MY EXAMPLES ARE PROBABLY OLD, BUT *GAKI-DEKA* HAD "DEATH PENALTY," "HMPH!" "I LOVE THOSE AFRICAN ELEPHANTS!" AND "A REEVES'S MUNTJAC FROM HAKKEIJIMA!"... OKAY, THOSE ARE OLD... "SHEE"-- UH, THAT'S EVEN OLDER. "MATANKI," "TOMODACHINKO."
YEAH, I GET IT.
AND FROM THE WORLD OF COMEDIANS, THERE'S "GETS." OH, THAT'S OLD TOO. "I WONDER WHY...", "LALALA LAI ATHLETICS," "GIRLFRIEND, PLEASE..." AND "YOU'RE NOT A WESTERNER."
I CAN'T THINK OF ANYTHING RECENT, BUT YOU MEAN THE KIND OF STUFF THAT WINS THE "PHRASE OF THE YEAR AWARD."
RIGHT! RE-USE CERTAIN PHRASES OVER AND OVER AGAIN.
I DON'T KNOW HOW I'LL DO IT, BUT I'LL TRY. IT MIGHT EVEN MAKE COMING UP WITH JOKES EASIER.
DEPENDING ON HOW THIS GOES, WE MIGHT ACTUALLY DO BETTER!

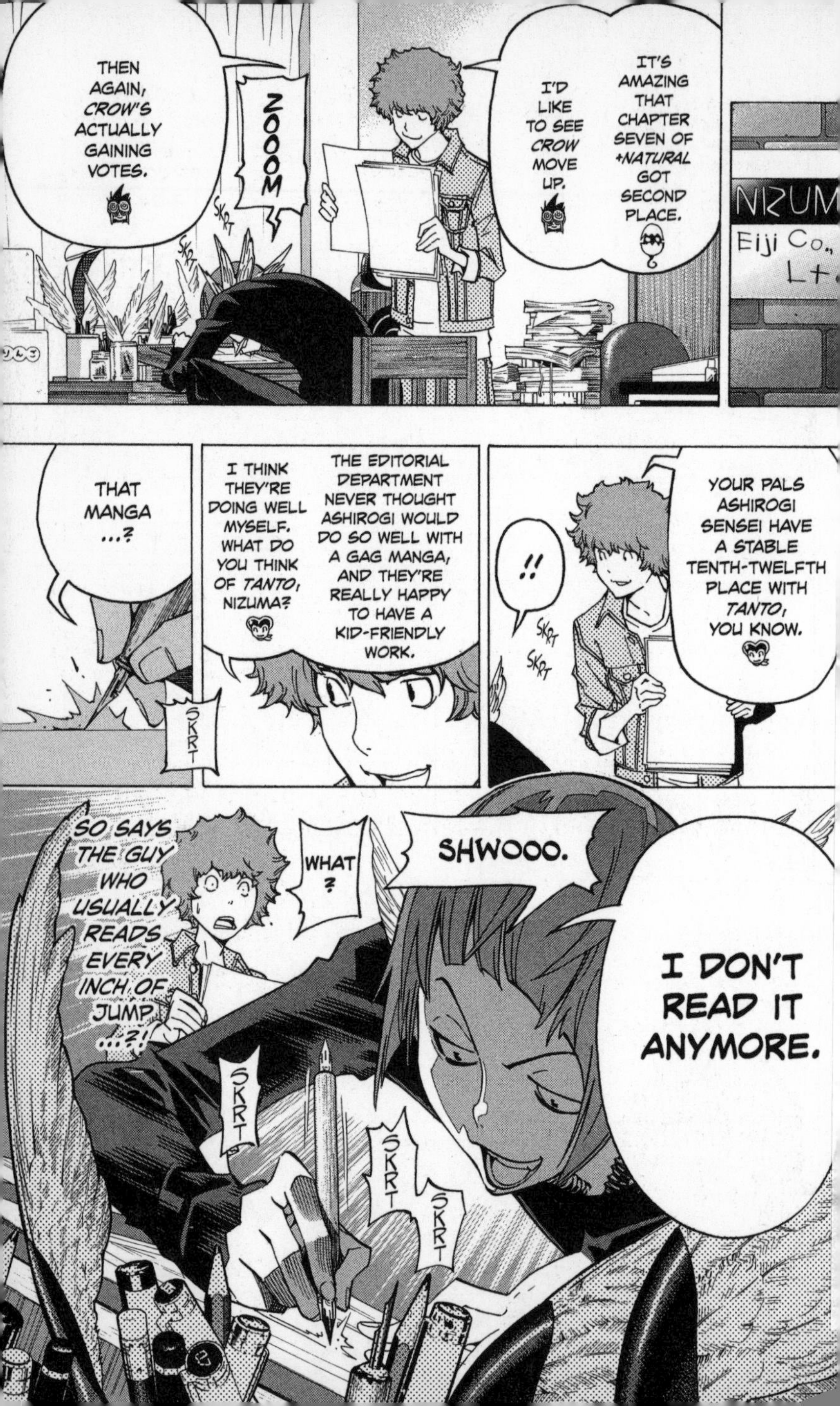
NIZUM
Eiji Co., Lt
IT'S AMAZING THAT CHAPTER SEVEN OF +NATURAL GOT SECOND PLACE.
I'D LIKE TO SEE CROW MOVE UP.
ZOOOOM
SKRT
SKRT
THEN AGAIN, CROW'S ACTUALLY GAINING VOTES.
YOUR PALS ASHIROGI SENSEI HAVE A STABLE TENTH-TWELFTH PLACE WITH TANTO, YOU KNOW.
!!
SKRT
SKRT
THE EDITORIAL DEPARTMENT NEVER THOUGHT ASHIROGI WOULD DO SO WELL WITH A GAG MANGA, AND THEY'RE REALLY HAPPY TO HAVE A KID-FRIENDLY WORK.
I THINK THEY'RE DOING WELL MYSELF. WHAT DO YOU THINK OF TANTO, NIZUMA?
SKRT
THAT MANGA ...?
I DON'T READ IT ANYMORE.
SHWOOO.
WHAT?
SO SAYS THE GUY WHO USUALLY READS EVERY INCH OF JUMP ...?!
SKRT
SKRT
SKRT

OHBA'S STORYBOARD

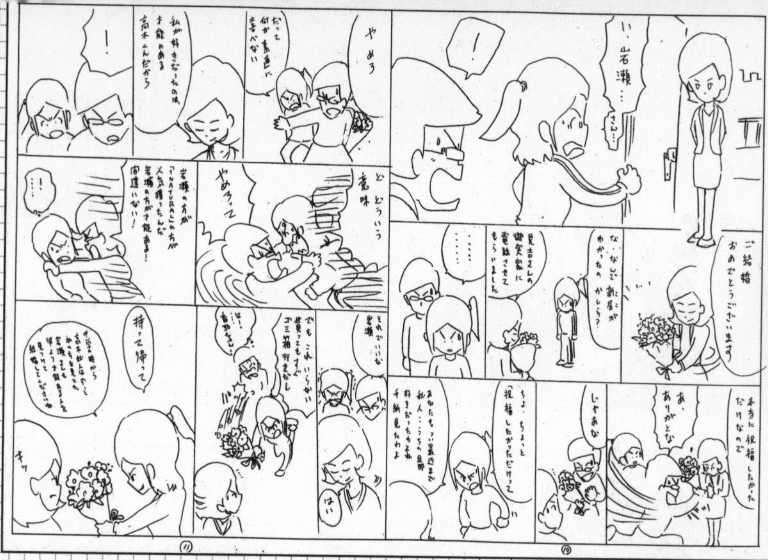

い、岩瀬…さん…
！
ご結婚おめでとうございます
…
な、なんで新居がわかったのかしら？
見吉さんの御実家に電話させてもらいました
……
本当に祝福したかっただけなので
あ、ありがとな
じゃあな
ちょ、ちょっと「祝福したかっただけ」って
あなたもつい最近まで秋人…うちの旦那が好きだったわよね 手紙見たわよ
やめろ
だって何か素直に喜べない
私が好きだったのは才能のある高木くんだから
！
どういう意味
やめろって
岩瀬の方が「+NATURAL」の方が人気獲ったんだ 岩瀬の方が才能ある！ 間違いない！
！……
それでいいな岩瀬
はい
でもこれいらない 貰ってもすぐゴミ箱行きだし
は…香耶ちゃん…
バッ
持って帰って
中学の時から高木くんはわたしを見てた 岩瀬さんも私より才能ある人を見つけて結婚してくださいね
キッ

OBATA'S STORYBOARD

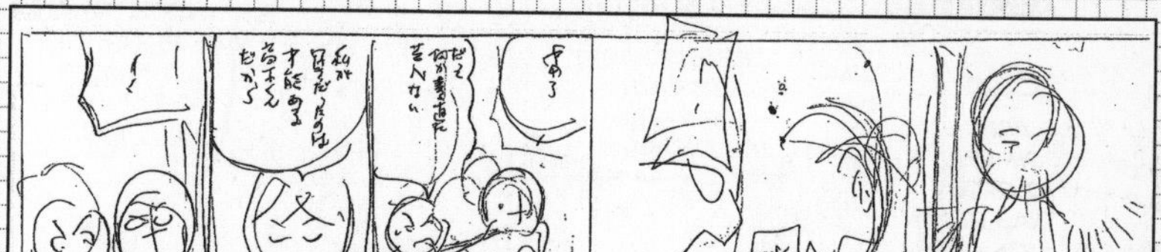

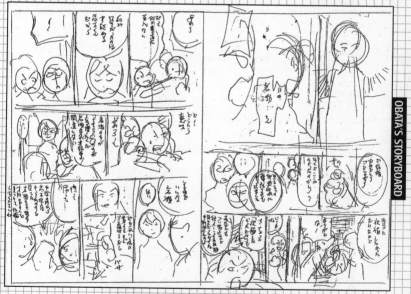

COMPLETE!

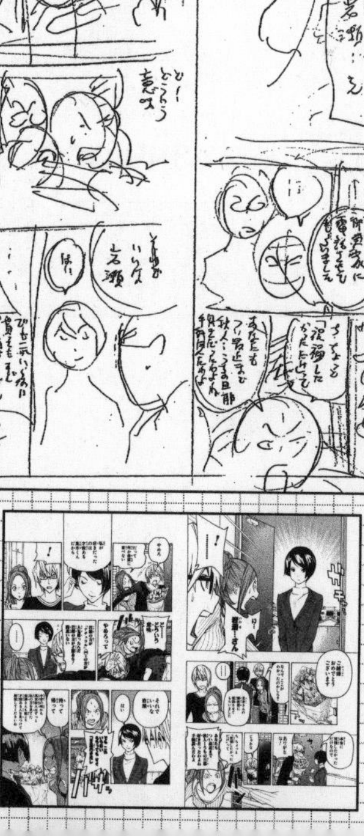

※CREATOR STORYBOARDS AND FINISHED PAGES IN JAPANESE

BAKUMAN。vol.9

"Until the Final Draft Is Complete"

Chapter 75, pp. 100-101

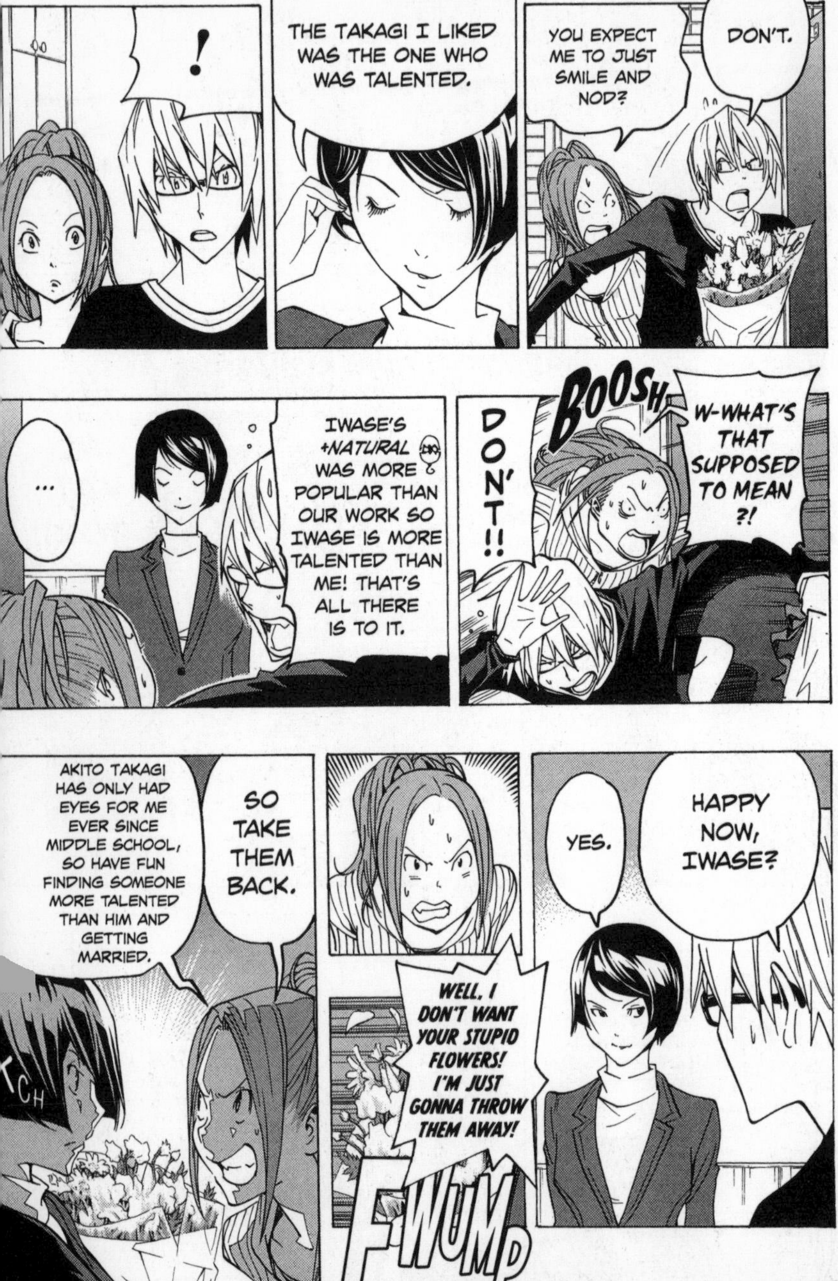
DON'T.
YOU EXPECT ME TO JUST SMILE AND NOD?
THE TAKAGI I LIKED WAS THE ONE WHO WAS TALENTED.
!
W-WHAT'S THAT SUPPOSED TO MEAN ?!
BOOSH
DON'T!!
IWASE'S +NATURAL WAS MORE POPULAR THAN OUR WORK SO IWASE IS MORE TALENTED THAN ME! THAT'S ALL THERE IS TO IT.
...
HAPPY NOW, IWASE?
YES.
WELL, I DON'T WANT YOUR STUPID FLOWERS! I'M JUST GONNA THROW THEM AWAY!
FWUMP
SO TAKE THEM BACK.
AKITO TAKAGI HAS ONLY HAD EYES FOR ME EVER SINCE MIDDLE SCHOOL, SO HAVE FUN FINDING SOMEONE MORE TALENTED THAN HIM AND GETTING MARRIED.
TCH

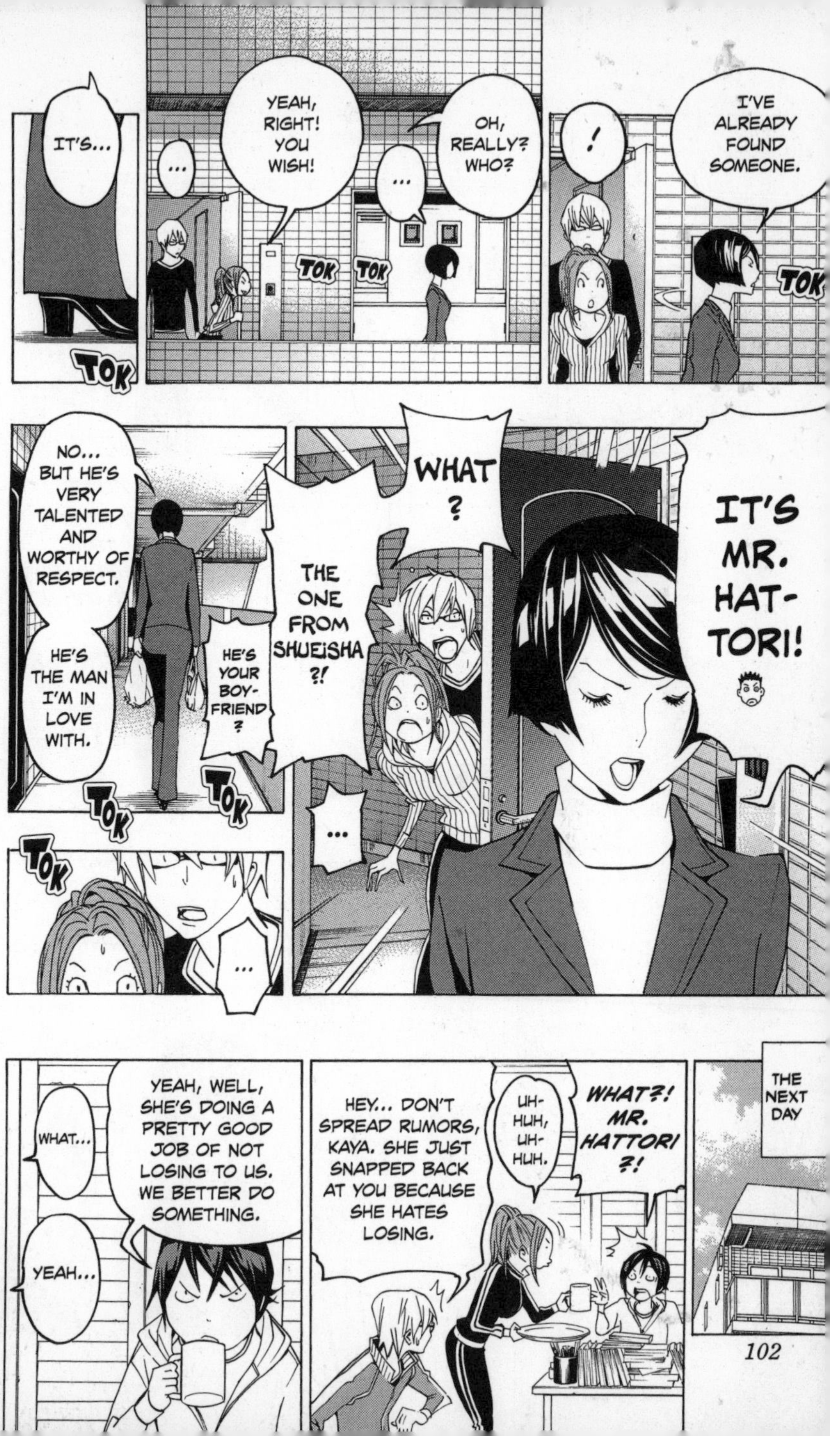
I'VE ALREADY FOUND SOMEONE.
!
TOK
OH, REALLY? WHO?
...
YEAH, RIGHT! YOU WISH!
...
TOK TOK
IT'S...
TOK
IT'S MR. HATTORI!
WHAT?
THE ONE FROM SHUEISHA?!
HE'S YOUR BOY-FRIEND?
...
NO... BUT HE'S VERY TALENTED AND WORTHY OF RESPECT.
HE'S THE MAN I'M IN LOVE WITH.
TOK
TOK
TOK
...
THE NEXT DAY
WHAT?! MR. HATTORI?!
UH-HUH, UH-HUH.
HEY... DON'T SPREAD RUMORS, KAYA. SHE JUST SNAPPED BACK AT YOU BECAUSE SHE HATES LOSING.
YEAH, WELL, SHE'S DOING A PRETTY GOOD JOB OF NOT LOSING TO US. WE BETTER DO SOMETHING.
WHAT...
YEAH...

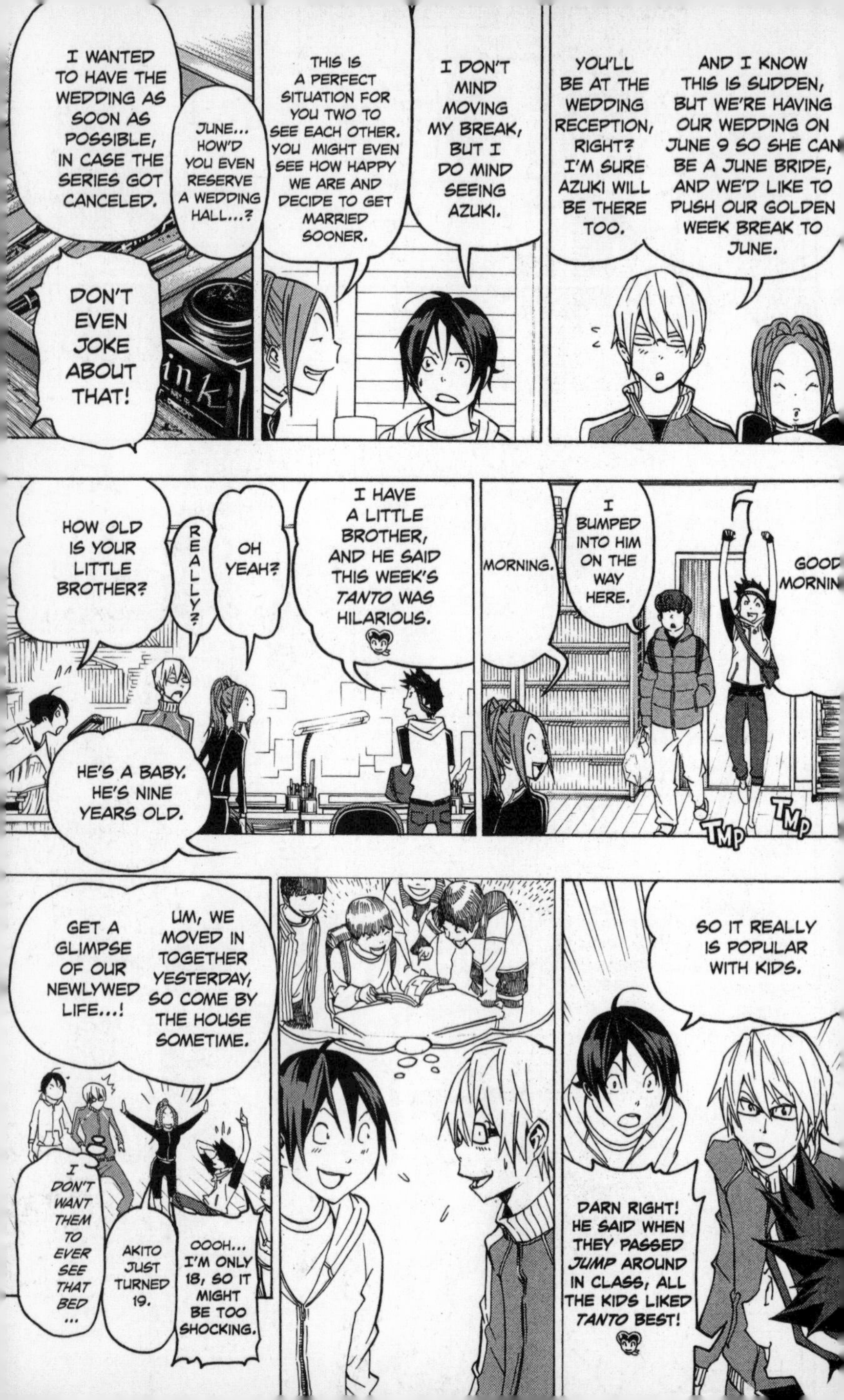
AND I KNOW THIS IS SUDDEN, BUT WE'RE HAVING OUR WEDDING ON JUNE 9 SO SHE CAN BE A JUNE BRIDE, AND WE'D LIKE TO PUSH OUR GOLDEN WEEK BREAK TO JUNE.
YOU'LL BE AT THE WEDDING RECEPTION, RIGHT? I'M SURE AZUKI WILL BE THERE TOO.
I DON'T MIND MOVING MY BREAK, BUT I DO MIND SEEING AZUKI.
THIS IS A PERFECT SITUATION FOR YOU TWO TO SEE EACH OTHER. YOU MIGHT EVEN SEE HOW HAPPY WE ARE AND DECIDE TO GET MARRIED SOONER.
JUNE... HOW'D YOU EVEN RESERVE A WEDDING HALL...?
I WANTED TO HAVE THE WEDDING AS SOON AS POSSIBLE, IN CASE THE SERIES GOT CANCELED.
DON'T EVEN JOKE ABOUT THAT!
GOOD MORNIN
TMP
TMP
I BUMPED INTO HIM ON THE WAY HERE.
MORNING.
I HAVE A LITTLE BROTHER, AND HE SAID THIS WEEK'S *TANTO* WAS HILARIOUS.
OH YEAH?
REALLY?
HOW OLD IS YOUR LITTLE BROTHER?
HE'S A BABY. HE'S NINE YEARS OLD.
SO IT REALLY IS POPULAR WITH KIDS.
DARN RIGHT! HE SAID WHEN THEY PASSED *JUMP* AROUND IN CLASS, ALL THE KIDS LIKED *TANTO* BEST!
UM, WE MOVED IN TOGETHER YESTERDAY, SO COME BY THE HOUSE SOMETIME.
GET A GLIMPSE OF OUR NEWLYWED LIFE...!
OOOH... I'M ONLY 18, SO IT MIGHT BE TOO SHOCKING.
AKITO JUST TURNED 19.
I DON'T WANT THEM TO EVER SEE THAT BED...

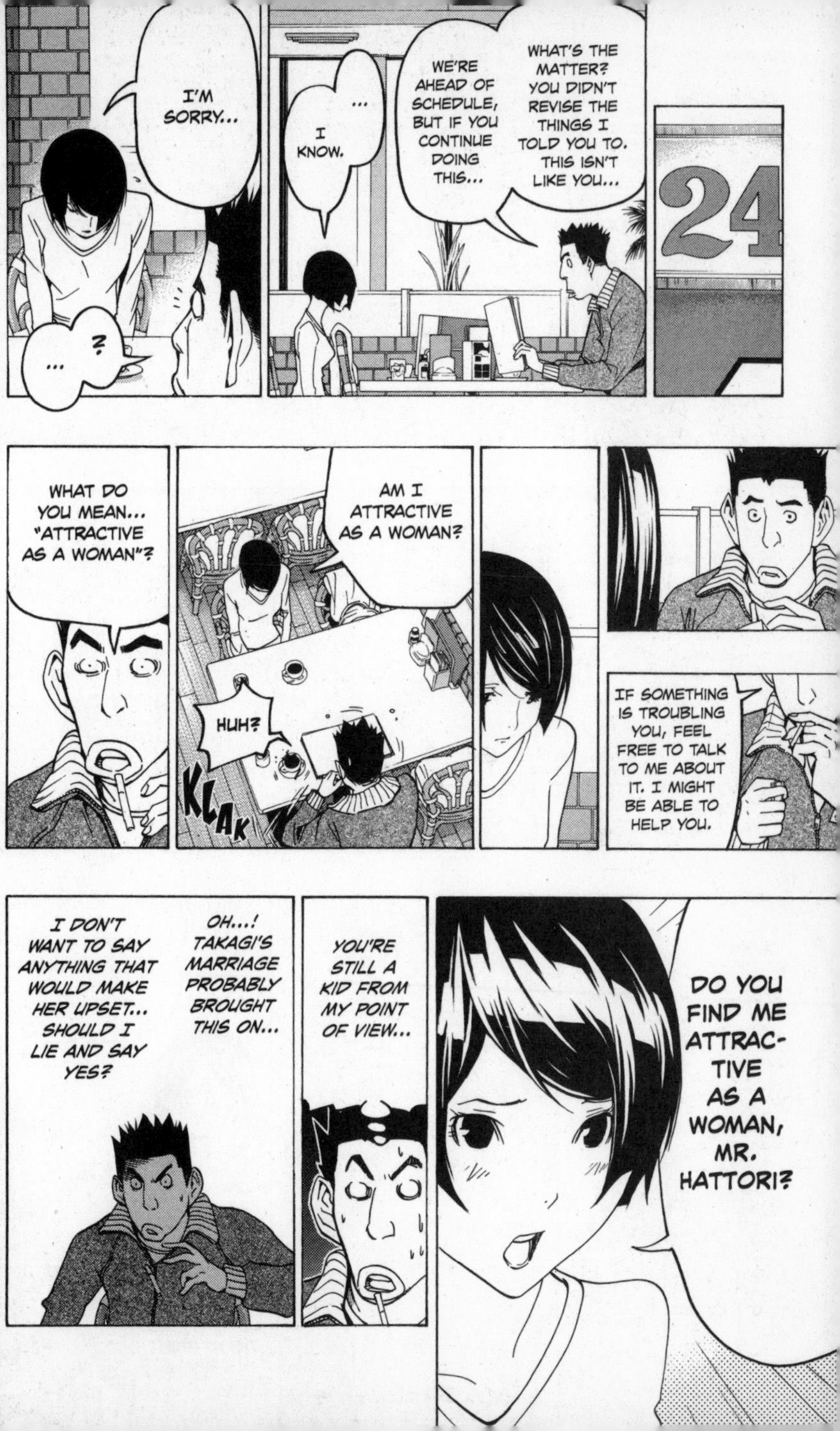
24
WHAT'S THE MATTER? YOU DIDN'T REVISE THE THINGS I TOLD YOU TO. THIS ISN'T LIKE YOU...
WE'RE AHEAD OF SCHEDULE, BUT IF YOU CONTINUE DOING THIS...
... I KNOW.
I'M SORRY...
? ...
IF SOMETHING IS TROUBLING YOU, FEEL FREE TO TALK TO ME ABOUT IT. I MIGHT BE ABLE TO HELP YOU.
AM I ATTRACTIVE AS A WOMAN?
HUH?
KLAK
WHAT DO YOU MEAN... "ATTRACTIVE AS A WOMAN"?
DO YOU FIND ME ATTRACTIVE AS A WOMAN, MR. HATTORI?
YOU'RE STILL A KID FROM MY POINT OF VIEW...
OH...! TAKAGI'S MARRIAGE PROBABLY BROUGHT THIS ON...
I DON'T WANT TO SAY ANYTHING THAT WOULD MAKE HER UPSET... SHOULD I LIE AND SAY YES?

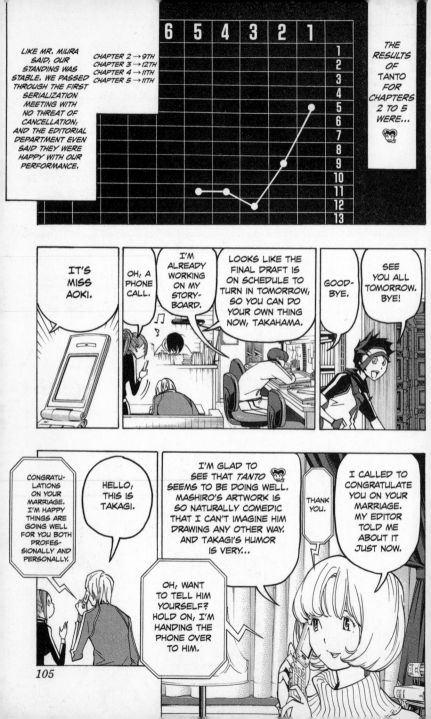

THE RESULTS OF *TANTO* FOR CHAPTERS 2 TO 5 WERE...

	6	5	4	3	2	1
1						
2						
3						
4						
5						
6						
7						
8						
9						
10						
11						
12						
13						

LIKE MR. MIURA SAID, OUR STANDING WAS STABLE. WE PASSED THROUGH THE FIRST SERIALIZATION MEETING WITH NO THREAT OF CANCELLATION, AND THE EDITORIAL DEPARTMENT EVEN SAID THEY WERE HAPPY WITH OUR PERFORMANCE.

CHAPTER 2 → 9TH
CHAPTER 3 → 12TH
CHAPTER 4 → 11TH
CHAPTER 5 → 11TH

IT'S MISS AOKI.

OH, A PHONE CALL.

I'M ALREADY WORKING ON MY STORYBOARD.

LOOKS LIKE THE FINAL DRAFT IS ON SCHEDULE TO TURN IN TOMORROW, SO YOU CAN DO YOUR OWN THING NOW, TAKAHAMA.

GOODBYE.

SEE YOU ALL TOMORROW. BYE!

CONGRATULATIONS ON YOUR MARRIAGE. I'M HAPPY THINGS ARE GOING WELL FOR YOU BOTH PROFESSIONALLY AND PERSONALLY.

HELLO, THIS IS TAKAGI.

I'M GLAD TO SEE THAT *TANTO* SEEMS TO BE DOING WELL. MASHIRO'S ARTWORK IS SO NATURALLY COMEDIC THAT I CAN'T IMAGINE HIM DRAWING ANY OTHER WAY. AND TAKAGI'S HUMOR IS VERY...

OH, WANT TO TELL HIM YOURSELF? HOLD ON, I'M HANDING THE PHONE OVER TO HIM.

THANK YOU.

I CALLED TO CONGRATULATE YOU ON YOUR MARRIAGE. MY EDITOR TOLD ME ABOUT IT JUST NOW.

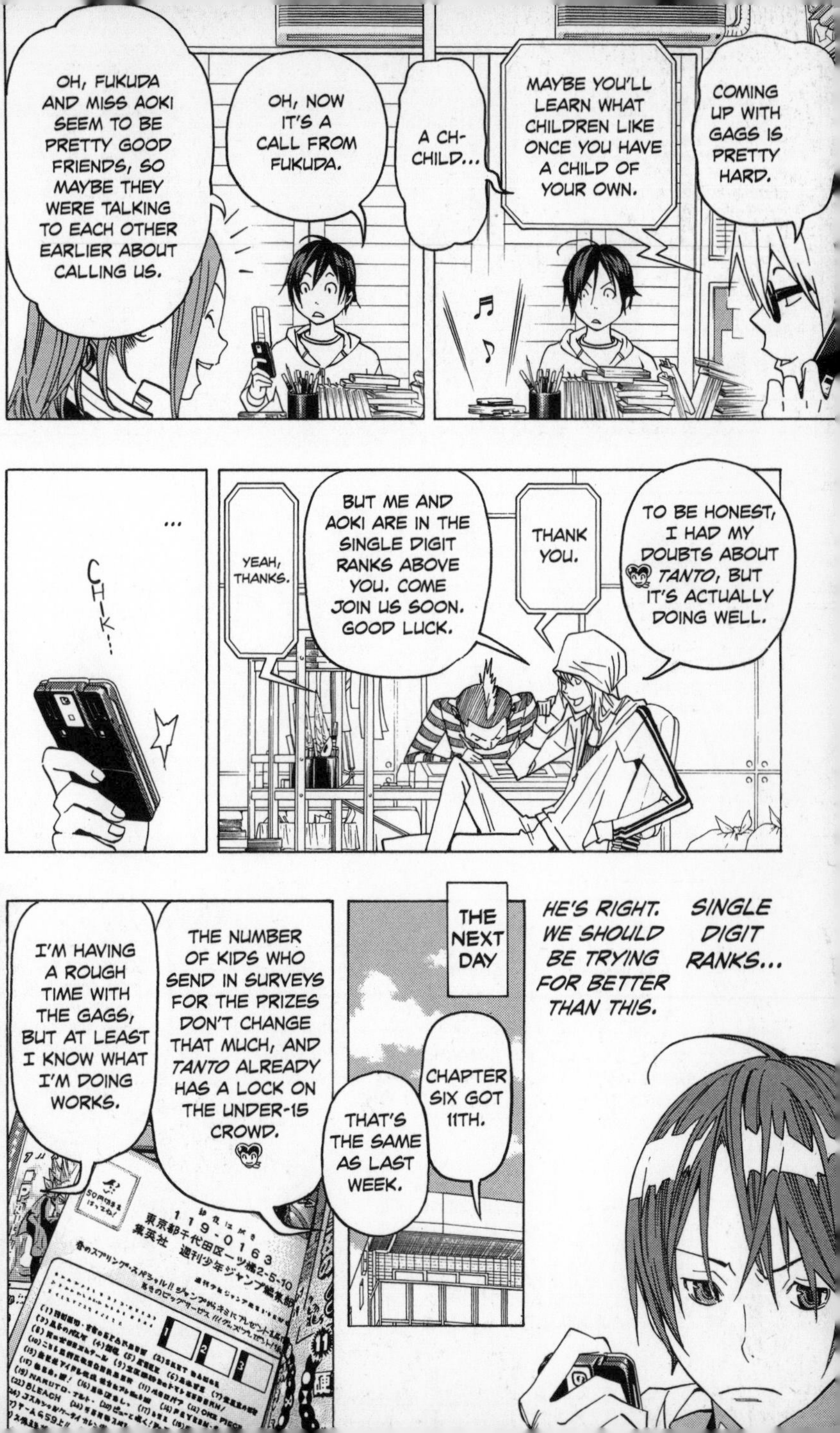
COMING UP WITH GAGS IS PRETTY HARD.
MAYBE YOU'LL LEARN WHAT CHILDREN LIKE ONCE YOU HAVE A CHILD OF YOUR OWN.
A CH-CHILD...
OH, NOW IT'S A CALL FROM FUKUDA.
OH, FUKUDA AND MISS AOKI SEEM TO BE PRETTY GOOD FRIENDS, SO MAYBE THEY WERE TALKING TO EACH OTHER EARLIER ABOUT CALLING US.
TO BE HONEST, I HAD MY DOUBTS ABOUT *TANTO*, BUT IT'S ACTUALLY DOING WELL.
THANK YOU.
BUT ME AND AOKI ARE IN THE SINGLE DIGIT RANKS ABOVE YOU. COME JOIN US SOON. GOOD LUCK.
YEAH, THANKS.
...
CHIK...
SINGLE DIGIT RANKS...
HE'S RIGHT. WE SHOULD BE TRYING FOR BETTER THAN THIS.
THE NEXT DAY
CHAPTER SIX GOT 11TH.
THAT'S THE SAME AS LAST WEEK.
THE NUMBER OF KIDS WHO SEND IN SURVEYS FOR THE PRIZES DON'T CHANGE THAT MUCH, AND *TANTO* ALREADY HAS A LOCK ON THE UNDER-15 CROWD.
I'M HAVING A ROUGH TIME WITH THE GAGS, BUT AT LEAST I KNOW WHAT I'M DOING WORKS.
119-0163
東京都千代田区一ツ橋2-5-10
集英社 週刊少年ジャンプ編集部

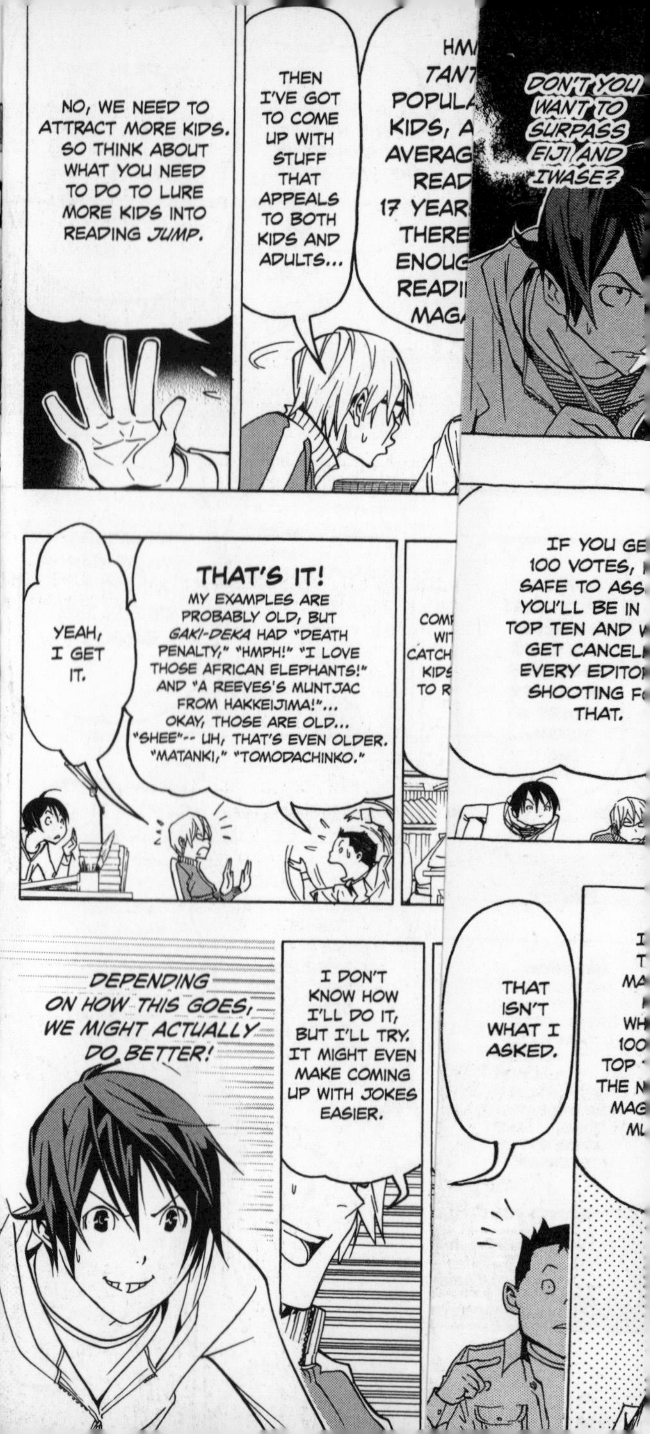
DON'T YOU WANT TO SURPASS EIJI AND IWASE?
THEN I'VE GOT TO COME UP WITH STUFF THAT APPEALS TO BOTH KIDS AND ADULTS...
NO, WE NEED TO ATTRACT MORE KIDS. SO THINK ABOUT WHAT YOU NEED TO DO TO LURE MORE KIDS INTO READING *JUMP*.
THAT'S IT! MY EXAMPLES ARE PROBABLY OLD, BUT *GAKI-DEKA* HAD "DEATH PENALTY," "HMPH!" "I LOVE THOSE AFRICAN ELEPHANTS!" AND "A REEVES'S MUNTJAC FROM HAKKEIJIMA!"... OKAY, THOSE ARE OLD... "SHEE"-- UH, THAT'S EVEN OLDER. "MATANKI," "TOMODACHINKO."
YEAH, I GET IT.
THAT ISN'T WHAT I ASKED.
I DON'T KNOW HOW I'LL DO IT, BUT I'LL TRY. IT MIGHT EVEN MAKE COMING UP WITH JOKES EASIER.
DEPENDING ON HOW THIS GOES, WE MIGHT ACTUALLY DO BETTER!

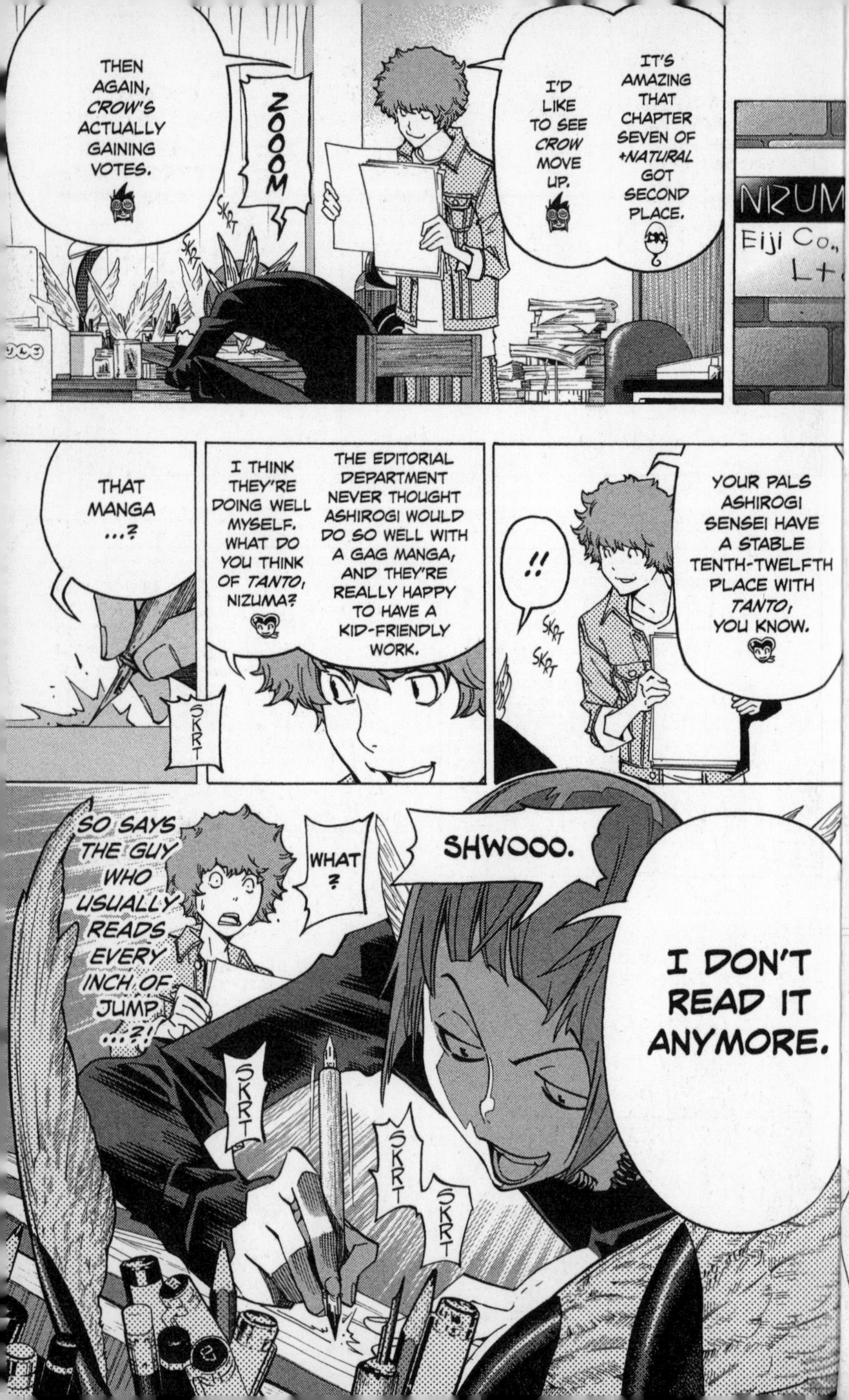
IT'S AMAZING THAT CHAPTER SEVEN OF *+NATURAL* GOT SECOND PLACE.
I'D LIKE TO SEE *CROW* MOVE UP.
ZOOOM
SKRT
SKRT
THEN AGAIN, *CROW'S* ACTUALLY GAINING VOTES.
YOUR PALS ASHIROGI SENSEI HAVE A STABLE TENTH-TWELFTH PLACE WITH *TANTO*, YOU KNOW.
!!
SKRT
SKRT
THE EDITORIAL DEPARTMENT NEVER THOUGHT ASHIROGI WOULD DO SO WELL WITH A GAG MANGA, AND THEY'RE REALLY HAPPY TO HAVE A KID-FRIENDLY WORK.
I THINK THEY'RE DOING WELL MYSELF. WHAT DO YOU THINK OF *TANTO*, NIZUMA?
THAT MANGA ...?
SKRT
SHWOOO.
I DON'T READ IT ANYMORE.
WHAT?
SO SAYS THE GUY WHO USUALLY READS EVERY INCH OF JUMP ...?!
SKRT
SKRT
SKRT

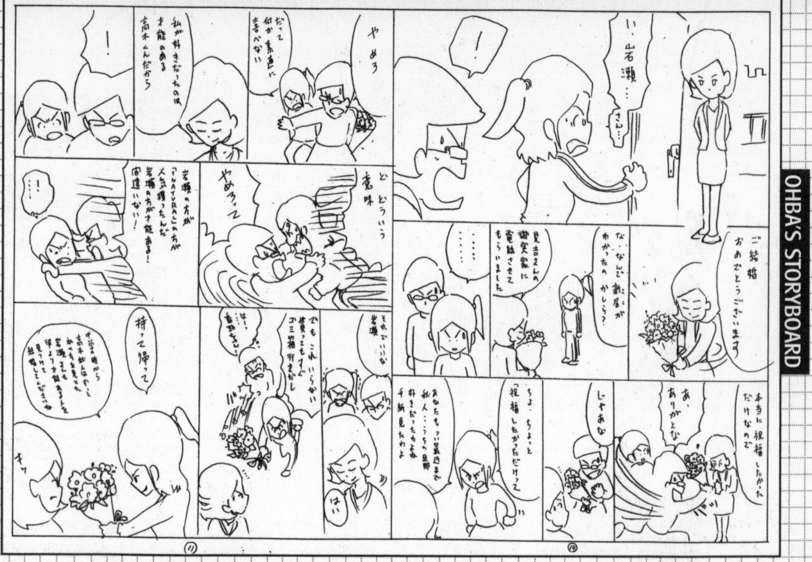

OHBA'S STORYBOARD

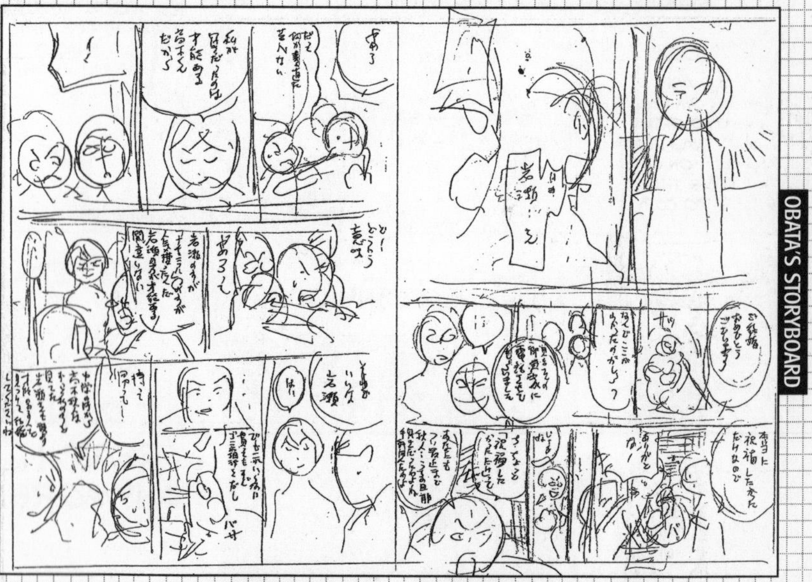

OBATA'S STORYBOARD

COMPLETE!

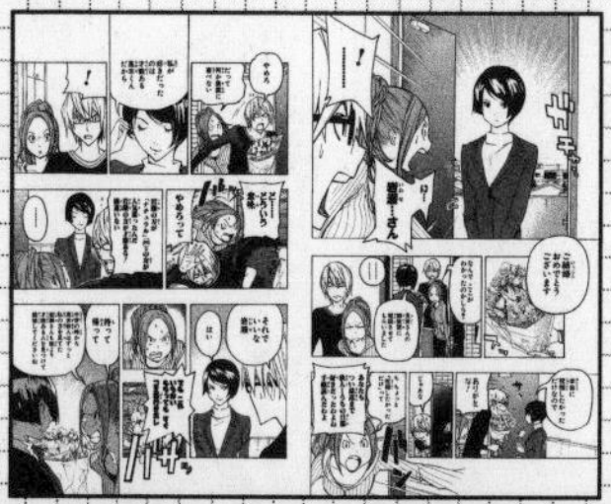

※CREATOR STORYBOARDS AND FINISHED PAGES IN JAPANESE

BAKUMAN。vol.9

"Until the Final Draft Is Complete"

Chapter 75, pp. 100-101

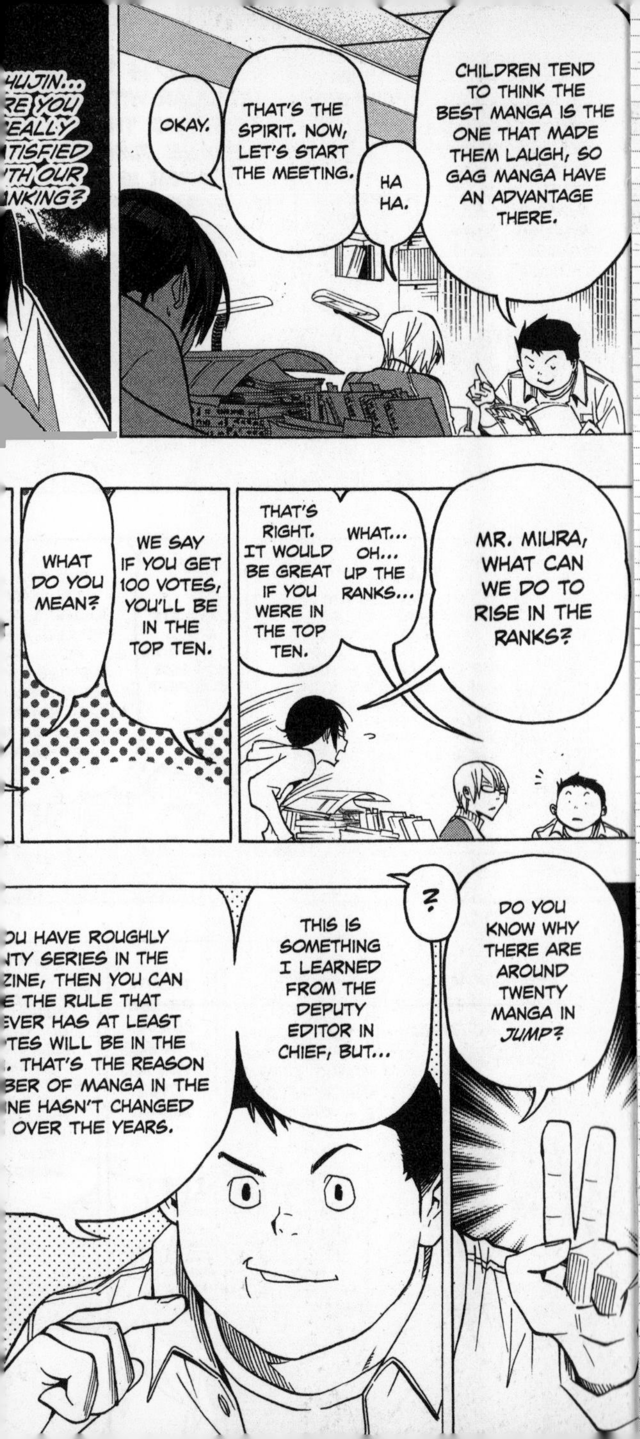
CHILDREN TEND TO THINK THE BEST MANGA IS THE ONE THAT MADE THEM LAUGH, SO GAG MANGA HAVE AN ADVANTAGE THERE.
HA HA.
THAT'S THE SPIRIT. NOW, LET'S START THE MEETING.
OKAY.
HUJIN... RE YOU EALLY TISFIED TH OUR NKING?
MR. MIURA, WHAT CAN WE DO TO RISE IN THE RANKS?
WHAT... OH... UP THE RANKS...
THAT'S RIGHT. IT WOULD BE GREAT IF YOU WERE IN THE TOP TEN.
WE SAY IF YOU GET 100 VOTES, YOU'LL BE IN THE TOP TEN.
WHAT DO YOU MEAN?
DO YOU KNOW WHY THERE ARE AROUND TWENTY MANGA IN *JUMP*?
?
THIS IS SOMETHING I LEARNED FROM THE DEPUTY EDITOR IN CHIEF, BUT...
OU HAVE ROUGHLY NTY SERIES IN THE ZINE, THEN YOU CAN E THE RULE THAT EVER HAS AT LEAST TES WILL BE IN THE . THAT'S THE REASON BER OF MANGA IN THE NE HASN'T CHANGED OVER THE YEARS.

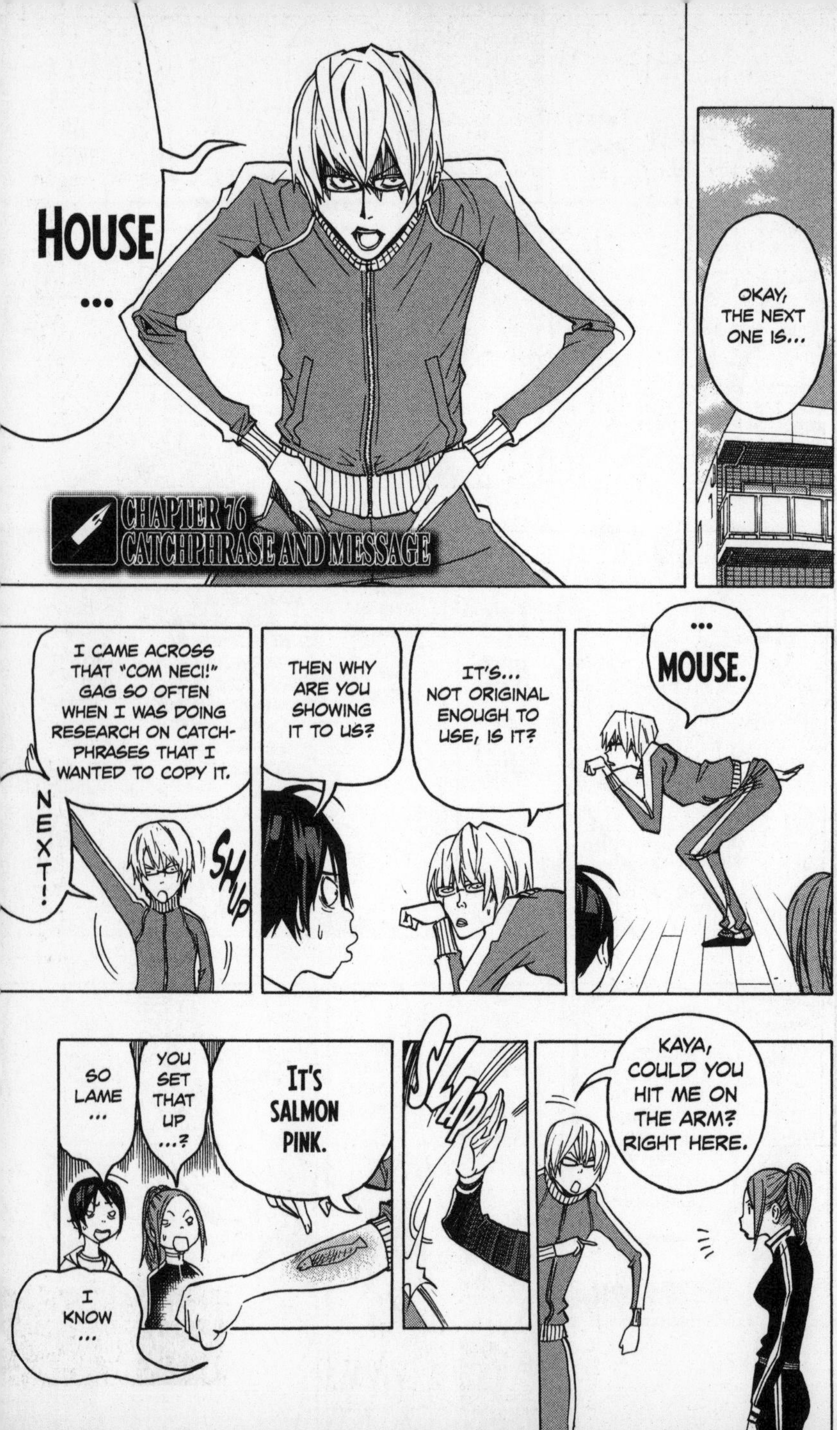
OKAY, THE NEXT ONE IS...
HOUSE ...
CHAPTER 76
CATCHPHRASE AND MESSAGE
... MOUSE.
IT'S... NOT ORIGINAL ENOUGH TO USE, IS IT?
THEN WHY ARE YOU SHOWING IT TO US?
I CAME ACROSS THAT "COM NECI!" GAG SO OFTEN WHEN I WAS DOING RESEARCH ON CATCH-PHRASES THAT I WANTED TO COPY IT.
SHUP
NEXT!
KAYA, COULD YOU HIT ME ON THE ARM? RIGHT HERE.
IT'S SALMON PINK.
YOU SET THAT UP ...?
SO LAME ...
I KNOW ...

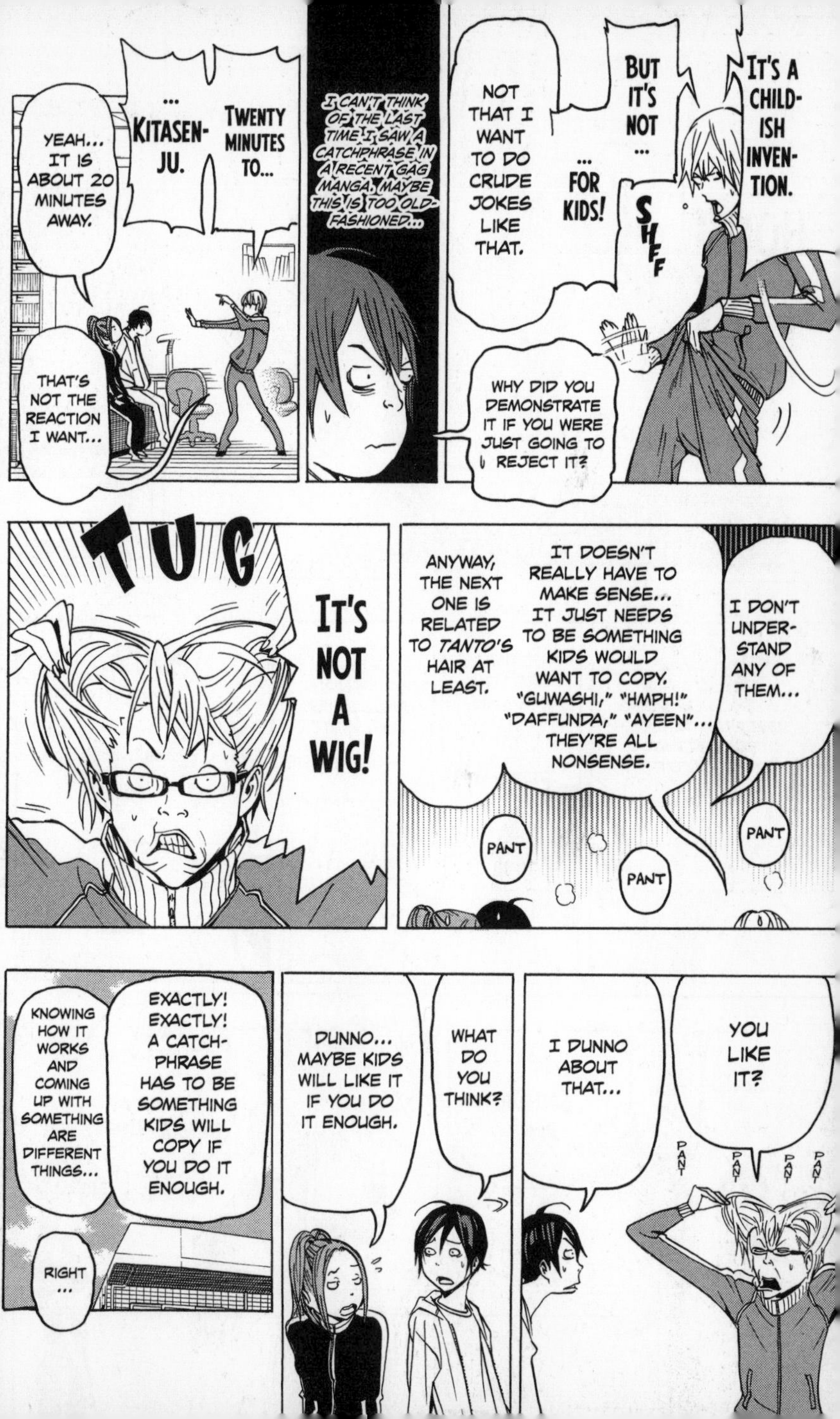
IT'S A CHILDISH INVENTION.
BUT IT'S NOT ... FOR KIDS!
SHFF
NOT THAT I WANT TO DO CRUDE JOKES LIKE THAT.
WHY DID YOU DEMONSTRATE IT IF YOU WERE JUST GOING TO REJECT IT?
I CAN'T THINK OF THE LAST TIME I SAW A CATCHPHRASE IN A RECENT GAG MANGA. MAYBE THIS IS TOO OLD-FASHIONED...
TWENTY MINUTES TO...
... KITASEN-JU.
YEAH... IT IS ABOUT 20 MINUTES AWAY.
THAT'S NOT THE REACTION I WANT...
I DON'T UNDERSTAND ANY OF THEM...
IT DOESN'T REALLY HAVE TO MAKE SENSE... IT JUST NEEDS TO BE SOMETHING KIDS WOULD WANT TO COPY. "GUWASHI," "HMPH!" "DAFFUNDA," "AYEEN"... THEY'RE ALL NONSENSE.
ANYWAY, THE NEXT ONE IS RELATED TO *TANTO*'S HAIR AT LEAST.
PANT
PANT
PANT
TUG
IT'S NOT A WIG!
YOU LIKE IT?
PANT PANT PANT PANT
I DUNNO ABOUT THAT...
WHAT DO YOU THINK?
DUNNO... MAYBE KIDS WILL LIKE IT IF YOU DO IT ENOUGH.
EXACTLY! EXACTLY! A CATCHPHRASE HAS TO BE SOMETHING KIDS WILL COPY IF YOU DO IT ENOUGH.
KNOWING HOW IT WORKS AND COMING UP WITH SOMETHING ARE DIFFERENT THINGS...
RIGHT...

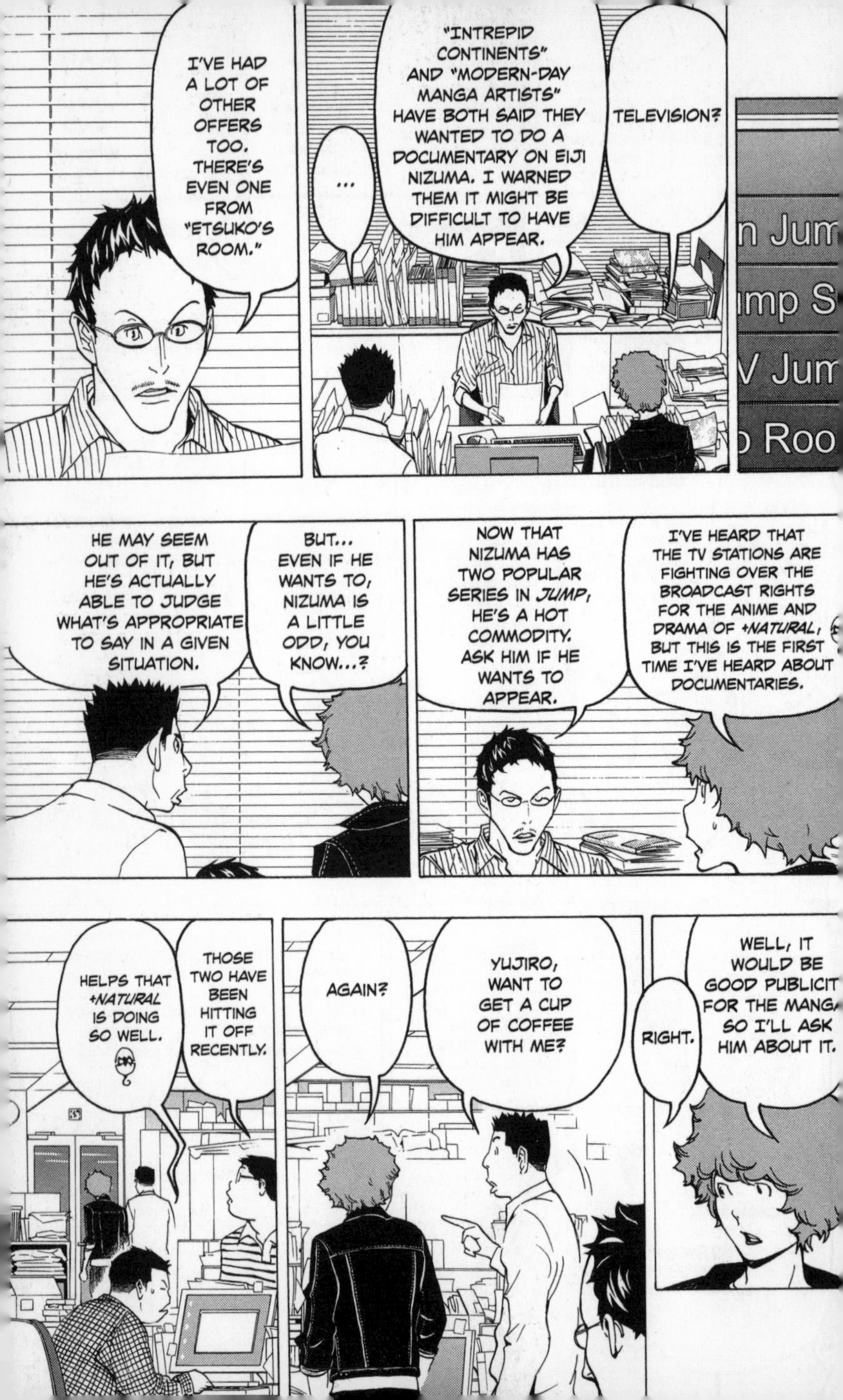
n Jum
mp S
V Jum
o Roo
TELEVISION?
"INTREPID CONTINENTS" AND "MODERN-DAY MANGA ARTISTS" HAVE BOTH SAID THEY WANTED TO DO A DOCUMENTARY ON EIJI NIZUMA. I WARNED THEM IT MIGHT BE DIFFICULT TO HAVE HIM APPEAR.
...
I'VE HAD A LOT OF OTHER OFFERS TOO. THERE'S EVEN ONE FROM "ETSUKO'S ROOM."
I'VE HEARD THAT THE TV STATIONS ARE FIGHTING OVER THE BROADCAST RIGHTS FOR THE ANIME AND DRAMA OF +NATURAL, BUT THIS IS THE FIRST TIME I'VE HEARD ABOUT DOCUMENTARIES.
NOW THAT NIZUMA HAS TWO POPULAR SERIES IN JUMP, HE'S A HOT COMMODITY. ASK HIM IF HE WANTS TO APPEAR.
BUT... EVEN IF HE WANTS TO, NIZUMA IS A LITTLE ODD, YOU KNOW...?
HE MAY SEEM OUT OF IT, BUT HE'S ACTUALLY ABLE TO JUDGE WHAT'S APPROPRIATE TO SAY IN A GIVEN SITUATION.
WELL, IT WOULD BE GOOD PUBLICIT FOR THE MANG SO I'LL ASK HIM ABOUT IT.
RIGHT.
YUJIRO, WANT TO GET A CUP OF COFFEE WITH ME?
AGAIN?
THOSE TWO HAVE BEEN HITTING IT OFF RECENTLY.
HELPS THAT +NATURAL IS DOING SO WELL.

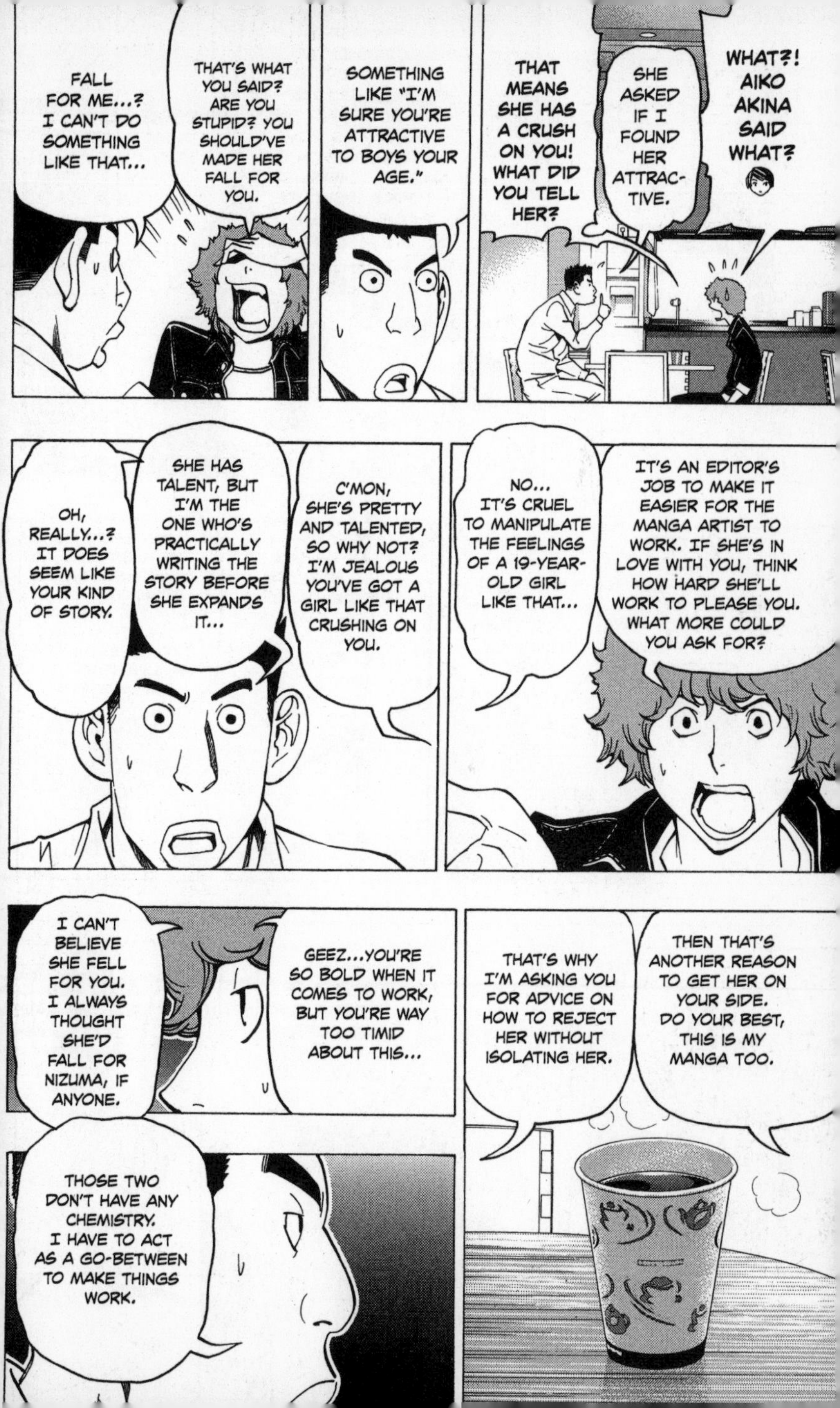
WHAT?! AIKO AKINA SAID WHAT?
SHE ASKED IF I FOUND HER ATTRACTIVE.
THAT MEANS SHE HAS A CRUSH ON YOU! WHAT DID YOU TELL HER?
SOMETHING LIKE "I'M SURE YOU'RE ATTRACTIVE TO BOYS YOUR AGE."
THAT'S WHAT YOU SAID? ARE YOU STUPID? YOU SHOULD'VE MADE HER FALL FOR YOU.
FALL FOR ME...? I CAN'T DO SOMETHING LIKE THAT...
IT'S AN EDITOR'S JOB TO MAKE IT EASIER FOR THE MANGA ARTIST TO WORK. IF SHE'S IN LOVE WITH YOU, THINK HOW HARD SHE'LL WORK TO PLEASE YOU. WHAT MORE COULD YOU ASK FOR?
NO... IT'S CRUEL TO MANIPULATE THE FEELINGS OF A 19-YEAR-OLD GIRL LIKE THAT...
C'MON, SHE'S PRETTY AND TALENTED, SO WHY NOT? I'M JEALOUS YOU'VE GOT A GIRL LIKE THAT CRUSHING ON YOU.
SHE HAS TALENT, BUT I'M THE ONE WHO'S PRACTICALLY WRITING THE STORY BEFORE SHE EXPANDS IT...
OH, REALLY...? IT DOES SEEM LIKE YOUR KIND OF STORY.
THEN THAT'S ANOTHER REASON TO GET HER ON YOUR SIDE. DO YOUR BEST, THIS IS MY MANGA TOO.
THAT'S WHY I'M ASKING YOU FOR ADVICE ON HOW TO REJECT HER WITHOUT ISOLATING HER.
GEEZ...YOU'RE SO BOLD WHEN IT COMES TO WORK, BUT YOU'RE WAY TOO TIMID ABOUT THIS...
I CAN'T BELIEVE SHE FELL FOR YOU. I ALWAYS THOUGHT SHE'D FALL FOR NIZUMA, IF ANYONE.
THOSE TWO DON'T HAVE ANY CHEMISTRY. I HAVE TO ACT AS A GO-BETWEEN TO MAKE THINGS WORK.

READ THIS WAY

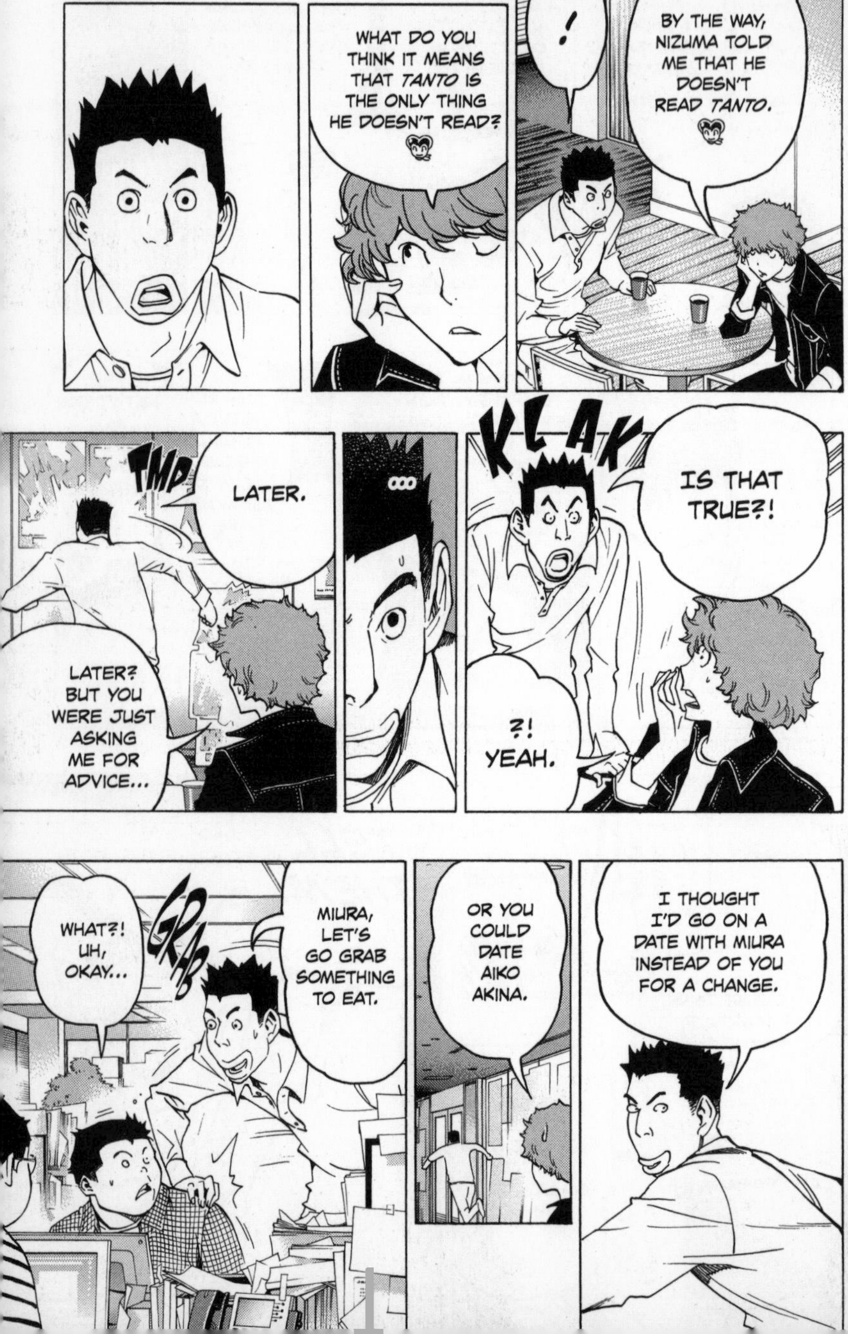

BY THE WAY, NIZUMA TOLD ME THAT HE DOESN'T READ *TANTO*.
!
WHAT DO YOU THINK IT MEANS THAT *TANTO* IS THE ONLY THING HE DOESN'T READ?
KLAK
IS THAT TRUE?!
?! YEAH.
...
LATER.
TMP
LATER? BUT YOU WERE JUST ASKING ME FOR ADVICE...
I THOUGHT I'D GO ON A DATE WITH MIURA INSTEAD OF YOU FOR A CHANGE.
OR YOU COULD DATE AIKO AKINA.
MIURA, LET'S GO GRAB SOMETHING TO EAT.
GRAB
WHAT?! UH, OKAY...

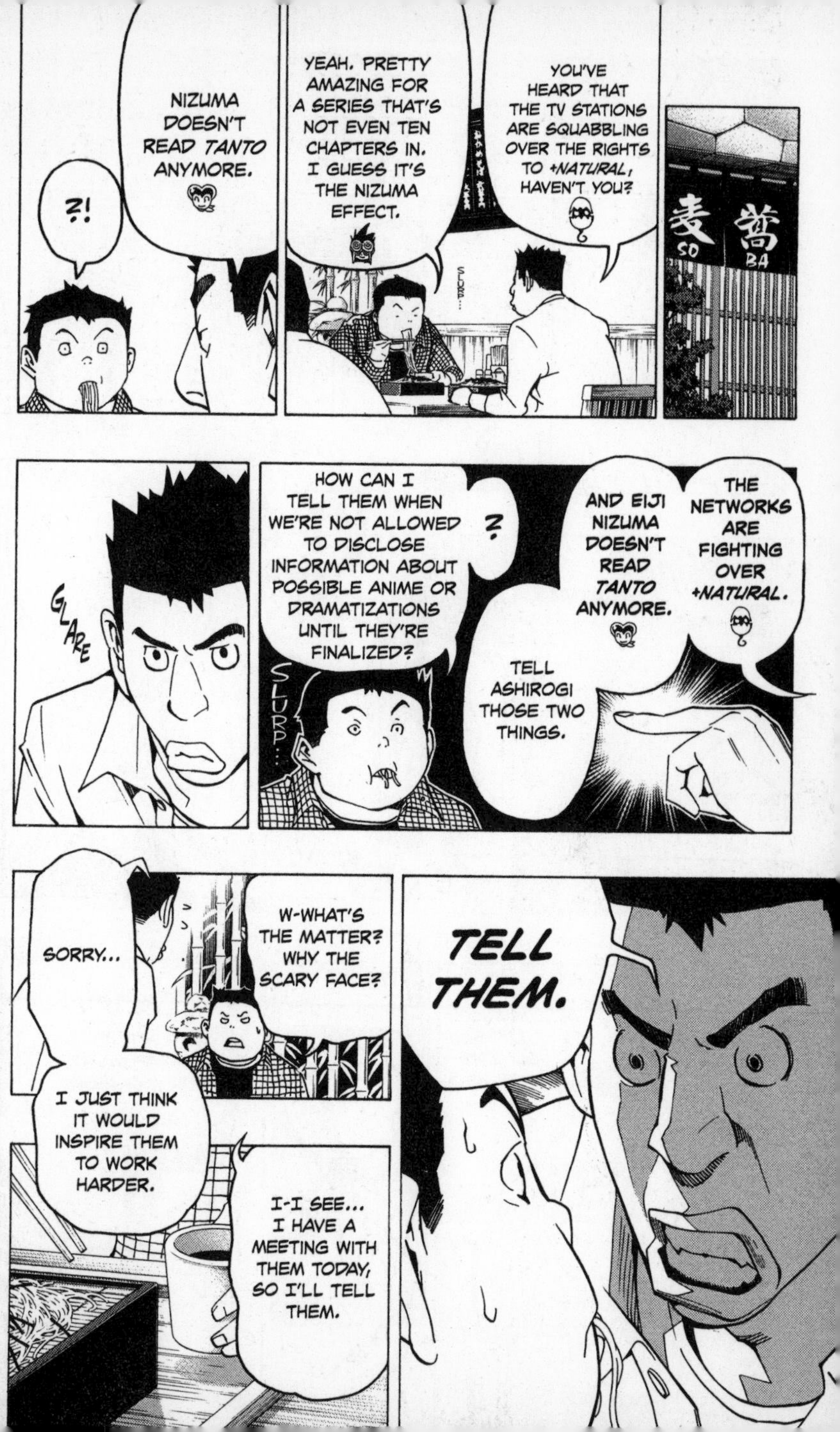
SO
BA
YOU'VE HEARD THAT THE TV STATIONS ARE SQUABBLING OVER THE RIGHTS TO +NATURAL, HAVEN'T YOU?
YEAH. PRETTY AMAZING FOR A SERIES THAT'S NOT EVEN TEN CHAPTERS IN. I GUESS IT'S THE NIZUMA EFFECT.
SLURP...
NIZUMA DOESN'T READ *TANTO* ANYMORE.
?!
THE NETWORKS ARE FIGHTING OVER +NATURAL.
AND EIJI NIZUMA DOESN'T READ *TANTO* ANYMORE.
TELL ASHIROGI THOSE TWO THINGS.
?
HOW CAN I TELL THEM WHEN WE'RE NOT ALLOWED TO DISCLOSE INFORMATION ABOUT POSSIBLE ANIME OR DRAMATIZATIONS UNTIL THEY'RE FINALIZED?
SLURP...
GLARE
TELL THEM.
W-WHAT'S THE MATTER? WHY THE SCARY FACE?
SORRY...
I JUST THINK IT WOULD INSPIRE THEM TO WORK HARDER.
I-I SEE... I HAVE A MEETING WITH THEM TODAY, SO I'LL TELL THEM.

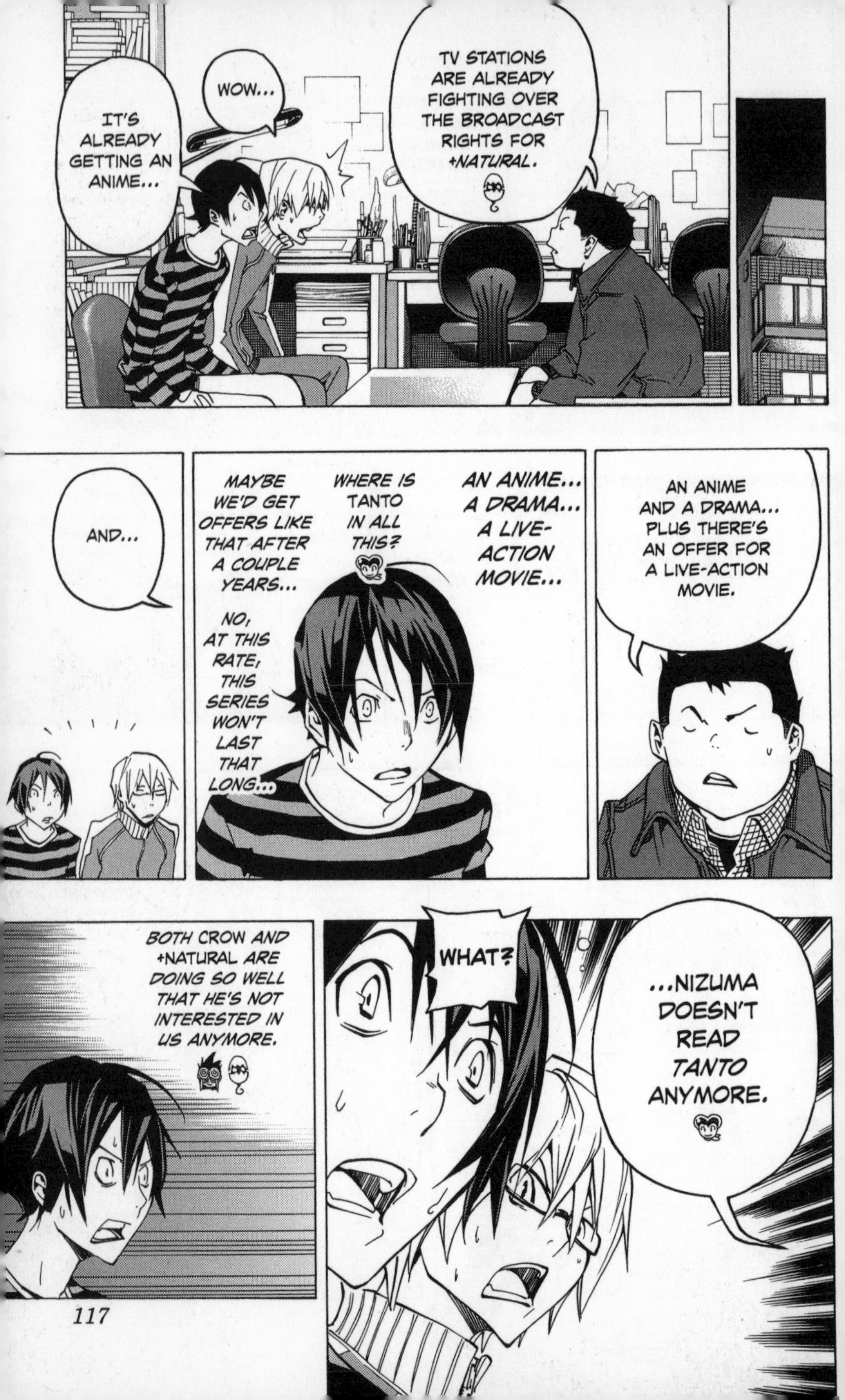

TV STATIONS ARE ALREADY FIGHTING OVER THE BROADCAST RIGHTS FOR +*NATURAL*.
WOW...
IT'S ALREADY GETTING AN ANIME...
AN ANIME AND A DRAMA... PLUS THERE'S AN OFFER FOR A LIVE-ACTION MOVIE.
AN ANIME... A DRAMA... A LIVE-ACTION MOVIE...
WHERE IS TANTO IN ALL THIS?
MAYBE WE'D GET OFFERS LIKE THAT AFTER A COUPLE YEARS...
NO, AT THIS RATE, THIS SERIES WON'T LAST THAT LONG...
AND...
...NIZUMA DOESN'T READ *TANTO* ANYMORE.
WHAT?
BOTH CROW AND +NATURAL ARE DOING SO WELL THAT HE'S NOT INTERESTED IN US ANYMORE.

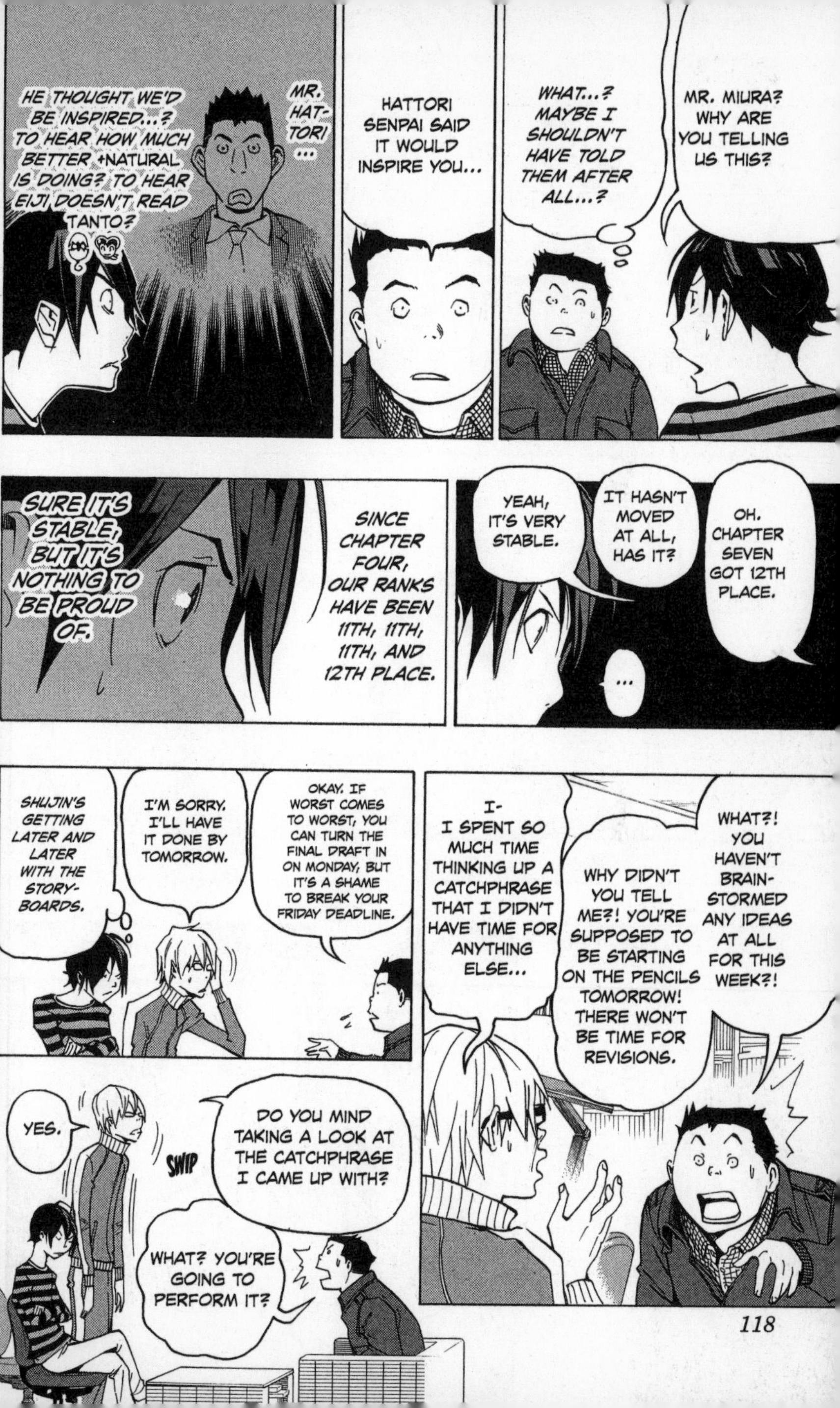

MR. MIURA? WHY ARE YOU TELLING US THIS?
WHAT...? MAYBE I SHOULDN'T HAVE TOLD THEM AFTER ALL...?
HATTORI SENPAI SAID IT WOULD INSPIRE YOU...
MR. HATTORI...
HE THOUGHT WE'D BE INSPIRED...? TO HEAR HOW MUCH BETTER +NATURAL IS DOING? TO HEAR EIJI DOESN'T READ TANTO?
OH. CHAPTER SEVEN GOT 12TH PLACE.
IT HASN'T MOVED AT ALL, HAS IT?
YEAH, IT'S VERY STABLE.
...
SINCE CHAPTER FOUR, OUR RANKS HAVE BEEN 11TH, 11TH, 11TH, AND 12TH PLACE.
SURE IT'S STABLE, BUT IT'S NOTHING TO BE PROUD OF.
WHAT?! YOU HAVEN'T BRAINSTORMED ANY IDEAS AT ALL FOR THIS WEEK?!
WHY DIDN'T YOU TELL ME?! YOU'RE SUPPOSED TO BE STARTING ON THE PENCILS TOMORROW! THERE WON'T BE TIME FOR REVISIONS.
I- I SPENT SO MUCH TIME THINKING UP A CATCHPHRASE THAT I DIDN'T HAVE TIME FOR ANYTHING ELSE...
OKAY. IF WORST COMES TO WORST, YOU CAN TURN THE FINAL DRAFT IN ON MONDAY, BUT IT'S A SHAME TO BREAK YOUR FRIDAY DEADLINE.
I'M SORRY. I'LL HAVE IT DONE BY TOMORROW.
SHUJIN'S GETTING LATER AND LATER WITH THE STORYBOARDS.
DO YOU MIND TAKING A LOOK AT THE CATCHPHRASE I CAME UP WITH?
YES.
SWIP
WHAT? YOU'RE GOING TO PERFORM IT?

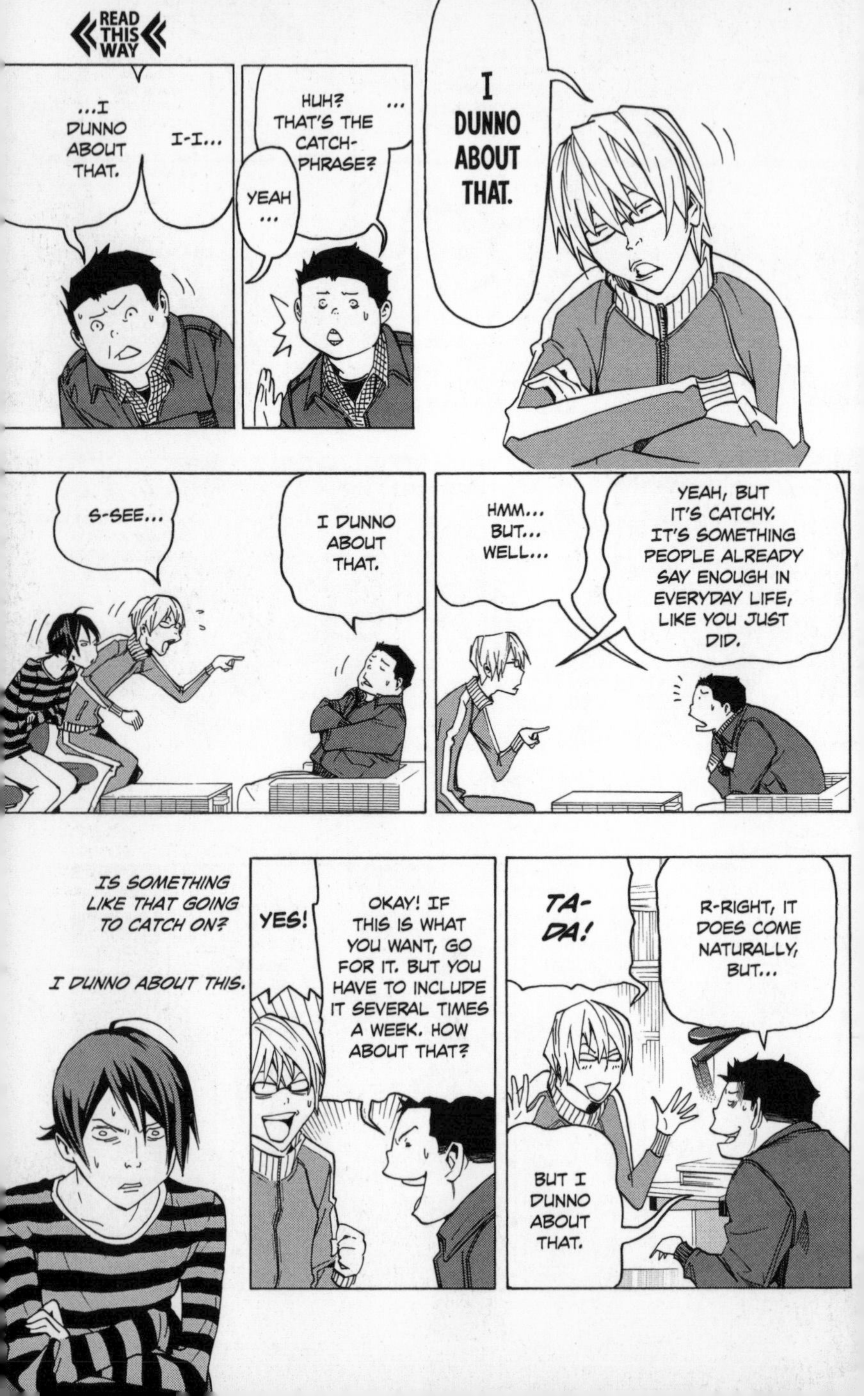
READ THIS WAY
I DUNNO ABOUT THAT.
...
HUH? THAT'S THE CATCH-PHRASE?
YEAH ...
I-I...
...I DUNNO ABOUT THAT.
YEAH, BUT IT'S CATCHY. IT'S SOMETHING PEOPLE ALREADY SAY ENOUGH IN EVERYDAY LIFE, LIKE YOU JUST DID.
HMM... BUT... WELL...
I DUNNO ABOUT THAT.
S-SEE...
R-RIGHT, IT DOES COME NATURALLY, BUT...
TA-DA!
BUT I DUNNO ABOUT THAT.
OKAY! IF THIS IS WHAT YOU WANT, GO FOR IT. BUT YOU HAVE TO INCLUDE IT SEVERAL TIMES A WEEK. HOW ABOUT THAT?
YES!
IS SOMETHING LIKE THAT GOING TO CATCH ON?
I DUNNO ABOUT THIS.

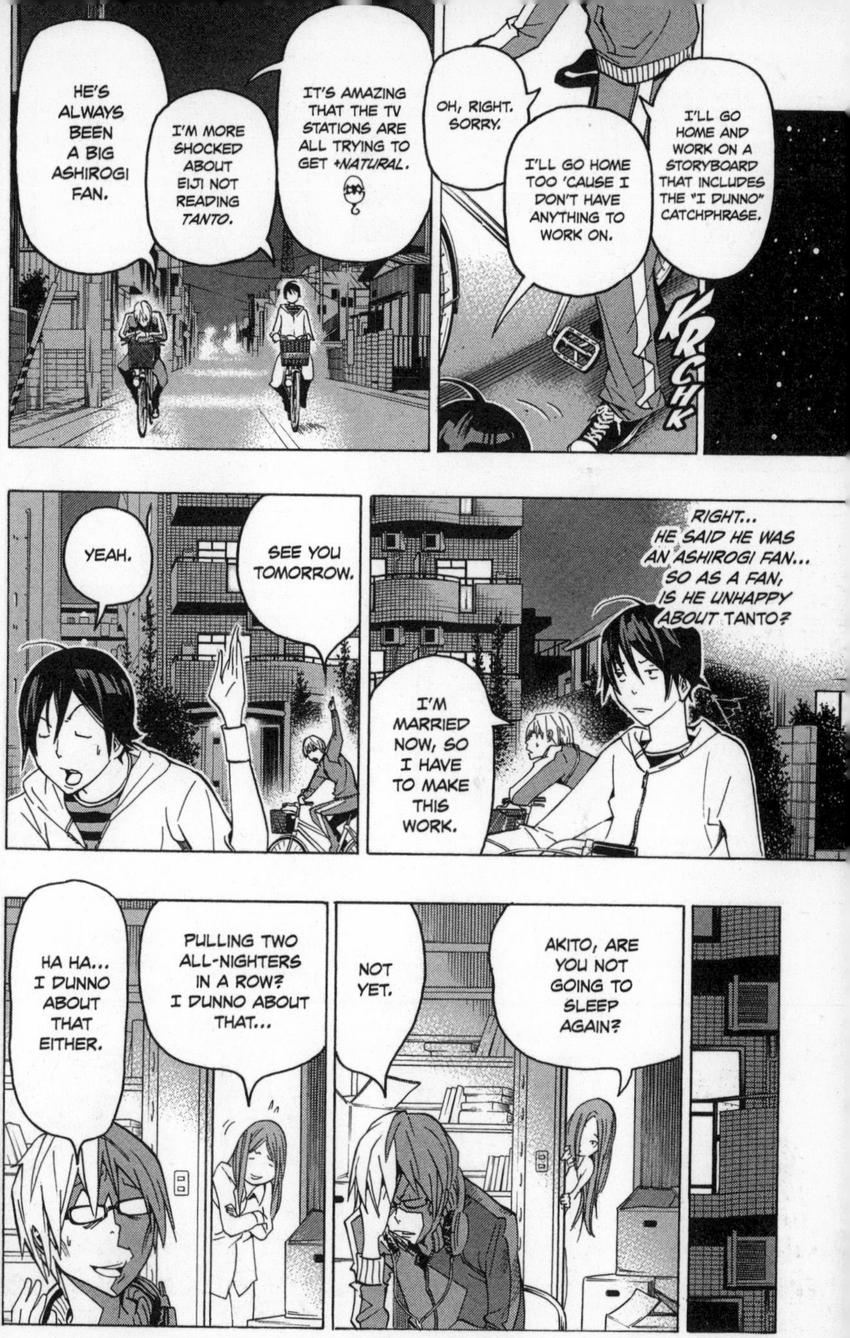
I'LL GO HOME AND WORK ON A STORYBOARD THAT INCLUDES THE "I DUNNO" CATCHPHRASE.
OH, RIGHT. SORRY.
I'LL GO HOME TOO 'CAUSE I DON'T HAVE ANYTHING TO WORK ON.
KRCHK
IT'S AMAZING THAT THE TV STATIONS ARE ALL TRYING TO GET +*NATURAL*.
I'M MORE SHOCKED ABOUT EIJI NOT READING *TANTO*.
HE'S ALWAYS BEEN A BIG ASHIROGI FAN.
RIGHT... HE SAID HE WAS AN ASHIROGI FAN... SO AS A FAN, IS HE UNHAPPY ABOUT TANTO*?*
I'M MARRIED NOW, SO I HAVE TO MAKE THIS WORK.
SEE YOU TOMORROW.
YEAH.
AKITO, ARE YOU NOT GOING TO SLEEP AGAIN?
NOT YET.
PULLING TWO ALL-NIGHTERS IN A ROW? I DUNNO ABOUT THAT...
HA HA... I DUNNO ABOUT THAT EITHER.

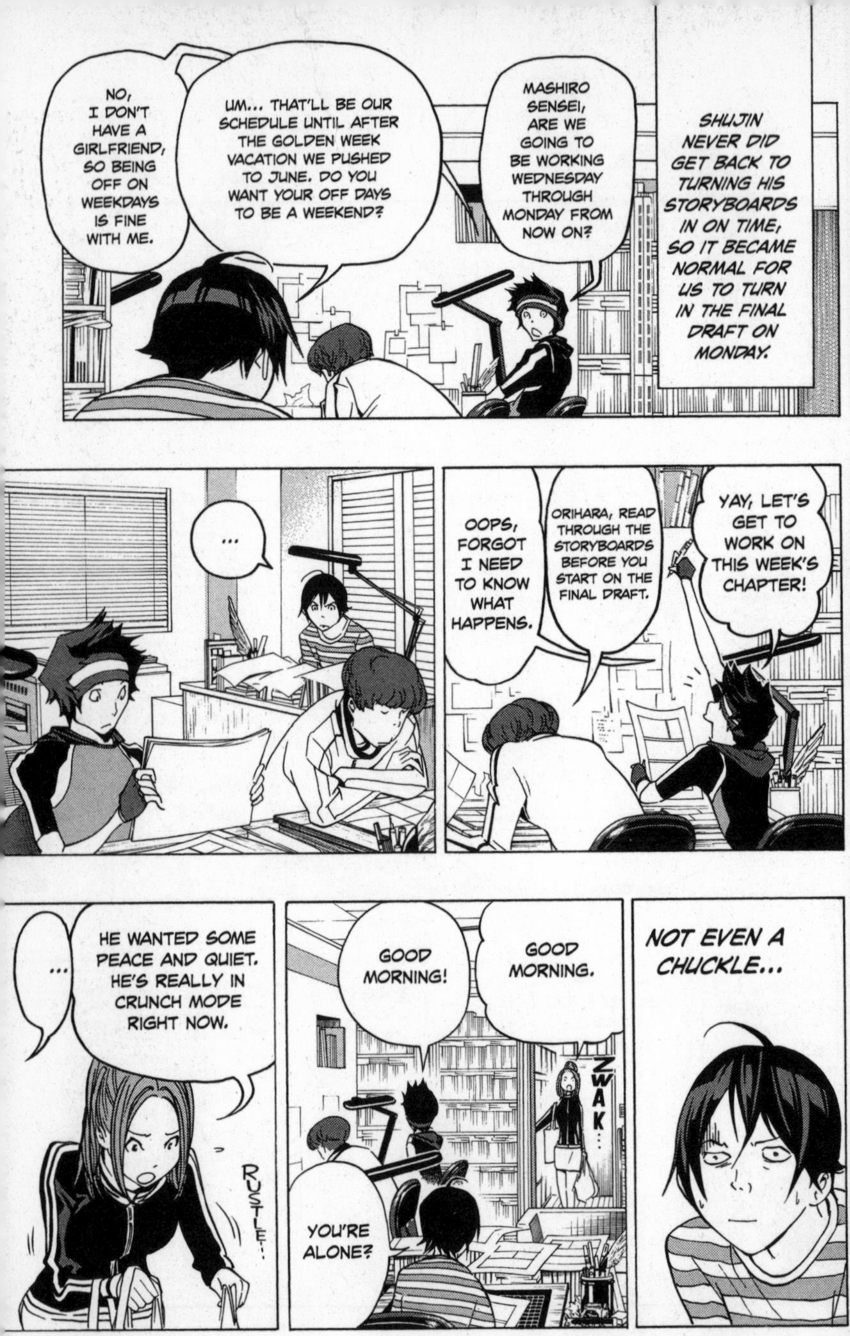
SHUJIN NEVER DID GET BACK TO TURNING HIS STORYBOARDS IN ON TIME, SO IT BECAME NORMAL FOR US TO TURN IN THE FINAL DRAFT ON MONDAY.
MASHIRO SENSEI, ARE WE GOING TO BE WORKING WEDNESDAY THROUGH MONDAY FROM NOW ON?
UM... THAT'LL BE OUR SCHEDULE UNTIL AFTER THE GOLDEN WEEK VACATION WE PUSHED TO JUNE. DO YOU WANT YOUR OFF DAYS TO BE A WEEKEND?
NO, I DON'T HAVE A GIRLFRIEND, SO BEING OFF ON WEEKDAYS IS FINE WITH ME.
YAY, LET'S GET TO WORK ON THIS WEEK'S CHAPTER!
ORIHARA, READ THROUGH THE STORYBOARDS BEFORE YOU START ON THE FINAL DRAFT.
OOPS, FORGOT I NEED TO KNOW WHAT HAPPENS.
...
NOT EVEN A CHUCKLE...
GOOD MORNING.
GOOD MORNING!
ZWAK...
YOU'RE ALONE?
HE WANTED SOME PEACE AND QUIET. HE'S REALLY IN CRUNCH MODE RIGHT NOW.
...
RUSTLE...

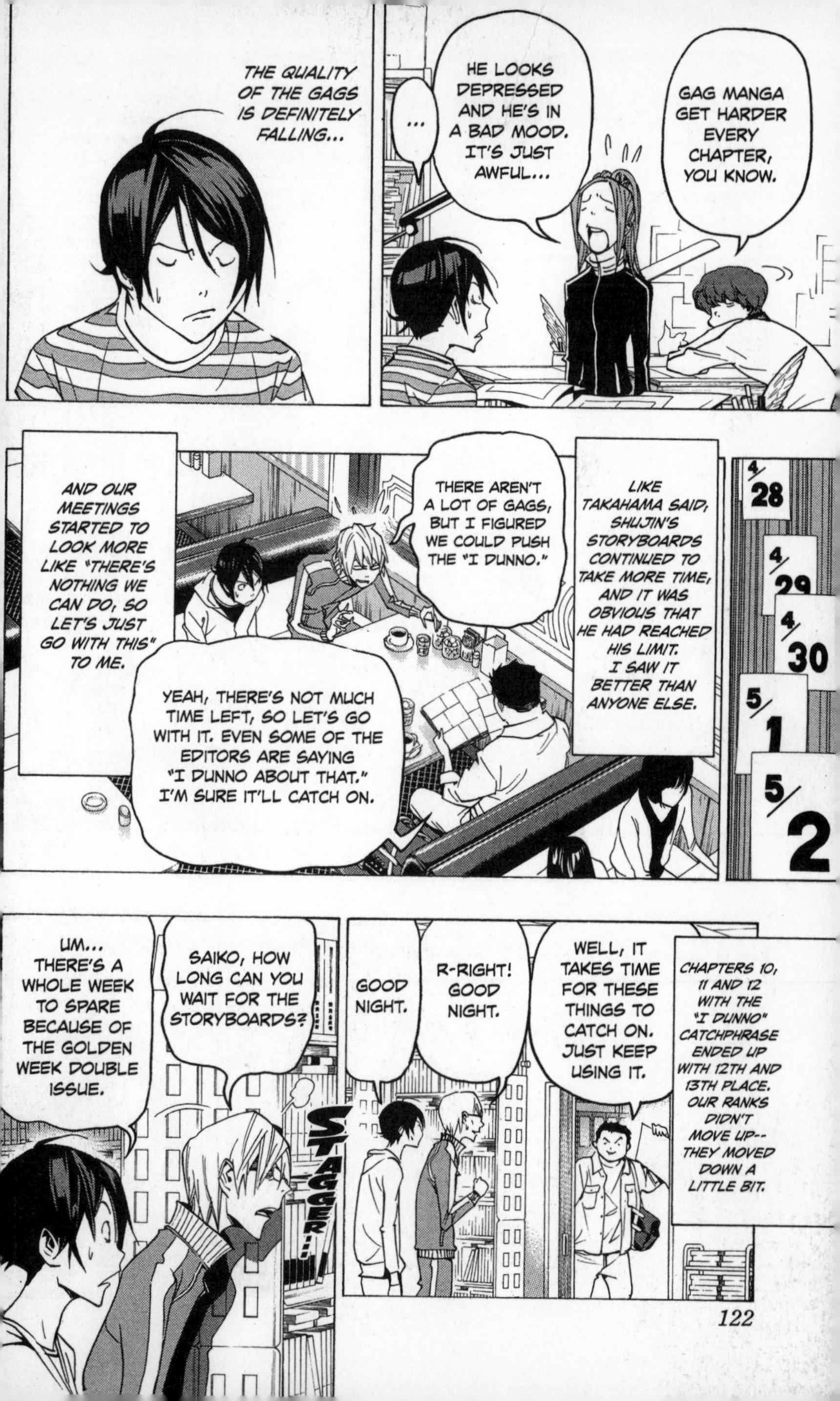
GAG MANGA GET HARDER EVERY CHAPTER, YOU KNOW.
HE LOOKS DEPRESSED AND HE'S IN A BAD MOOD. IT'S JUST AWFUL...
...
THE QUALITY OF THE GAGS IS DEFINITELY FALLING...
4/28
4/29
4/30
5/1
5/2
LIKE TAKAHAMA SAID, SHUJIN'S STORYBOARDS CONTINUED TO TAKE MORE TIME, AND IT WAS OBVIOUS THAT HE HAD REACHED HIS LIMIT. I SAW IT BETTER THAN ANYONE ELSE.
THERE AREN'T A LOT OF GAGS, BUT I FIGURED WE COULD PUSH THE "I DUNNO."
AND OUR MEETINGS STARTED TO LOOK MORE LIKE "THERE'S NOTHING WE CAN DO, SO LET'S JUST GO WITH THIS" TO ME.
YEAH, THERE'S NOT MUCH TIME LEFT, SO LET'S GO WITH IT. EVEN SOME OF THE EDITORS ARE SAYING "I DUNNO ABOUT THAT." I'M SURE IT'LL CATCH ON.
CHAPTERS 10, 11 AND 12 WITH THE "I DUNNO" CATCHPHRASE ENDED UP WITH 12TH AND 13TH PLACE. OUR RANKS DIDN'T MOVE UP-- THEY MOVED DOWN A LITTLE BIT.
WELL, IT TAKES TIME FOR THESE THINGS TO CATCH ON. JUST KEEP USING IT.
R-RIGHT! GOOD NIGHT.
GOOD NIGHT.
STAGGER...
SAIKO, HOW LONG CAN YOU WAIT FOR THE STORYBOARDS?
UM... THERE'S A WHOLE WEEK TO SPARE BECAUSE OF THE GOLDEN WEEK DOUBLE ISSUE.

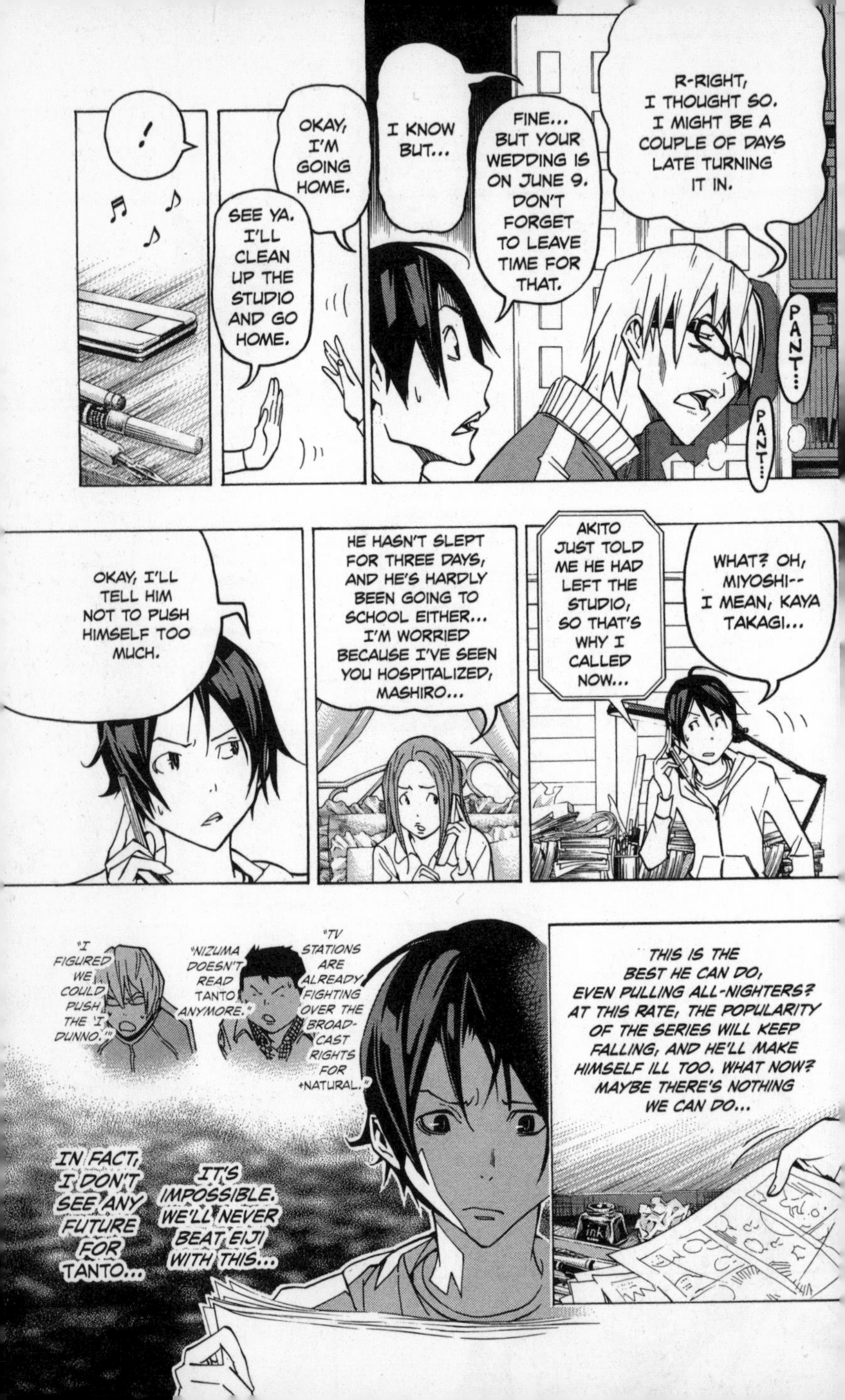
R-RIGHT, I THOUGHT SO. I MIGHT BE A COUPLE OF DAYS LATE TURNING IT IN.
PANT...
PANT...
FINE... BUT YOUR WEDDING IS ON JUNE 9. DON'T FORGET TO LEAVE TIME FOR THAT.
I KNOW BUT...
OKAY, I'M GOING HOME.
SEE YA. I'LL CLEAN UP THE STUDIO AND GO HOME.
!
WHAT? OH, MIYOSHI-- I MEAN, KAYA TAKAGI...
AKITO JUST TOLD ME HE HAD LEFT THE STUDIO, SO THAT'S WHY I CALLED NOW...
HE HASN'T SLEPT FOR THREE DAYS, AND HE'S HARDLY BEEN GOING TO SCHOOL EITHER... I'M WORRIED BECAUSE I'VE SEEN YOU HOSPITALIZED, MASHIRO...
OKAY, I'LL TELL HIM NOT TO PUSH HIMSELF TOO MUCH.
THIS IS THE BEST HE CAN DO, EVEN PULLING ALL-NIGHTERS? AT THIS RATE, THE POPULARITY OF THE SERIES WILL KEEP FALLING, AND HE'LL MAKE HIMSELF ILL TOO. WHAT NOW? MAYBE THERE'S NOTHING WE CAN DO...
"TV STATIONS ARE ALREADY FIGHTING OVER THE BROAD-CAST RIGHTS FOR +NATURAL."
"NIZUMA DOESN'T READ TANTO ANYMORE."
"I FIGURED WE COULD PUSH THE 'I DUNNO.'"
IT'S IMPOSSIBLE. WE'LL NEVER BEAT EIJI WITH THIS...
IN FACT, I DON'T SEE ANY FUTURE FOR TANTO...

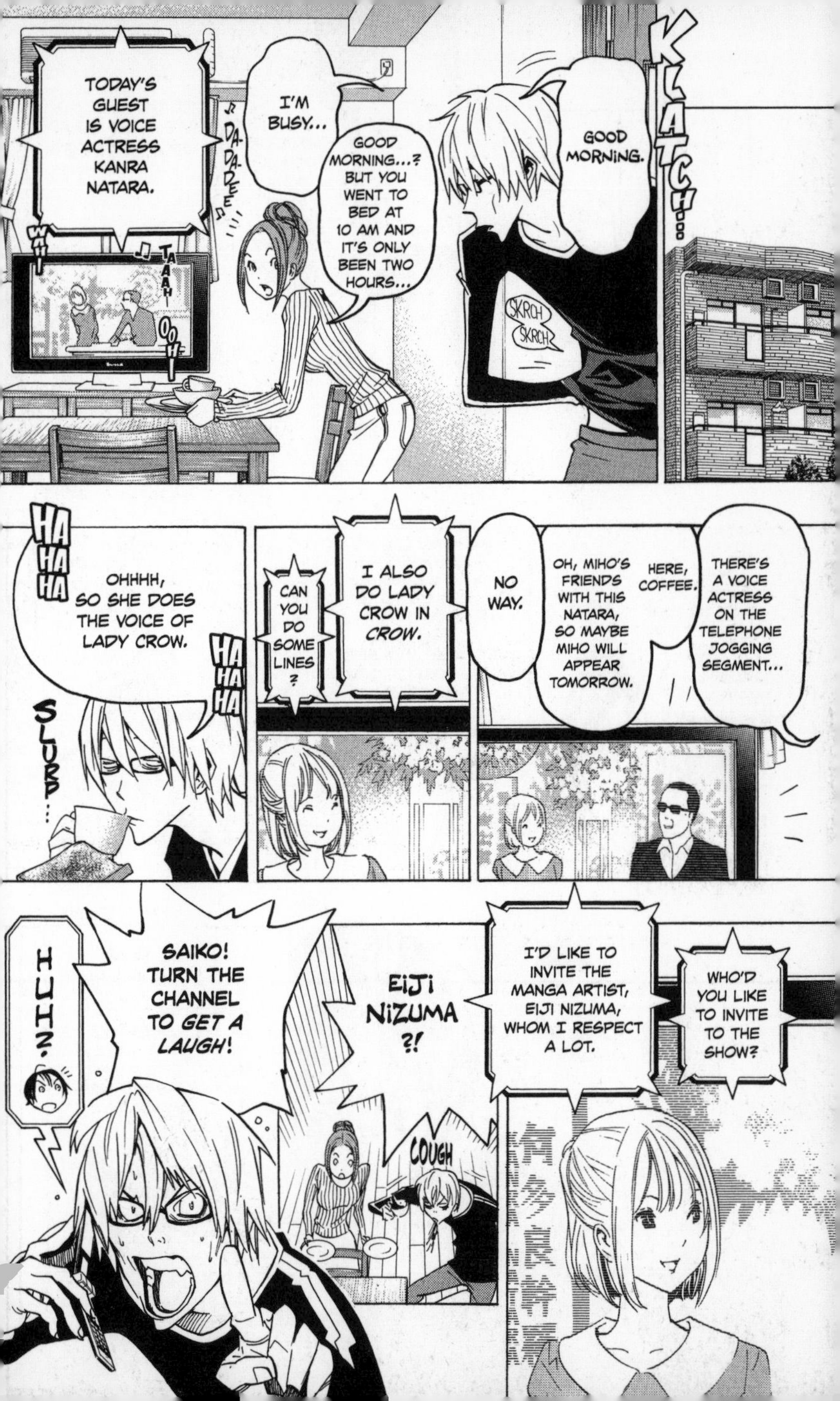
KLATCH...
GOOD MORNING.
SKRCH SKRCH
I'M BUSY...
GOOD MORNING...? BUT YOU WENT TO BED AT 10 AM AND IT'S ONLY BEEN TWO HOURS...
TODAY'S GUEST IS VOICE ACTRESS KANRA NATARA.
DA-DA-DEE
TAAAH
OOH
WAH
THERE'S A VOICE ACTRESS ON THE TELEPHONE JOGGING SEGMENT...
HERE, COFFEE.
OH, MIHO'S FRIENDS WITH THIS NATARA, SO MAYBE MIHO WILL APPEAR TOMORROW.
NO WAY.
I ALSO DO LADY CROW IN *CROW*.
CAN YOU DO SOME LINES?
HA HA HA
OHHHH, SO SHE DOES THE VOICE OF LADY CROW.
HA HA HA
SLURP...
WHO'D YOU LIKE TO INVITE TO THE SHOW?
I'D LIKE TO INVITE THE MANGA ARTIST, EIJI NIZUMA, WHOM I RESPECT A LOT.
EIJI NIZUMA?!
COUGH
SAIKO! TURN THE CHANNEL TO *GET A LAUGH*!
HUH?

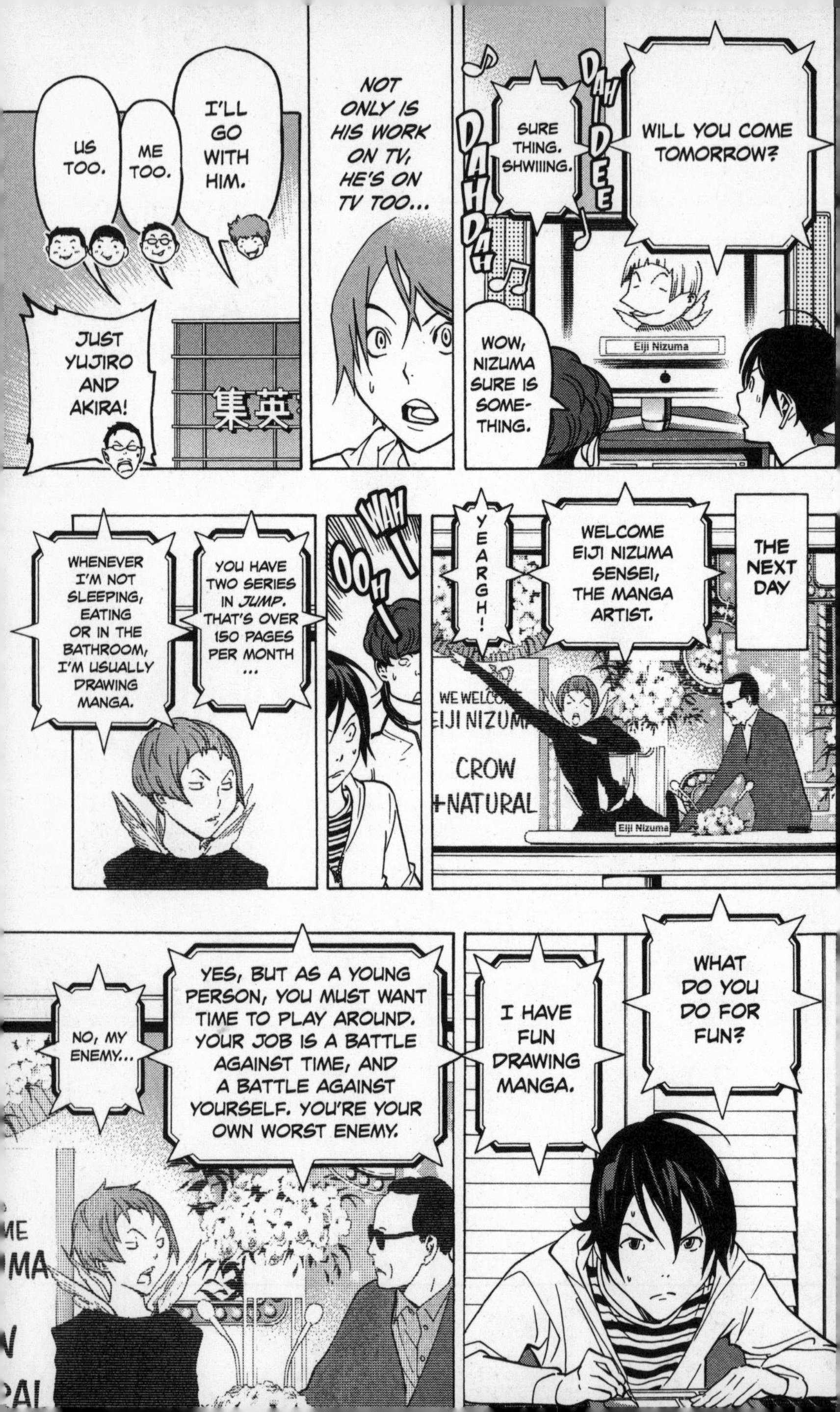

WILL YOU COME TOMORROW?
DAH DEE
SURE THING. SHWIIING.
DAH DAH DAH
Eiji Nizuma
WOW, NIZUMA SURE IS SOME-THING.
NOT ONLY IS HIS WORK ON TV, HE'S ON TV TOO...
I'LL GO WITH HIM.
ME TOO.
US TOO.
JUST YUJIRO AND AKIRA!
集英
THE NEXT DAY
WELCOME EIJI NIZUMA SENSEI, THE MANGA ARTIST.
YEARGH!
CROW
+NATURAL
Eiji Nizuma
WAH
OOH
YOU HAVE TWO SERIES IN *JUMP*. THAT'S OVER 150 PAGES PER MONTH ...
WHENEVER I'M NOT SLEEPING, EATING OR IN THE BATHROOM, I'M USUALLY DRAWING MANGA.
WHAT DO YOU DO FOR FUN?
I HAVE FUN DRAWING MANGA.
YES, BUT AS A YOUNG PERSON, YOU MUST WANT TIME TO PLAY AROUND. YOUR JOB IS A BATTLE AGAINST TIME, AND A BATTLE AGAINST YOURSELF. YOU'RE YOUR OWN WORST ENEMY.
NO, MY ENEMY...

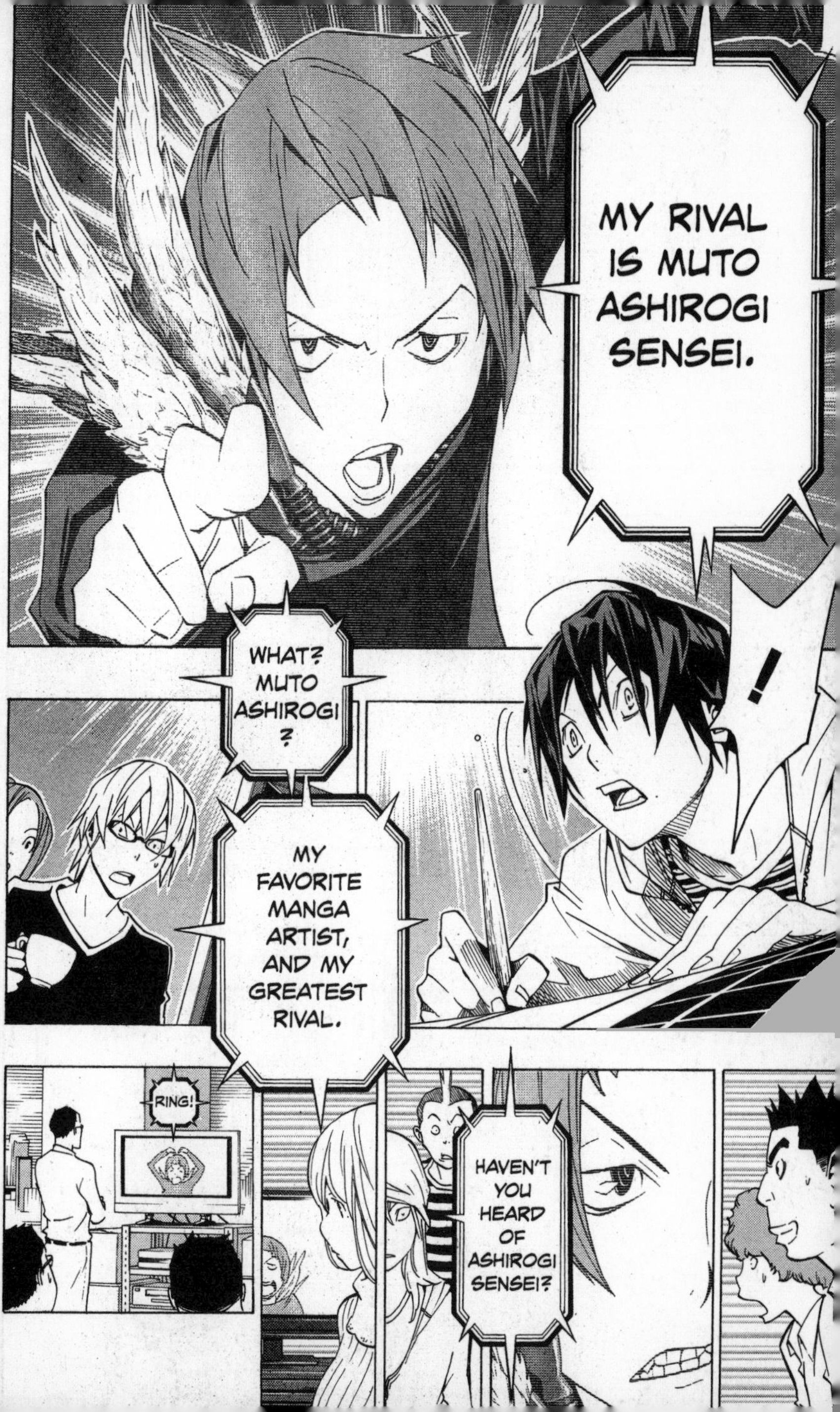
MY RIVAL IS MUTO ASHIROGI SENSEI.
!
WHAT? MUTO ASHIROGI?
MY FAVORITE MANGA ARTIST, AND MY GREATEST RIVAL.
HAVEN'T YOU HEARD OF ASHIROGI SENSEI?
RING!

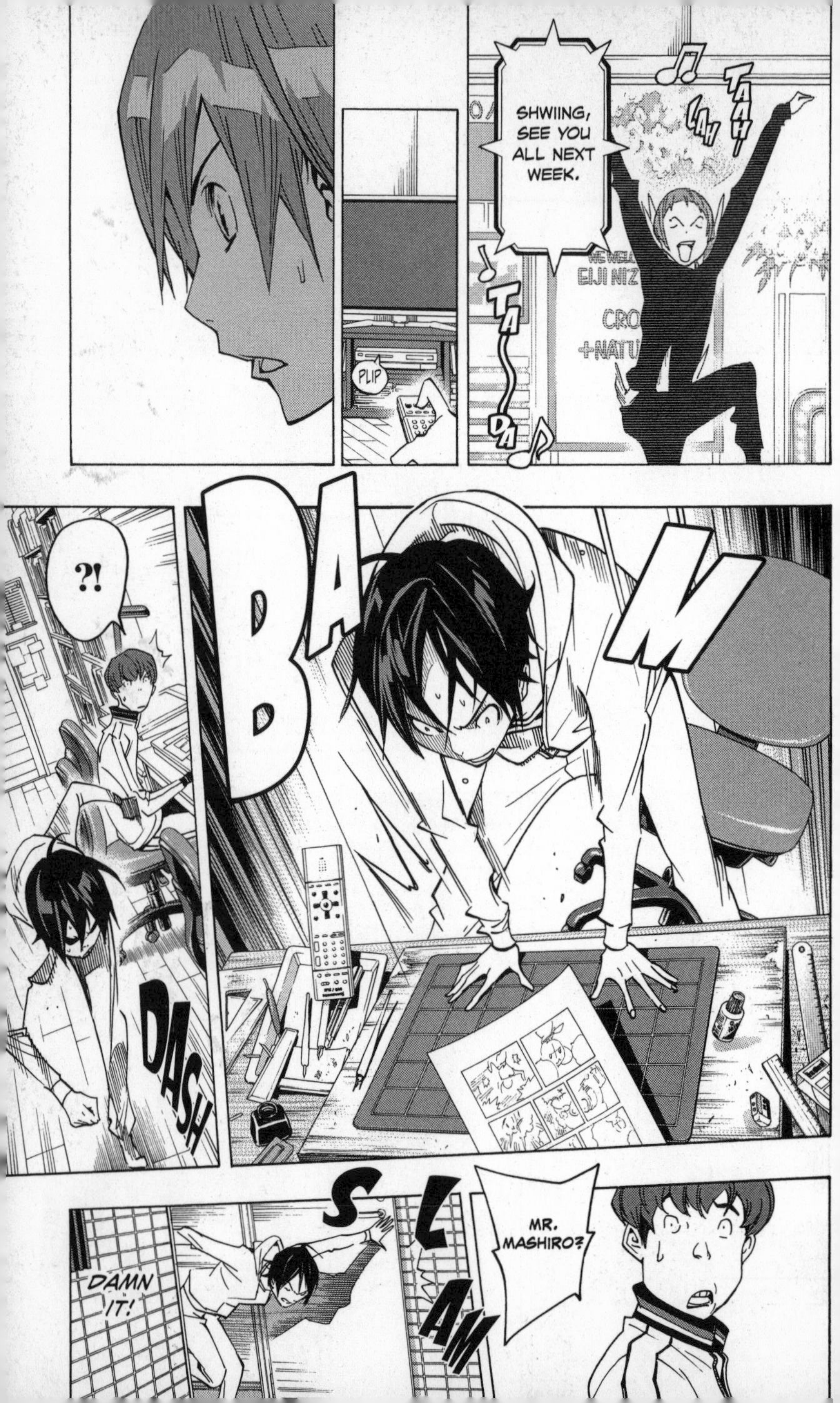
TAAH
LAH
SHWIING, SEE YOU ALL NEXT WEEK.
TA
DA
PLIP
BAM
?!
DASH
MR. MASHIRO?
SLAM
DAMN IT!

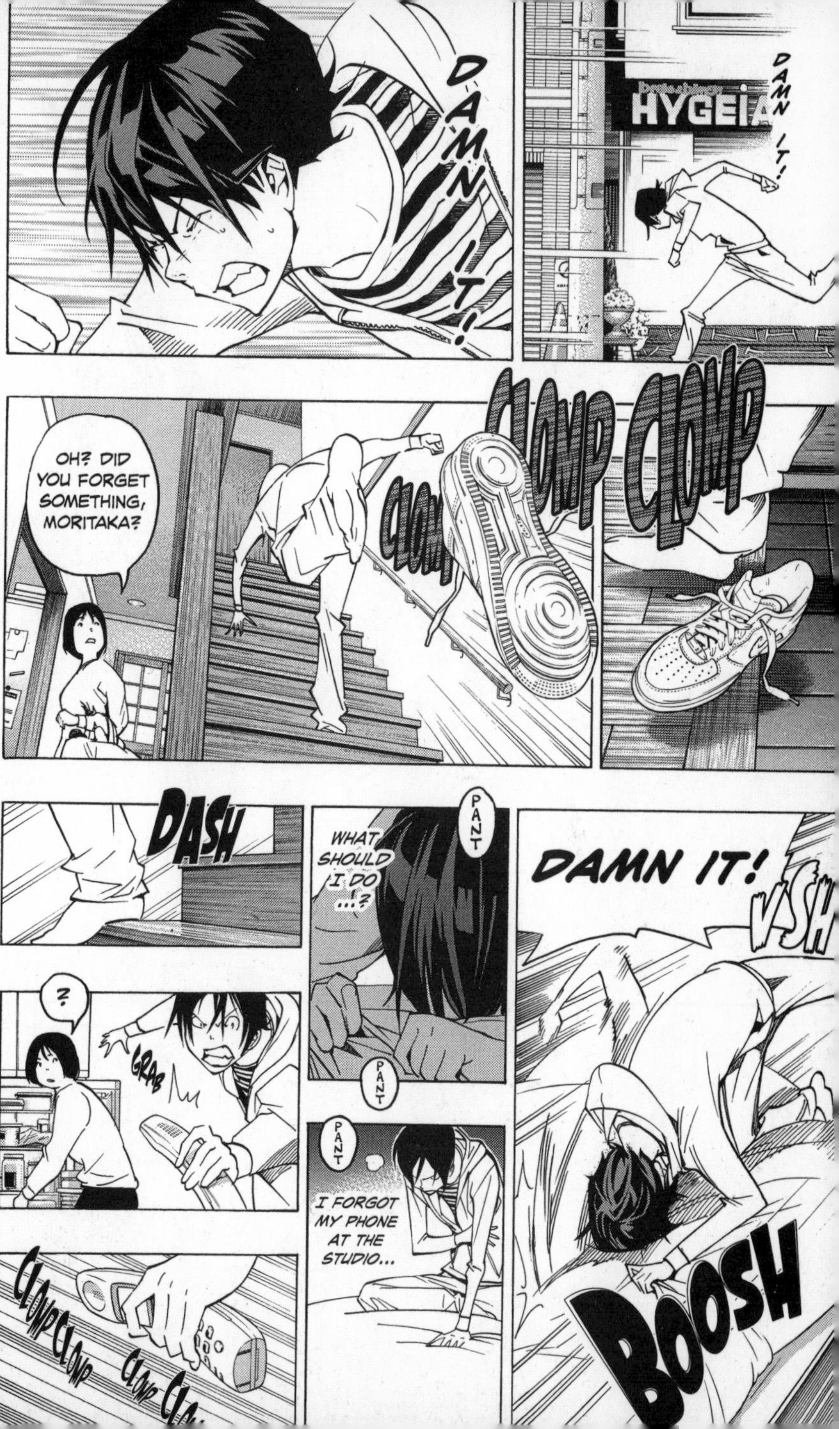
HYGEIA
DAMN IT!
DAMN IT!
CLOMP CLOMP
CLOMP
OH? DID YOU FORGET SOMETHING, MORITAKA?
DAMN IT!
VSH
BOOSH
PANT
WHAT SHOULD I DO ...?
PANT
PANT
I FORGOT MY PHONE AT THE STUDIO...
DASH
?
GRAB
CLOMP CLOMP
CLOMP CLOMP

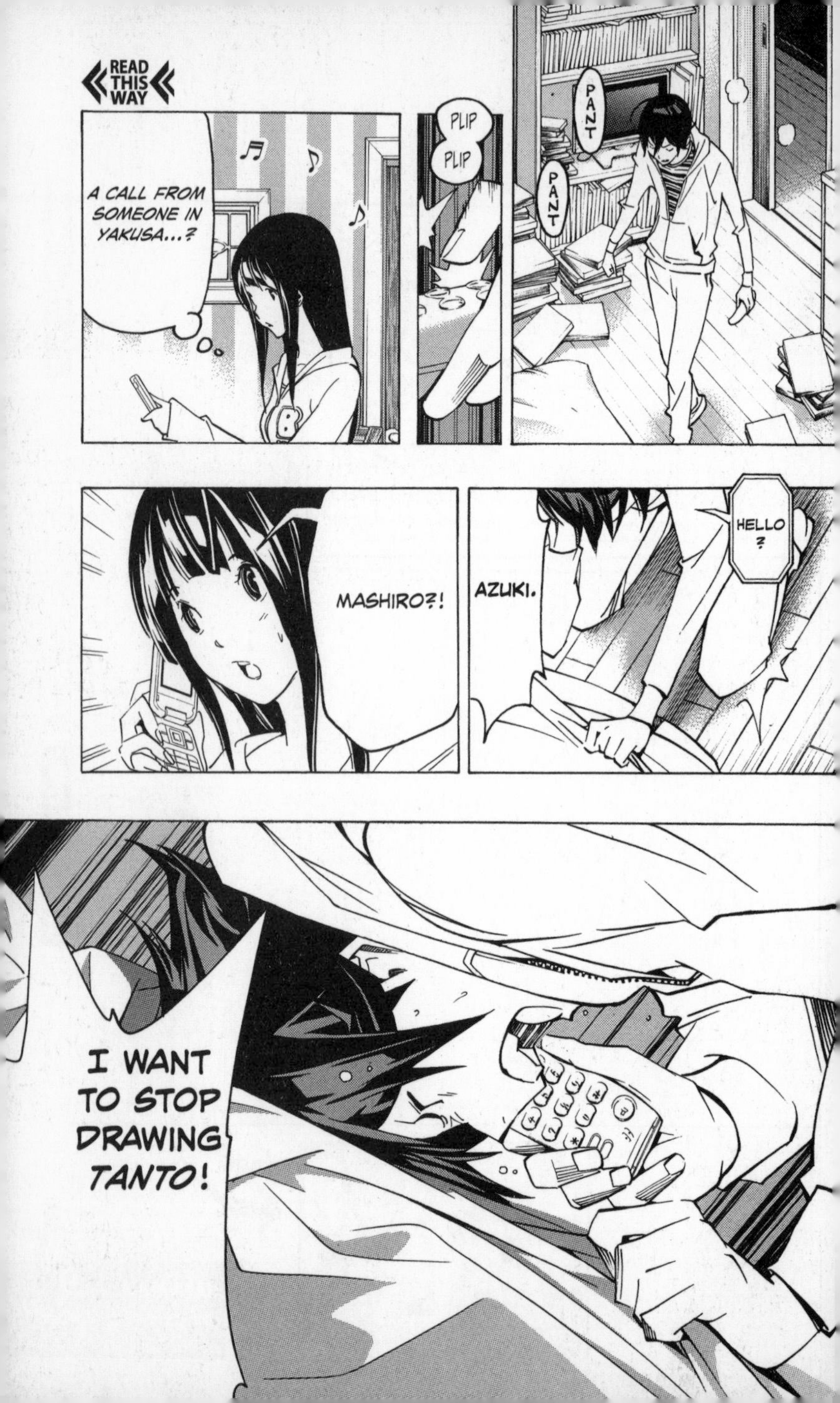
READ THIS WAY
PANT
PANT
PLIP
PLIP
A CALL FROM SOMEONE IN YAKUSA...?
HELLO?
AZUKI.
MASHIRO?!
I WANT TO STOP DRAWING *TANTO*!

OHBA'S STORYBOARD

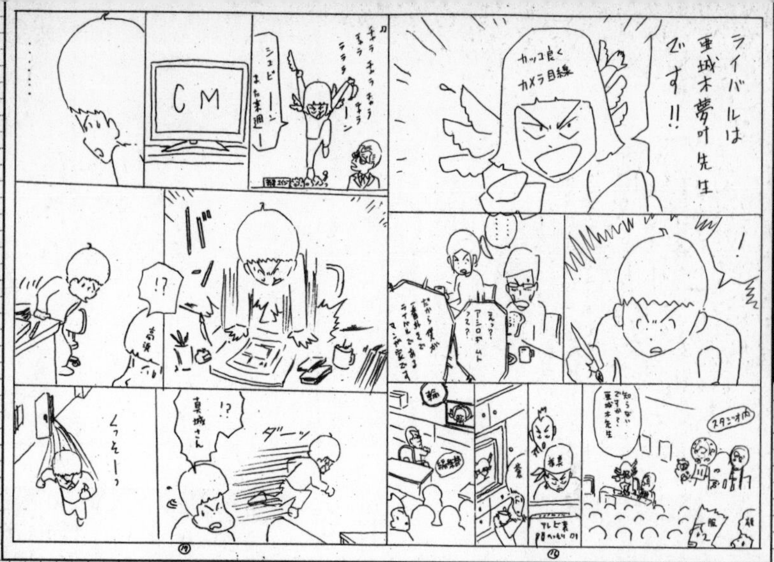
ライバルは亜城木夢叶先生です!!
カッコ良くカメラ目線
!
シュピーン また来週ー
CM
!?
ダーッ
!?
真城さん
くっそー
知らない? ですか? 亜城木先生
スタジオ内

OBATA'S STORYBOARD

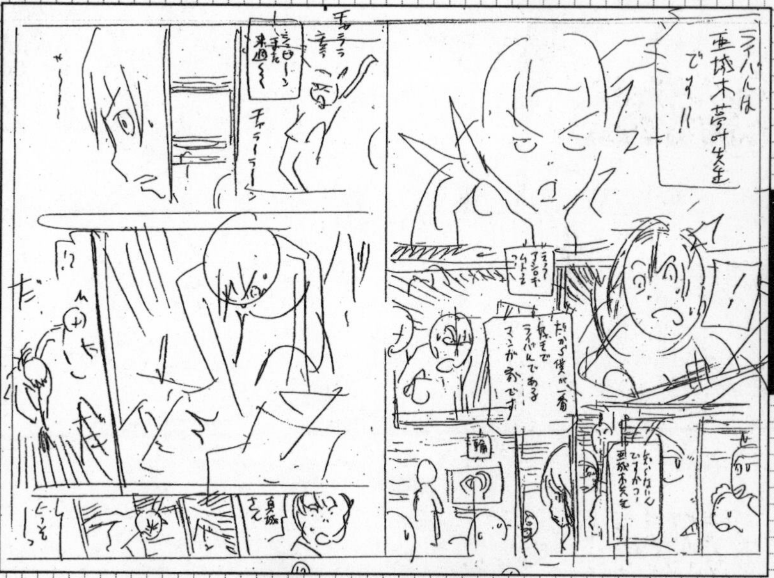
ライバルは亜城木夢叶先生です!!
!
!?

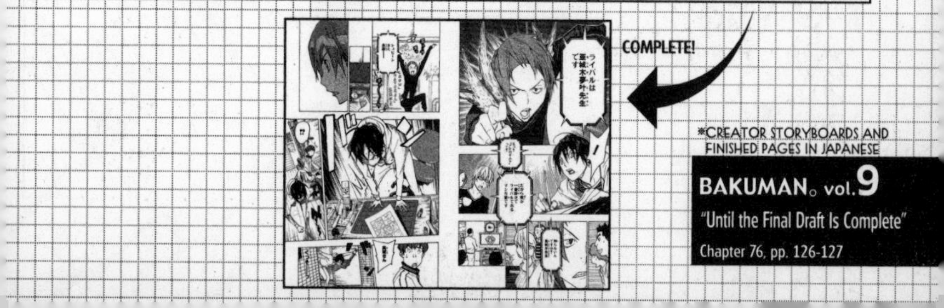
ライバルは亜城木夢叶先生です

COMPLETE!

*CREATOR STORYBOARDS AND FINISHED PAGES IN JAPANESE

BAKUMAN。 vol.9

"Until the Final Draft Is Complete"

Chapter 76, pp. 126-127

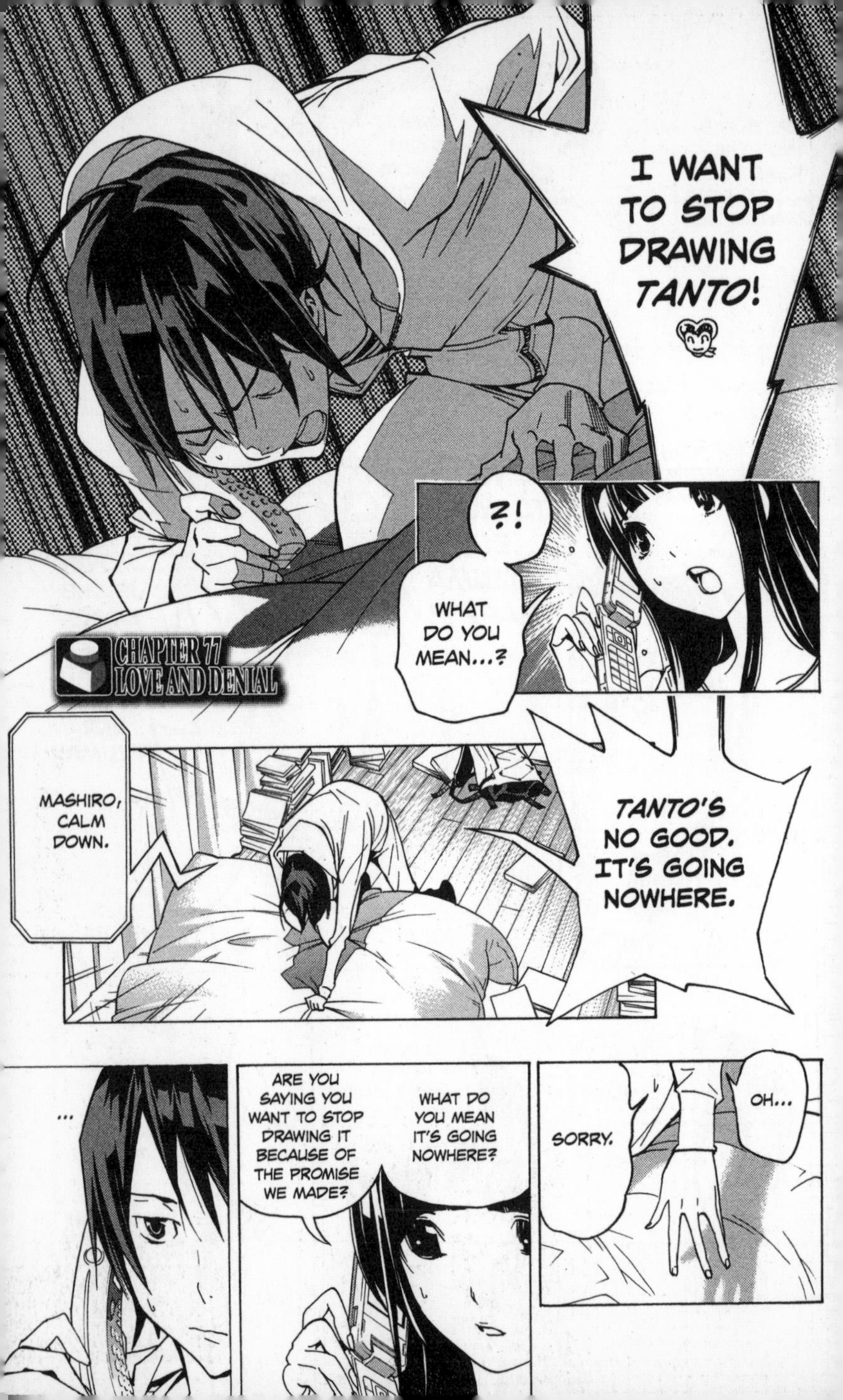
I WANT TO STOP DRAWING TANTO!
CHAPTER 77 LOVE AND DENIAL
?!
WHAT DO YOU MEAN...?
TANTO'S NO GOOD. IT'S GOING NOWHERE.
MASHIRO, CALM DOWN.
OH...
SORRY.
WHAT DO YOU MEAN IT'S GOING NOWHERE?
ARE YOU SAYING YOU WANT TO STOP DRAWING IT BECAUSE OF THE PROMISE WE MADE?
...

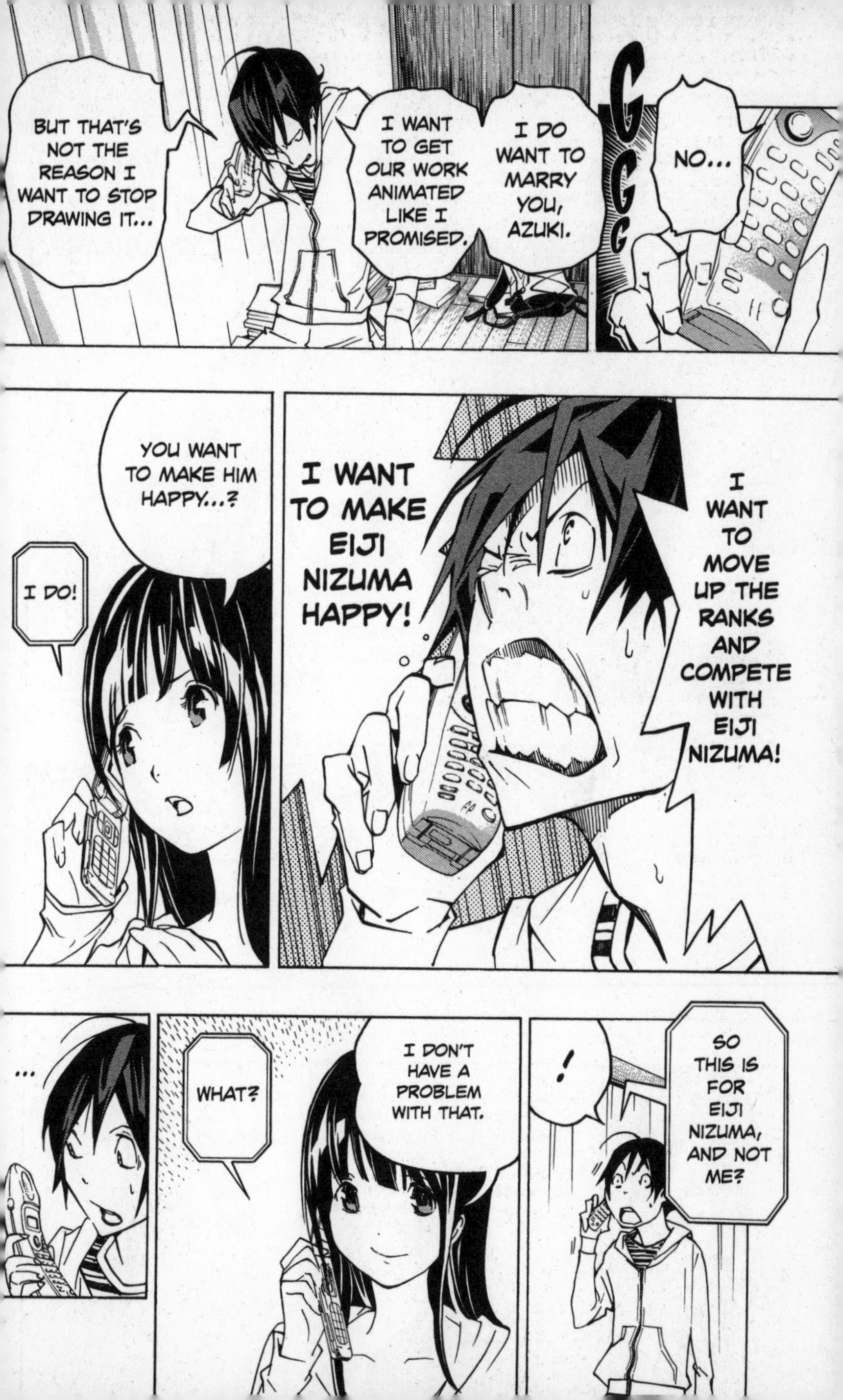
GGG
NO...
I DO WANT TO MARRY YOU, AZUKI.
I WANT TO GET OUR WORK ANIMATED LIKE I PROMISED.
BUT THAT'S NOT THE REASON I WANT TO STOP DRAWING IT...
I WANT TO MOVE UP THE RANKS AND COMPETE WITH EIJI NIZUMA!
I WANT TO MAKE EIJI NIZUMA HAPPY!
YOU WANT TO MAKE HIM HAPPY...?
I DO!
!
SO THIS IS FOR EIJI NIZUMA, AND NOT ME?
I DON'T HAVE A PROBLEM WITH THAT.
WHAT?
...

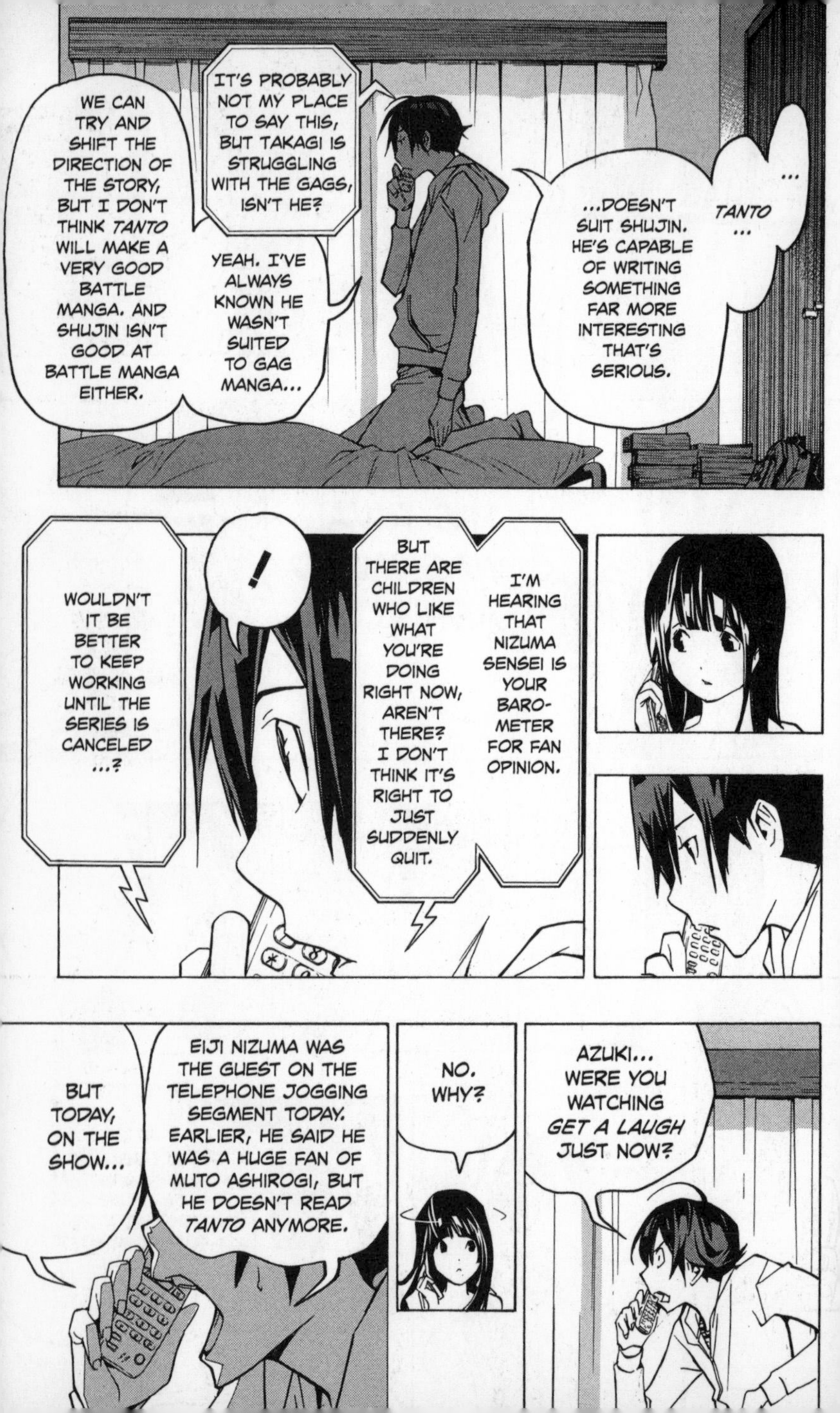
...
TANTO ...
...DOESN'T SUIT SHUJIN. HE'S CAPABLE OF WRITING SOMETHING FAR MORE INTERESTING THAT'S SERIOUS.
IT'S PROBABLY NOT MY PLACE TO SAY THIS, BUT TAKAGI IS STRUGGLING WITH THE GAGS, ISN'T HE?
YEAH. I'VE ALWAYS KNOWN HE WASN'T SUITED TO GAG MANGA...
WE CAN TRY AND SHIFT THE DIRECTION OF THE STORY, BUT I DON'T THINK *TANTO* WILL MAKE A VERY GOOD BATTLE MANGA. AND SHUJIN ISN'T GOOD AT BATTLE MANGA EITHER.
I'M HEARING THAT NIZUMA SENSEI IS YOUR BARO-METER FOR FAN OPINION.
BUT THERE ARE CHILDREN WHO LIKE WHAT YOU'RE DOING RIGHT NOW, AREN'T THERE? I DON'T THINK IT'S RIGHT TO JUST SUDDENLY QUIT.
!
WOULDN'T IT BE BETTER TO KEEP WORKING UNTIL THE SERIES IS CANCELED ...?
AZUKI... WERE YOU WATCHING *GET A LAUGH* JUST NOW?
NO. WHY?
EIJI NIZUMA WAS THE GUEST ON THE TELEPHONE JOGGING SEGMENT TODAY. EARLIER, HE SAID HE WAS A HUGE FAN OF MUTO ASHIROGI, BUT HE DOESN'T READ *TANTO* ANYMORE.
BUT TODAY, ON THE SHOW...

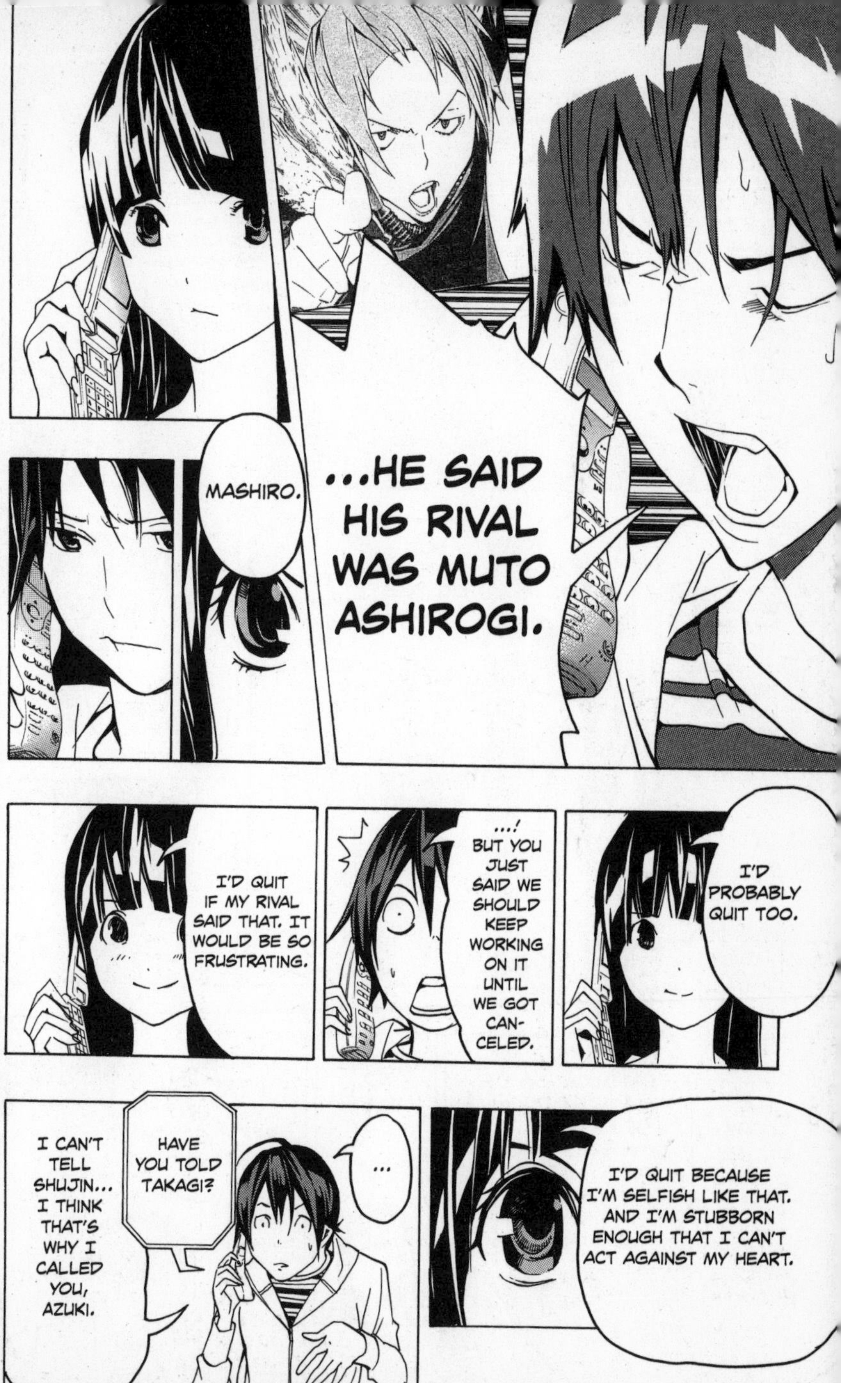
...HE SAID HIS RIVAL WAS MUTO ASHIROGI.
MASHIRO.
I'D PROBABLY QUIT TOO.
...! BUT YOU JUST SAID WE SHOULD KEEP WORKING ON IT UNTIL WE GOT CAN-CELED.
I'D QUIT IF MY RIVAL SAID THAT. IT WOULD BE SO FRUSTRATING.
I'D QUIT BECAUSE I'M SELFISH LIKE THAT. AND I'M STUBBORN ENOUGH THAT I CAN'T ACT AGAINST MY HEART.
...
HAVE YOU TOLD TAKAGI?
I CAN'T TELL SHUJIN... I THINK THAT'S WHY I CALLED YOU, AZUKI.

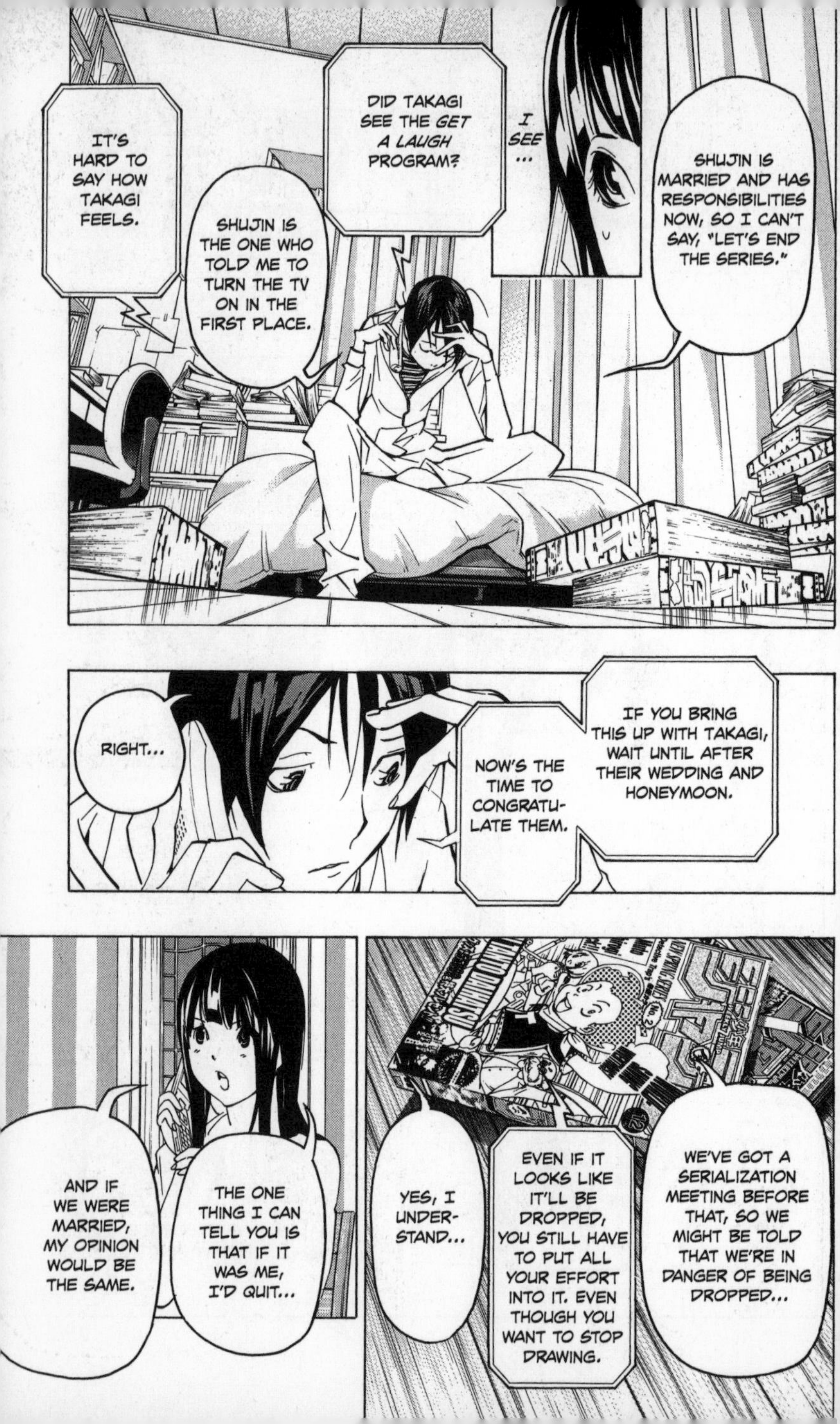
SHUJIN IS MARRIED AND HAS RESPONSIBILITIES NOW, SO I CAN'T SAY, "LET'S END THE SERIES."
I SEE...
DID TAKAGI SEE THE *GET A LAUGH* PROGRAM?
SHUJIN IS THE ONE WHO TOLD ME TO TURN THE TV ON IN THE FIRST PLACE.
IT'S HARD TO SAY HOW TAKAGI FEELS.
IF YOU BRING THIS UP WITH TAKAGI, WAIT UNTIL AFTER THEIR WEDDING AND HONEYMOON.
NOW'S THE TIME TO CONGRATU-LATE THEM.
RIGHT...
WE'VE GOT A SERIALIZATION MEETING BEFORE THAT, SO WE MIGHT BE TOLD THAT WE'RE IN DANGER OF BEING DROPPED...
EVEN IF IT LOOKS LIKE IT'LL BE DROPPED, YOU STILL HAVE TO PUT ALL YOUR EFFORT INTO IT. EVEN THOUGH YOU WANT TO STOP DRAWING.
YES, I UNDER-STAND...
THE ONE THING I CAN TELL YOU IS THAT IF IT WAS ME, I'D QUIT...
AND IF WE WERE MARRIED, MY OPINION WOULD BE THE SAME.

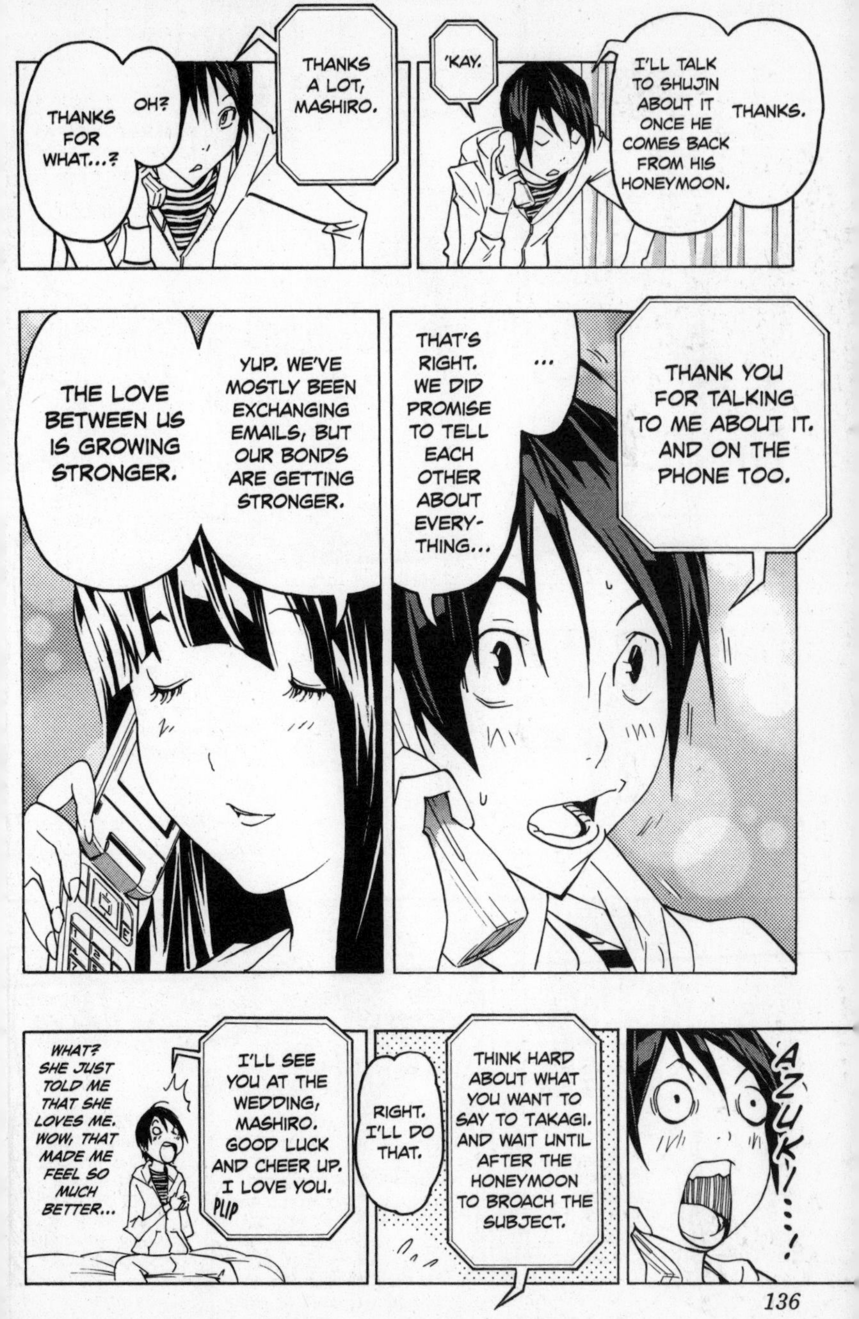
THANKS.
I'LL TALK TO SHUJIN ABOUT IT ONCE HE COMES BACK FROM HIS HONEYMOON.
'KAY.
THANKS A LOT, MASHIRO.
OH? THANKS FOR WHAT...?
THANK YOU FOR TALKING TO ME ABOUT IT. AND ON THE PHONE TOO.
...
THAT'S RIGHT. WE DID PROMISE TO TELL EACH OTHER ABOUT EVERY-THING...
YUP. WE'VE MOSTLY BEEN EXCHANGING EMAILS, BUT OUR BONDS ARE GETTING STRONGER.
THE LOVE BETWEEN US IS GROWING STRONGER.
AZUKI...!
THINK HARD ABOUT WHAT YOU WANT TO SAY TO TAKAGI. AND WAIT UNTIL AFTER THE HONEYMOON TO BROACH THE SUBJECT.
RIGHT. I'LL DO THAT.
I'LL SEE YOU AT THE WEDDING, MASHIRO. GOOD LUCK AND CHEER UP. I LOVE YOU.
PLIP
WHAT? SHE JUST TOLD ME THAT SHE LOVES ME. WOW, THAT MADE ME FEEL SO MUCH BETTER...

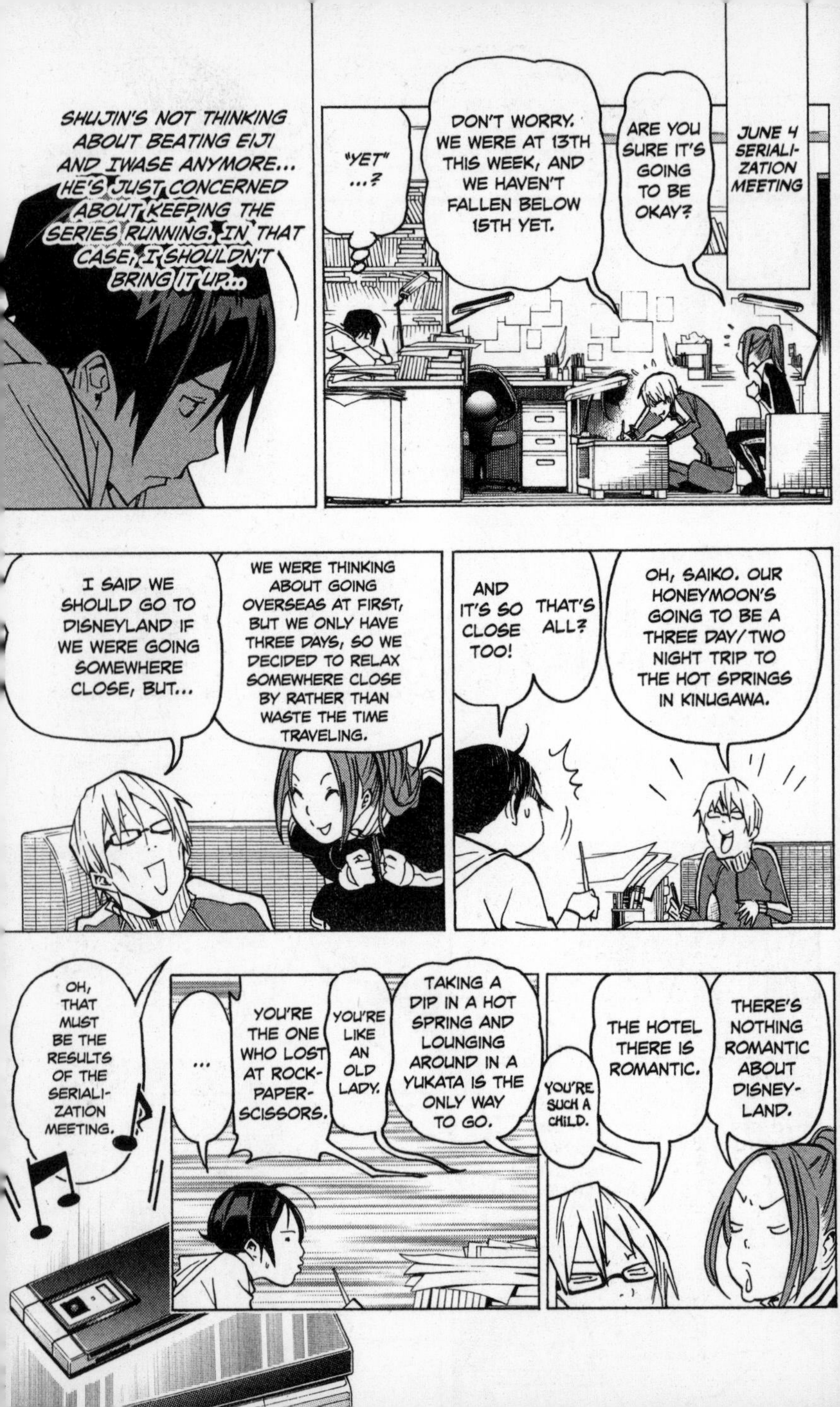
JUNE 4 SERIALIZATION MEETING
ARE YOU SURE IT'S GOING TO BE OKAY?
DON'T WORRY. WE WERE AT 13TH THIS WEEK, AND WE HAVEN'T FALLEN BELOW 15TH YET.
"YET" ...?
SHUJIN'S NOT THINKING ABOUT BEATING EIJI AND IWASE ANYMORE... HE'S JUST CONCERNED ABOUT KEEPING THE SERIES RUNNING. IN THAT CASE, I SHOULDN'T BRING IT UP...
OH, SAIKO. OUR HONEYMOON'S GOING TO BE A THREE DAY/TWO NIGHT TRIP TO THE HOT SPRINGS IN KINUGAWA.
THAT'S ALL?
AND IT'S SO CLOSE TOO!
WE WERE THINKING ABOUT GOING OVERSEAS AT FIRST, BUT WE ONLY HAVE THREE DAYS, SO WE DECIDED TO RELAX SOMEWHERE CLOSE BY RATHER THAN WASTE THE TIME TRAVELING.
I SAID WE SHOULD GO TO DISNEYLAND IF WE WERE GOING SOMEWHERE CLOSE, BUT...
THERE'S NOTHING ROMANTIC ABOUT DISNEYLAND.
THE HOTEL THERE IS ROMANTIC.
YOU'RE SUCH A CHILD.
TAKING A DIP IN A HOT SPRING AND LOUNGING AROUND IN A YUKATA IS THE ONLY WAY TO GO.
YOU'RE LIKE AN OLD LADY.
YOU'RE THE ONE WHO LOST AT ROCK-PAPER-SCISSORS.
...
OH, THAT MUST BE THE RESULTS OF THE SERIALIZATION MEETING.

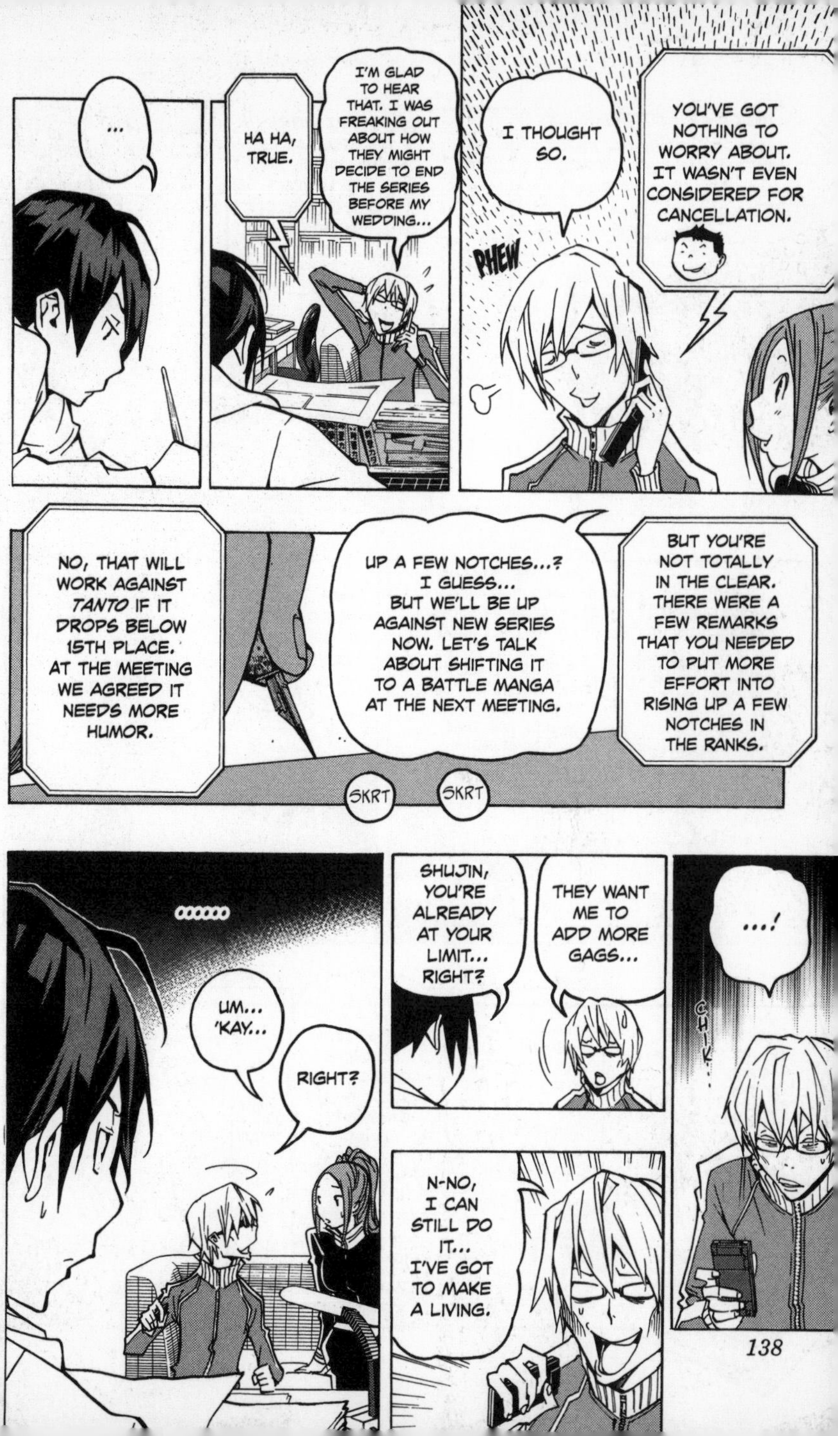
YOU'VE GOT NOTHING TO WORRY ABOUT. IT WASN'T EVEN CONSIDERED FOR CANCELLATION.
I THOUGHT SO.
PHEW
I'M GLAD TO HEAR THAT. I WAS FREAKING OUT ABOUT HOW THEY MIGHT DECIDE TO END THE SERIES BEFORE MY WEDDING...
HA HA, TRUE.
...
BUT YOU'RE NOT TOTALLY IN THE CLEAR. THERE WERE A FEW REMARKS THAT YOU NEEDED TO PUT MORE EFFORT INTO RISING UP A FEW NOTCHES IN THE RANKS.
UP A FEW NOTCHES...? I GUESS... BUT WE'LL BE UP AGAINST NEW SERIES NOW. LET'S TALK ABOUT SHIFTING IT TO A BATTLE MANGA AT THE NEXT MEETING.
NO, THAT WILL WORK AGAINST *TANTO* IF IT DROPS BELOW 15TH PLACE. AT THE MEETING WE AGREED IT NEEDS MORE HUMOR.
SKRT
SKRT
...!
CHIK...
THEY WANT ME TO ADD MORE GAGS...
SHUJIN, YOU'RE ALREADY AT YOUR LIMIT... RIGHT?
N-NO, I CAN STILL DO IT... I'VE GOT TO MAKE A LIVING.
RIGHT?
UM... 'KAY...

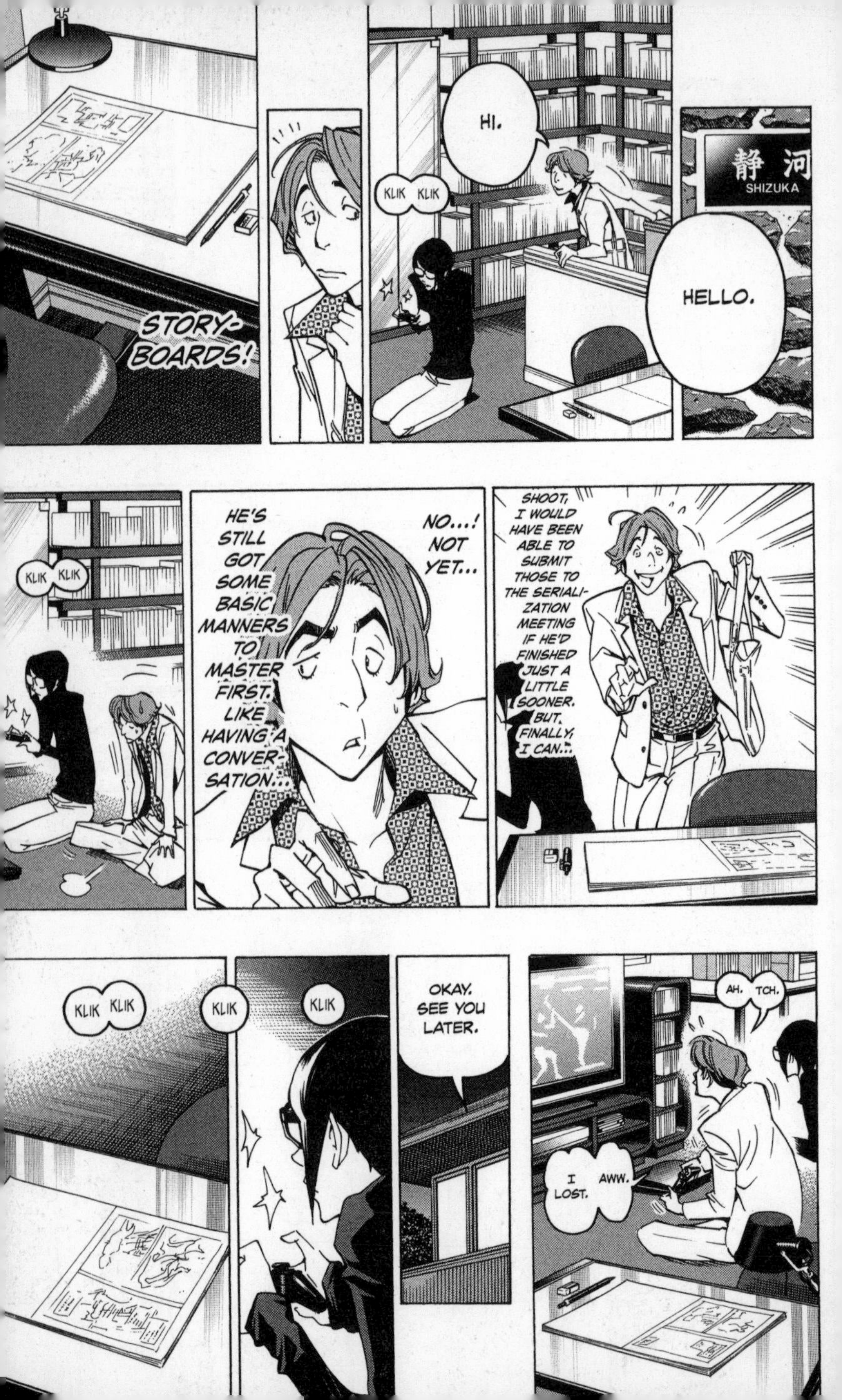

静河
SHIZUKA
HELLO.
HI.
KLIK KLIK
STORY-BOARDS!
SHOOT, I WOULD HAVE BEEN ABLE TO SUBMIT THOSE TO THE SERIALI-ZATION MEETING IF HE'D FINISHED JUST A LITTLE SOONER. BUT, FINALLY, I CAN...
NO...! NOT YET...
HE'S STILL GOT SOME BASIC MANNERS TO MASTER FIRST. LIKE HAVING A CONVER-SATION...
KLIK KLIK
AH. TCH.
AWW.
I LOST.
OKAY. SEE YOU LATER.
KLIK
KLIK
KLIK KLIK

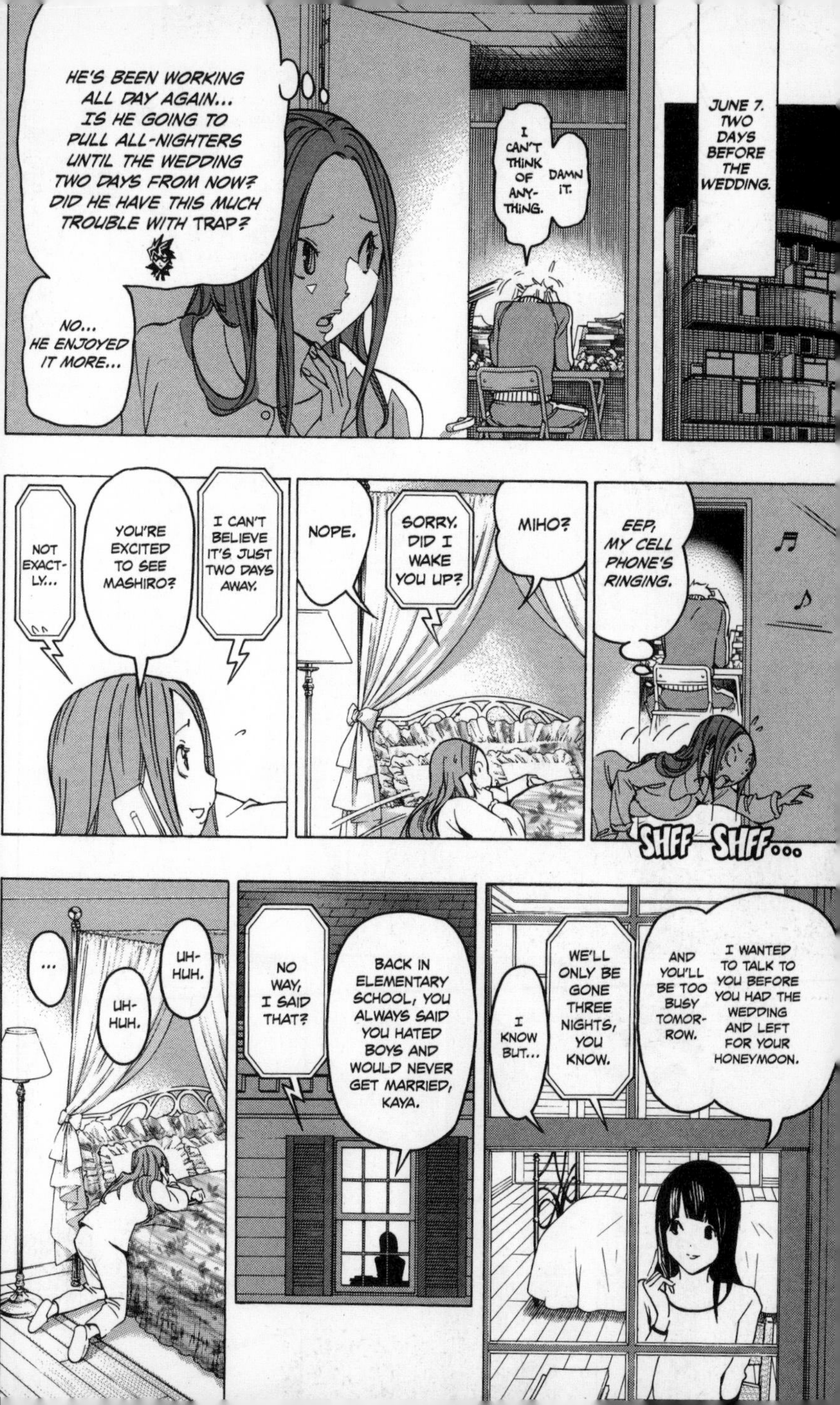
JUNE 7. TWO DAYS BEFORE THE WEDDING.
I CAN'T THINK OF ANYTHING.
DAMN IT.
HE'S BEEN WORKING ALL DAY AGAIN... IS HE GOING TO PULL ALL-NIGHTERS UNTIL THE WEDDING TWO DAYS FROM NOW? DID HE HAVE THIS MUCH TROUBLE WITH TRAP?
NO... HE ENJOYED IT MORE...
EEP, MY CELL PHONE'S RINGING.
SHFF SHFF...
MIHO?
SORRY. DID I WAKE YOU UP?
NOPE.
I CAN'T BELIEVE IT'S JUST TWO DAYS AWAY.
YOU'RE EXCITED TO SEE MASHIRO?
NOT EXACTLY...
I WANTED TO TALK TO YOU BEFORE YOU HAD THE WEDDING AND LEFT FOR YOUR HONEYMOON.
AND YOU'LL BE TOO BUSY TOMORROW.
WE'LL ONLY BE GONE THREE NIGHTS, YOU KNOW.
I KNOW BUT...
BACK IN ELEMENTARY SCHOOL, YOU ALWAYS SAID YOU HATED BOYS AND WOULD NEVER GET MARRIED, KAYA.
NO WAY, I SAID THAT?
UH-HUH.
UH-HUH.
...

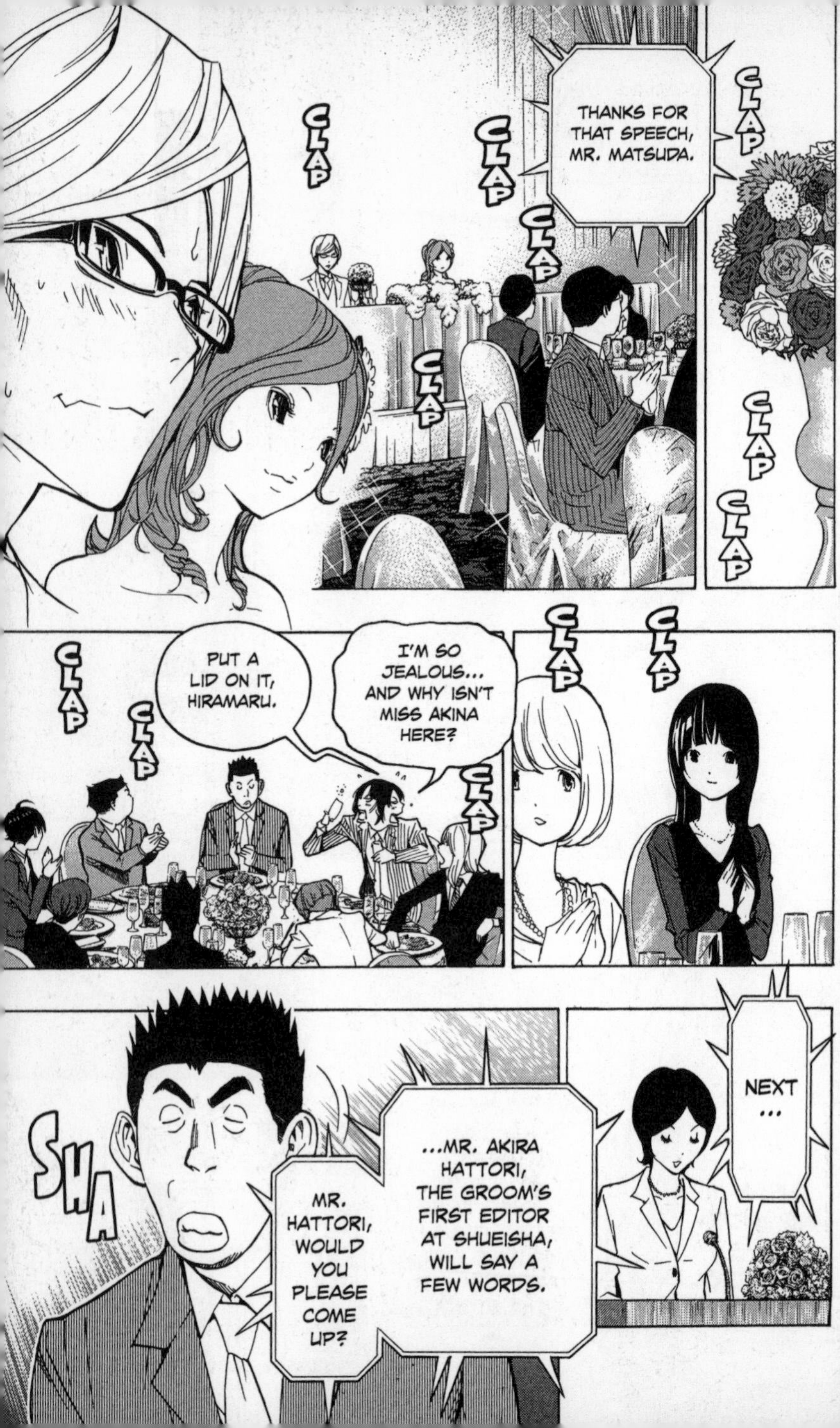
THANKS FOR THAT SPEECH, MR. MATSUDA.
CLAP
CLAP
CLAP
CLAP
CLAP
CLAP
CLAP
CLAP
CLAP
I'M SO JEALOUS... AND WHY ISN'T MISS AKINA HERE?
PUT A LID ON IT, HIRAMARU.
CLAP
CLAP
CLAP
NEXT...
...MR. AKIRA HATTORI, THE GROOM'S FIRST EDITOR AT SHUEISHA, WILL SAY A FEW WORDS.
MR. HATTORI, WOULD YOU PLEASE COME UP?
SHA

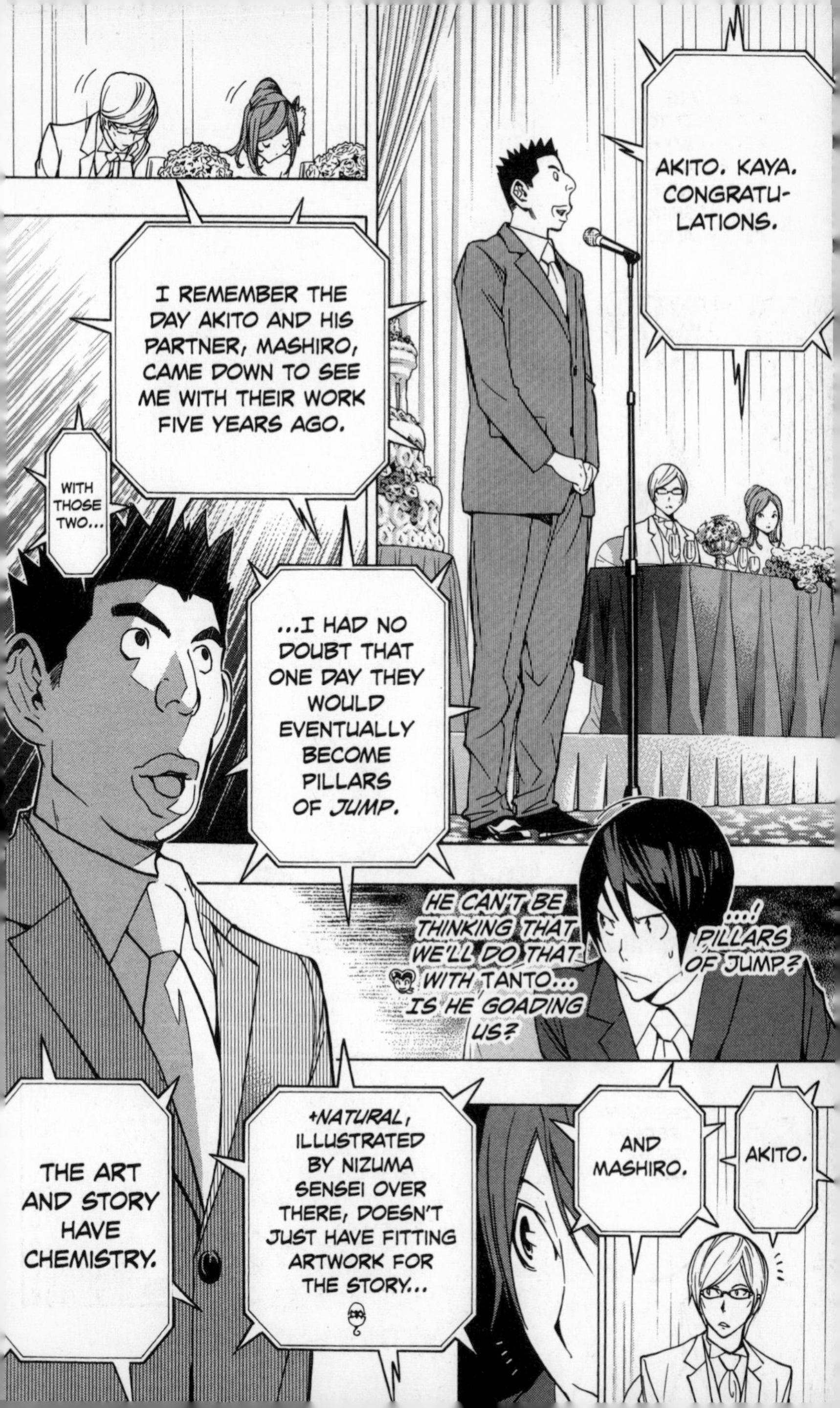
AKITO. KAYA. CONGRATULATIONS.
I REMEMBER THE DAY AKITO AND HIS PARTNER, MASHIRO, CAME DOWN TO SEE ME WITH THEIR WORK FIVE YEARS AGO.
WITH THOSE TWO...
...I HAD NO DOUBT THAT ONE DAY THEY WOULD EVENTUALLY BECOME PILLARS OF *JUMP*.
...! PILLARS OF *JUMP*?
HE CAN'T BE THINKING THAT WE'LL DO THAT WITH TANTO... IS HE GOADING US?
AKITO.
AND MASHIRO.
+NATURAL, ILLUSTRATED BY NIZUMA SENSEI OVER THERE, DOESN'T JUST HAVE FITTING ARTWORK FOR THE STORY...
THE ART AND STORY HAVE CHEMISTRY.

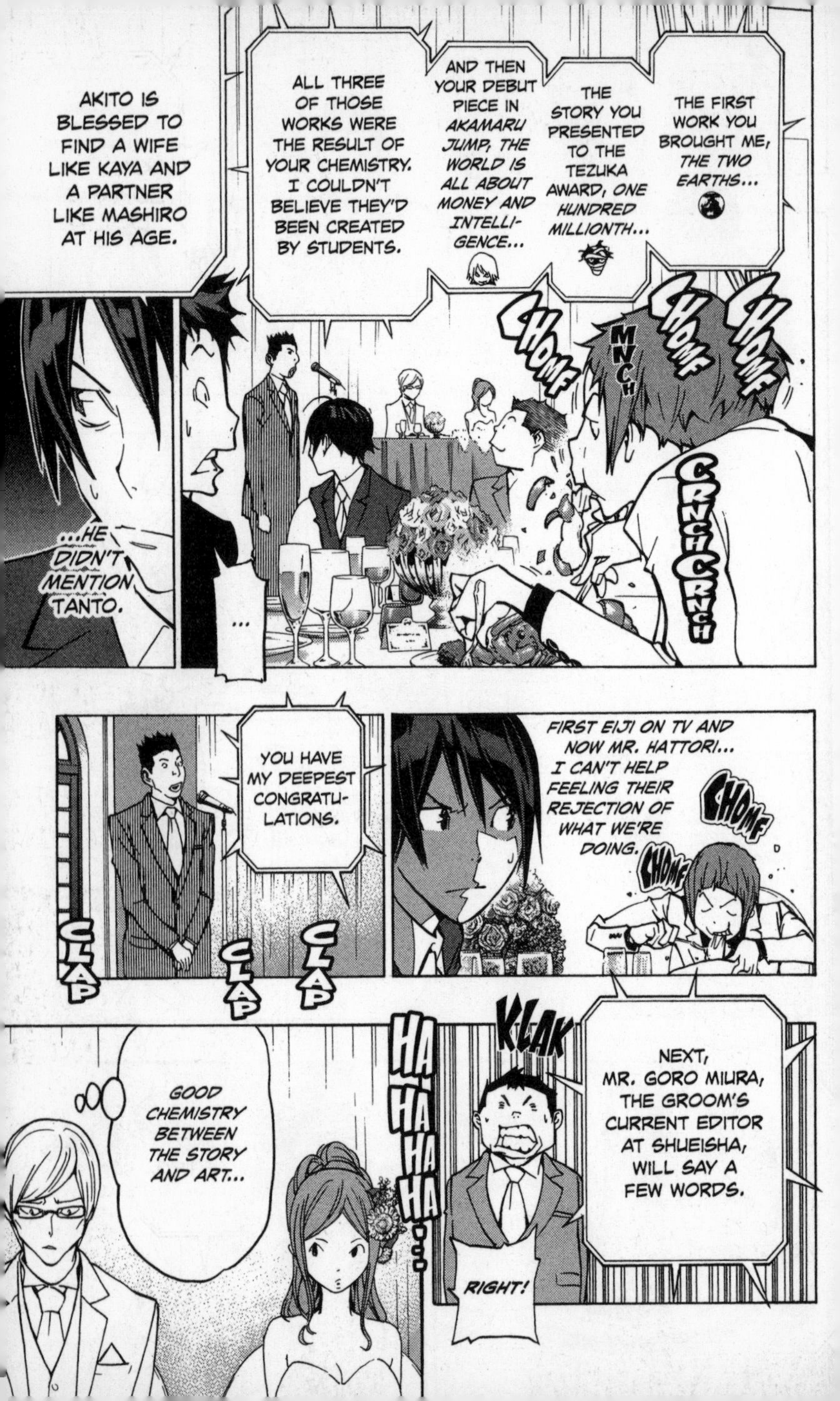
THE FIRST WORK YOU BROUGHT ME, *THE TWO EARTHS*...
THE STORY YOU PRESENTED TO THE TEZUKA AWARD, *ONE HUNDRED MILLIONTH*...
AND THEN YOUR DEBUT PIECE IN *AKAMARU JUMP*, *THE WORLD IS ALL ABOUT MONEY AND INTELLIGENCE*...
ALL THREE OF THOSE WORKS WERE THE RESULT OF YOUR CHEMISTRY. I COULDN'T BELIEVE THEY'D BEEN CREATED BY STUDENTS.
AKITO IS BLESSED TO FIND A WIFE LIKE KAYA AND A PARTNER LIKE MASHIRO AT HIS AGE.
CHOMF
CHOMF
CHOMF
MNCH
CRNCH CRNCH CRNCH
...
...HE DIDN'T MENTION TANTO.
FIRST EIJI ON TV AND NOW MR. HATTORI... I CAN'T HELP FEELING THEIR REJECTION OF WHAT WE'RE DOING.
CHOMF
CHOMF
YOU HAVE MY DEEPEST CONGRATULATIONS.
CLAP
CLAP
CLAP
KLAK
NEXT, MR. GORO MIURA, THE GROOM'S CURRENT EDITOR AT SHUEISHA, WILL SAY A FEW WORDS.
RIGHT!
HA HA HA HA HA
GOOD CHEMISTRY BETWEEN THE STORY AND ART...

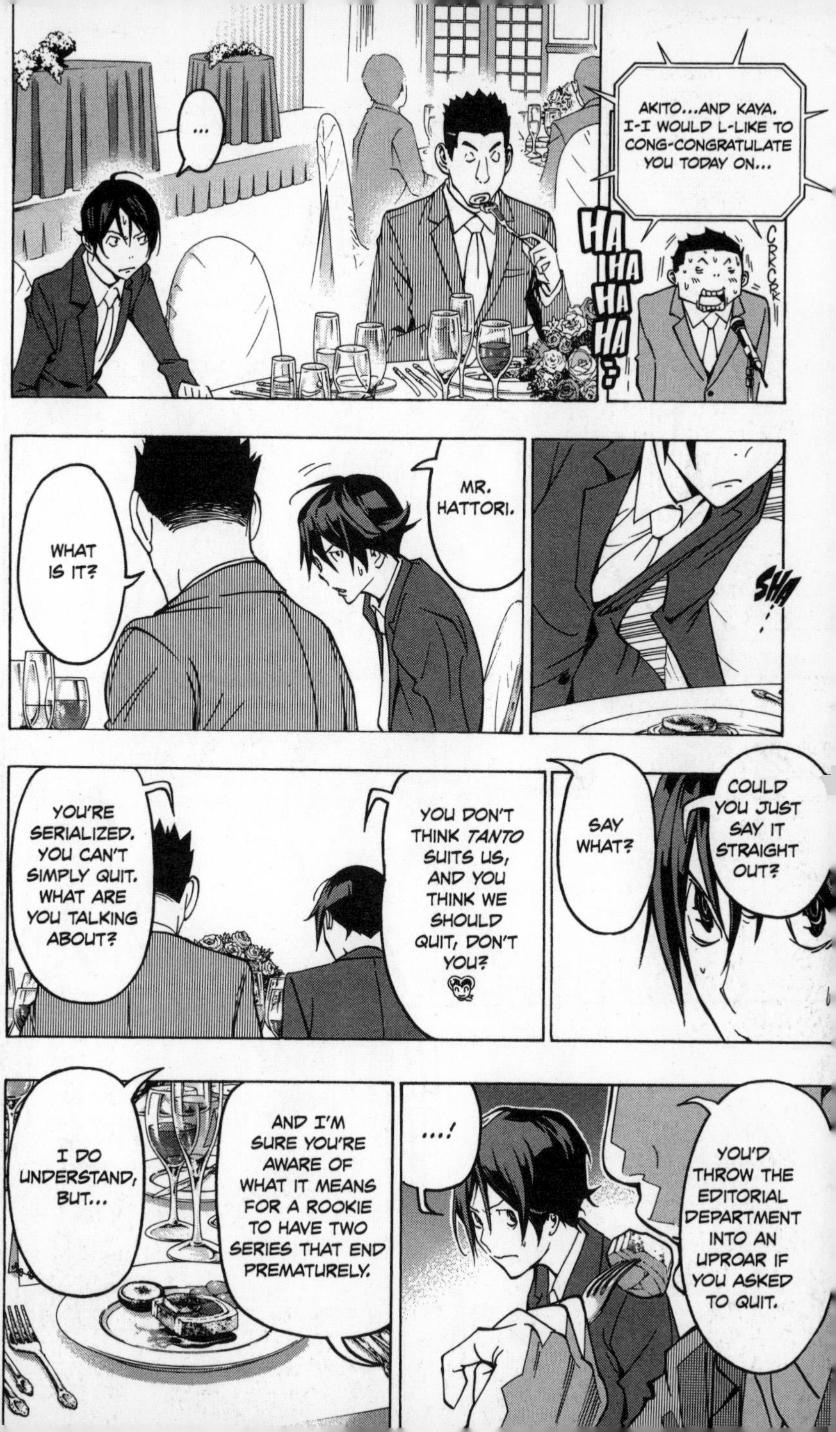
AKITO...AND KAYA. I-I WOULD L-LIKE TO CONG-CONGRATULATE YOU TODAY ON...
HA HA HA HA
CRK CRK
...
SHA
MR. HATTORI.
WHAT IS IT?
COULD YOU JUST SAY IT STRAIGHT OUT?
SAY WHAT?
YOU DON'T THINK *TANTO* SUITS US, AND YOU THINK WE SHOULD QUIT, DON'T YOU?
YOU'RE SERIALIZED. YOU CAN'T SIMPLY QUIT. WHAT ARE YOU TALKING ABOUT?
YOU'D THROW THE EDITORIAL DEPARTMENT INTO AN UPROAR IF YOU ASKED TO QUIT.
...!
AND I'M SURE YOU'RE AWARE OF WHAT IT MEANS FOR A ROOKIE TO HAVE TWO SERIES THAT END PREMATURELY.
I DO UNDERSTAND, BUT...

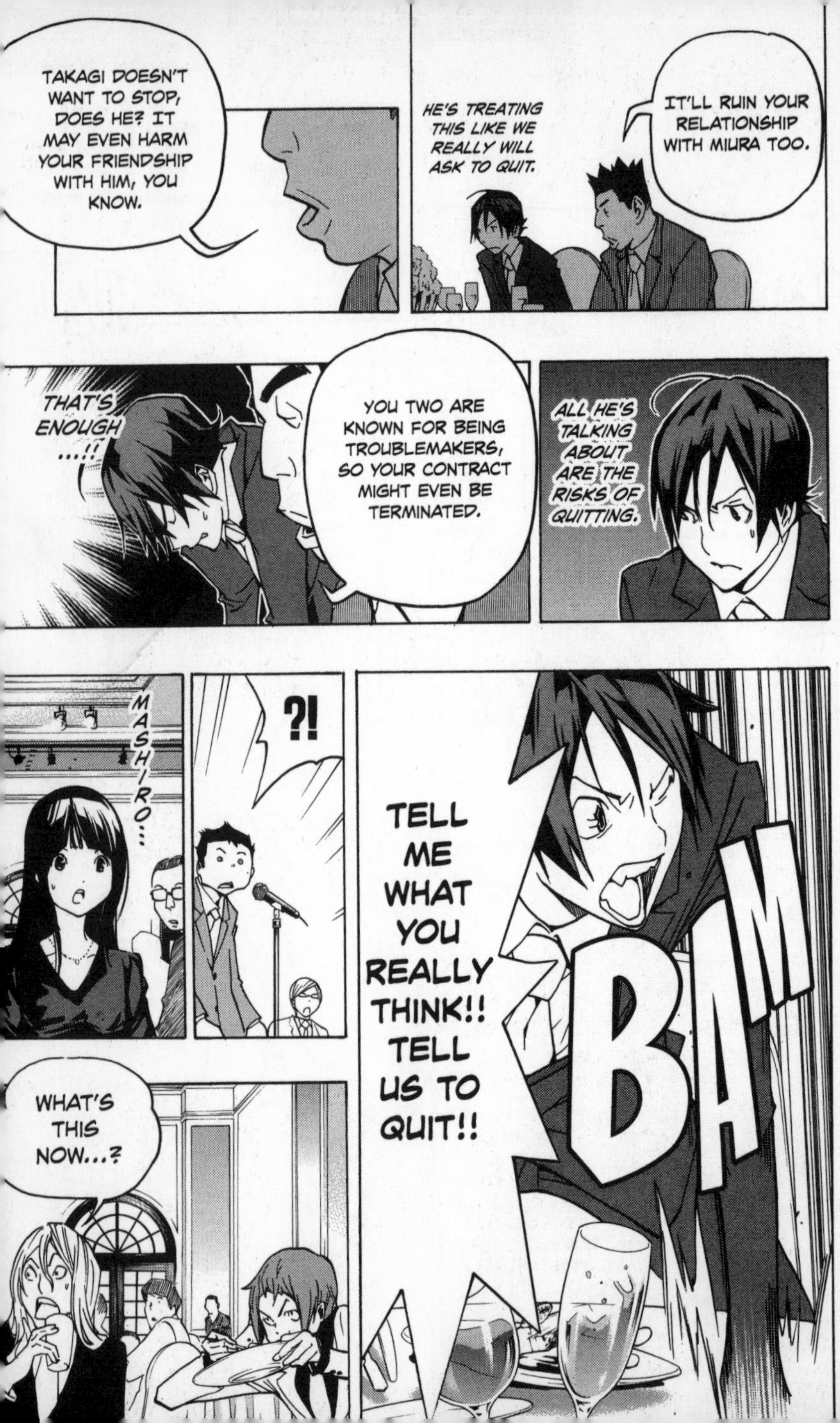
IT'LL RUIN YOUR RELATIONSHIP WITH MIURA TOO.
HE'S TREATING THIS LIKE WE REALLY WILL ASK TO QUIT.
TAKAGI DOESN'T WANT TO STOP, DOES HE? IT MAY EVEN HARM YOUR FRIENDSHIP WITH HIM, YOU KNOW.
ALL HE'S TALKING ABOUT ARE THE RISKS OF QUITTING.
YOU TWO ARE KNOWN FOR BEING TROUBLEMAKERS, SO YOUR CONTRACT MIGHT EVEN BE TERMINATED.
THAT'S ENOUGH ...!!
TELL ME WHAT YOU REALLY THINK!! TELL US TO QUIT!!
BAM
?!
MASHIRO...
WHAT'S THIS NOW...?

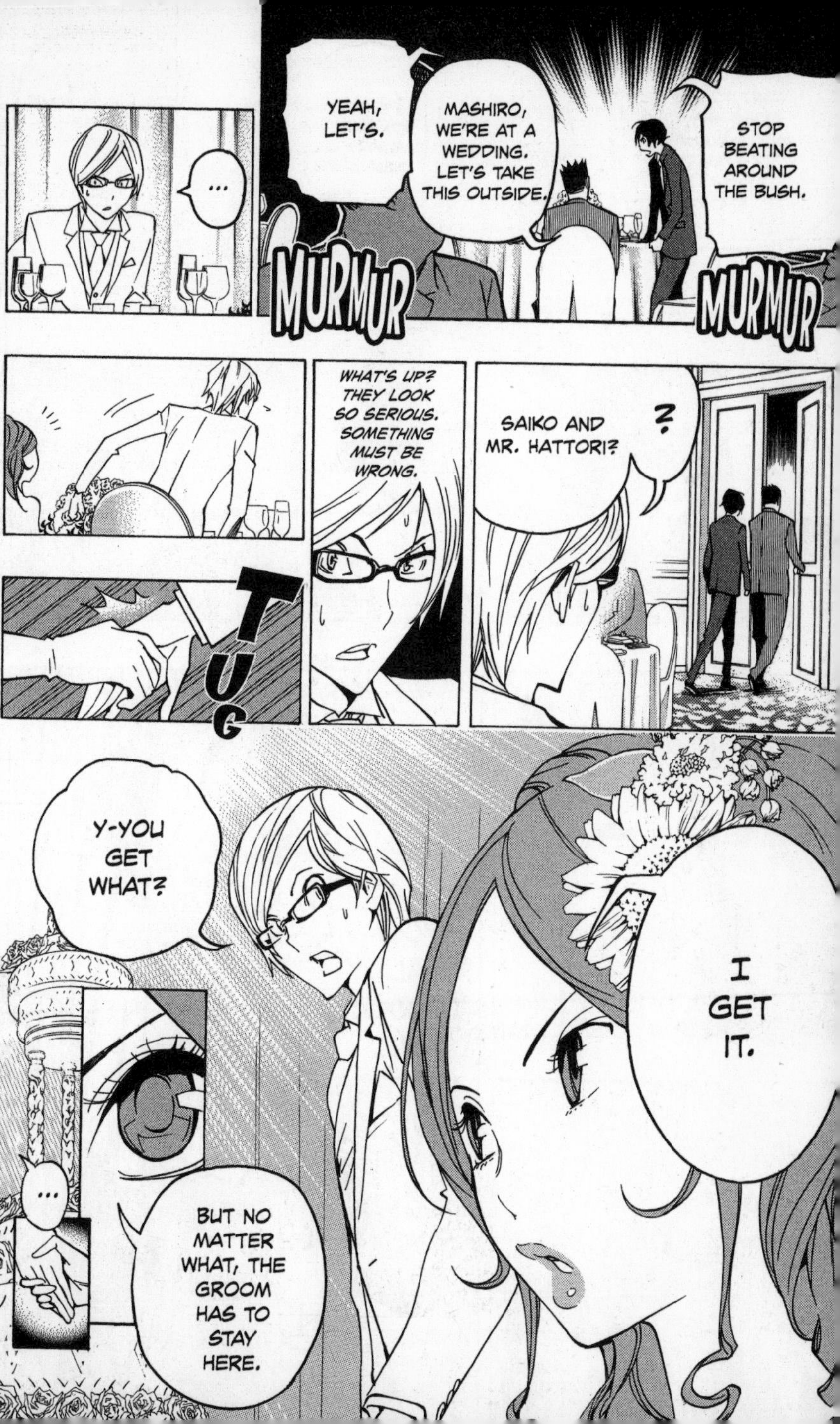
STOP BEATING AROUND THE BUSH.
MURMUR
MASHIRO, WE'RE AT A WEDDING. LET'S TAKE THIS OUTSIDE.
YEAH, LET'S.
MURMUR
...
SAIKO AND MR. HATTORI?
?
WHAT'S UP? THEY LOOK SO SERIOUS. SOMETHING MUST BE WRONG.
TUG
I GET IT.
Y-YOU GET WHAT?
...
BUT NO MATTER WHAT, THE GROOM HAS TO STAY HERE.

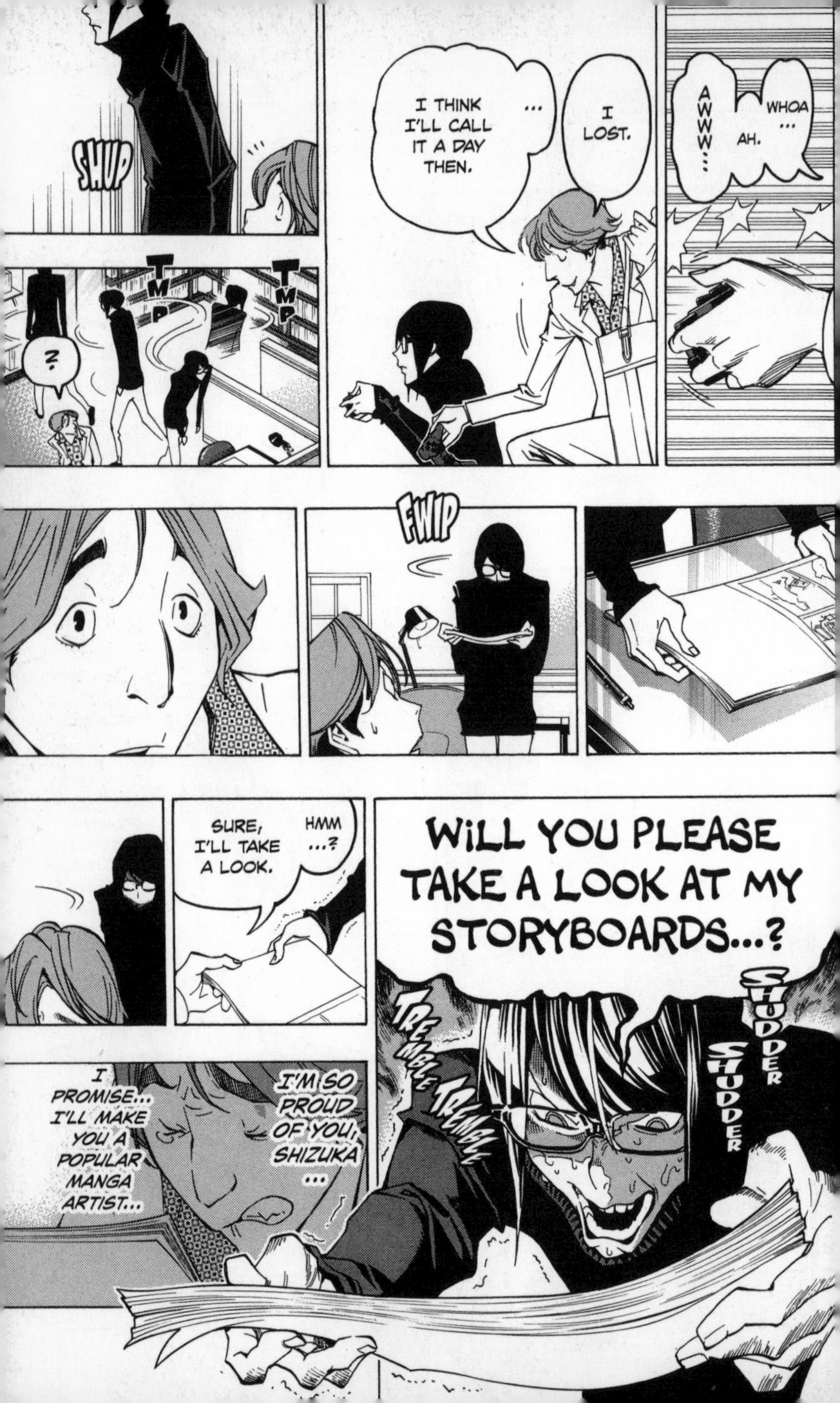
WHOA...
AH.
AWWW...
...
I LOST.
I THINK I'LL CALL IT A DAY THEN.
SHUP
?
TMP
TMP
FWIP
WILL YOU PLEASE TAKE A LOOK AT MY STORYBOARDS...?
SHUDDER
SHUDDER
TREMBLE TREMBLE
HMM...?
SURE, I'LL TAKE A LOOK.
I'M SO PROUD OF YOU, SHIZUKA...
I PROMISE... I'LL MAKE YOU A POPULAR MANGA ARTIST...

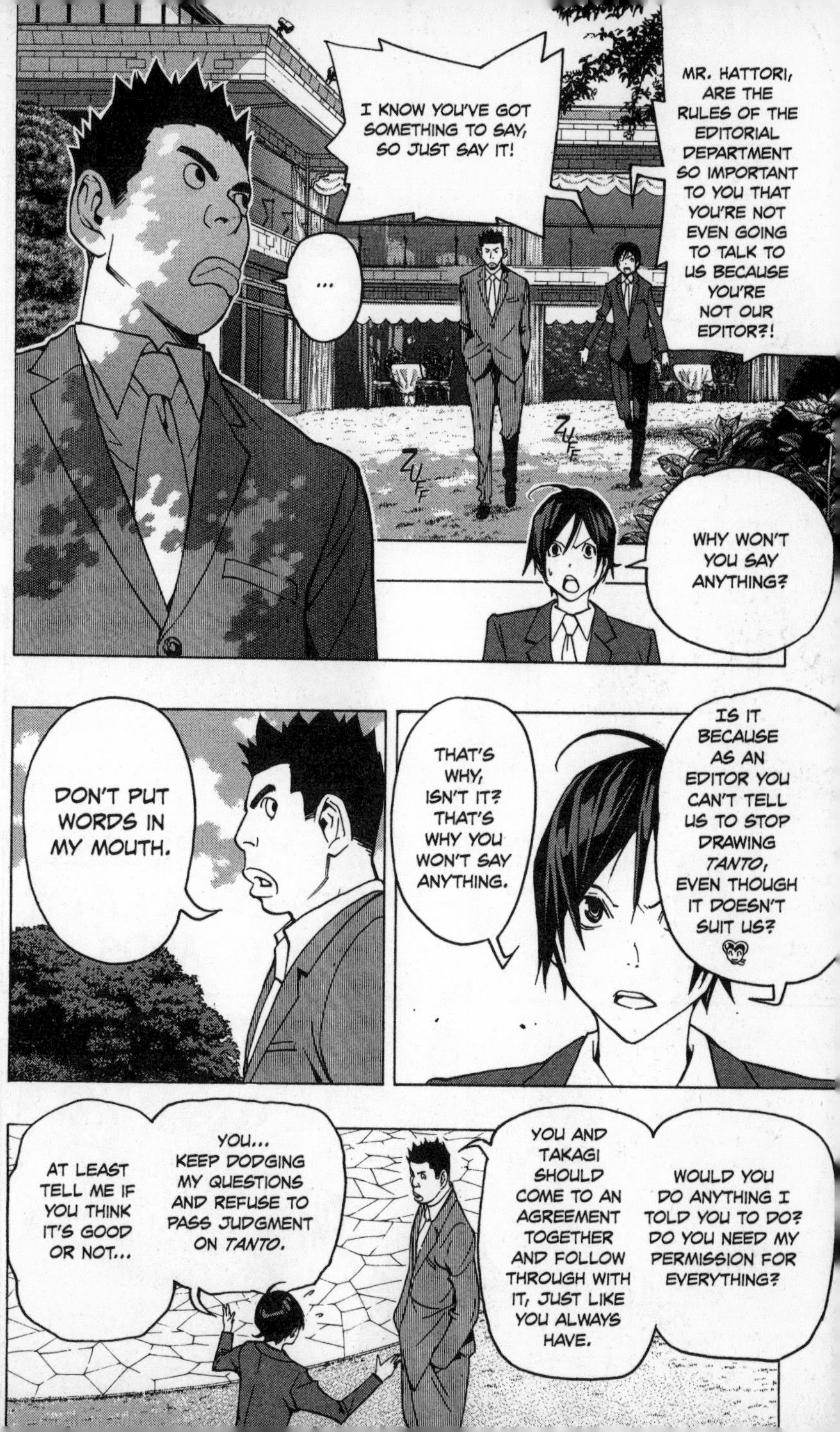
MR. HATTORI, ARE THE RULES OF THE EDITORIAL DEPARTMENT SO IMPORTANT TO YOU THAT YOU'RE NOT EVEN GOING TO TALK TO US BECAUSE YOU'RE NOT OUR EDITOR?!
I KNOW YOU'VE GOT SOMETHING TO SAY, SO JUST SAY IT!
...
ZUFF
ZUFF
WHY WON'T YOU SAY ANYTHING?
IS IT BECAUSE AS AN EDITOR YOU CAN'T TELL US TO STOP DRAWING *TANTO*, EVEN THOUGH IT DOESN'T SUIT US?
THAT'S WHY, ISN'T IT? THAT'S WHY YOU WON'T SAY ANYTHING.
DON'T PUT WORDS IN MY MOUTH.
WOULD YOU DO ANYTHING I TOLD YOU TO DO? DO YOU NEED MY PERMISSION FOR EVERYTHING?
YOU AND TAKAGI SHOULD COME TO AN AGREEMENT TOGETHER AND FOLLOW THROUGH WITH IT, JUST LIKE YOU ALWAYS HAVE.
YOU... KEEP DODGING MY QUESTIONS AND REFUSE TO PASS JUDGMENT ON *TANTO*.
AT LEAST TELL ME IF YOU THINK IT'S GOOD OR NOT...

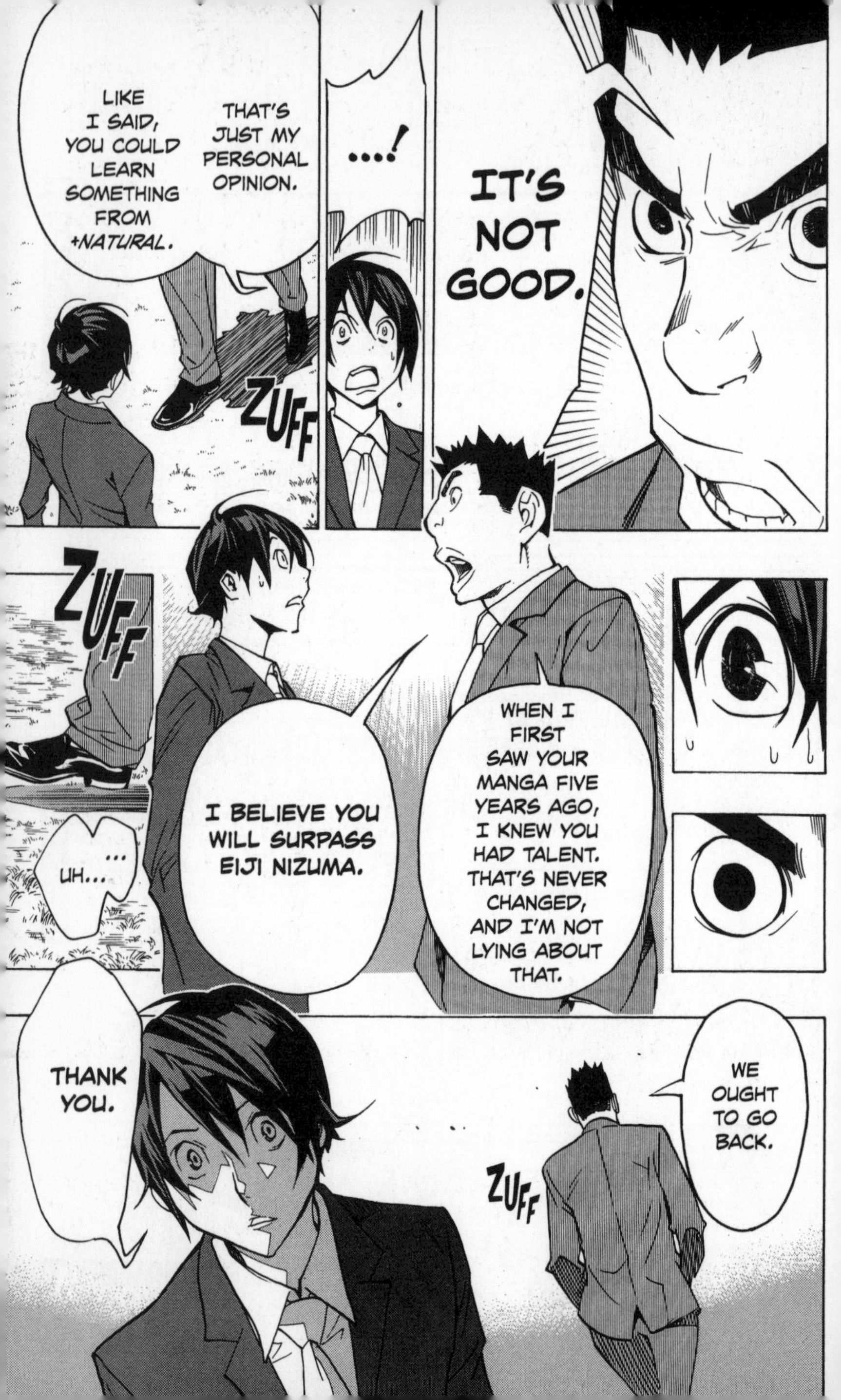
IT'S NOT GOOD.
....!
THAT'S JUST MY PERSONAL OPINION.
LIKE I SAID, YOU COULD LEARN SOMETHING FROM +NATURAL.
ZUFF
WHEN I FIRST SAW YOUR MANGA FIVE YEARS AGO, I KNEW YOU HAD TALENT. THAT'S NEVER CHANGED, AND I'M NOT LYING ABOUT THAT.
I BELIEVE YOU WILL SURPASS EIJI NIZUMA.
ZUFF
... UH...
WE OUGHT TO GO BACK.
ZUFF
THANK YOU.

OHBA'S STORYBOARD

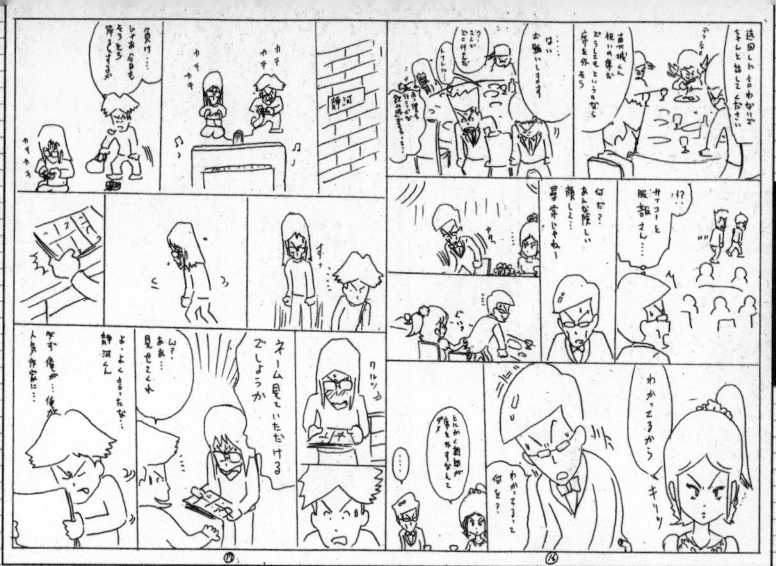
服部さん……
!?
わかってるから
キリッ
わかってるって何を?
カチ カチ
静河
ネーム見ていただけるでしょうか
ん? ああ… 見せてくれ
クルッ
よ…よく言ったな… 静河くん

OBATA'S STORYBOARD

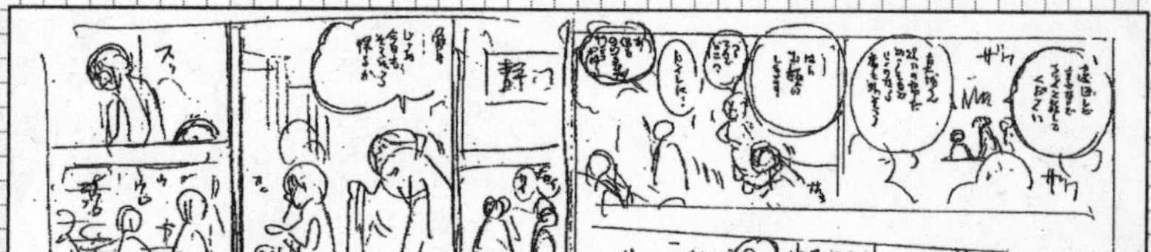
わかってるから
ネーム見ていただけるでしょうか

COMPLETE!

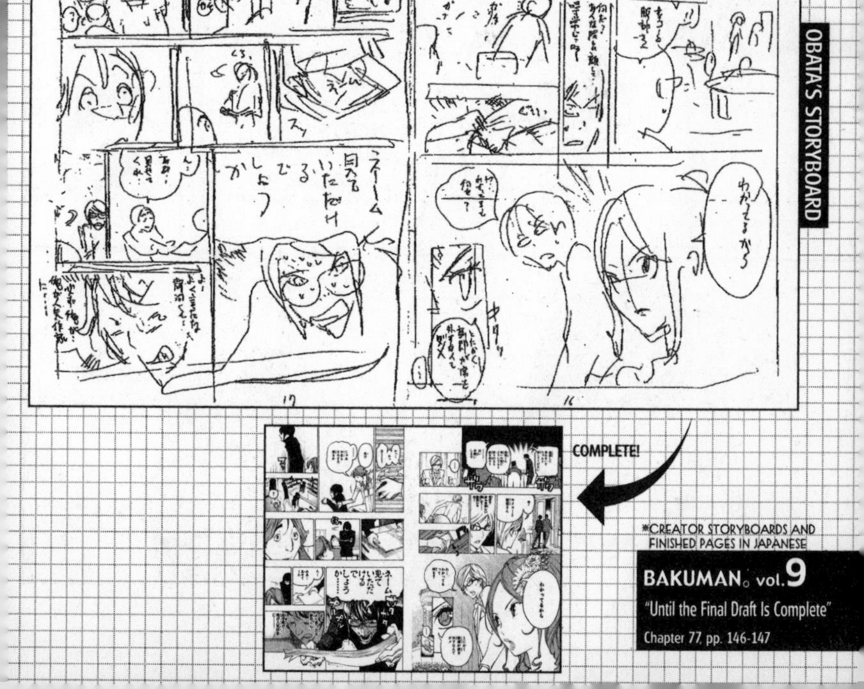

※CREATOR STORYBOARDS AND FINISHED PAGES IN JAPANESE

BAKUMAN。 vol.9

"Until the Final Draft Is Complete"

Chapter 77, pp. 146-147

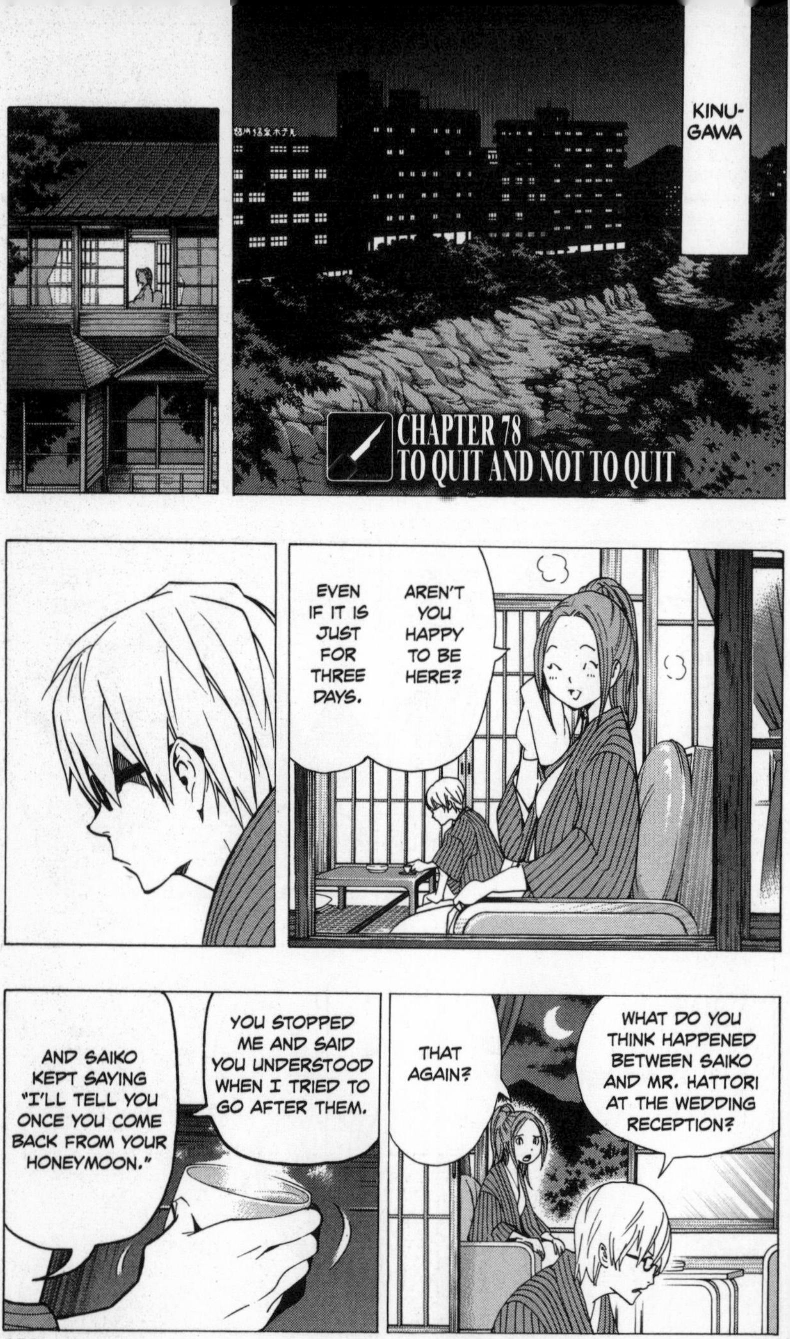
KINU-GAWA
CHAPTER 78
TO QUIT AND NOT TO QUIT
AREN'T YOU HAPPY TO BE HERE?
EVEN IF IT IS JUST FOR THREE DAYS.
WHAT DO YOU THINK HAPPENED BETWEEN SAIKO AND MR. HATTORI AT THE WEDDING RECEPTION?
THAT AGAIN?
YOU STOPPED ME AND SAID YOU UNDERSTOOD WHEN I TRIED TO GO AFTER THEM.
AND SAIKO KEPT SAYING "I'LL TELL YOU ONCE YOU COME BACK FROM YOUR HONEYMOON."

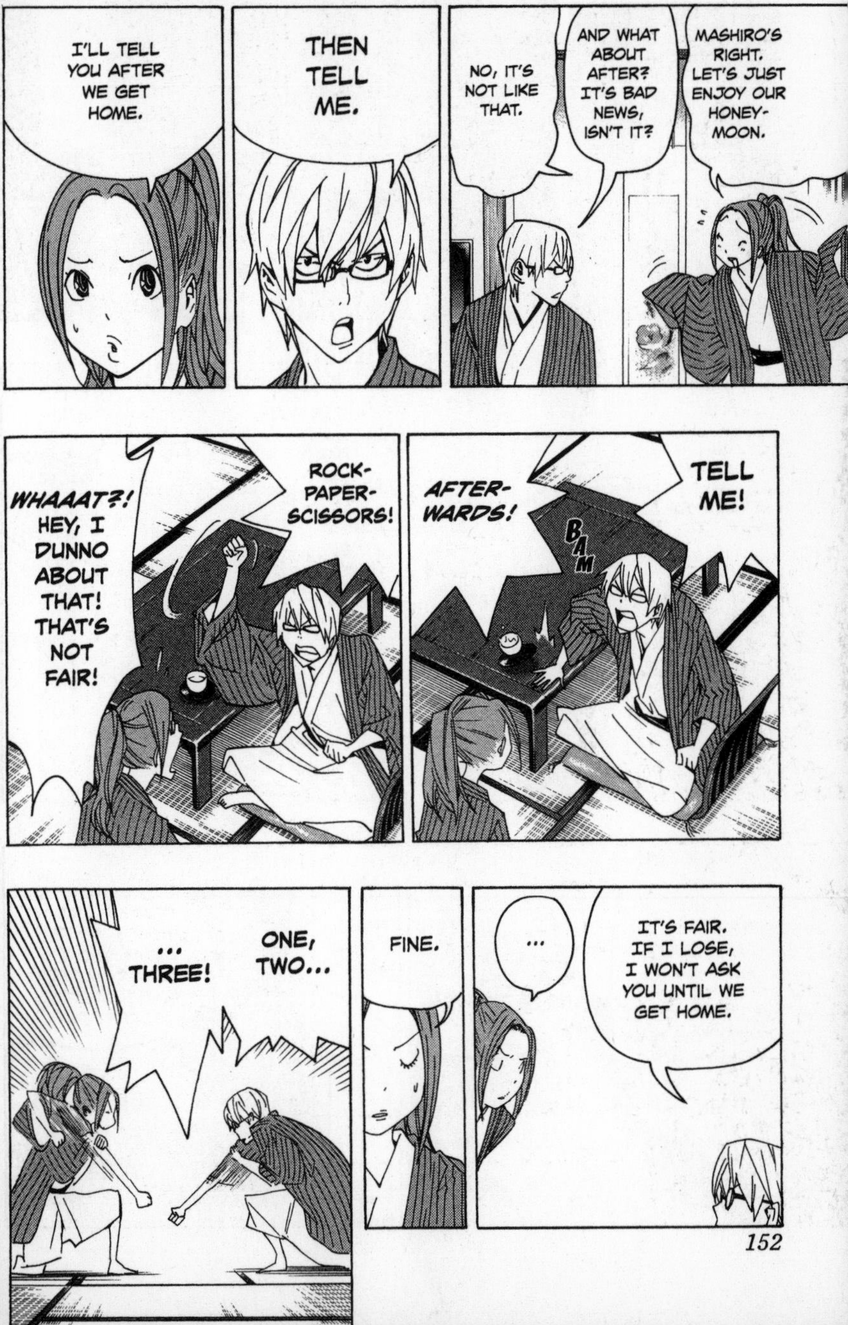
MASHIRO'S RIGHT. LET'S JUST ENJOY OUR HONEY-MOON.
AND WHAT ABOUT AFTER? IT'S BAD NEWS, ISN'T IT?
NO, IT'S NOT LIKE THAT.
THEN TELL ME.
I'LL TELL YOU AFTER WE GET HOME.
TELL ME!
BAM
AFTER-WARDS!
ROCK-PAPER-SCISSORS!
WHAAAT?! HEY, I DUNNO ABOUT THAT! THAT'S NOT FAIR!
IT'S FAIR. IF I LOSE, I WON'T ASK YOU UNTIL WE GET HOME.
...
FINE.
ONE, TWO...
... THREE!

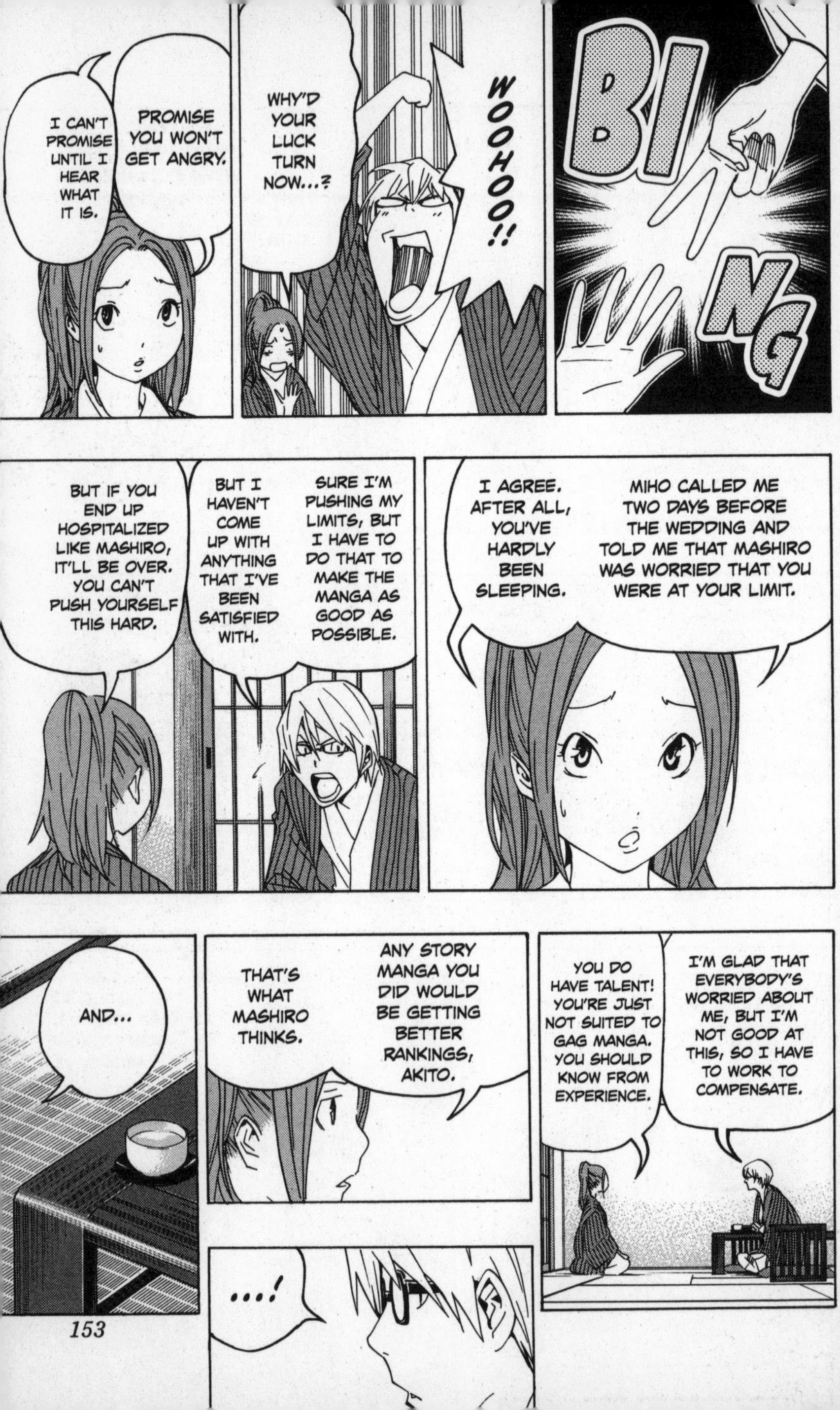
BING
WOOHOO!!
WHY'D YOUR LUCK TURN NOW...?
PROMISE YOU WON'T GET ANGRY.
I CAN'T PROMISE UNTIL I HEAR WHAT IT IS.
MIHO CALLED ME TWO DAYS BEFORE THE WEDDING AND TOLD ME THAT MASHIRO WAS WORRIED THAT YOU WERE AT YOUR LIMIT.
I AGREE. AFTER ALL, YOU'VE HARDLY BEEN SLEEPING.
SURE I'M PUSHING MY LIMITS, BUT I HAVE TO DO THAT TO MAKE THE MANGA AS GOOD AS POSSIBLE.
BUT I HAVEN'T COME UP WITH ANYTHING THAT I'VE BEEN SATISFIED WITH.
BUT IF YOU END UP HOSPITALIZED LIKE MASHIRO, IT'LL BE OVER. YOU CAN'T PUSH YOURSELF THIS HARD.
I'M GLAD THAT EVERYBODY'S WORRIED ABOUT ME, BUT I'M NOT GOOD AT THIS, SO I HAVE TO WORK TO COMPENSATE.
YOU DO HAVE TALENT! YOU'RE JUST NOT SUITED TO GAG MANGA. YOU SHOULD KNOW FROM EXPERIENCE.
ANY STORY MANGA YOU DID WOULD BE GETTING BETTER RANKINGS, AKITO.
THAT'S WHAT MASHIRO THINKS.
...!
AND...

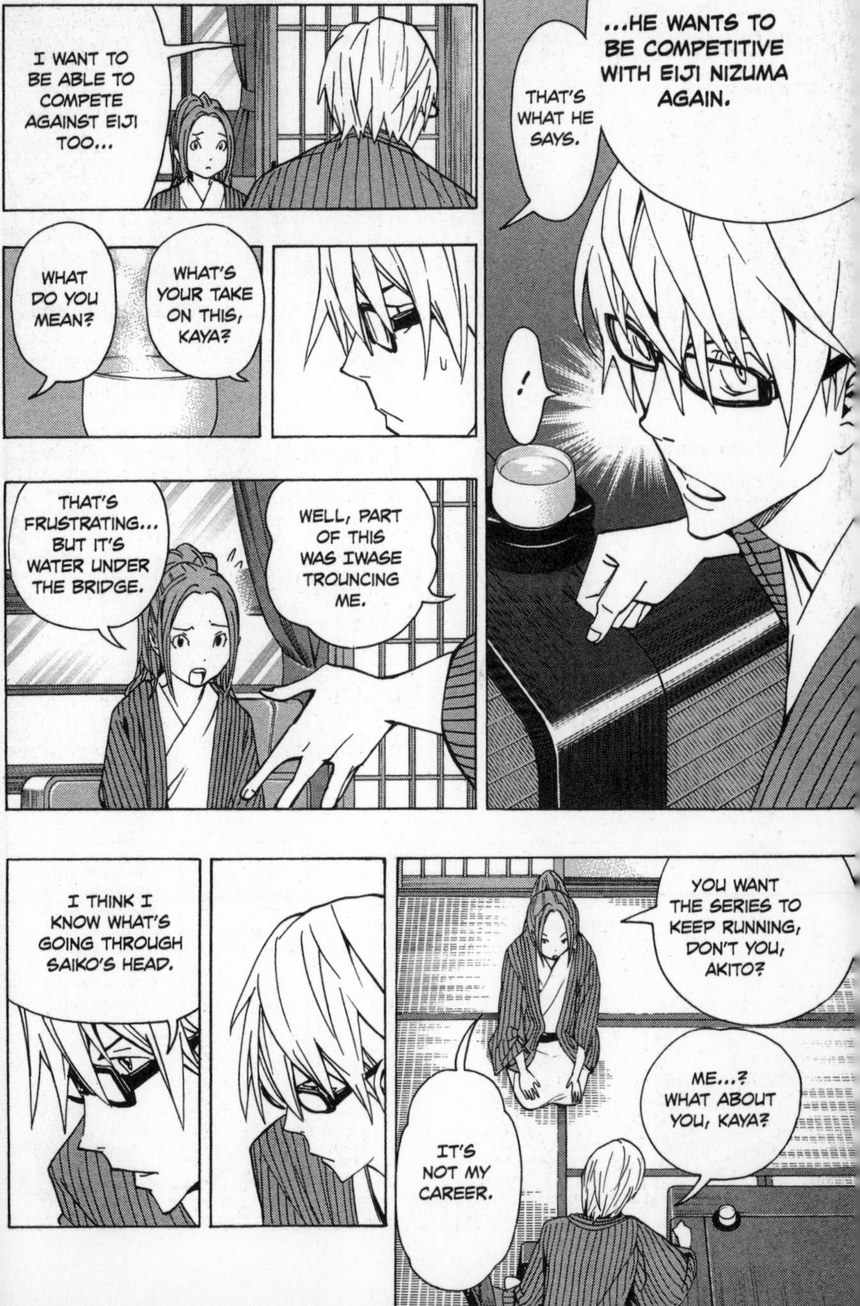
...HE WANTS TO BE COMPETITIVE WITH EIJI NIZUMA AGAIN.
THAT'S WHAT HE SAYS.
!
I WANT TO BE ABLE TO COMPETE AGAINST EIJI TOO...
WHAT'S YOUR TAKE ON THIS, KAYA?
WHAT DO YOU MEAN?
WELL, PART OF THIS WAS IWASE TROUNCING ME.
THAT'S FRUSTRATING... BUT IT'S WATER UNDER THE BRIDGE.
YOU WANT THE SERIES TO KEEP RUNNING, DON'T YOU, AKITO?
ME...? WHAT ABOUT YOU, KAYA?
IT'S NOT MY CAREER.
I THINK I KNOW WHAT'S GOING THROUGH SAIKO'S HEAD.

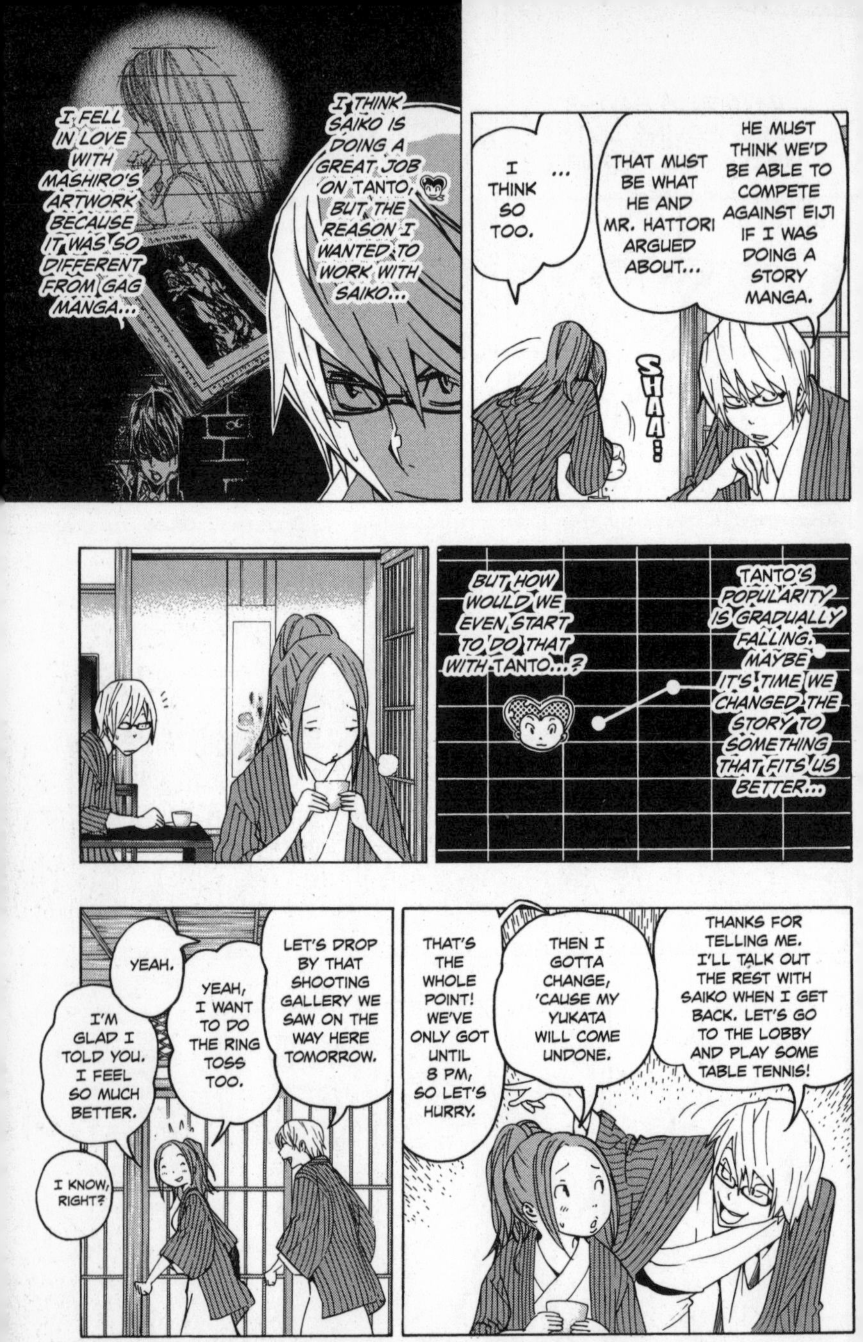
HE MUST THINK WE'D BE ABLE TO COMPETE AGAINST EIJI IF I WAS DOING A STORY MANGA.
THAT MUST BE WHAT HE AND MR. HATTORI ARGUED ABOUT...
I ... THINK SO TOO.
SHAA!!
I THINK SAIKO IS DOING A GREAT JOB ON TANTO, BUT THE REASON I WANTED TO WORK WITH SAIKO...
I FELL IN LOVE WITH MASHIRO'S ARTWORK BECAUSE IT WAS SO DIFFERENT FROM GAG MANGA...
TANTO'S POPULARITY IS GRADUALLY FALLING. MAYBE IT'S TIME WE CHANGED THE STORY TO SOMETHING THAT FITS US BETTER...
BUT HOW WOULD WE EVEN START TO DO THAT WITH TANTO...?
THANKS FOR TELLING ME. I'LL TALK OUT THE REST WITH SAIKO WHEN I GET BACK. LET'S GO TO THE LOBBY AND PLAY SOME TABLE TENNIS!
THEN I GOTTA CHANGE, 'CAUSE MY YUKATA WILL COME UNDONE.
THAT'S THE WHOLE POINT! WE'VE ONLY GOT UNTIL 8 PM, SO LET'S HURRY.
LET'S DROP BY THAT SHOOTING GALLERY WE SAW ON THE WAY HERE TOMORROW.
YEAH, I WANT TO DO THE RING TOSS TOO.
YEAH.
I'M GLAD I TOLD YOU. I FEEL SO MUCH BETTER.
I KNOW, RIGHT?

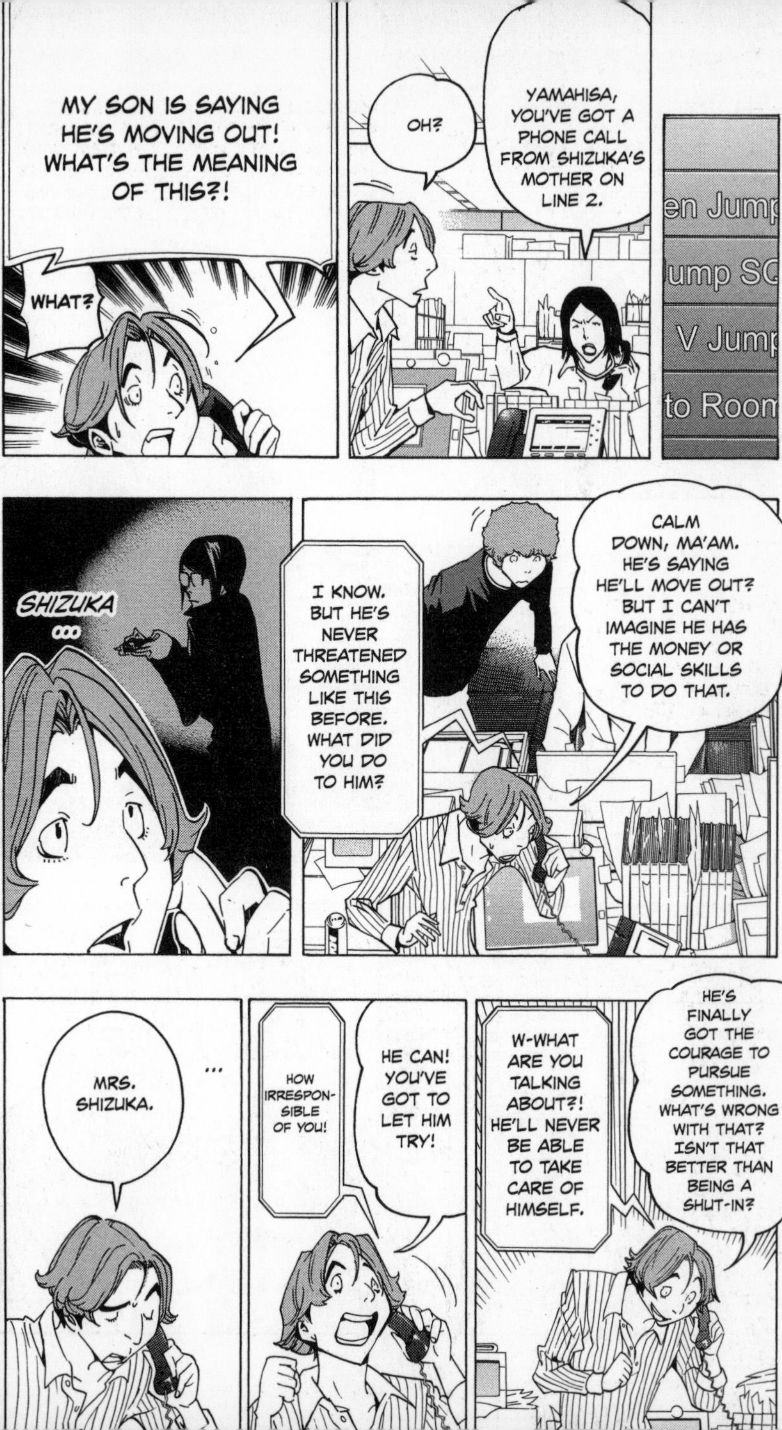

en Jump
ump SQ
V Jump
to Room
YAMAHISA, YOU'VE GOT A PHONE CALL FROM SHIZUKA'S MOTHER ON LINE 2.
OH?
MY SON IS SAYING HE'S MOVING OUT! WHAT'S THE MEANING OF THIS?!
WHAT?
CALM DOWN, MA'AM. HE'S SAYING HE'LL MOVE OUT? BUT I CAN'T IMAGINE HE HAS THE MONEY OR SOCIAL SKILLS TO DO THAT.
I KNOW. BUT HE'S NEVER THREATENED SOMETHING LIKE THIS BEFORE. WHAT DID YOU DO TO HIM?
SHIZUKA ...
HE'S FINALLY GOT THE COURAGE TO PURSUE SOMETHING. WHAT'S WRONG WITH THAT? ISN'T THAT BETTER THAN BEING A SHUT-IN?
W-WHAT ARE YOU TALKING ABOUT?! HE'LL NEVER BE ABLE TO TAKE CARE OF HIMSELF.
HE CAN! YOU'VE GOT TO LET HIM TRY!
HOW IRRESPON-SIBLE OF YOU!
...
MRS. SHIZUKA.

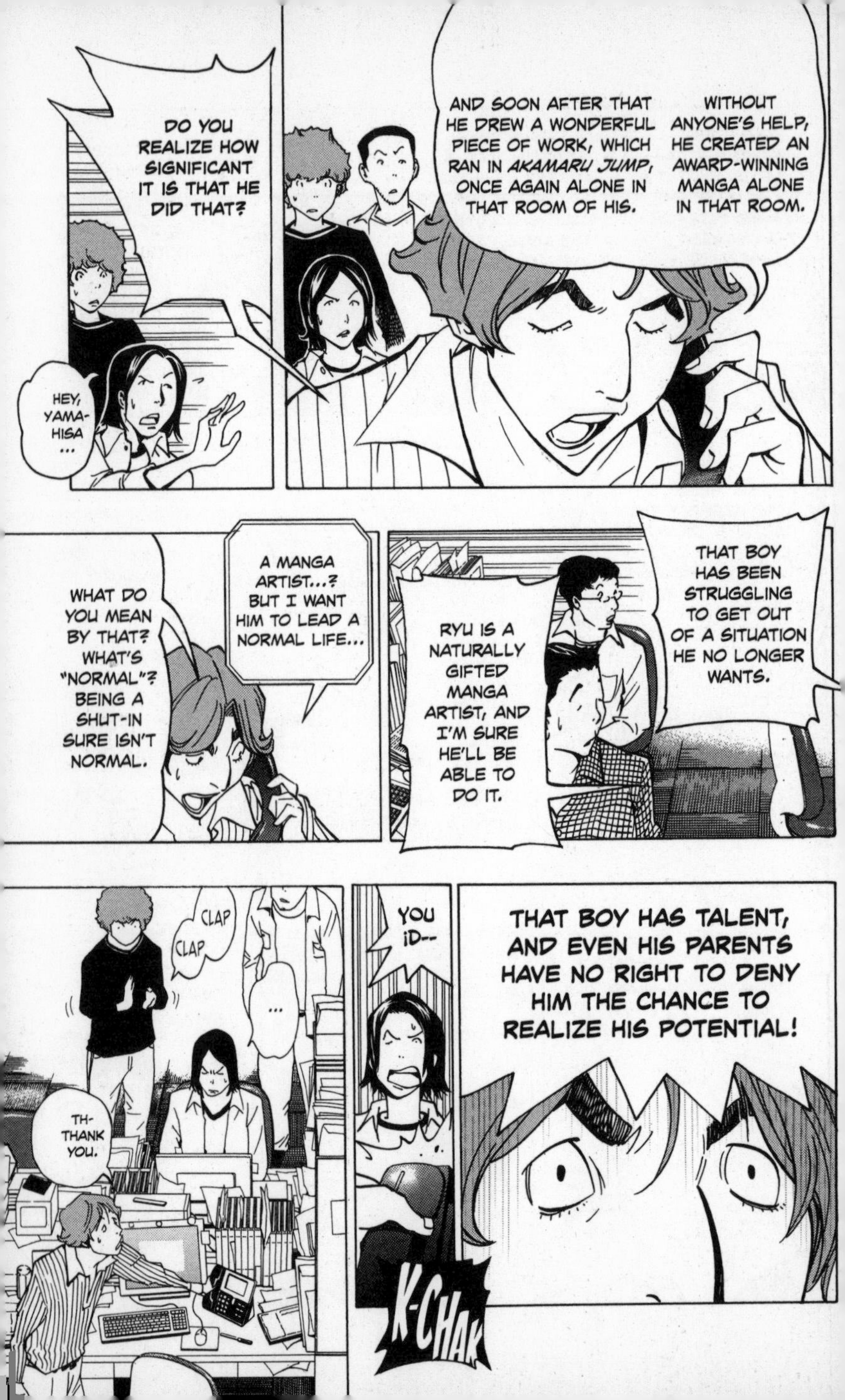

WITHOUT ANYONE'S HELP, HE CREATED AN AWARD-WINNING MANGA ALONE IN THAT ROOM.
AND SOON AFTER THAT HE DREW A WONDERFUL PIECE OF WORK, WHICH RAN IN *AKAMARU JUMP*, ONCE AGAIN ALONE IN THAT ROOM OF HIS.
DO YOU REALIZE HOW SIGNIFICANT IT IS THAT HE DID THAT?
HEY, YAMAHISA...
THAT BOY HAS BEEN STRUGGLING TO GET OUT OF A SITUATION HE NO LONGER WANTS.
RYU IS A NATURALLY GIFTED MANGA ARTIST, AND I'M SURE HE'LL BE ABLE TO DO IT.
A MANGA ARTIST...? BUT I WANT HIM TO LEAD A NORMAL LIFE...
WHAT DO YOU MEAN BY THAT? WHAT'S "NORMAL"? BEING A SHUT-IN SURE ISN'T NORMAL.
THAT BOY HAS TALENT, AND EVEN HIS PARENTS HAVE NO RIGHT TO DENY HIM THE CHANCE TO REALIZE HIS POTENTIAL!
YOU iD--
K-CHAK
CLAP
CLAP
...
TH-THANK YOU.

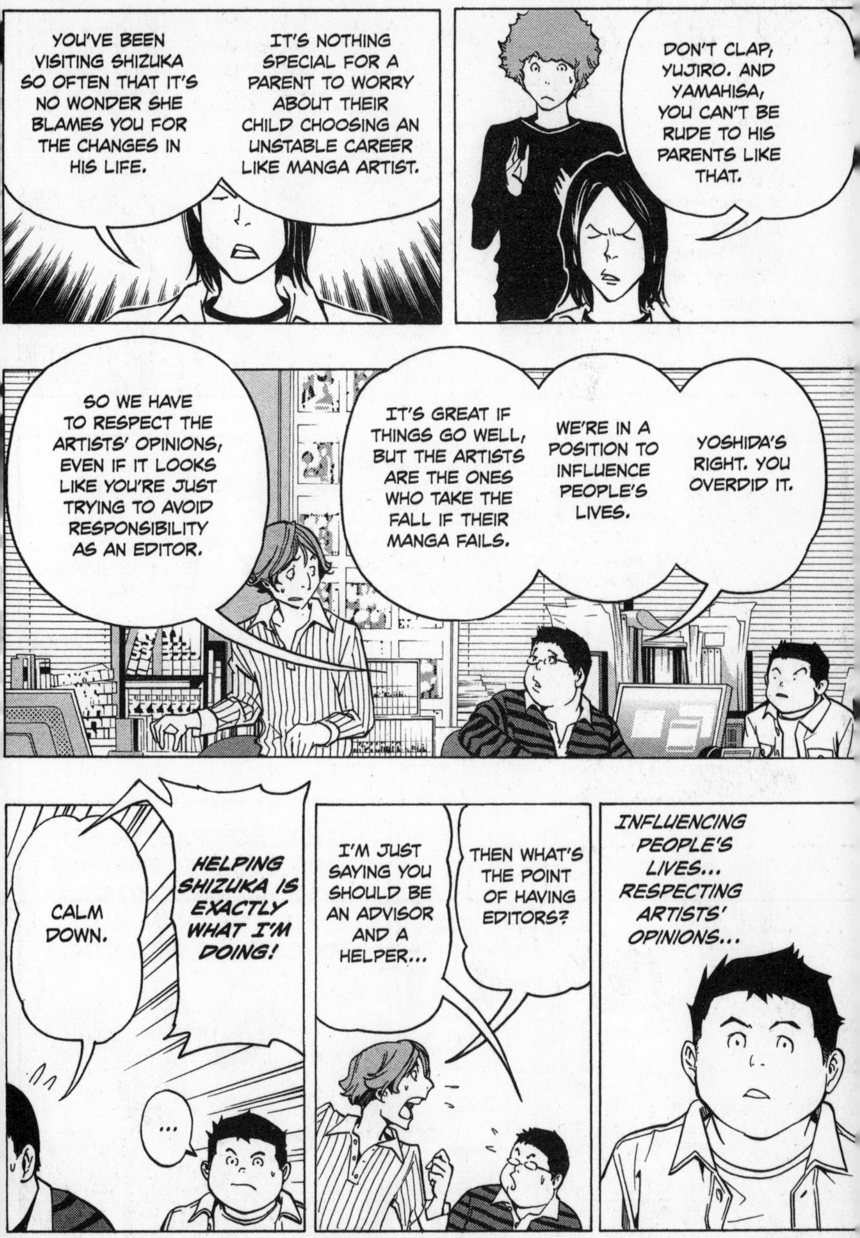
DON'T CLAP, YUJIRO. AND YAMAHISA, YOU CAN'T BE RUDE TO HIS PARENTS LIKE THAT.
IT'S NOTHING SPECIAL FOR A PARENT TO WORRY ABOUT THEIR CHILD CHOOSING AN UNSTABLE CAREER LIKE MANGA ARTIST.
YOU'VE BEEN VISITING SHIZUKA SO OFTEN THAT IT'S NO WONDER SHE BLAMES YOU FOR THE CHANGES IN HIS LIFE.
YOSHIDA'S RIGHT. YOU OVERDID IT.
WE'RE IN A POSITION TO INFLUENCE PEOPLE'S LIVES.
IT'S GREAT IF THINGS GO WELL, BUT THE ARTISTS ARE THE ONES WHO TAKE THE FALL IF THEIR MANGA FAILS.
SO WE HAVE TO RESPECT THE ARTISTS' OPINIONS, EVEN IF IT LOOKS LIKE YOU'RE JUST TRYING TO AVOID RESPONSIBILITY AS AN EDITOR.
INFLUENCING PEOPLE'S LIVES... RESPECTING ARTISTS' OPINIONS...
THEN WHAT'S THE POINT OF HAVING EDITORS?
I'M JUST SAYING YOU SHOULD BE AN ADVISOR AND A HELPER...
HELPING SHIZUKA IS EXACTLY WHAT I'M DOING!
CALM DOWN.
...

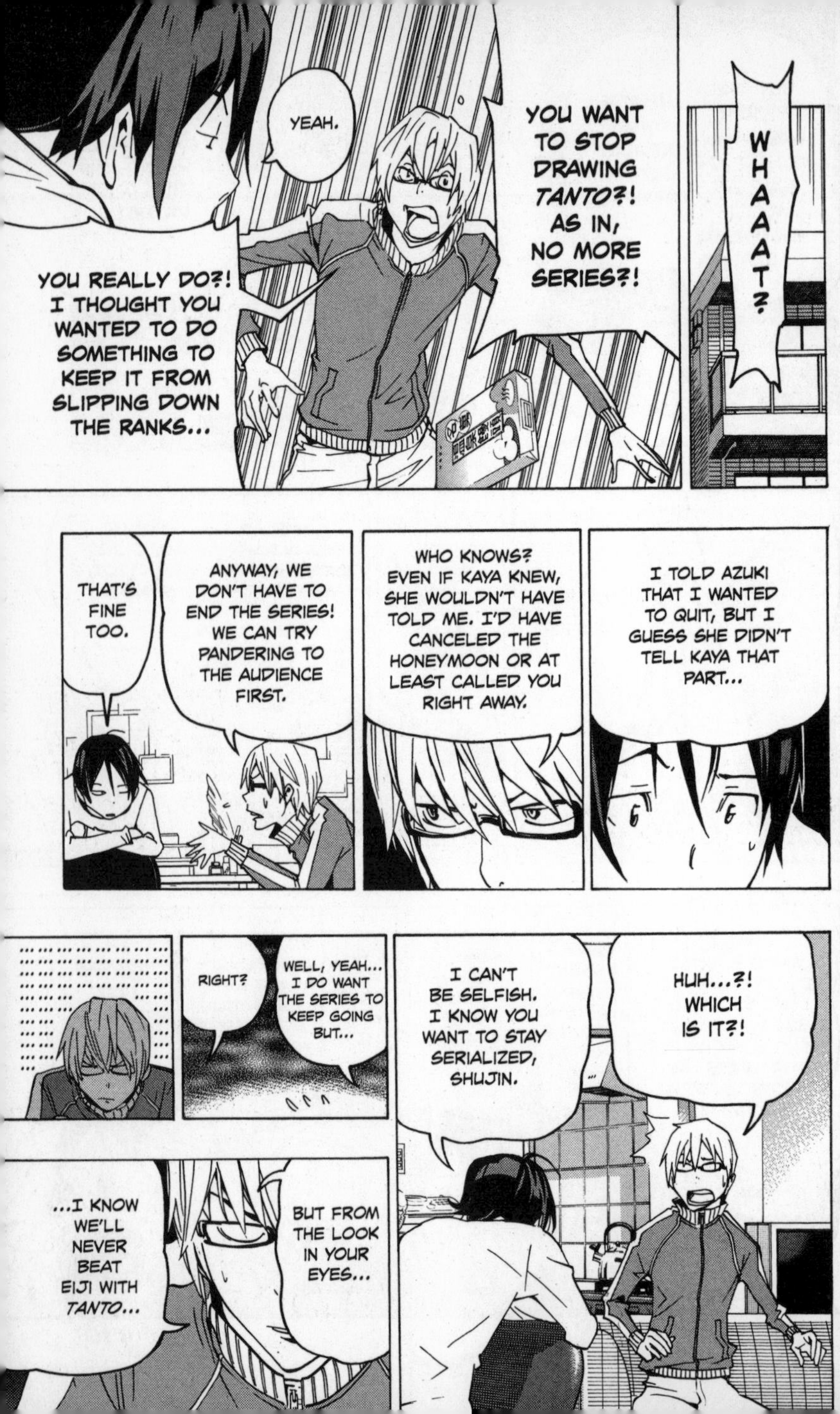
WHAAAT?!
YOU WANT TO STOP DRAWING *TANTO*?! AS IN, NO MORE SERIES?!
YEAH.
YOU REALLY DO?! I THOUGHT YOU WANTED TO DO SOMETHING TO KEEP IT FROM SLIPPING DOWN THE RANKS...
I TOLD AZUKI THAT I WANTED TO QUIT, BUT I GUESS SHE DIDN'T TELL KAYA THAT PART...
WHO KNOWS? EVEN IF KAYA KNEW, SHE WOULDN'T HAVE TOLD ME. I'D HAVE CANCELED THE HONEYMOON OR AT LEAST CALLED YOU RIGHT AWAY.
ANYWAY, WE DON'T HAVE TO END THE SERIES! WE CAN TRY PANDERING TO THE AUDIENCE FIRST.
THAT'S FINE TOO.
HUH...?! WHICH IS IT?!
I CAN'T BE SELFISH. I KNOW YOU WANT TO STAY SERIALIZED, SHUJIN.
WELL, YEAH... I DO WANT THE SERIES TO KEEP GOING BUT...
RIGHT?
......
BUT FROM THE LOOK IN YOUR EYES...
...I KNOW WE'LL NEVER BEAT EIJI WITH *TANTO*...

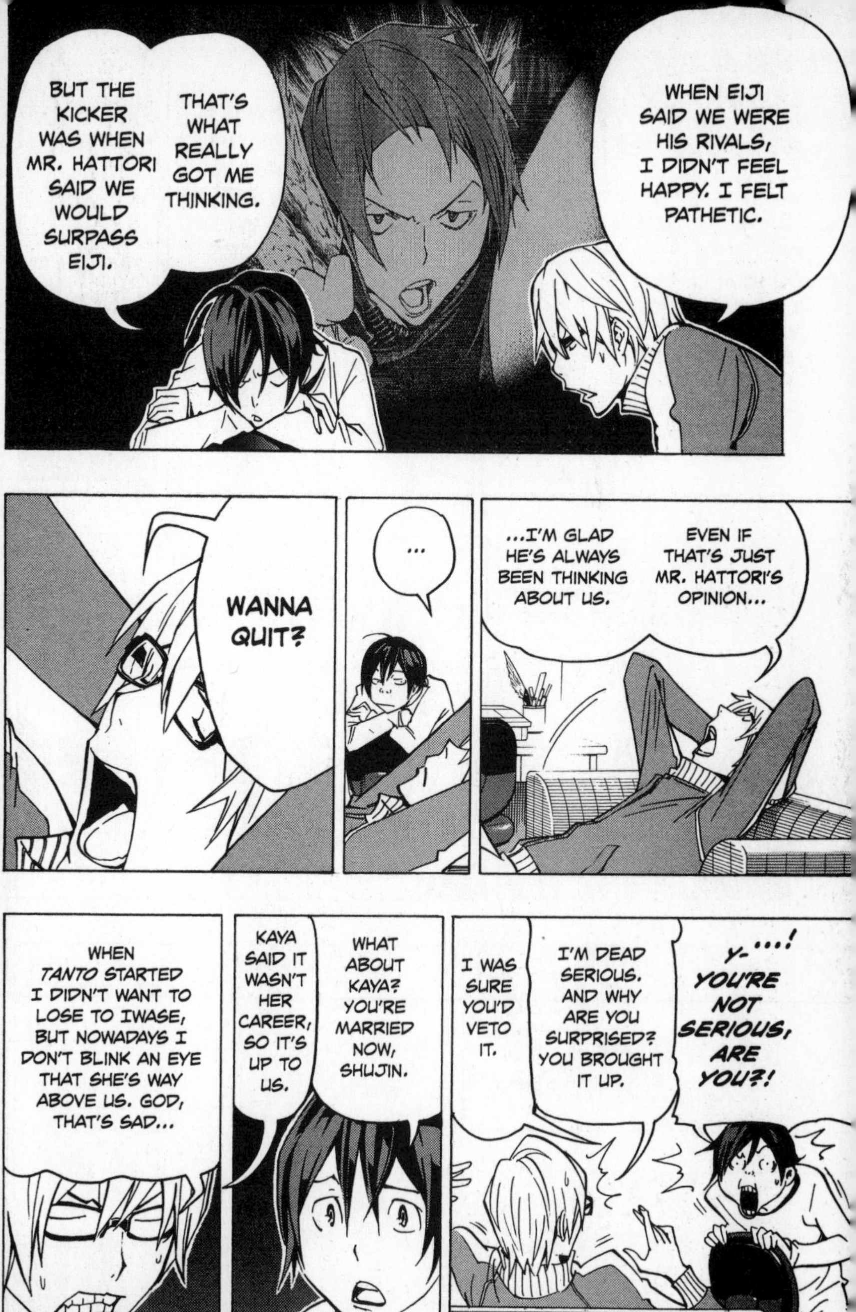
WHEN EIJI SAID WE WERE HIS RIVALS, I DIDN'T FEEL HAPPY. I FELT PATHETIC.
THAT'S WHAT REALLY GOT ME THINKING.
BUT THE KICKER WAS WHEN MR. HATTORI SAID WE WOULD SURPASS EIJI.
EVEN IF THAT'S JUST MR. HATTORI'S OPINION...
...I'M GLAD HE'S ALWAYS BEEN THINKING ABOUT US.
...
WANNA QUIT?
Y-...! YOU'RE NOT SERIOUS, ARE YOU?!
I'M DEAD SERIOUS. AND WHY ARE YOU SURPRISED? YOU BROUGHT IT UP.
I WAS SURE YOU'D VETO IT.
WHAT ABOUT KAYA? YOU'RE MARRIED NOW, SHUJIN.
KAYA SAID IT WASN'T HER CAREER, SO IT'S UP TO US.
WHEN TANTO STARTED I DIDN'T WANT TO LOSE TO IWASE, BUT NOWADAYS I DON'T BLINK AN EYE THAT SHE'S WAY ABOVE US. GOD, THAT'S SAD...

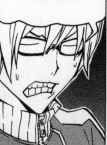

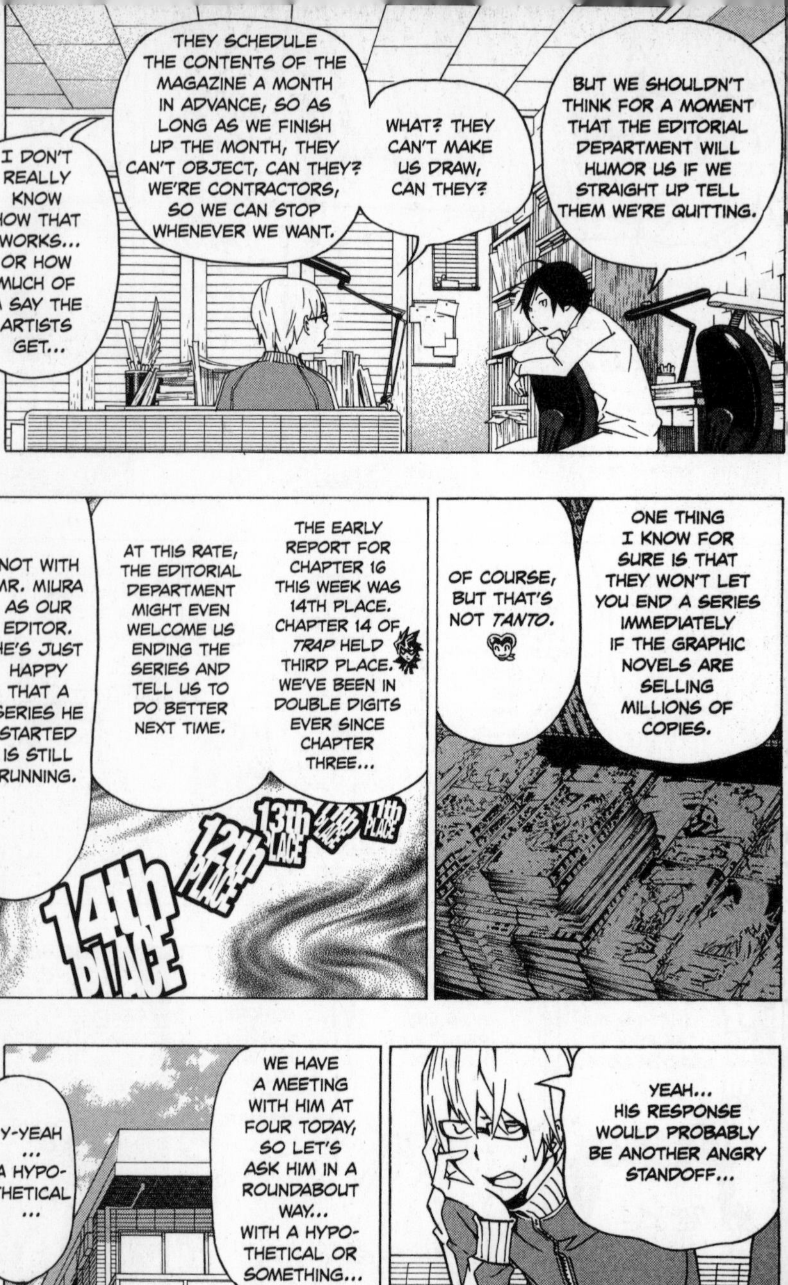
BUT WE SHOULDN'T THINK FOR A MOMENT THAT THE EDITORIAL DEPARTMENT WILL HUMOR US IF WE STRAIGHT UP TELL THEM WE'RE QUITTING.
WHAT? THEY CAN'T MAKE US DRAW, CAN THEY?
THEY SCHEDULE THE CONTENTS OF THE MAGAZINE A MONTH IN ADVANCE, SO AS LONG AS WE FINISH UP THE MONTH, THEY CAN'T OBJECT, CAN THEY? WE'RE CONTRACTORS, SO WE CAN STOP WHENEVER WE WANT.
I DON'T REALLY KNOW HOW THAT WORKS... OR HOW MUCH OF A SAY THE ARTISTS GET...
ONE THING I KNOW FOR SURE IS THAT THEY WON'T LET YOU END A SERIES IMMEDIATELY IF THE GRAPHIC NOVELS ARE SELLING MILLIONS OF COPIES.
OF COURSE, BUT THAT'S NOT *TANTO*.
THE EARLY REPORT FOR CHAPTER 16 THIS WEEK WAS 14TH PLACE. CHAPTER 14 OF *TRAP* HELD THIRD PLACE. WE'VE BEEN IN DOUBLE DIGITS EVER SINCE CHAPTER THREE...
AT THIS RATE, THE EDITORIAL DEPARTMENT MIGHT EVEN WELCOME US ENDING THE SERIES AND TELL US TO DO BETTER NEXT TIME.
NOT WITH MR. MIURA AS OUR EDITOR. HE'S JUST HAPPY THAT A SERIES HE STARTED IS STILL RUNNING.
13th PLACE
12th PLACE
14th PLACE
YEAH... HIS RESPONSE WOULD PROBABLY BE ANOTHER ANGRY STANDOFF...
WE HAVE A MEETING WITH HIM AT FOUR TODAY, SO LET'S ASK HIM IN A ROUNDABOUT WAY... WITH A HYPOTHETICAL OR SOMETHING...
Y-YEAH... A HYPOTHETICAL...

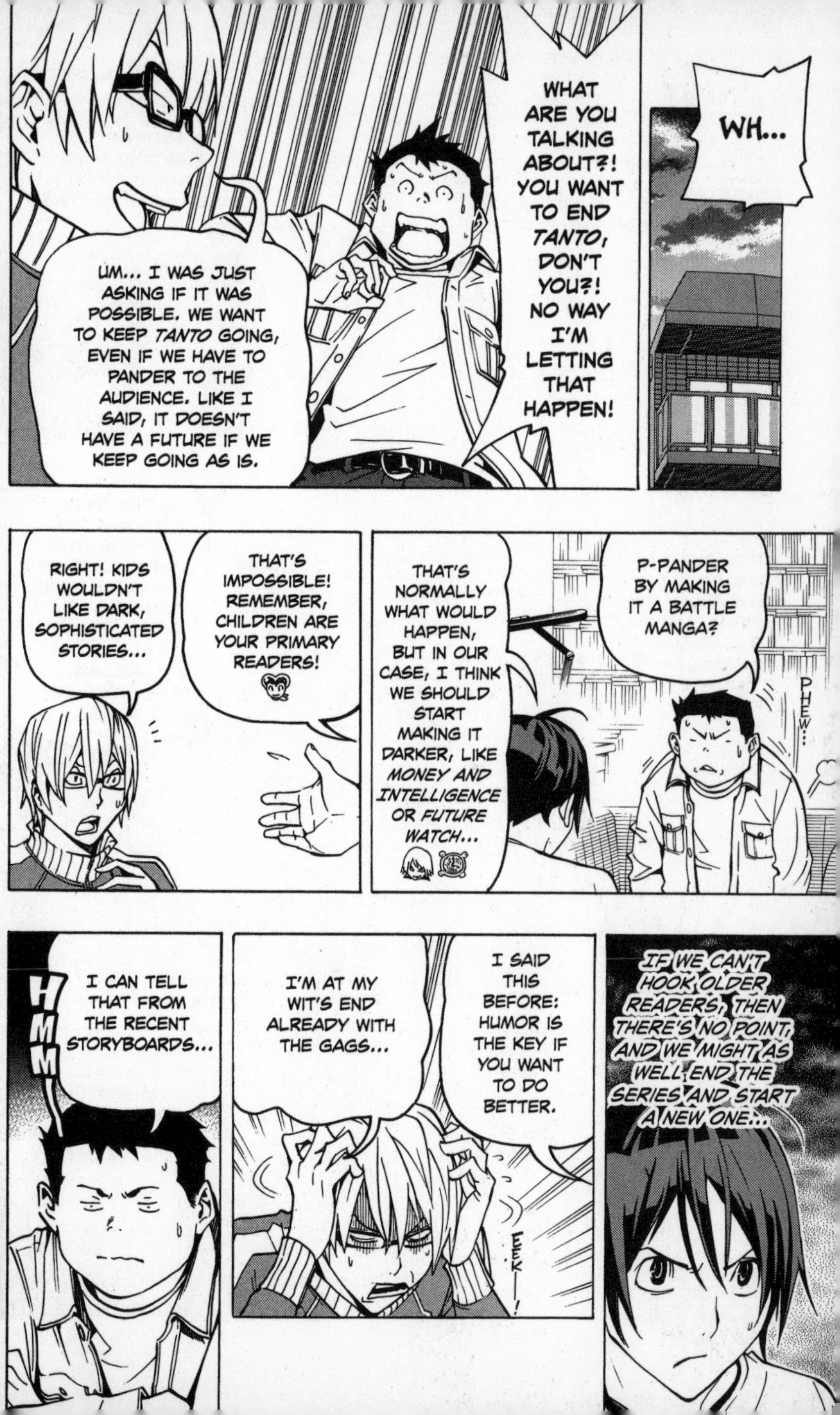
WH...
WHAT ARE YOU TALKING ABOUT?! YOU WANT TO END TANTO, DON'T YOU?! NO WAY I'M LETTING THAT HAPPEN!
UM... I WAS JUST ASKING IF IT WAS POSSIBLE. WE WANT TO KEEP TANTO GOING, EVEN IF WE HAVE TO PANDER TO THE AUDIENCE. LIKE I SAID, IT DOESN'T HAVE A FUTURE IF WE KEEP GOING AS IS.
P-PANDER BY MAKING IT A BATTLE MANGA?
PHEW...
THAT'S NORMALLY WHAT WOULD HAPPEN, BUT IN OUR CASE, I THINK WE SHOULD START MAKING IT DARKER, LIKE MONEY AND INTELLIGENCE OR FUTURE WATCH...
THAT'S IMPOSSIBLE! REMEMBER, CHILDREN ARE YOUR PRIMARY READERS!
RIGHT! KIDS WOULDN'T LIKE DARK, SOPHISTICATED STORIES...
IF WE CAN'T HOOK OLDER READERS, THEN THERE'S NO POINT, AND WE MIGHT AS WELL END THE SERIES AND START A NEW ONE...
I SAID THIS BEFORE: HUMOR IS THE KEY IF YOU WANT TO DO BETTER.
I'M AT MY WIT'S END ALREADY WITH THE GAGS...
EEK!
HMM
I CAN TELL THAT FROM THE RECENT STORYBOARDS...

READ THIS WAY

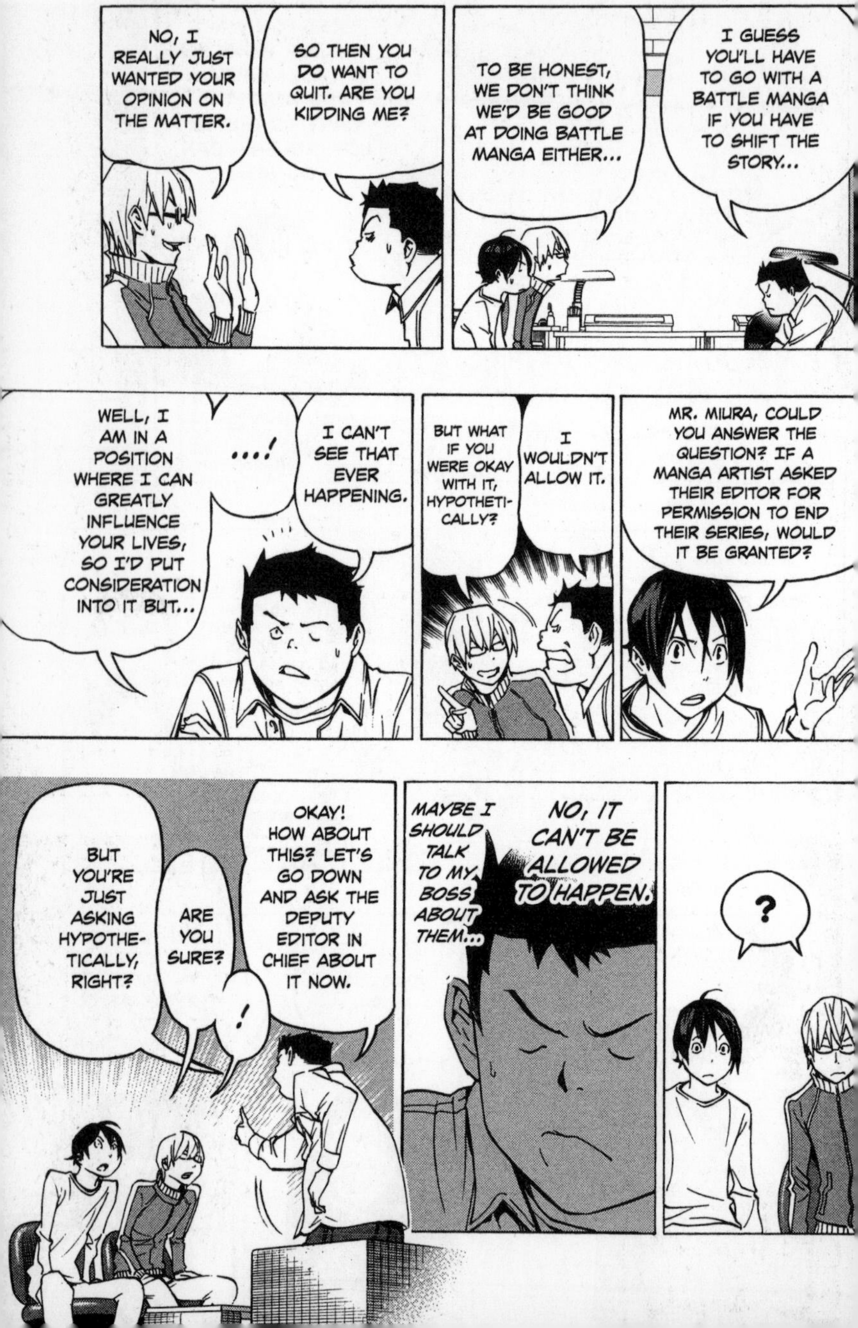

I GUESS YOU'LL HAVE TO GO WITH A BATTLE MANGA IF YOU HAVE TO SHIFT THE STORY...
TO BE HONEST, WE DON'T THINK WE'D BE GOOD AT DOING BATTLE MANGA EITHER...
SO THEN YOU DO WANT TO QUIT. ARE YOU KIDDING ME?
NO, I REALLY JUST WANTED YOUR OPINION ON THE MATTER.
MR. MIURA, COULD YOU ANSWER THE QUESTION? IF A MANGA ARTIST ASKED THEIR EDITOR FOR PERMISSION TO END THEIR SERIES, WOULD IT BE GRANTED?
I WOULDN'T ALLOW IT.
BUT WHAT IF YOU WERE OKAY WITH IT, HYPOTHETICALLY?
I CAN'T SEE THAT EVER HAPPENING.
...!
WELL, I AM IN A POSITION WHERE I CAN GREATLY INFLUENCE YOUR LIVES, SO I'D PUT CONSIDERATION INTO IT BUT...
?
NO, IT CAN'T BE ALLOWED TO HAPPEN.
MAYBE I SHOULD TALK TO MY BOSS ABOUT THEM...
OKAY! HOW ABOUT THIS? LET'S GO DOWN AND ASK THE DEPUTY EDITOR IN CHIEF ABOUT IT NOW.
ARE YOU SURE?
!
BUT YOU'RE JUST ASKING HYPOTHETICALLY, RIGHT?

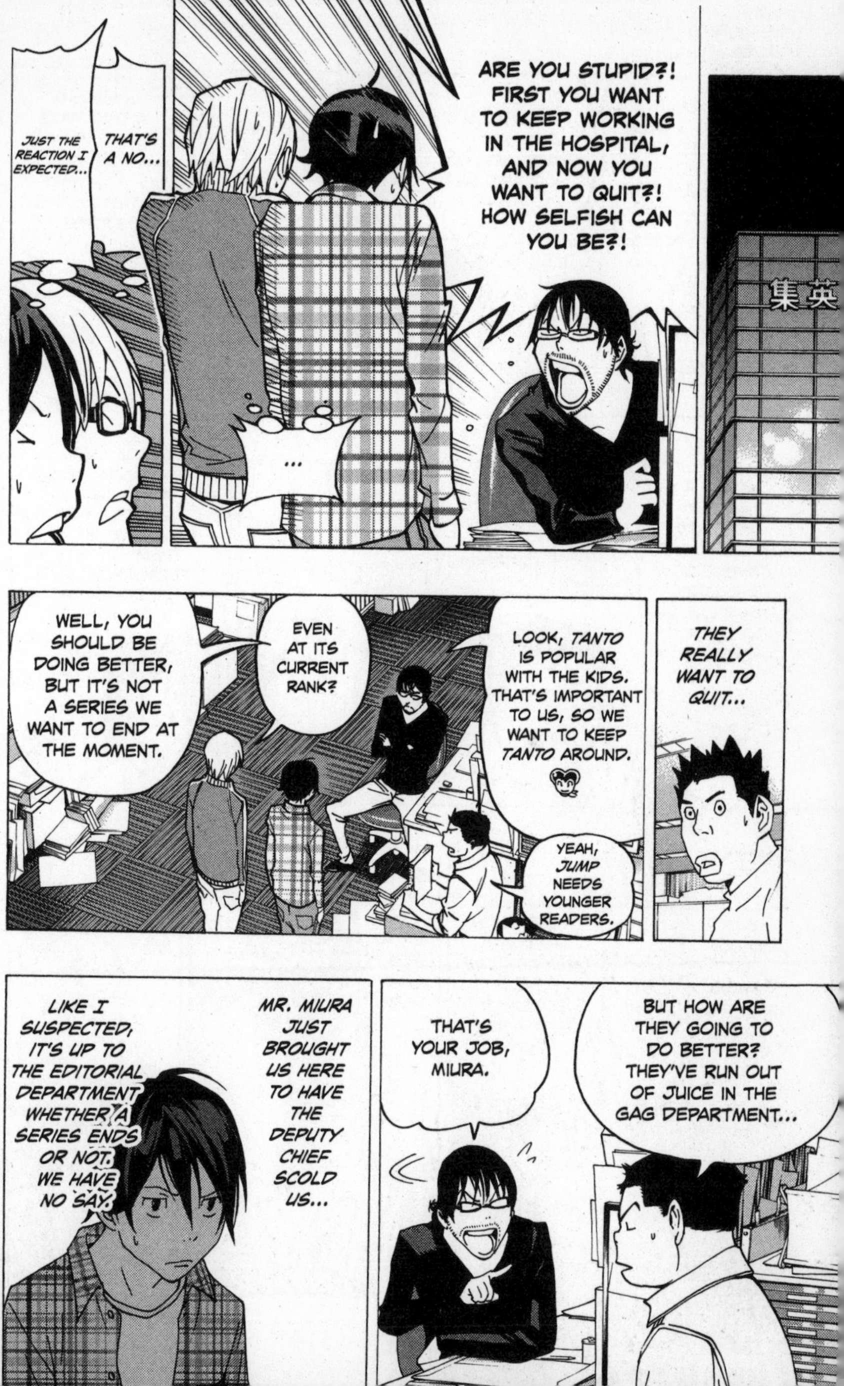
集英
ARE YOU STUPID?! FIRST YOU WANT TO KEEP WORKING IN THE HOSPITAL, AND NOW YOU WANT TO QUIT?! HOW SELFISH CAN YOU BE?!
...
THAT'S A NO...
JUST THE REACTION I EXPECTED...
THEY REALLY WANT TO QUIT...
LOOK, TANTO IS POPULAR WITH THE KIDS. THAT'S IMPORTANT TO US, SO WE WANT TO KEEP TANTO AROUND.
YEAH, JUMP NEEDS YOUNGER READERS.
EVEN AT ITS CURRENT RANK?
WELL, YOU SHOULD BE DOING BETTER, BUT IT'S NOT A SERIES WE WANT TO END AT THE MOMENT.
BUT HOW ARE THEY GOING TO DO BETTER? THEY'VE RUN OUT OF JUICE IN THE GAG DEPARTMENT...
THAT'S YOUR JOB, MIURA.
MR. MIURA JUST BROUGHT US HERE TO HAVE THE DEPUTY CHIEF SCOLD US...
LIKE I SUSPECTED, IT'S UP TO THE EDITORIAL DEPARTMENT WHETHER A SERIES ENDS OR NOT. WE HAVE NO SAY.

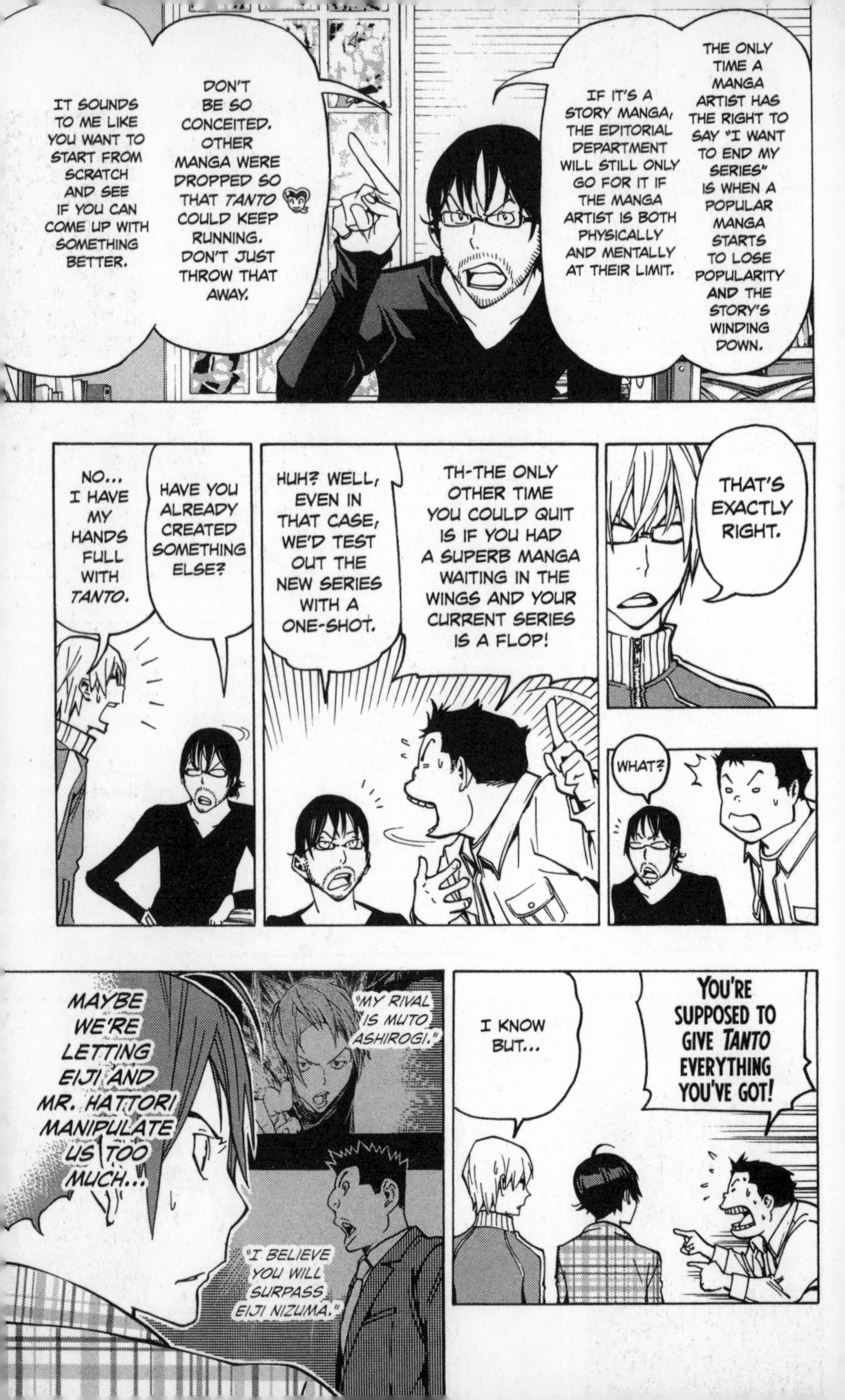
THE ONLY TIME A MANGA ARTIST HAS THE RIGHT TO SAY "I WANT TO END MY SERIES" IS WHEN A POPULAR MANGA STARTS TO LOSE POPULARITY AND THE STORY'S WINDING DOWN.
IF IT'S A STORY MANGA, THE EDITORIAL DEPARTMENT WILL STILL ONLY GO FOR IT IF THE MANGA ARTIST IS BOTH PHYSICALLY AND MENTALLY AT THEIR LIMIT.
DON'T BE SO CONCEITED. OTHER MANGA WERE DROPPED SO THAT *TANTO* COULD KEEP RUNNING. DON'T JUST THROW THAT AWAY.
IT SOUNDS TO ME LIKE YOU WANT TO START FROM SCRATCH AND SEE IF YOU CAN COME UP WITH SOMETHING BETTER.
THAT'S EXACTLY RIGHT.
WHAT?
TH-THE ONLY OTHER TIME YOU COULD QUIT IS IF YOU HAD A SUPERB MANGA WAITING IN THE WINGS AND YOUR CURRENT SERIES IS A FLOP!
HUH? WELL, EVEN IN THAT CASE, WE'D TEST OUT THE NEW SERIES WITH A ONE-SHOT.
HAVE YOU ALREADY CREATED SOMETHING ELSE?
NO... I HAVE MY HANDS FULL WITH *TANTO*.
YOU'RE SUPPOSED TO GIVE *TANTO* EVERYTHING YOU'VE GOT!
I KNOW BUT...
"MY RIVAL IS MUTO ASHIROGI."
MAYBE WE'RE LETTING EIJI AND MR. HATTORI MANIPULATE US TOO MUCH...
"I BELIEVE YOU WILL SURPASS EIJI NIZUMA."

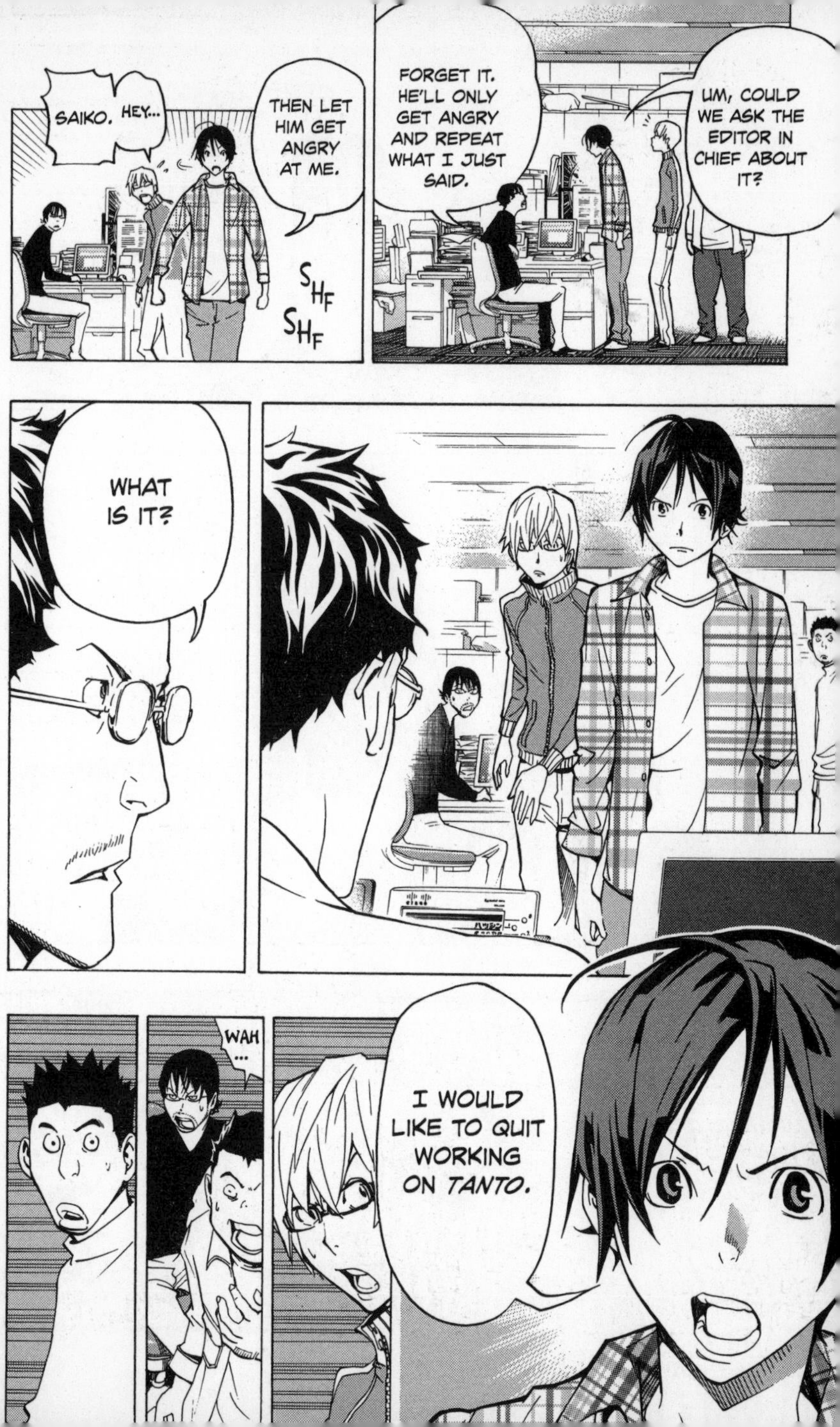
UM, COULD WE ASK THE EDITOR IN CHIEF ABOUT IT?
FORGET IT. HE'LL ONLY GET ANGRY AND REPEAT WHAT I JUST SAID.
THEN LET HIM GET ANGRY AT ME.
SAIKO. HEY...
SHF SHF
WHAT IS IT?
I WOULD LIKE TO QUIT WORKING ON *TANTO*.
WAH...

READ THIS WAY

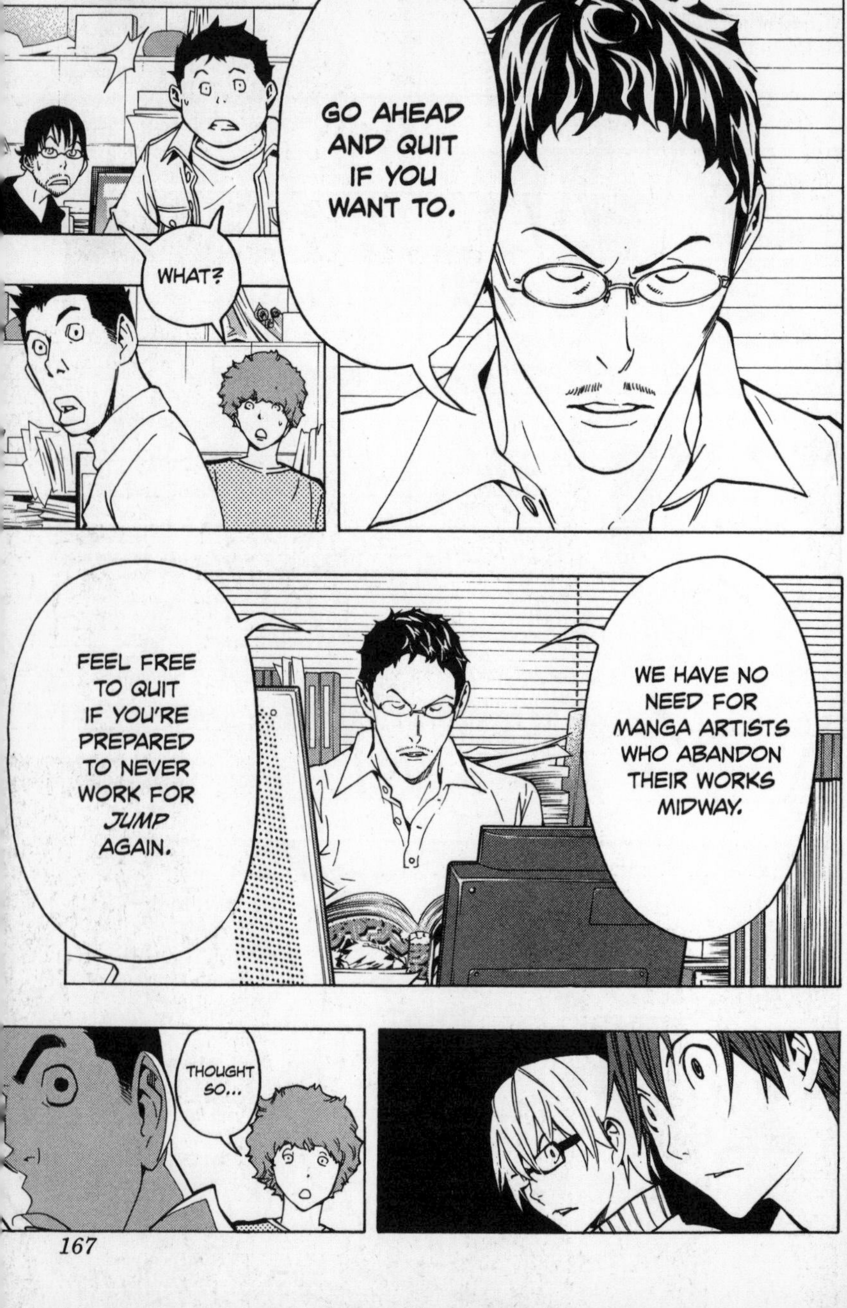
GO AHEAD AND QUIT IF YOU WANT TO.
WHAT?
WE HAVE NO NEED FOR MANGA ARTISTS WHO ABANDON THEIR WORKS MIDWAY.
FEEL FREE TO QUIT IF YOU'RE PREPARED TO NEVER WORK FOR *JUMP* AGAIN.
THOUGHT SO...

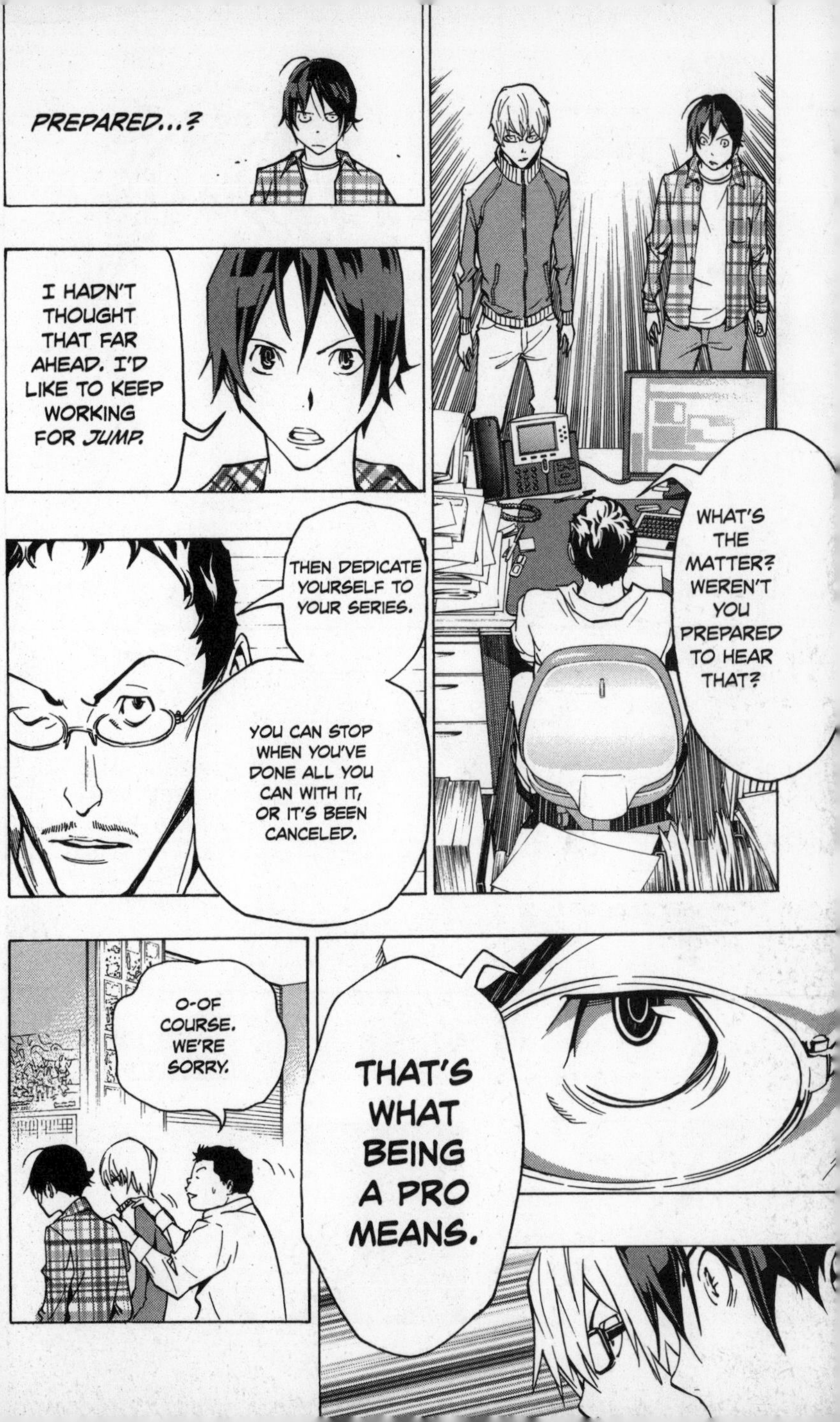
WHAT'S THE MATTER? WEREN'T YOU PREPARED TO HEAR THAT?
PREPARED...?
I HADN'T THOUGHT THAT FAR AHEAD. I'D LIKE TO KEEP WORKING FOR *JUMP*.
THEN DEDICATE YOURSELF TO YOUR SERIES.
YOU CAN STOP WHEN YOU'VE DONE ALL YOU CAN WITH IT, OR IT'S BEEN CANCELED.
THAT'S WHAT BEING A PRO MEANS.
O-OF COURSE. WE'RE SORRY.

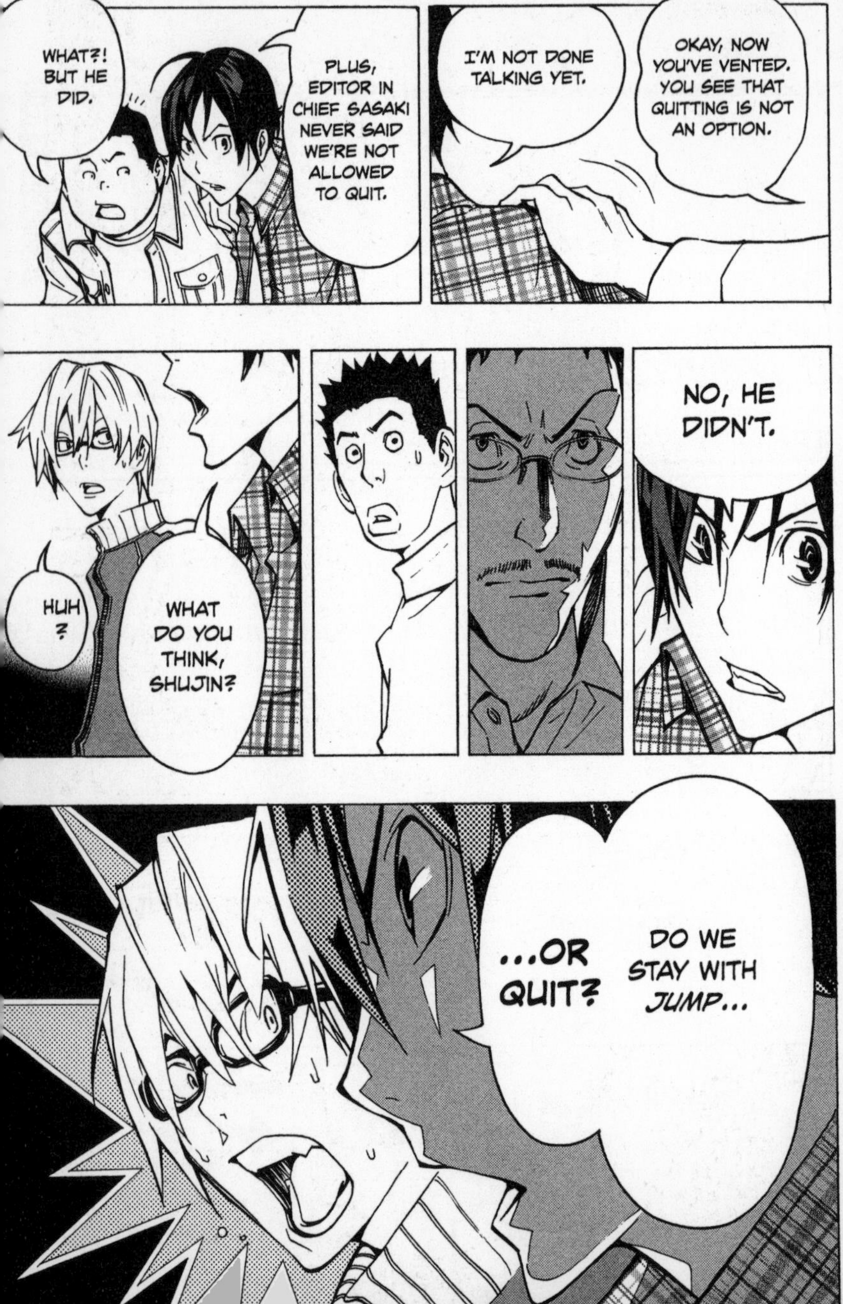
OKAY, NOW YOU'VE VENTED. YOU SEE THAT QUITTING IS NOT AN OPTION.
I'M NOT DONE TALKING YET.
PLUS, EDITOR IN CHIEF SASAKI NEVER SAID WE'RE NOT ALLOWED TO QUIT.
WHAT?! BUT HE DID.
NO, HE DIDN'T.
WHAT DO YOU THINK, SHUJIN?
HUH?
DO WE STAY WITH *JUMP*...
...OR QUIT?

OHBA'S STORYBOARD

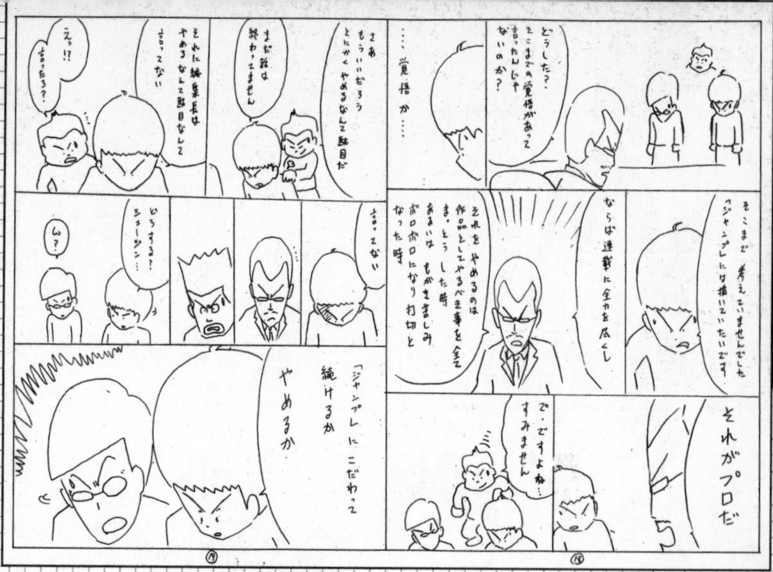

どうした？ そこまでの覚悟があって言ったんじゃないのか？
……覚悟か……
そこまで考えていませんでした 「ジャンプ」に描いていたいです
ならば連載に全力を尽くし
それをやめるのは 作品としてやるべき事を全て まっとうした時 あるいは もがき苦しみ ボロボロになり 打切となった時
それがプロだ
で、ですよね…… すみません
さあ もういいだろう とにかくやめるなんて駄目だ
まだ話は終わってません
それに編集長はやめるなんて駄目なんて言ってない
えっ!? 言ってたろ？
言ってない
どうする？ シュージン……
ん？
「ジャンプ」にこだわって続けるか やめるか

OBATA'S STORYBOARD

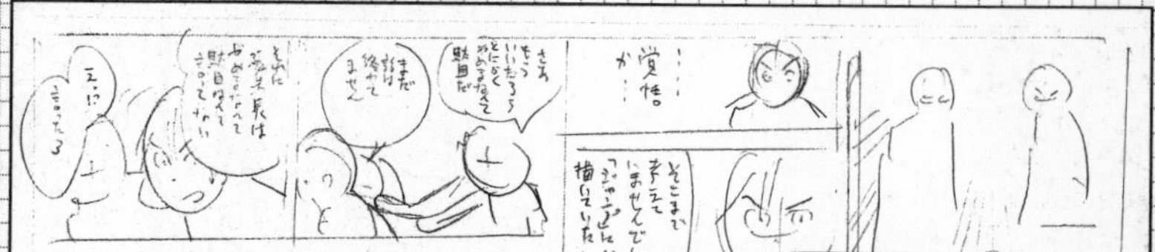

どうしたっ そこまでの覚悟があって言ったんじゃないのか？
覚悟か……
そこまで考えていませんでした 「ジャンプ」には描いていたいです
ならば連載に全力を尽くし それをやめるのは作品としてやるべき事を全てまっとうした時
あるいは もがき苦しみ ボロボロになり 打ち切りとなった時
それがプロだ
で、ですよね すみません
さあ もういいだろう とにかくやめるなんて駄目だ
まだ話は終わってません
それに編集長はやめるなんて駄目なんて言ってない
え!? 言ってたろ
言ってない
どうする シュージン
ん？
ジャンプにこだわって続けるか やめるか

COMPLETE!

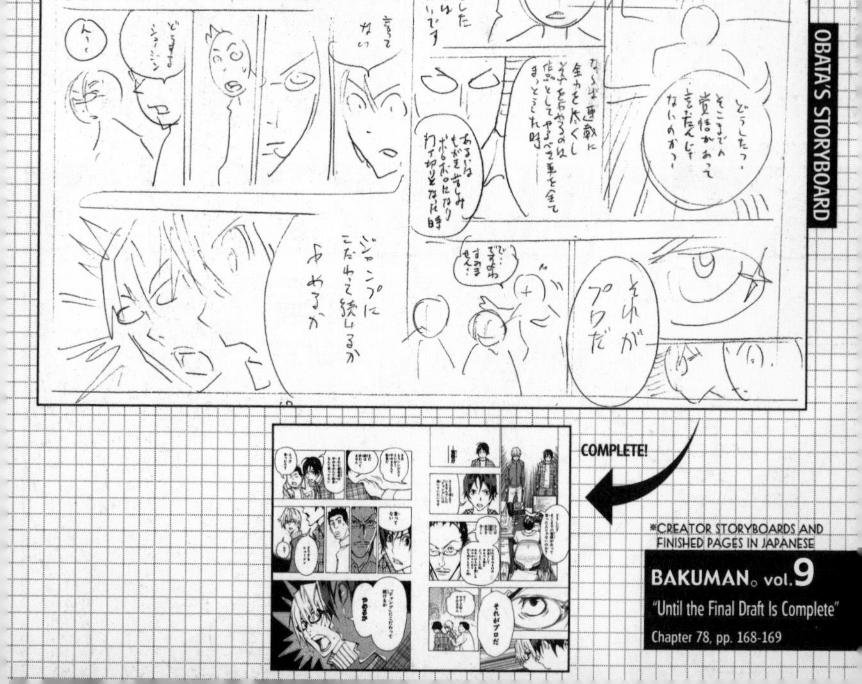

*CREATOR STORYBOARDS AND FINISHED PAGES IN JAPANESE

BAKUMAN。 vol.9

"Until the Final Draft Is Complete"

Chapter 78, pp. 168-169

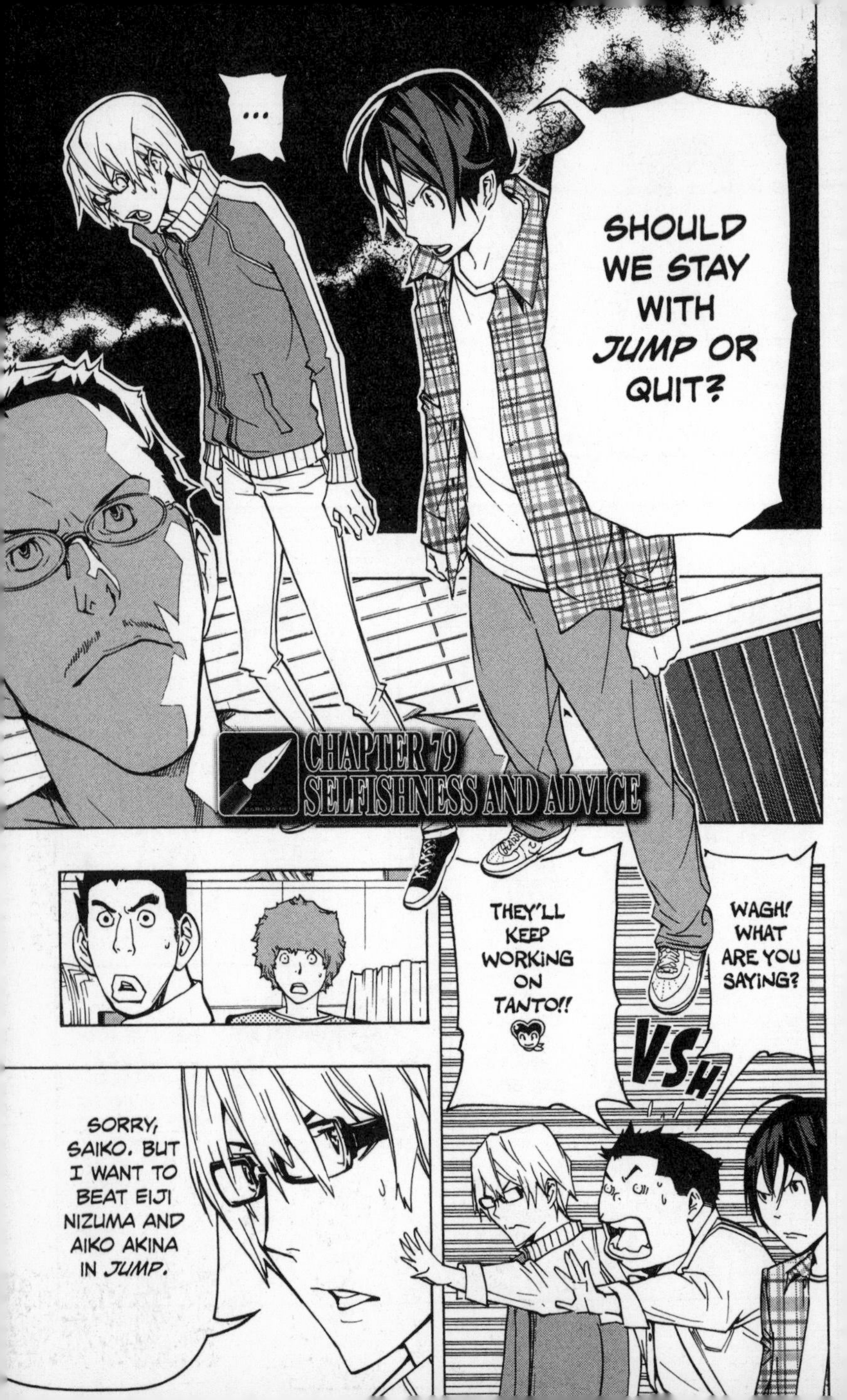
SHOULD WE STAY WITH JUMP OR QUIT?
...
CHAPTER 79
SELFISHNESS AND ADVICE
WAGH! WHAT ARE YOU SAYING?
THEY'LL KEEP WORKING ON TANTO!!
VSH
SORRY, SAIKO. BUT I WANT TO BEAT EIJI NIZUMA AND AIKO AKINA IN JUMP.

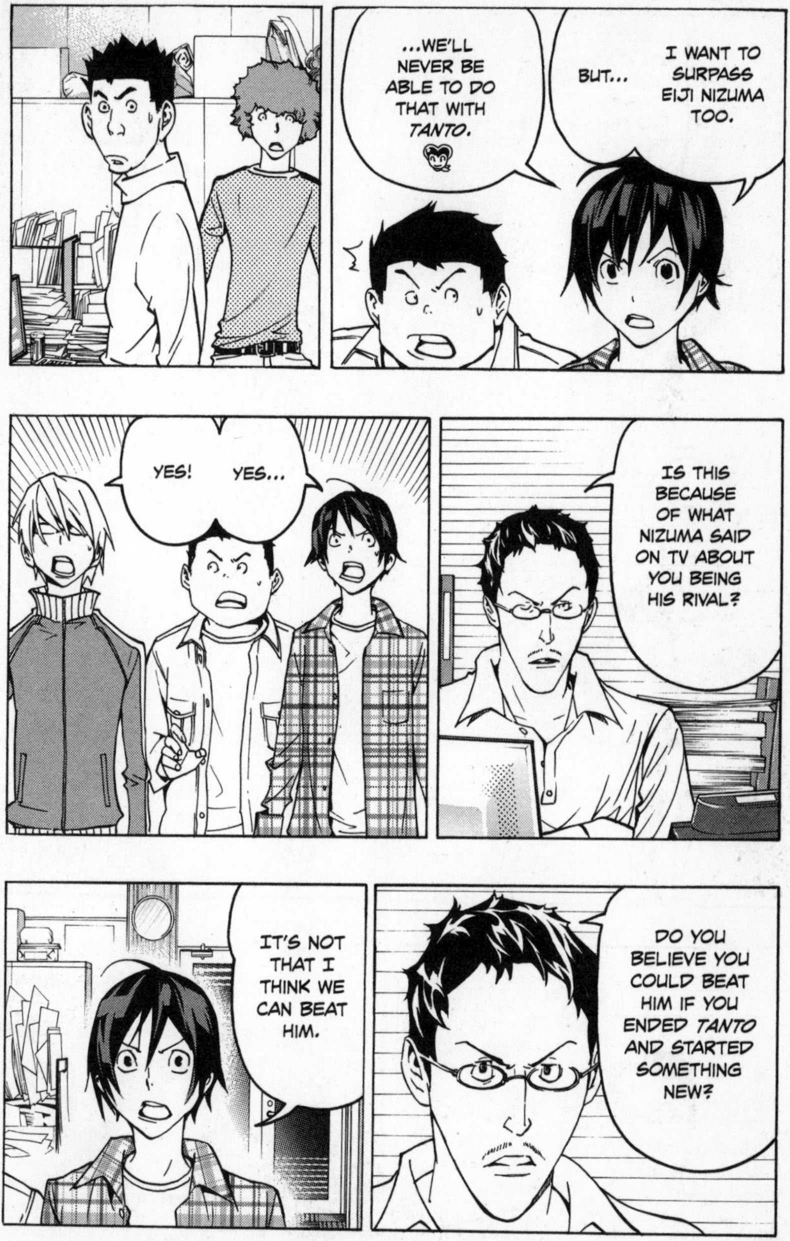
I WANT TO SURPASS EIJI NIZUMA TOO.
BUT...
...WE'LL NEVER BE ABLE TO DO THAT WITH *TANTO*.
IS THIS BECAUSE OF WHAT NIZUMA SAID ON TV ABOUT YOU BEING HIS RIVAL?
YES...
YES!
DO YOU BELIEVE YOU COULD BEAT HIM IF YOU ENDED *TANTO* AND STARTED SOMETHING NEW?
IT'S NOT THAT I THINK WE CAN BEAT HIM.

READ THIS WAY

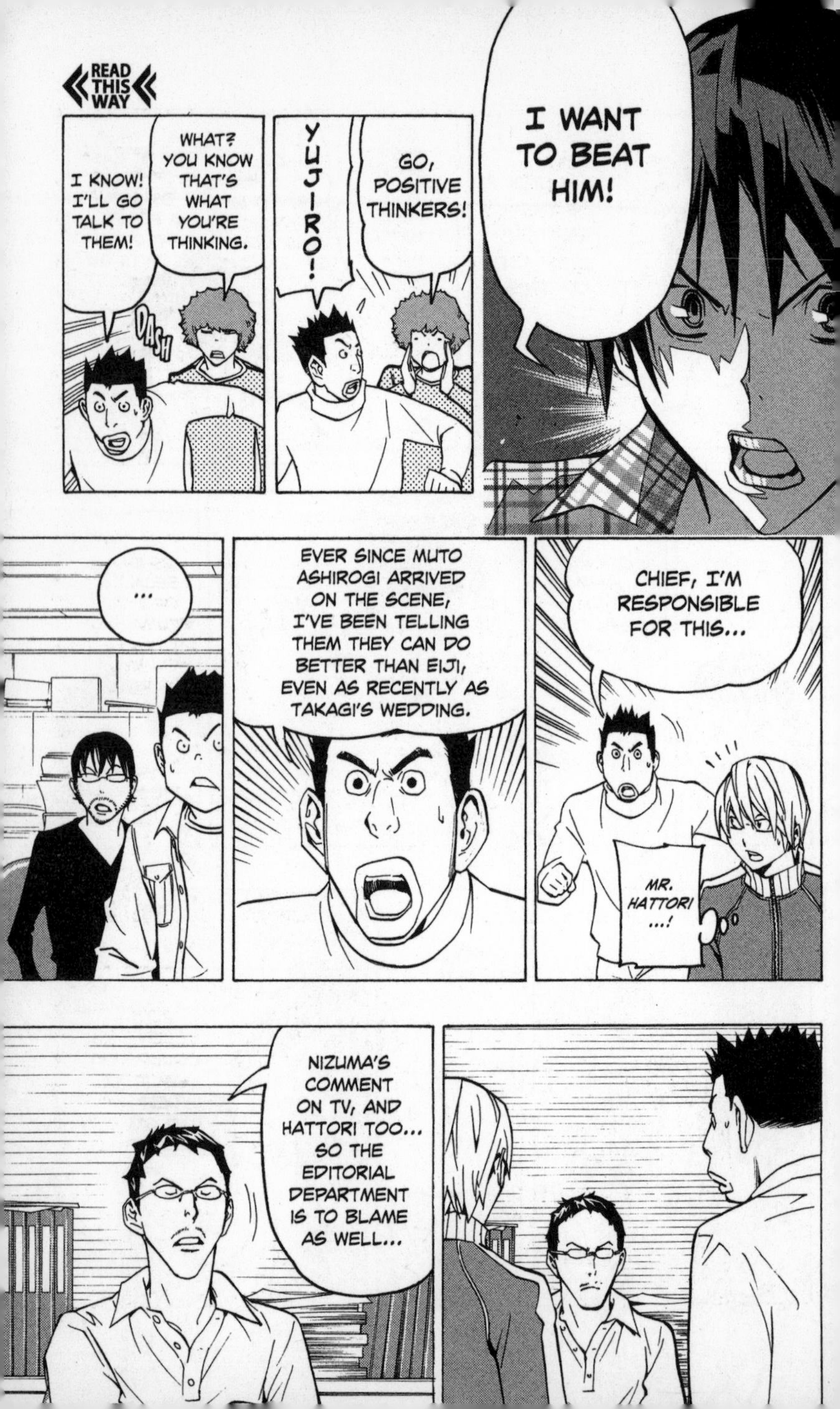

I WANT TO BEAT HIM!
GO, POSITIVE THINKERS!
YUJIRO!
WHAT? YOU KNOW THAT'S WHAT YOU'RE THINKING.
I KNOW! I'LL GO TALK TO THEM!
DASH
CHIEF, I'M RESPONSIBLE FOR THIS...
MR. HATTORI ...!
EVER SINCE MUTO ASHIROGI ARRIVED ON THE SCENE, I'VE BEEN TELLING THEM THEY CAN DO BETTER THAN EIJI, EVEN AS RECENTLY AS TAKAGI'S WEDDING.
...
NIZUMA'S COMMENT ON TV, AND HATTORI TOO... SO THE EDITORIAL DEPARTMENT IS TO BLAME AS WELL...

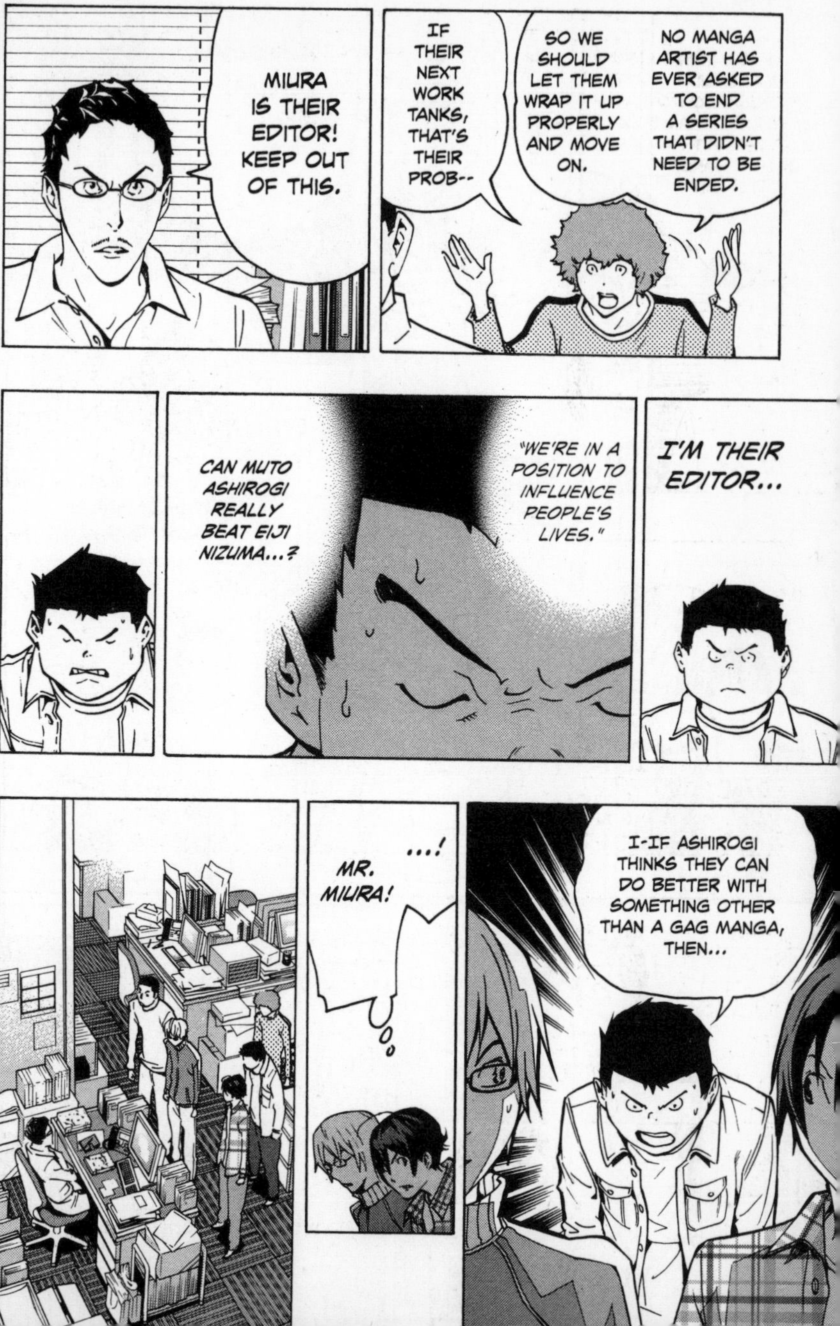
NO MANGA ARTIST HAS EVER ASKED TO END A SERIES THAT DIDN'T NEED TO BE ENDED.
SO WE SHOULD LET THEM WRAP IT UP PROPERLY AND MOVE ON.
IF THEIR NEXT WORK TANKS, THAT'S THEIR PROB--
MIURA IS THEIR EDITOR! KEEP OUT OF THIS.
I'M THEIR EDITOR...
"WE'RE IN A POSITION TO INFLUENCE PEOPLE'S LIVES."
CAN MUTO ASHIROGI REALLY BEAT EIJI NIZUMA...?
I-IF ASHIROGI THINKS THEY CAN DO BETTER WITH SOMETHING OTHER THAN A GAG MANGA, THEN...
...!
MR. MIURA!

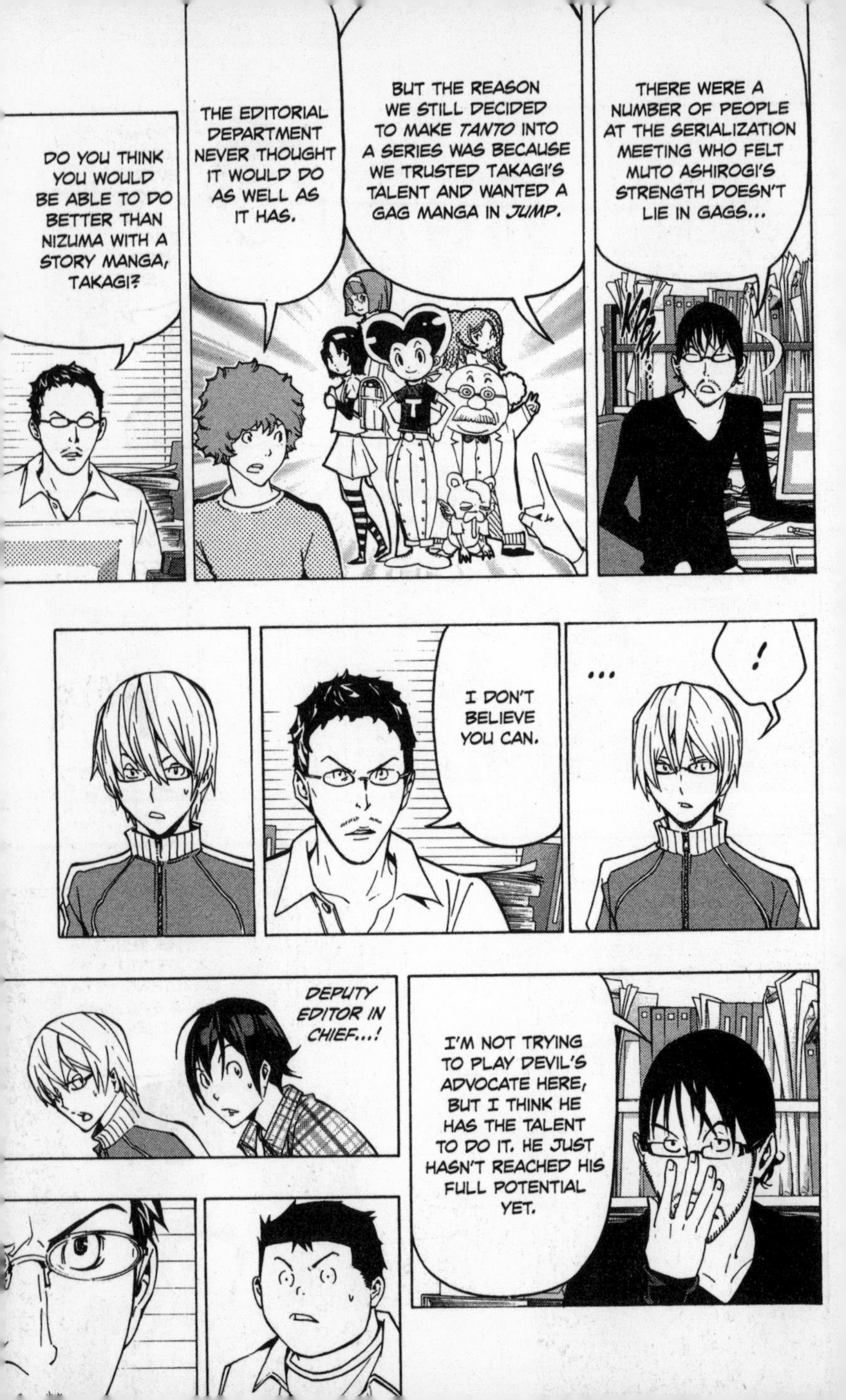
THERE WERE A NUMBER OF PEOPLE AT THE SERIALIZATION MEETING WHO FELT MUTO ASHIROGI'S STRENGTH DOESN'T LIE IN GAGS...
BUT THE REASON WE STILL DECIDED TO MAKE *TANTO* INTO A SERIES WAS BECAUSE WE TRUSTED TAKAGI'S TALENT AND WANTED A GAG MANGA IN *JUMP*.
THE EDITORIAL DEPARTMENT NEVER THOUGHT IT WOULD DO AS WELL AS IT HAS.
DO YOU THINK YOU WOULD BE ABLE TO DO BETTER THAN NIZUMA WITH A STORY MANGA, TAKAGI?
!
...
I DON'T BELIEVE YOU CAN.
I'M NOT TRYING TO PLAY DEVIL'S ADVOCATE HERE, BUT I THINK HE HAS THE TALENT TO DO IT. HE JUST HASN'T REACHED HIS FULL POTENTIAL YET.
DEPUTY EDITOR IN CHIEF...!

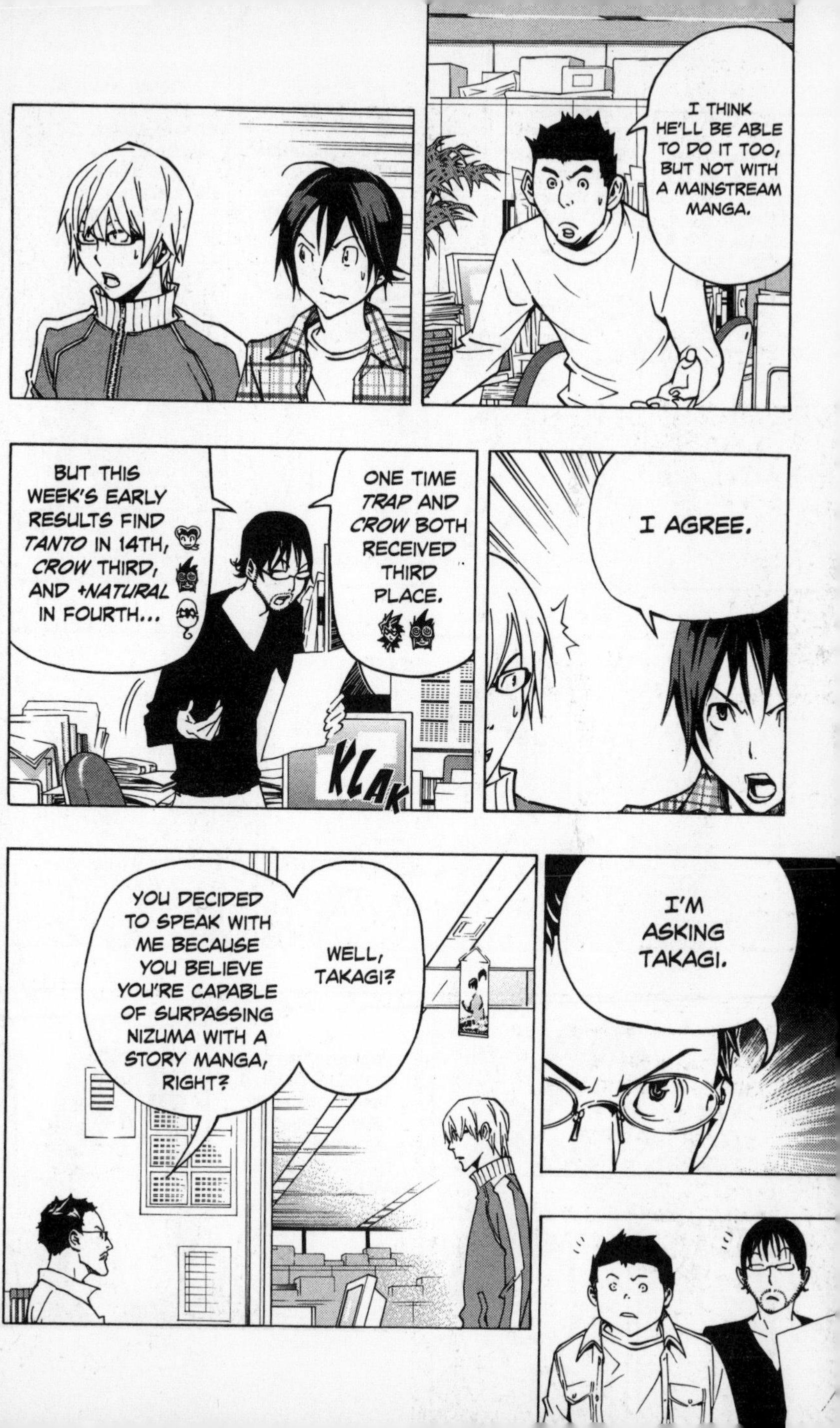
I THINK HE'LL BE ABLE TO DO IT TOO, BUT NOT WITH A MAINSTREAM MANGA.
I AGREE.
ONE TIME TRAP AND CROW BOTH RECEIVED THIRD PLACE.
BUT THIS WEEK'S EARLY RESULTS FIND TANTO IN 14TH, CROW THIRD, AND +NATURAL IN FOURTH...
KLAK
I'M ASKING TAKAGI.
WELL, TAKAGI?
YOU DECIDED TO SPEAK WITH ME BECAUSE YOU BELIEVE YOU'RE CAPABLE OF SURPASSING NIZUMA WITH A STORY MANGA, RIGHT?

READ THIS WAY

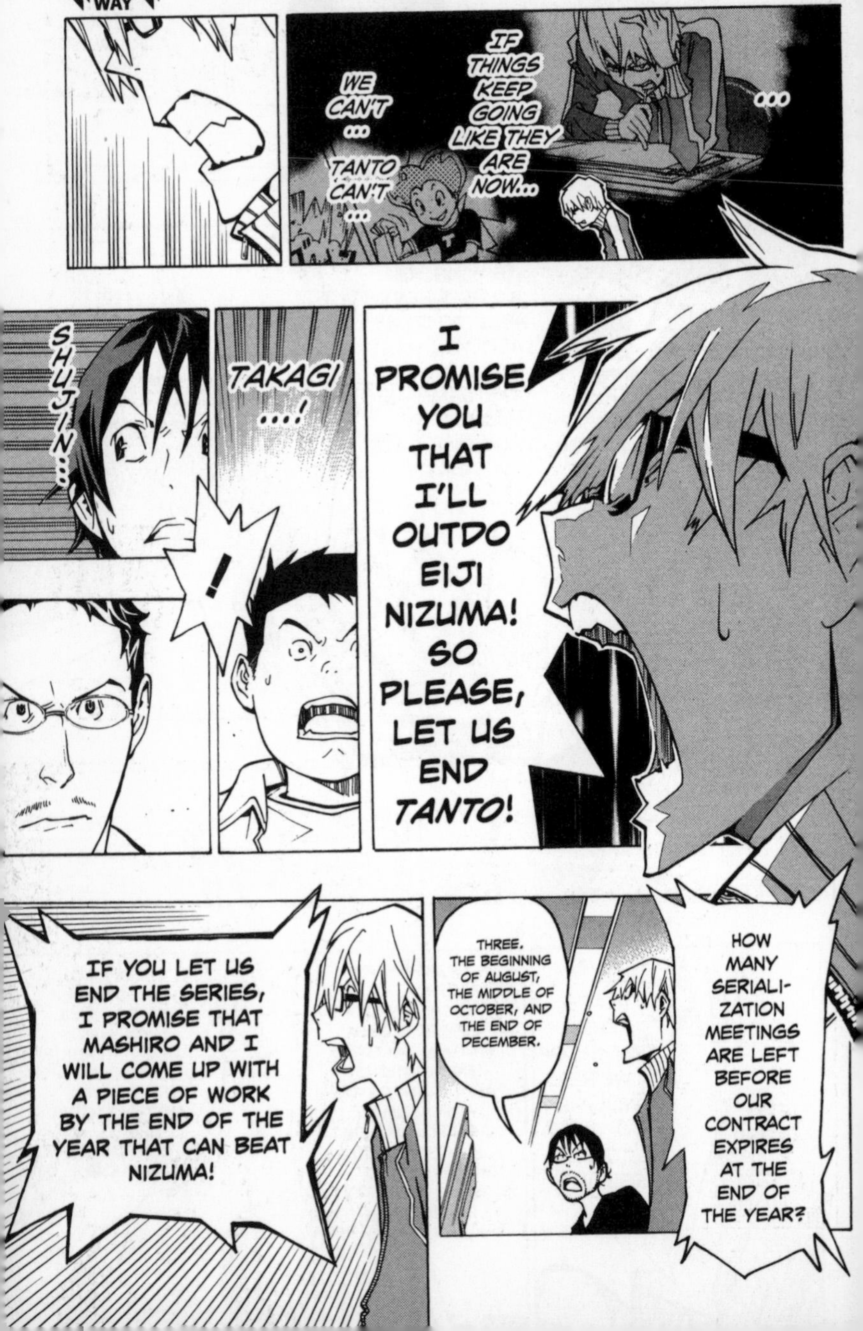

...
IF THINGS KEEP GOING LIKE THEY ARE NOW...
WE CAN'T ...
TANTO CAN'T ...
I PROMISE YOU THAT I'LL OUTDO EIJI NIZUMA! SO PLEASE, LET US END TANTO!
TAKAGI ...!
SHUJIN...
!
HOW MANY SERIALIZATION MEETINGS ARE LEFT BEFORE OUR CONTRACT EXPIRES AT THE END OF THE YEAR?
THREE. THE BEGINNING OF AUGUST, THE MIDDLE OF OCTOBER, AND THE END OF DECEMBER.
IF YOU LET US END THE SERIES, I PROMISE THAT MASHIRO AND I WILL COME UP WITH A PIECE OF WORK BY THE END OF THE YEAR THAT CAN BEAT NIZUMA!

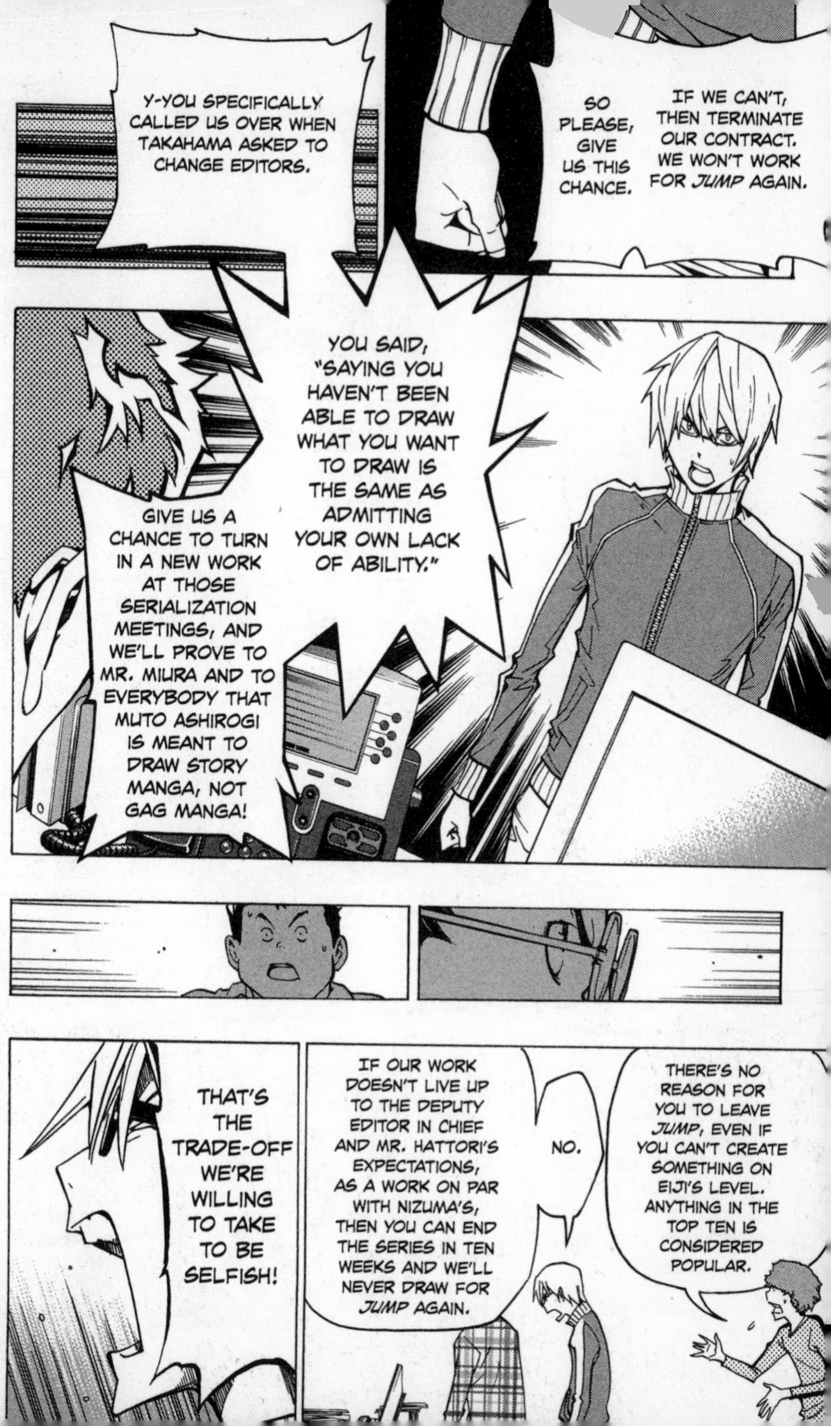
IF WE CAN'T, THEN TERMINATE OUR CONTRACT. WE WON'T WORK FOR *JUMP* AGAIN.
SO PLEASE, GIVE US THIS CHANCE.
Y-YOU SPECIFICALLY CALLED US OVER WHEN TAKAHAMA ASKED TO CHANGE EDITORS.
YOU SAID, "SAYING YOU HAVEN'T BEEN ABLE TO DRAW WHAT YOU WANT TO DRAW IS THE SAME AS ADMITTING YOUR OWN LACK OF ABILITY."
GIVE US A CHANCE TO TURN IN A NEW WORK AT THOSE SERIALIZATION MEETINGS, AND WE'LL PROVE TO MR. MIURA AND TO EVERYBODY THAT MUTO ASHIROGI IS MEANT TO DRAW STORY MANGA, NOT GAG MANGA!
THERE'S NO REASON FOR YOU TO LEAVE *JUMP*, EVEN IF YOU CAN'T CREATE SOMETHING ON EIJI'S LEVEL. ANYTHING IN THE TOP TEN IS CONSIDERED POPULAR.
NO.
IF OUR WORK DOESN'T LIVE UP TO THE DEPUTY EDITOR IN CHIEF AND MR. HATTORI'S EXPECTATIONS, AS A WORK ON PAR WITH NIZUMA'S, THEN YOU CAN END THE SERIES IN TEN WEEKS AND WE'LL NEVER DRAW FOR *JUMP* AGAIN.
THAT'S THE TRADE-OFF WE'RE WILLING TO TAKE TO BE SELFISH!

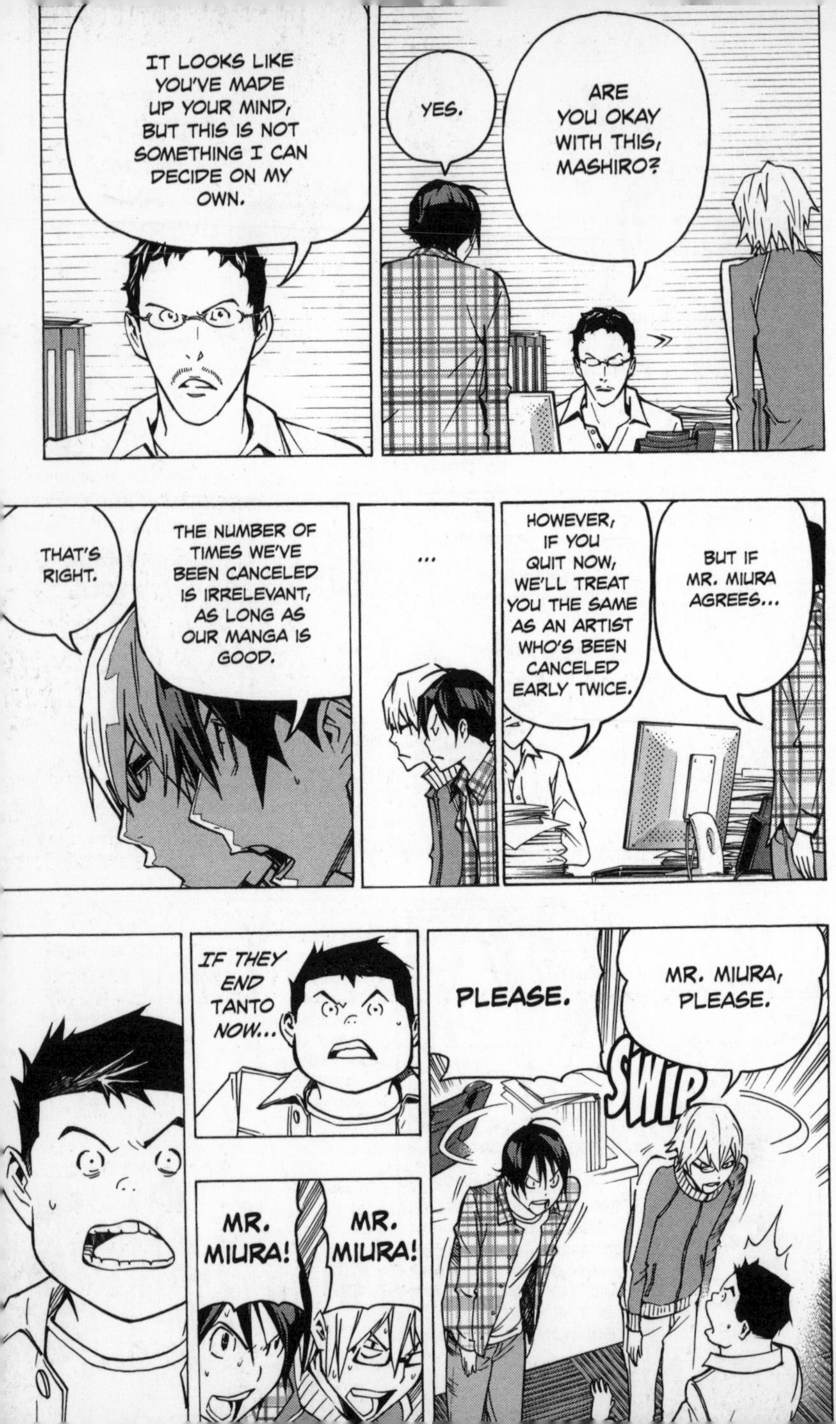
ARE YOU OKAY WITH THIS, MASHIRO?
YES.
IT LOOKS LIKE YOU'VE MADE UP YOUR MIND, BUT THIS IS NOT SOMETHING I CAN DECIDE ON MY OWN.
BUT IF MR. MIURA AGREES...
HOWEVER, IF YOU QUIT NOW, WE'LL TREAT YOU THE SAME AS AN ARTIST WHO'S BEEN CANCELED EARLY TWICE.
...
THE NUMBER OF TIMES WE'VE BEEN CANCELED IS IRRELEVANT, AS LONG AS OUR MANGA IS GOOD.
THAT'S RIGHT.
MR. MIURA, PLEASE.
PLEASE.
SWIP
IF THEY END TANTO NOW...
MR. MIURA!
MR. MIURA!

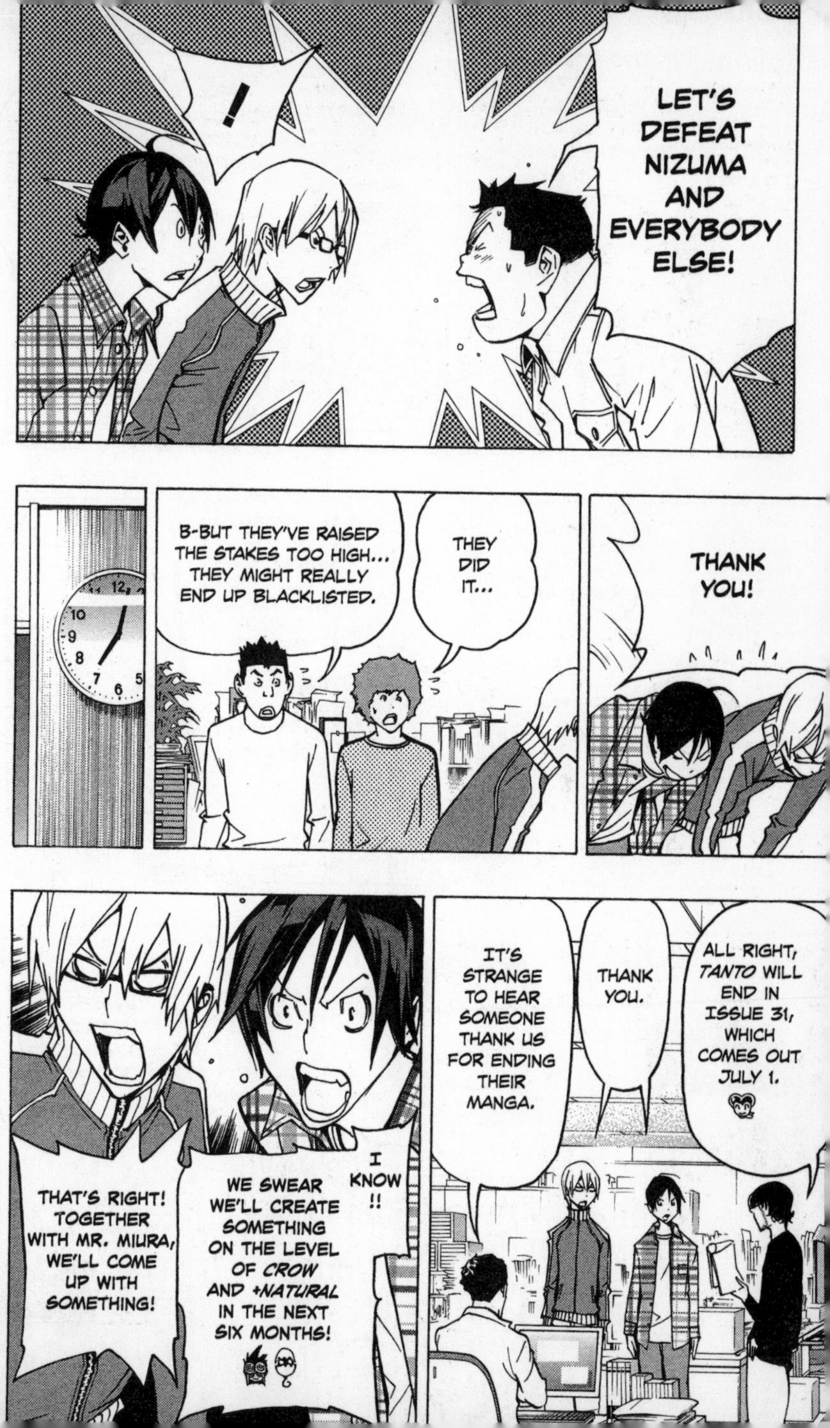
LET'S DEFEAT NIZUMA AND EVERYBODY ELSE!
!
THANK YOU!
THEY DID IT...
B-BUT THEY'VE RAISED THE STAKES TOO HIGH... THEY MIGHT REALLY END UP BLACKLISTED.
ALL RIGHT, *TANTO* WILL END IN ISSUE 31, WHICH COMES OUT JULY 1.
THANK YOU.
IT'S STRANGE TO HEAR SOMEONE THANK US FOR ENDING THEIR MANGA.
I KNOW!!
WE SWEAR WE'LL CREATE SOMETHING ON THE LEVEL OF *CROW* AND *+NATURAL* IN THE NEXT SIX MONTHS!
THAT'S RIGHT! TOGETHER WITH MR. MIURA, WE'LL COME UP WITH SOMETHING!

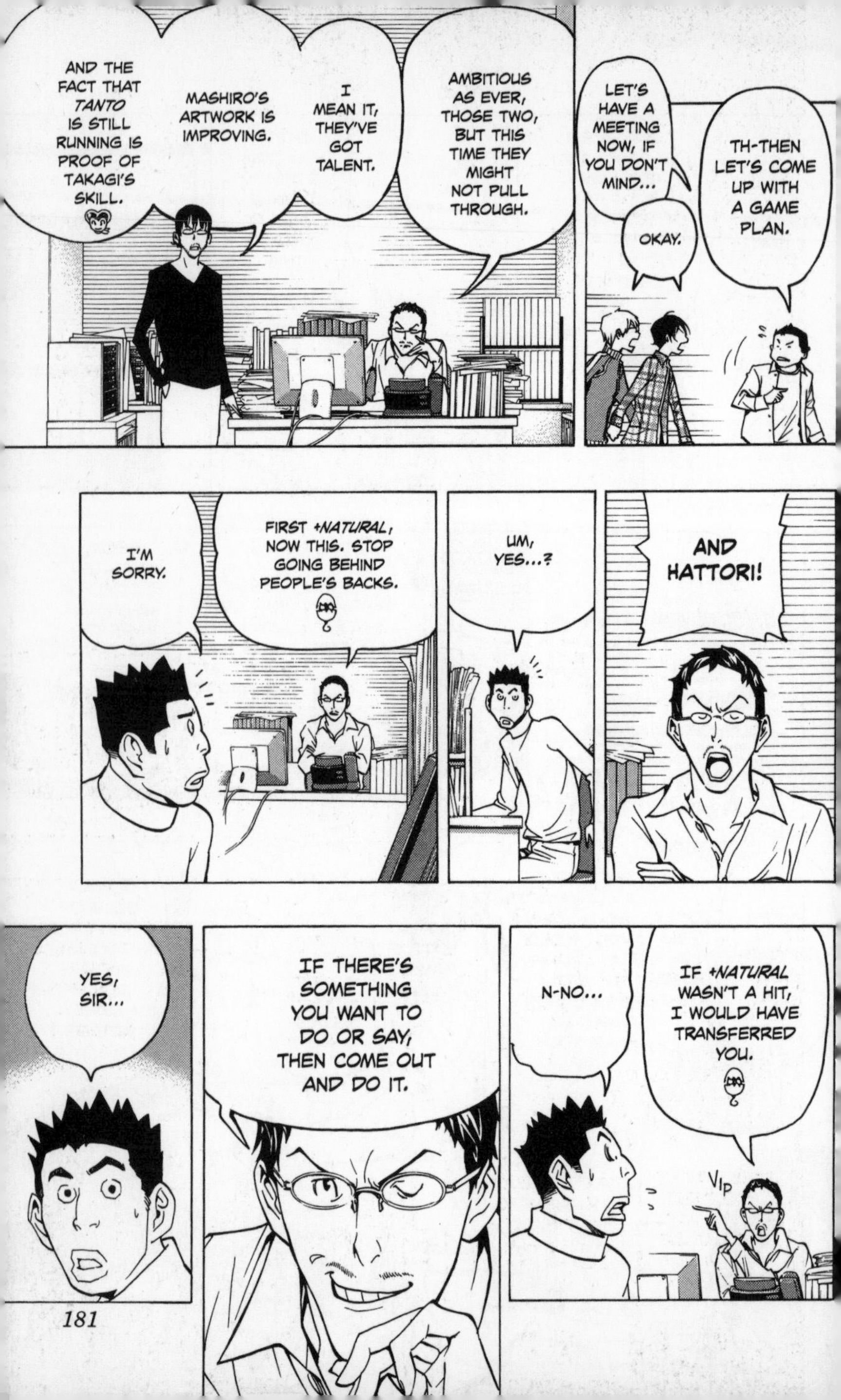

TH-THEN LET'S COME UP WITH A GAME PLAN.
LET'S HAVE A MEETING NOW, IF YOU DON'T MIND...
OKAY.
AMBITIOUS AS EVER, THOSE TWO, BUT THIS TIME THEY MIGHT NOT PULL THROUGH.
I MEAN IT, THEY'VE GOT TALENT.
MASHIRO'S ARTWORK IS IMPROVING.
AND THE FACT THAT *TANTO* IS STILL RUNNING IS PROOF OF TAKAGI'S SKILL.
AND HATTORI!
UM, YES...?
FIRST *+NATURAL*, NOW THIS. STOP GOING BEHIND PEOPLE'S BACKS.
I'M SORRY.
IF *+NATURAL* WASN'T A HIT, I WOULD HAVE TRANSFERRED YOU.
N-NO...
IF THERE'S SOMETHING YOU WANT TO DO OR SAY, THEN COME OUT AND DO IT.
YES, SIR...

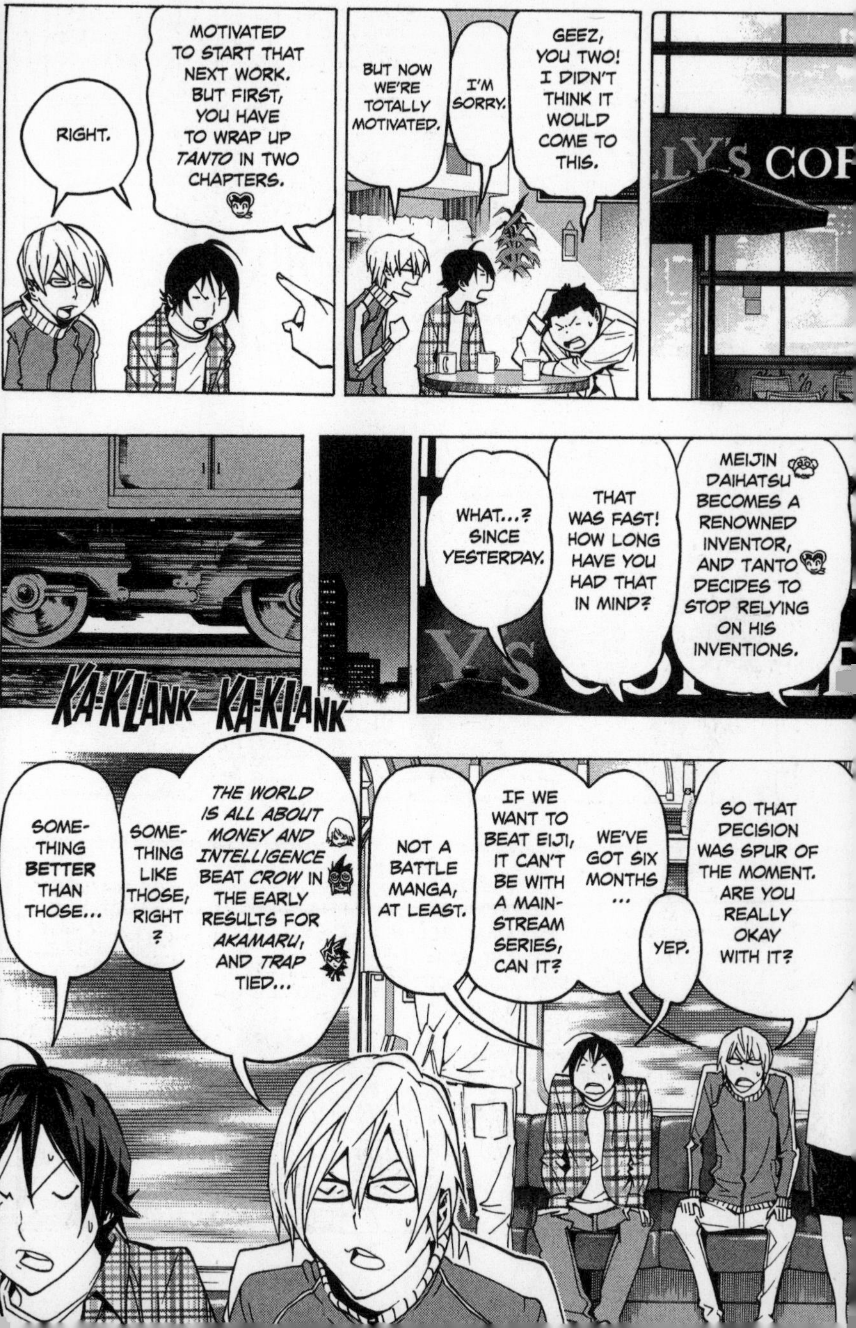
LLY'S COF
GEEZ, YOU TWO! I DIDN'T THINK IT WOULD COME TO THIS.
I'M SORRY.
BUT NOW WE'RE TOTALLY MOTIVATED.
MOTIVATED TO START THAT NEXT WORK. BUT FIRST, YOU HAVE TO WRAP UP *TANTO* IN TWO CHAPTERS.
RIGHT.
MEIJIN DAIHATSU BECOMES A RENOWNED INVENTOR, AND TANTO DECIDES TO STOP RELYING ON HIS INVENTIONS.
THAT WAS FAST! HOW LONG HAVE YOU HAD THAT IN MIND?
WHAT...? SINCE YESTERDAY.
KA-KLANK KA-KLANK
SO THAT DECISION WAS SPUR OF THE MOMENT. ARE YOU REALLY OKAY WITH IT?
YEP.
WE'VE GOT SIX MONTHS...
IF WE WANT TO BEAT EIJI, IT CAN'T BE WITH A MAIN-STREAM SERIES, CAN IT?
NOT A BATTLE MANGA, AT LEAST.
THE WORLD IS ALL ABOUT MONEY AND INTELLIGENCE BEAT *CROW* IN THE EARLY RESULTS FOR *AKAMARU*, AND *TRAP* TIED...
SOMETHING LIKE THOSE, RIGHT?
SOMETHING BETTER THAN THOSE...

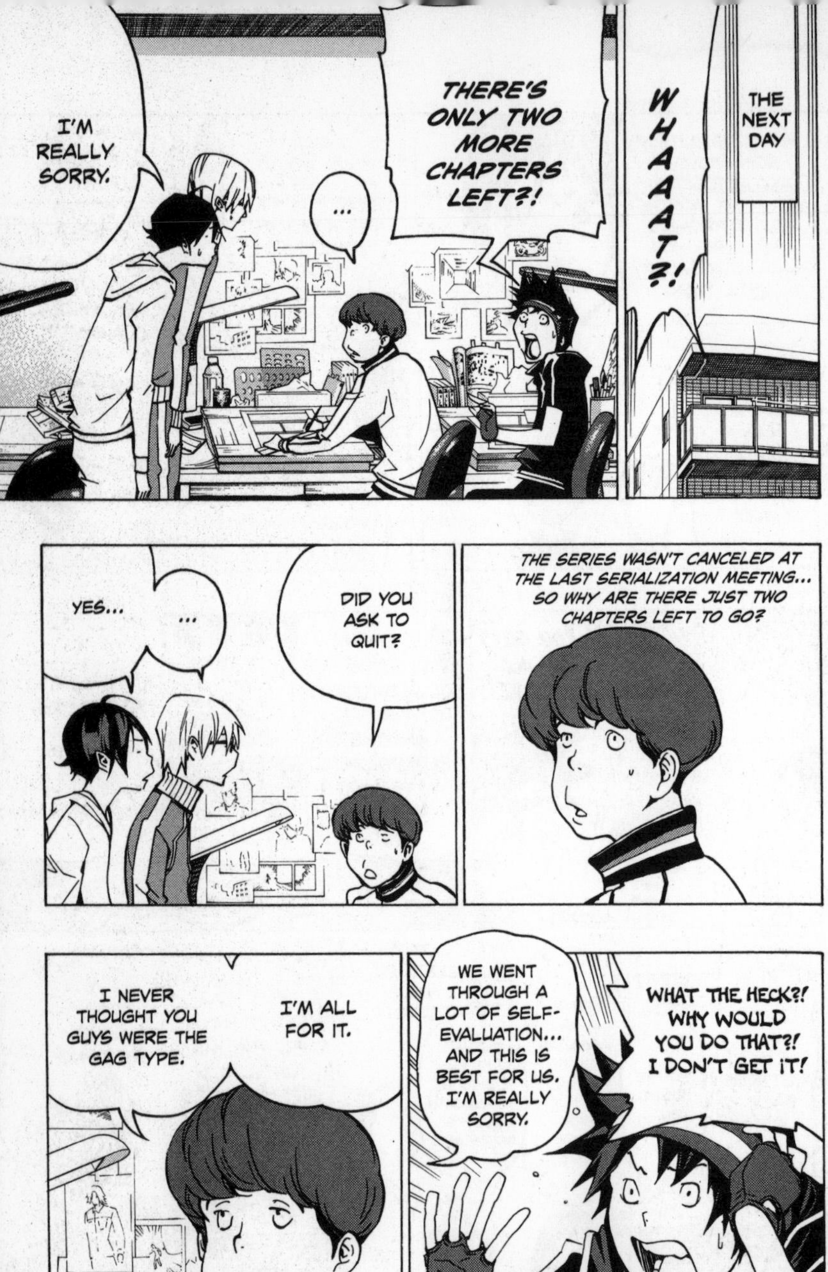
THE NEXT DAY
WHAAAT?!
THERE'S ONLY TWO MORE CHAPTERS LEFT?!
...
I'M REALLY SORRY.
THE SERIES WASN'T CANCELED AT THE LAST SERIALIZATION MEETING... SO WHY ARE THERE JUST TWO CHAPTERS LEFT TO GO?
DID YOU ASK TO QUIT?
...
YES...
WHAT THE HECK?! WHY WOULD YOU DO THAT?! I DON'T GET IT!
WE WENT THROUGH A LOT OF SELF-EVALUATION... AND THIS IS BEST FOR US. I'M REALLY SORRY.
I'M ALL FOR IT.
I NEVER THOUGHT YOU GUYS WERE THE GAG TYPE.

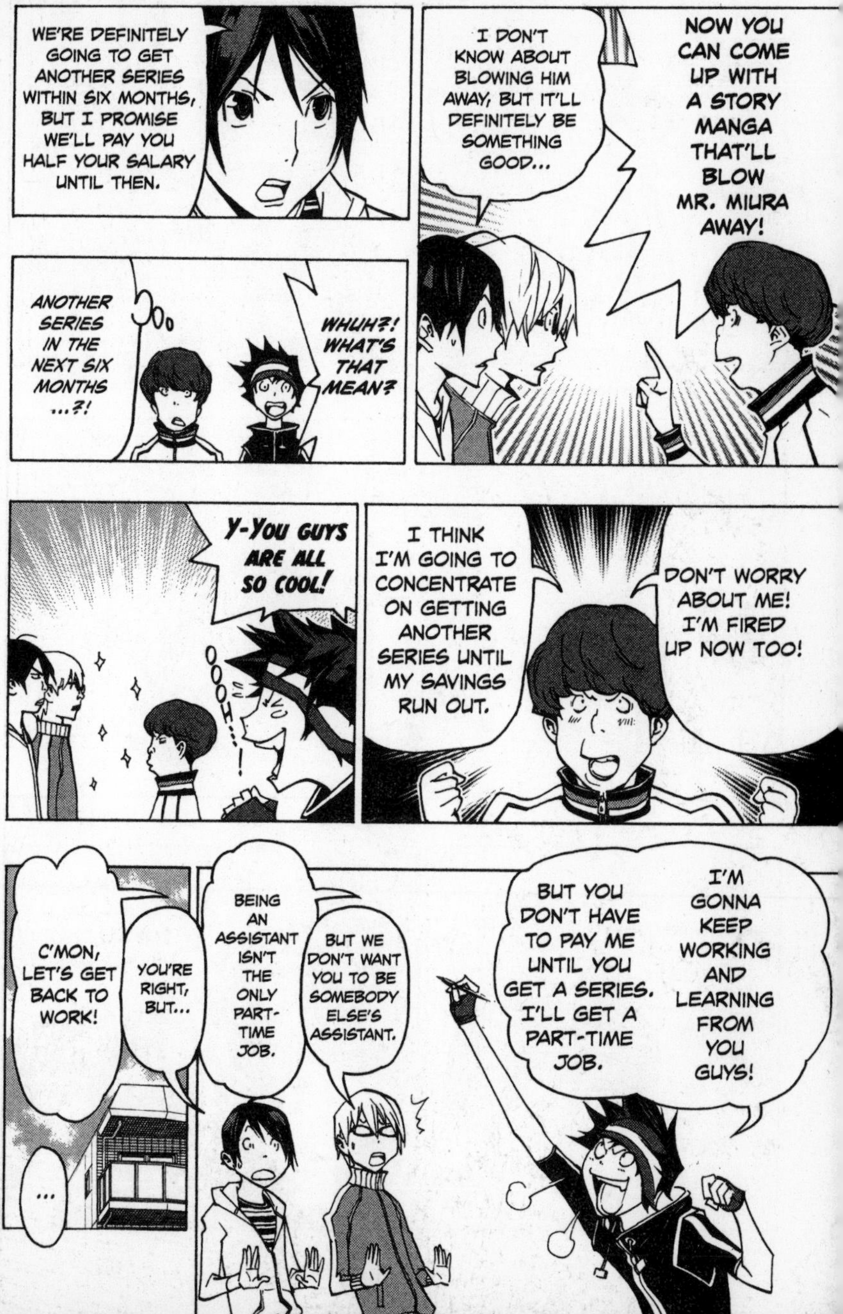
NOW YOU CAN COME UP WITH A STORY MANGA THAT'LL BLOW MR. MIURA AWAY!
I DON'T KNOW ABOUT BLOWING HIM AWAY, BUT IT'LL DEFINITELY BE SOMETHING GOOD...
WE'RE DEFINITELY GOING TO GET ANOTHER SERIES WITHIN SIX MONTHS, BUT I PROMISE WE'LL PAY YOU HALF YOUR SALARY UNTIL THEN.
WHUH?! WHAT'S THAT MEAN?
ANOTHER SERIES IN THE NEXT SIX MONTHS ...?!
DON'T WORRY ABOUT ME! I'M FIRED UP NOW TOO!
I THINK I'M GOING TO CONCENTRATE ON GETTING ANOTHER SERIES UNTIL MY SAVINGS RUN OUT.
Y-YOU GUYS ARE ALL SO COOL!
OOOH...!
I'M GONNA KEEP WORKING AND LEARNING FROM YOU GUYS!
BUT YOU DON'T HAVE TO PAY ME UNTIL YOU GET A SERIES. I'LL GET A PART-TIME JOB.
BUT WE DON'T WANT YOU TO BE SOMEBODY ELSE'S ASSISTANT.
BEING AN ASSISTANT ISN'T THE ONLY PART-TIME JOB.
YOU'RE RIGHT, BUT...
C'MON, LET'S GET BACK TO WORK!
...

READ THIS WAY

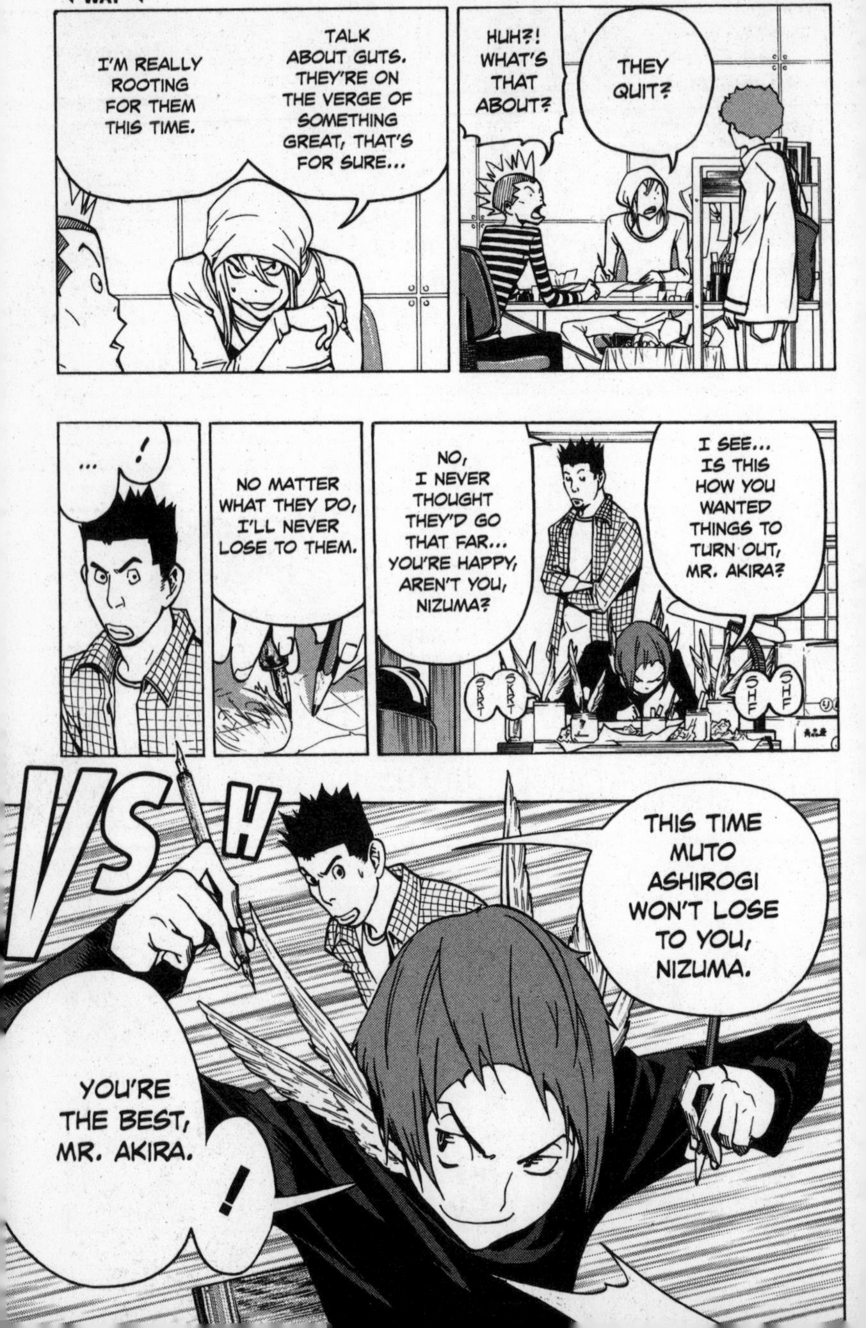
THEY QUIT?
HUH?! WHAT'S THAT ABOUT?
TALK ABOUT GUTS. THEY'RE ON THE VERGE OF SOMETHING GREAT, THAT'S FOR SURE...
I'M REALLY ROOTING FOR THEM THIS TIME.
I SEE... IS THIS HOW YOU WANTED THINGS TO TURN OUT, MR. AKIRA?
SHF SHF
NO, I NEVER THOUGHT THEY'D GO THAT FAR... YOU'RE HAPPY, AREN'T YOU, NIZUMA?
SKRT SKRT
NO MATTER WHAT THEY DO, I'LL NEVER LOSE TO THEM.
!
...
THIS TIME MUTO ASHIROGI WON'T LOSE TO YOU, NIZUMA.
VSH
!
YOU'RE THE BEST, MR. AKIRA.

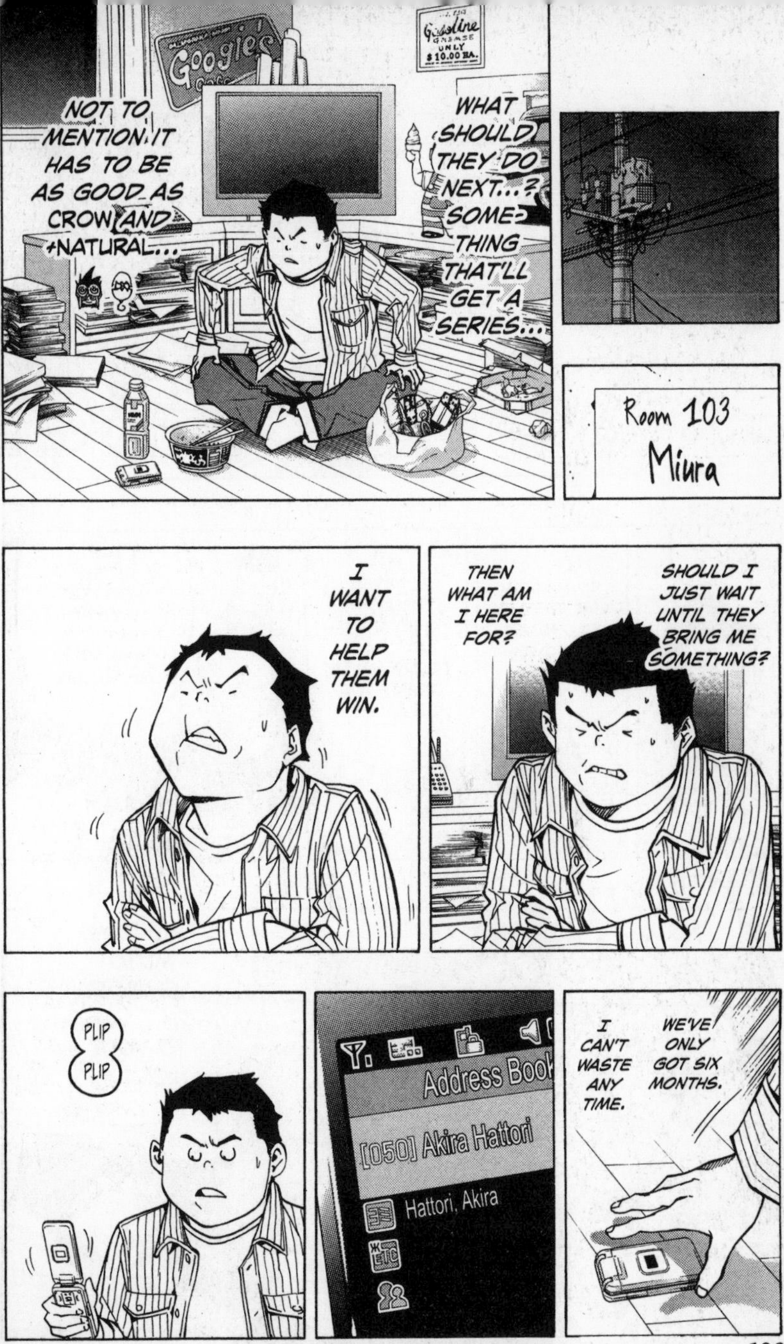
Room 103
Miura
Googie's
WHAT SHOULD THEY DO NEXT...? SOMETHING THAT'LL GET A SERIES...
NOT TO MENTION IT HAS TO BE AS GOOD AS CROW AND NATURAL...
SHOULD I JUST WAIT UNTIL THEY BRING ME SOMETHING?
THEN WHAT AM I HERE FOR?
I WANT TO HELP THEM WIN.
WE'VE ONLY GOT SIX MONTHS.
I CAN'T WASTE ANY TIME.
Address Book
[050] Akira Hattori
Hattori, Akira
PLIP
PLIP

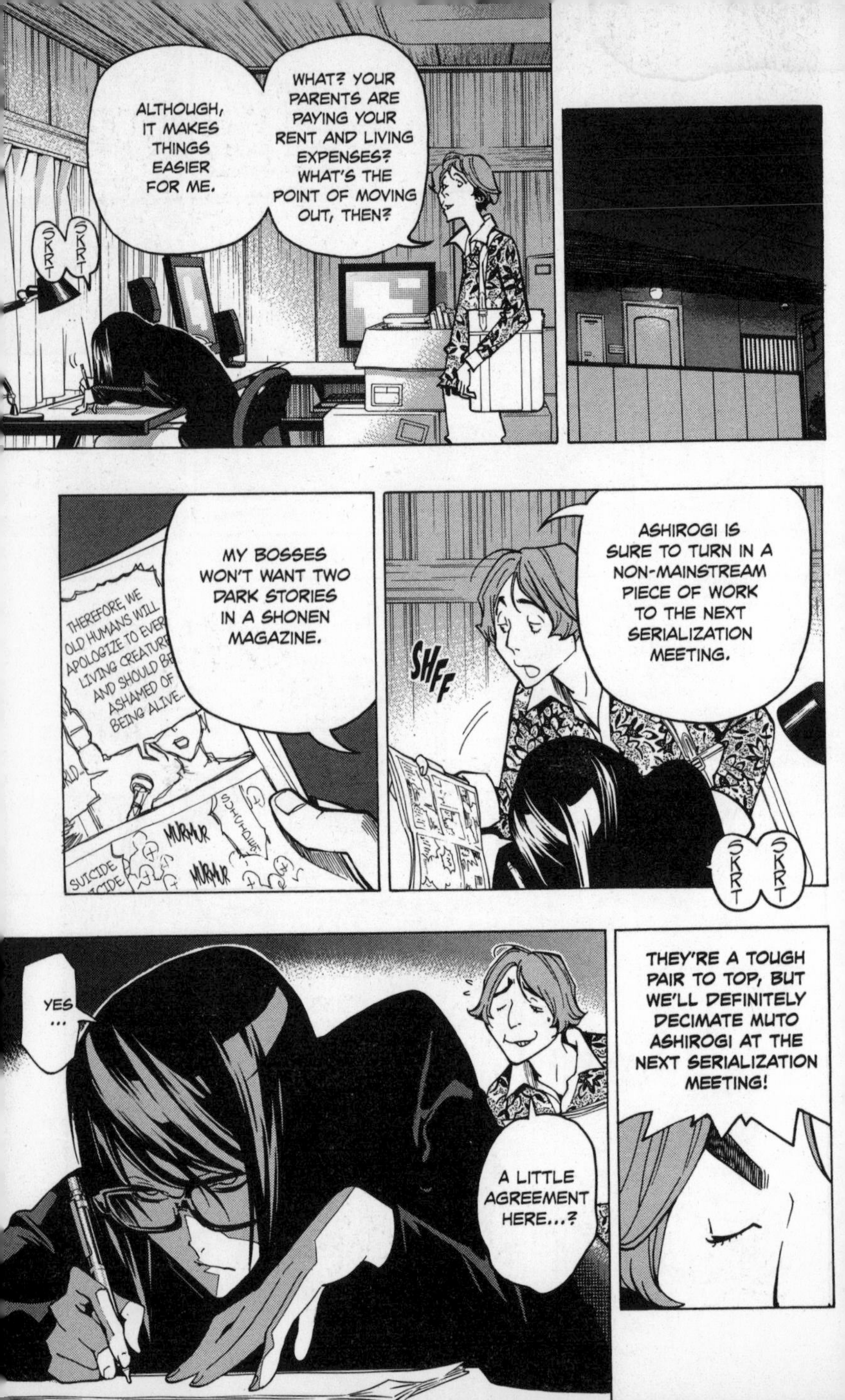
WHAT? YOUR PARENTS ARE PAYING YOUR RENT AND LIVING EXPENSES? WHAT'S THE POINT OF MOVING OUT, THEN?
ALTHOUGH, IT MAKES THINGS EASIER FOR ME.
SKRT SKRT
ASHIROGI IS SURE TO TURN IN A NON-MAINSTREAM PIECE OF WORK TO THE NEXT SERIALIZATION MEETING.
SHFF
SKRT SKRT
MY BOSSES WON'T WANT TWO DARK STORIES IN A SHONEN MAGAZINE.
THEREFORE, WE OLD HUMANS WILL APOLOGIZE TO EVER LIVING CREATURE AND SHOULD BE ASHAMED OF BEING ALIVE...
SUICIDE
MURMUR
MURMUR
SUICIDE
THEY'RE A TOUGH PAIR TO TOP, BUT WE'LL DEFINITELY DECIMATE MUTO ASHIROGI AT THE NEXT SERIALIZATION MEETING!
A LITTLE AGREEMENT HERE...?
YES...

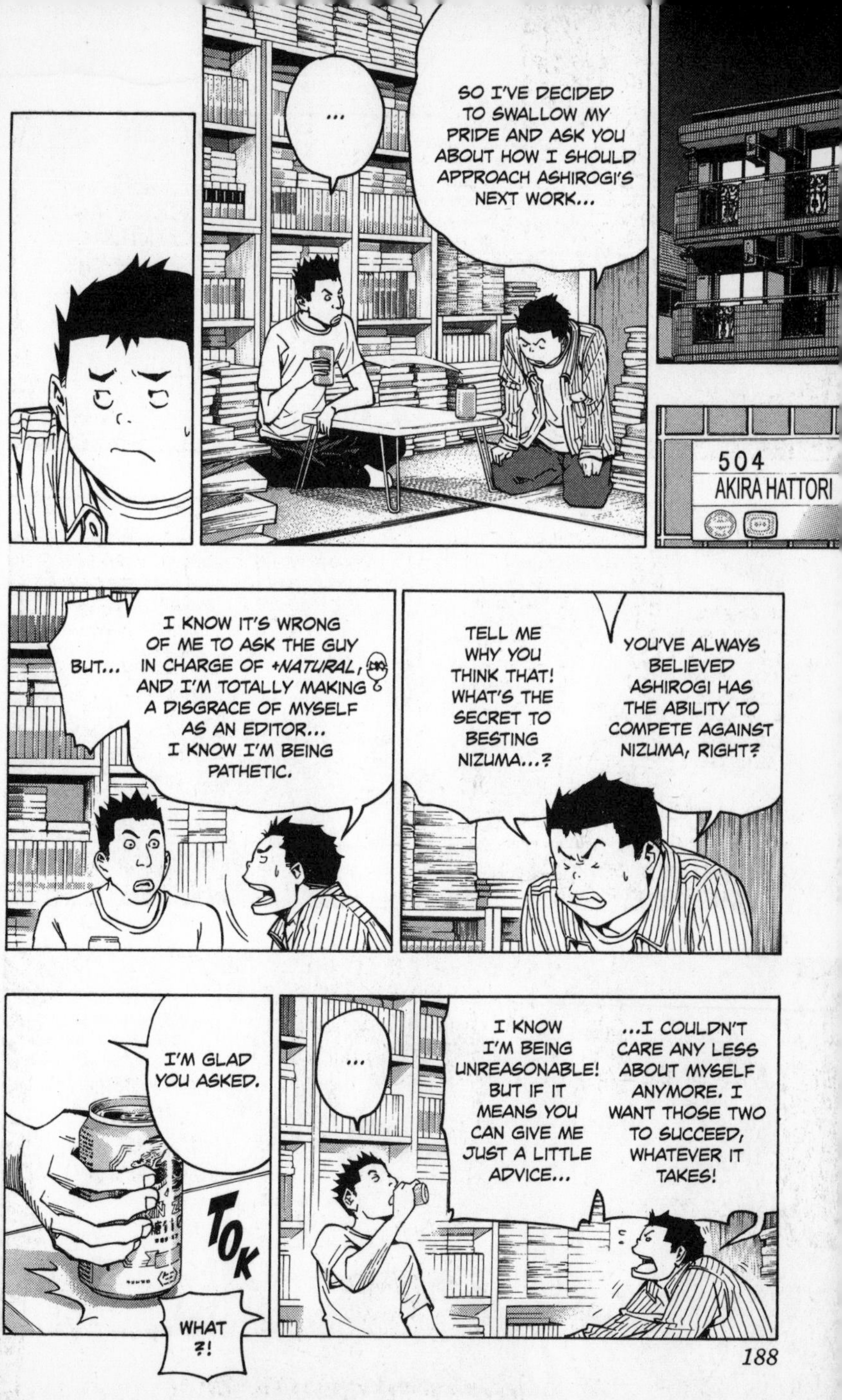
504
AKIRA HATTORI
SO I'VE DECIDED TO SWALLOW MY PRIDE AND ASK YOU ABOUT HOW I SHOULD APPROACH ASHIROGI'S NEXT WORK...
...
YOU'VE ALWAYS BELIEVED ASHIROGI HAS THE ABILITY TO COMPETE AGAINST NIZUMA, RIGHT?
TELL ME WHY YOU THINK THAT! WHAT'S THE SECRET TO BESTING NIZUMA...?
I KNOW IT'S WRONG OF ME TO ASK THE GUY IN CHARGE OF +NATURAL, AND I'M TOTALLY MAKING A DISGRACE OF MYSELF AS AN EDITOR... I KNOW I'M BEING PATHETIC.
BUT...
I KNOW I'M BEING UNREASONABLE! BUT IF IT MEANS YOU CAN GIVE ME JUST A LITTLE ADVICE...
...I COULDN'T CARE ANY LESS ABOUT MYSELF ANYMORE. I WANT THOSE TWO TO SUCCEED, WHATEVER IT TAKES!
...
I'M GLAD YOU ASKED.
TOK
WHAT ?!

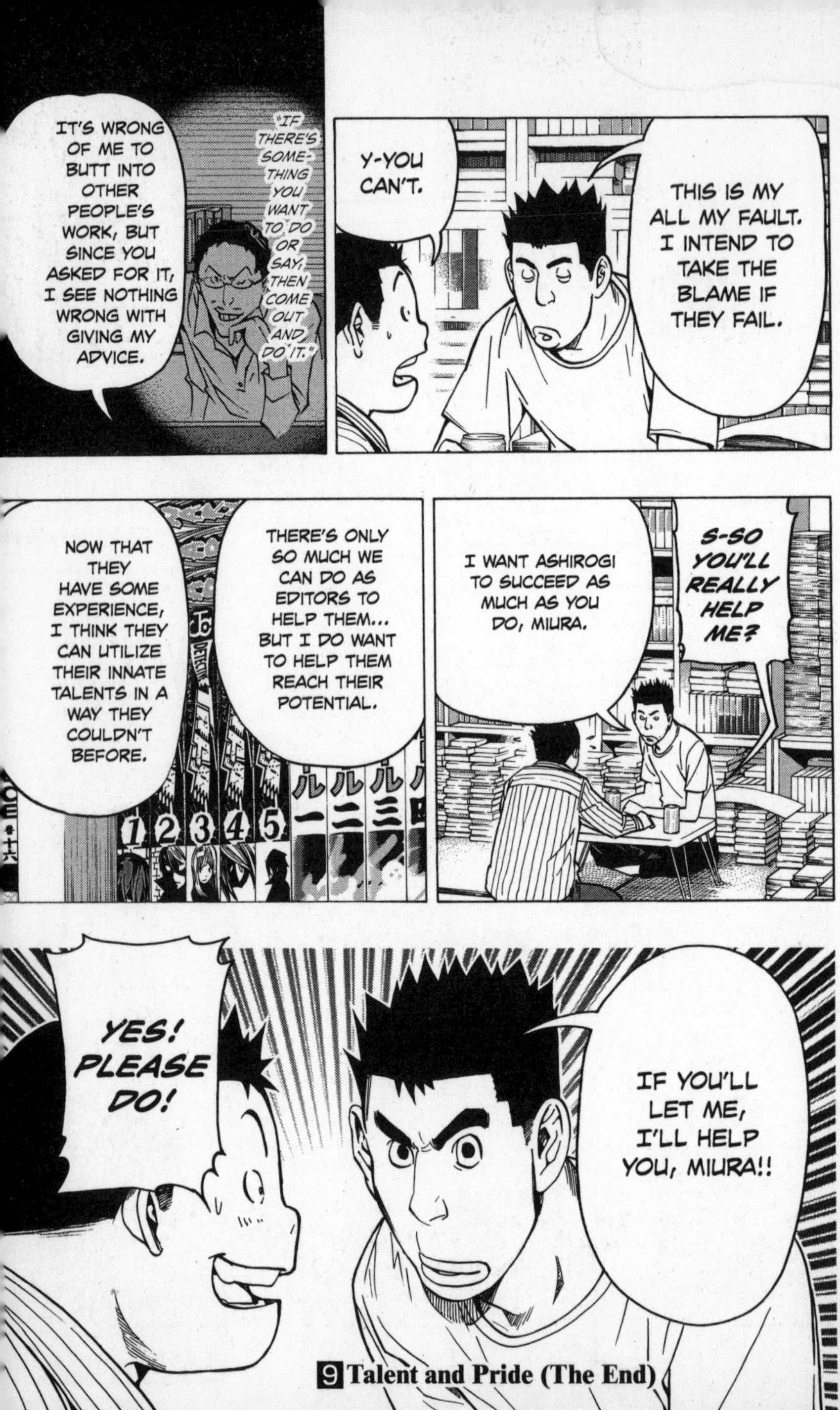
THIS IS MY ALL MY FAULT. I INTEND TO TAKE THE BLAME IF THEY FAIL.
Y-YOU CAN'T.
"IF THERE'S SOMETHING YOU WANT TO DO OR SAY, THEN COME OUT AND DO IT."
IT'S WRONG OF ME TO BUTT INTO OTHER PEOPLE'S WORK, BUT SINCE YOU ASKED FOR IT, I SEE NOTHING WRONG WITH GIVING MY ADVICE.
S-SO YOU'LL REALLY HELP ME?
I WANT ASHIROGI TO SUCCEED AS MUCH AS YOU DO, MIURA.
THERE'S ONLY SO MUCH WE CAN DO AS EDITORS TO HELP THEM... BUT I DO WANT TO HELP THEM REACH THEIR POTENTIAL.
NOW THAT THEY HAVE SOME EXPERIENCE, I THINK THEY CAN UTILIZE THEIR INNATE TALENTS IN A WAY THEY COULDN'T BEFORE.
IF YOU'LL LET ME, I'LL HELP YOU, MIURA!!
YES! PLEASE DO!

9 Talent and Pride (The End)

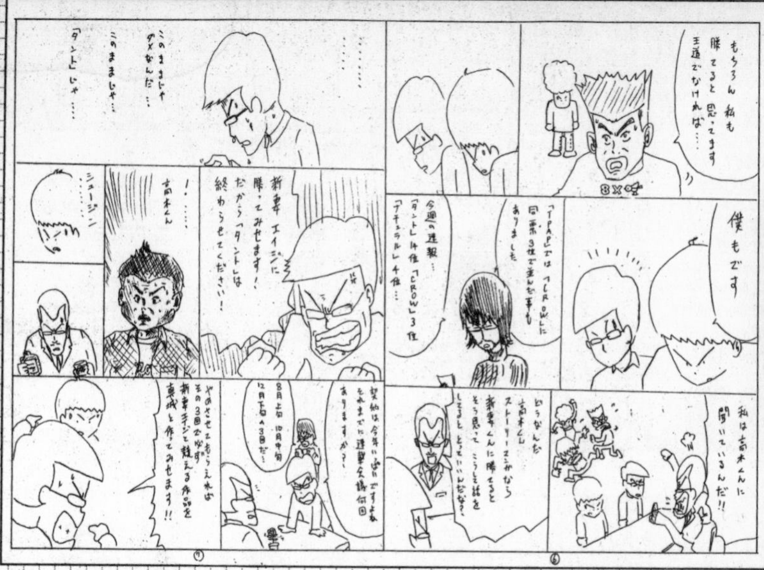
もちろん 私も 勝てると 思ってます 王道でなければ…
僕もです
「TRAP」では「CROW」に 同票3位で並んだ事も ありました
今週の速報… 「タント」14位 「CROW」3位 「ナチュラル」4位…
私は高木くんに 聞いているんだ!!
どうなんだ 高木くん ストーリーだけなら 新妻くんに勝てると そう思ってこういう話を しているととっていいんだな?
……
このままじゃ ダメなんだ…
このままじゃ…
「タント」じゃ……
新妻エイジに 勝ってみせます! だから「タント」は 終わらせてください!
!……
高木くん
シュージン……
契約は今年いっぱいですよね それまでに連載会議何回 ありますか?
8月上旬 10月中旬 12月下旬の3回だ…
やめさせてもらえれば その3回で必ず 新妻エイジを越える作品を 真城と作ってみせます!!

OHBA'S STORYBOARD

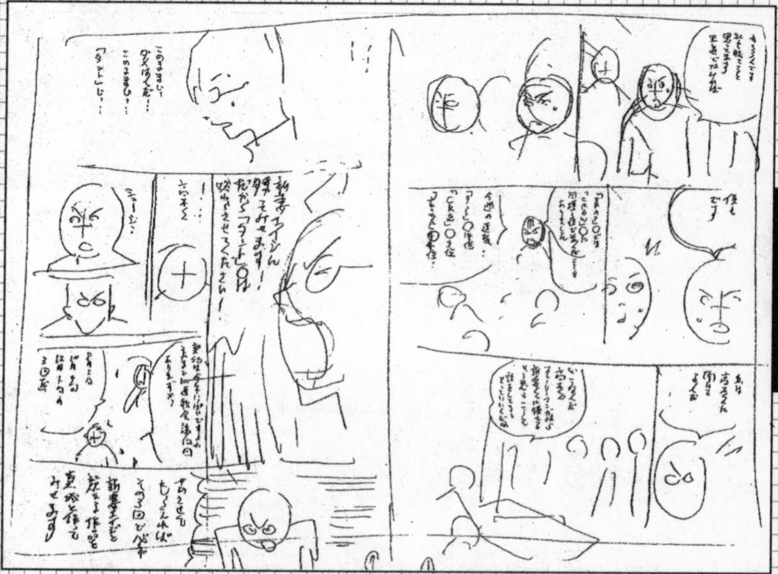

OBATA'S STORYBOARD

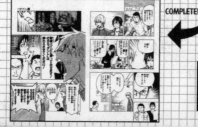

COMPLETE!

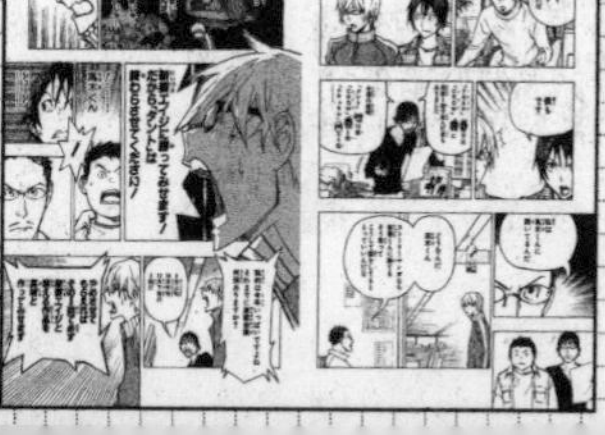

※CREATOR STORYBOARDS AND FINISHED PAGES IN JAPANESE

BAKUMAN。 vol. 9

"Until the Final Draft Is Complete"

Chapter 79, pp. 176-177

BAKUMAN。

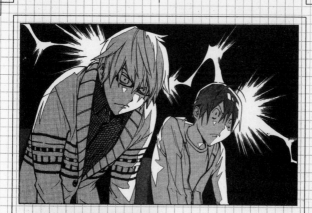

In the NEXT VOLUME

**Moritaka and Akito have only three
chances to created a brilliant new series
or they'll have to leave *Shonen Jump*
forever. They might have a chance with
their old editor, Hattori, helping them,
but they're going to need inspiration
from the unlikeliest of sources!**

Available April 2011